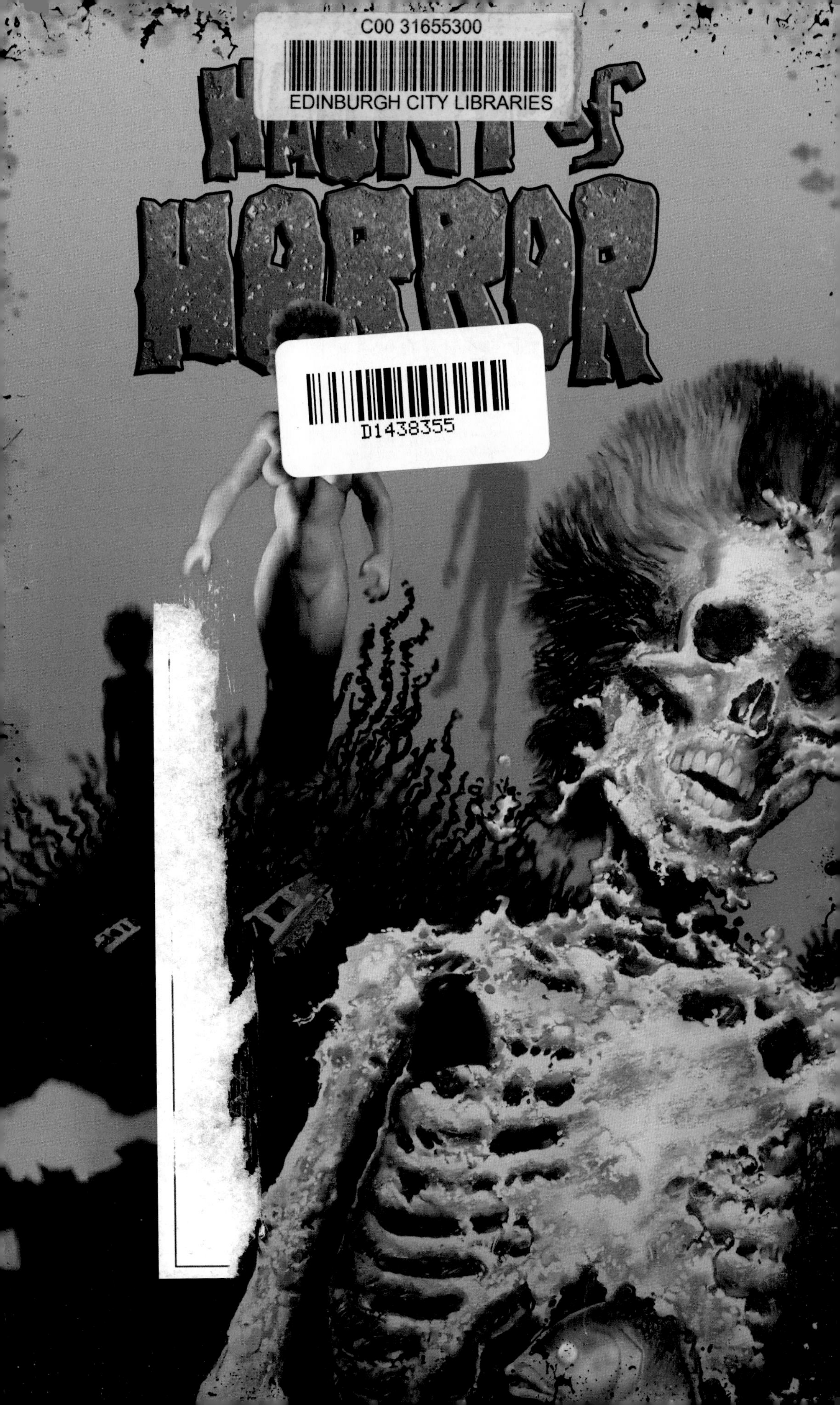

HAUNT of
HORROR

# HAUNT of HORROR

ADAPTED BY RICHARD CORBEN
STORY, ART & GRAYTONES

AFTER ORIGINAL STORIES
AND POEMS BY
EDGAR ALLAN POE & H.P. LOVECRAFT

WITH RICHARD MARGOPOULOS | PLOT AND SCRIPT (POE)

VC'S RANDY GENTILE & JEFF ECKLEBERRY | LETTERS

CORY SEDLMEIER & DANIEL KETCHUM EDITORS

AXEL ALONSO EXECUTIVE EDITOR

COVER ART RICHARD CORBEN

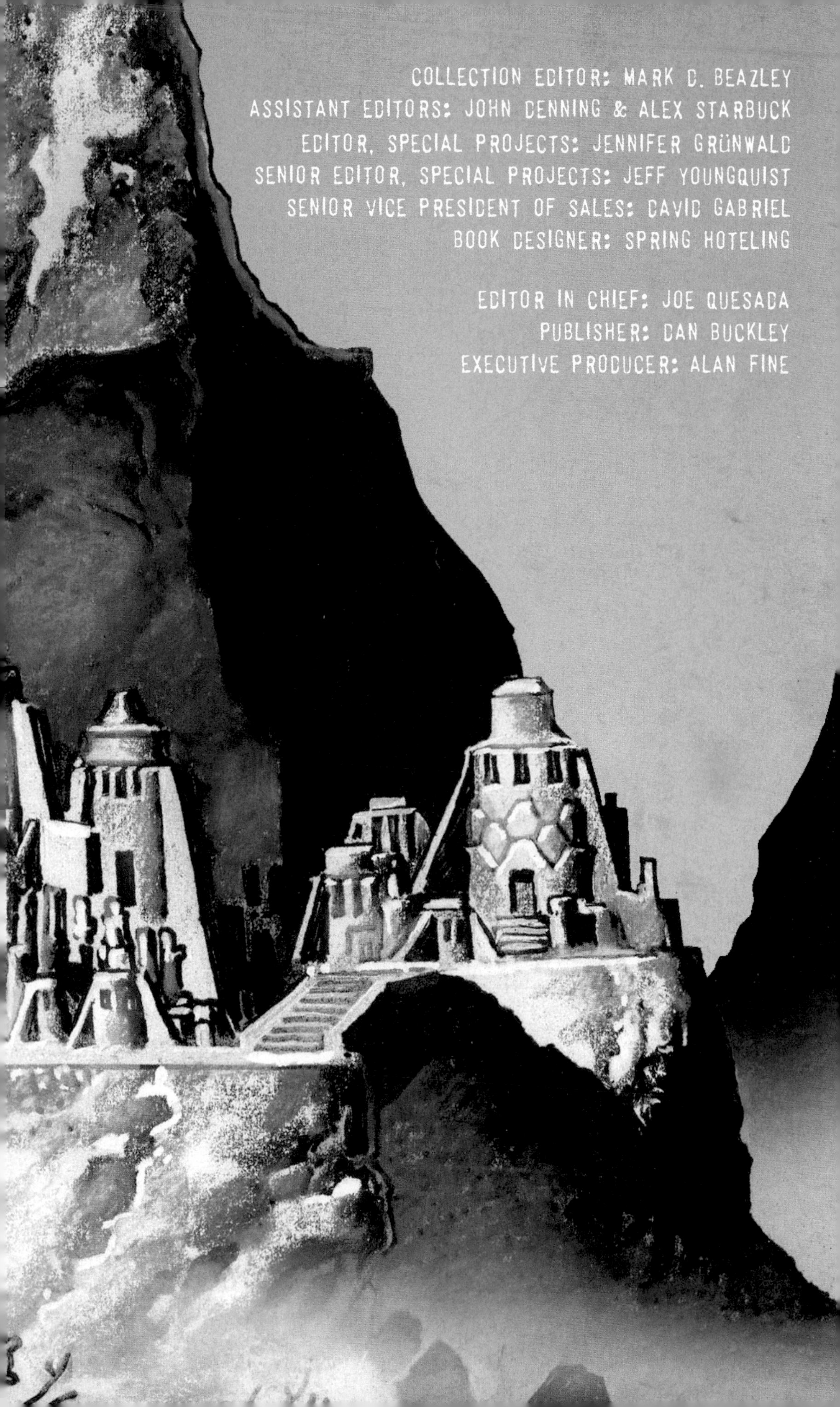


COLLECTION EDITOR: MARK D. BEAZLEY
ASSISTANT EDITORS: JOHN DENNING & ALEX STARBUCK
EDITOR, SPECIAL PROJECTS: JENNIFER GRÜNWALD
SENIOR EDITOR, SPECIAL PROJECTS: JEFF YOUNGQUIST
SENIOR VICE PRESIDENT OF SALES: DAVID GABRIEL
BOOK DESIGNER: SPRING HOTELING

EDITOR IN CHIEF: JOE QUESADA
PUBLISHER: DAN BUCKLEY
EXECUTIVE PRODUCER: ALAN FINE

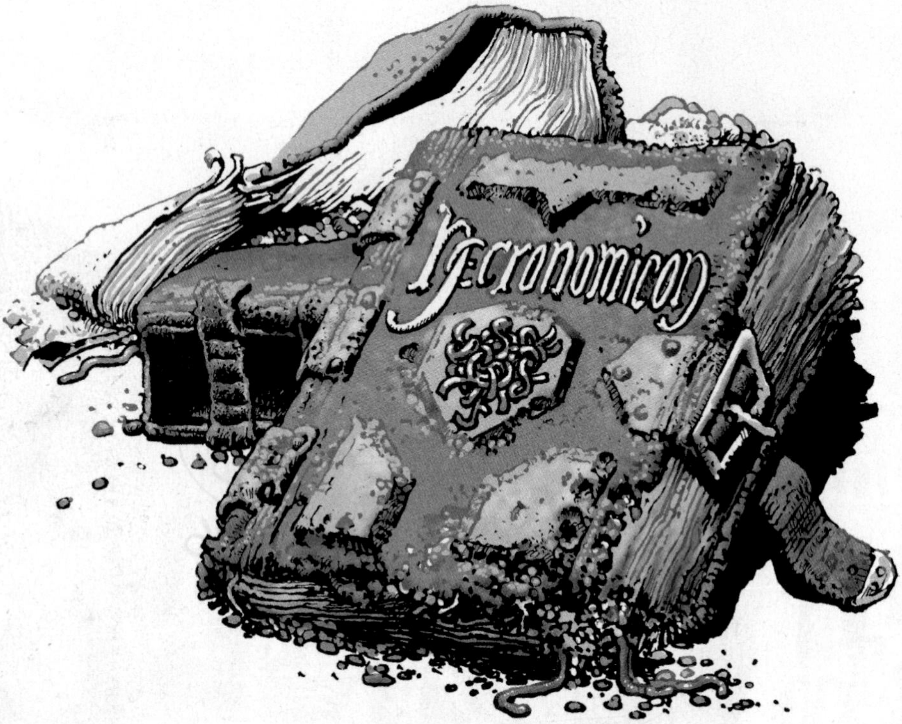
Necronomicon

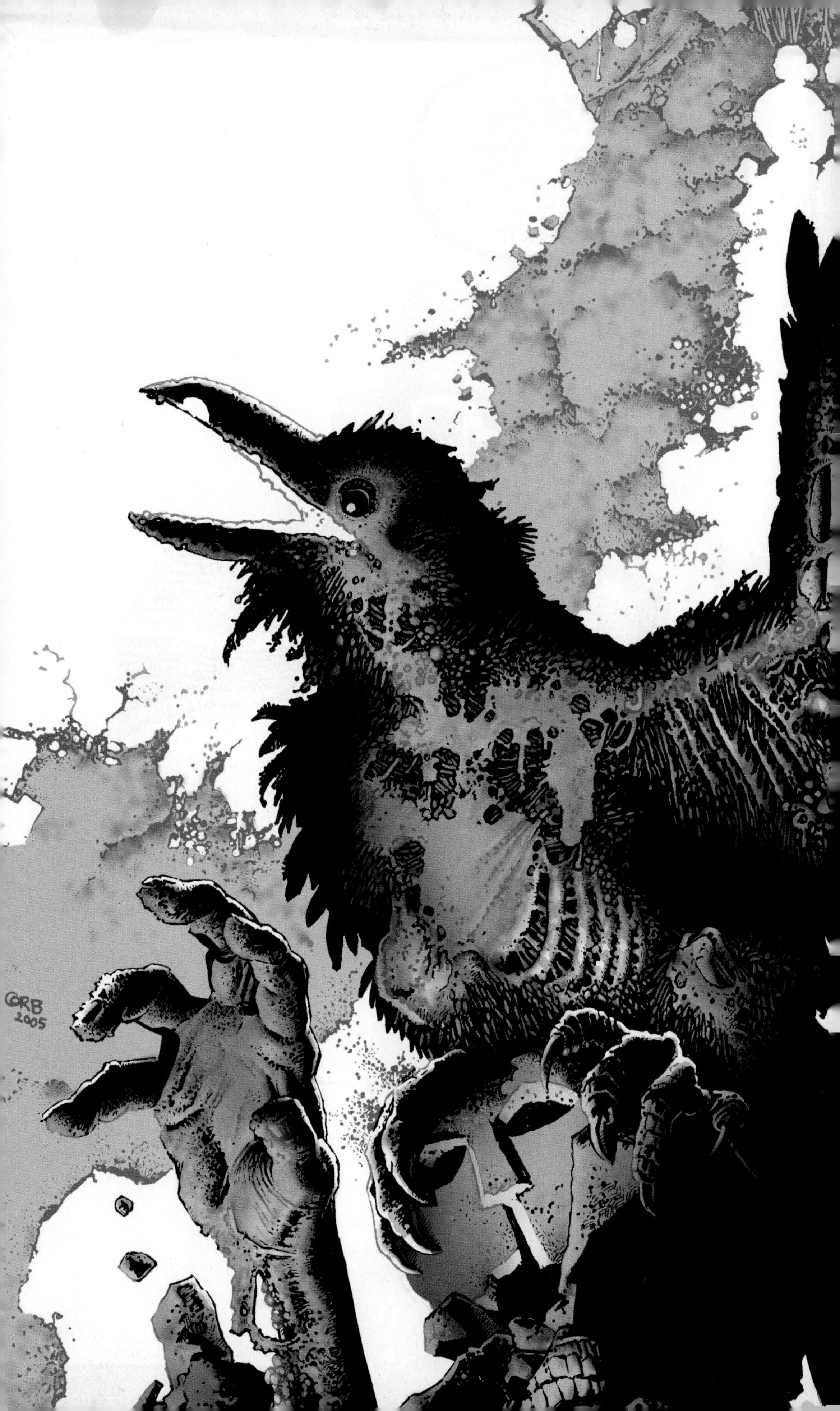
©RB
2005

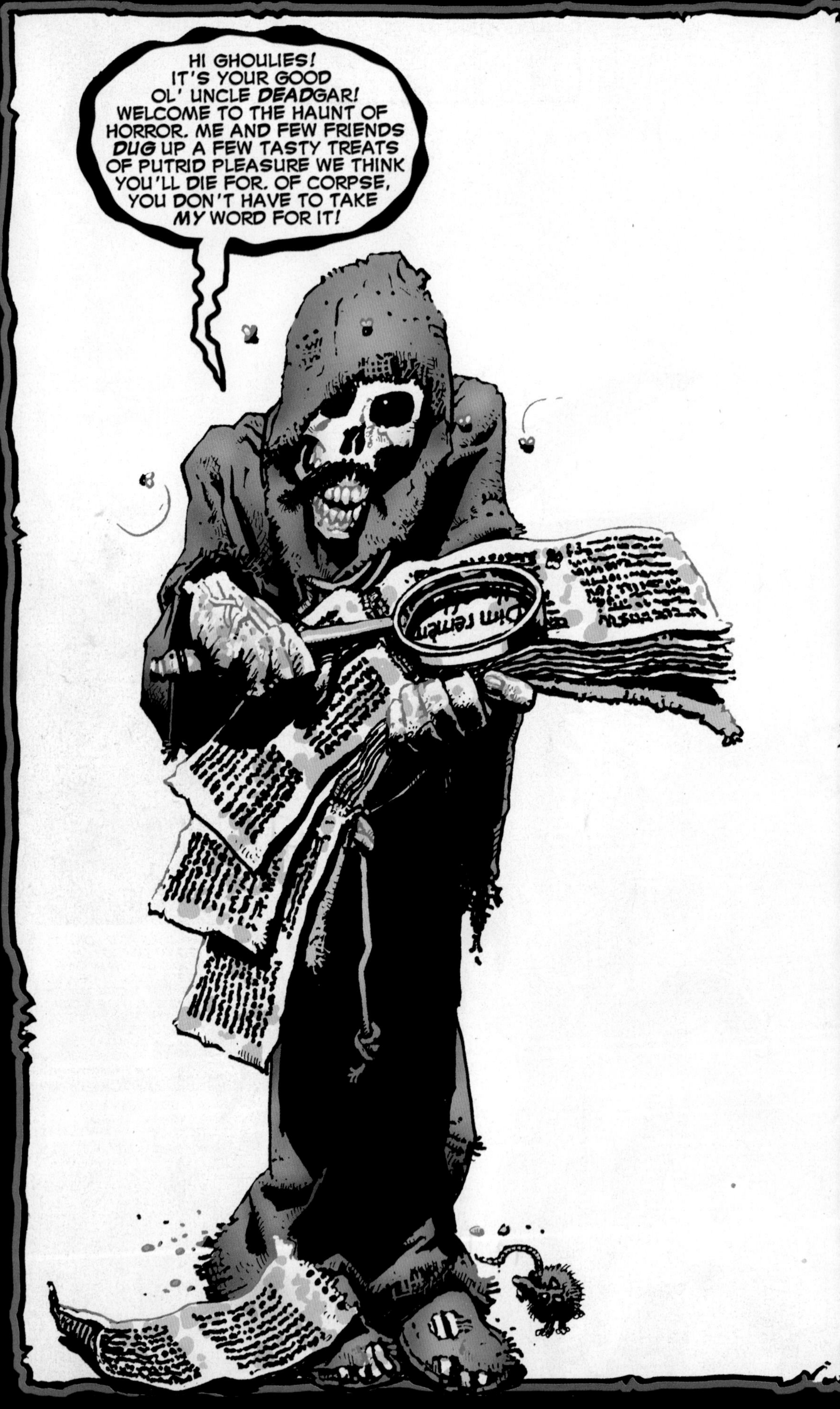
HI GHOULIES! IT'S YOUR GOOD OL' UNCLE DEADGAR! WELCOME TO THE HAUNT OF HORROR. ME AND FEW FRIENDS DUG UP A FEW TASTY TREATS OF PUTRID PLEASURE WE THINK YOU'LL DIE FOR. OF CORPSE, YOU DON'T HAVE TO TAKE MY WORD FOR IT!

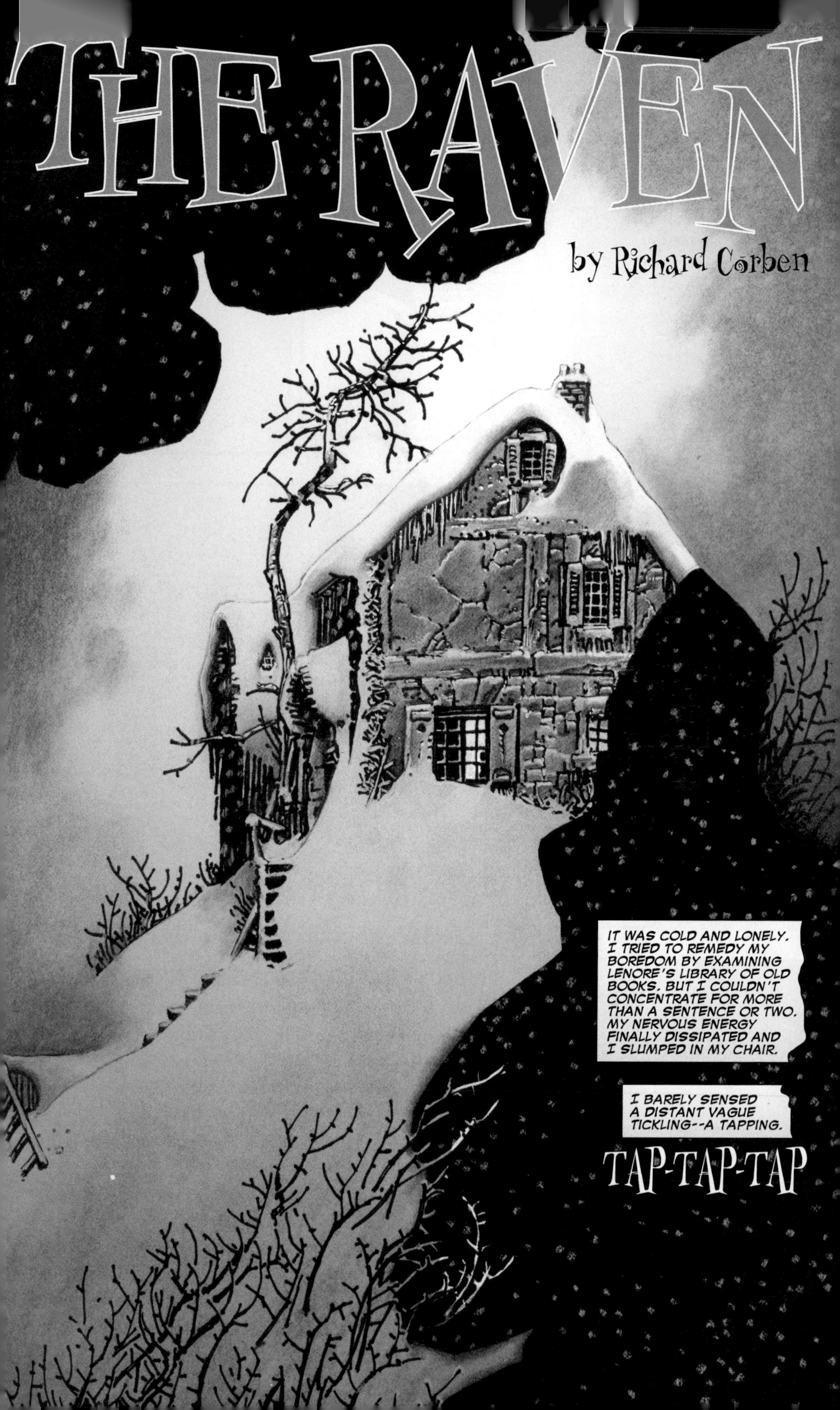
THE RAVEN
by Richard Corben
IT WAS COLD AND LONELY. I TRIED TO REMEDY MY BOREDOM BY EXAMINING LENORE'S LIBRARY OF OLD BOOKS, BUT I COULDN'T CONCENTRATE FOR MORE THAN A SENTENCE OR TWO. MY NERVOUS ENERGY FINALLY DISSIPATED AND I SLUMPED IN MY CHAIR.
I BARELY SENSED A DISTANT VAGUE TICKLING--A TAPPING.
TAP-TAP-TAP

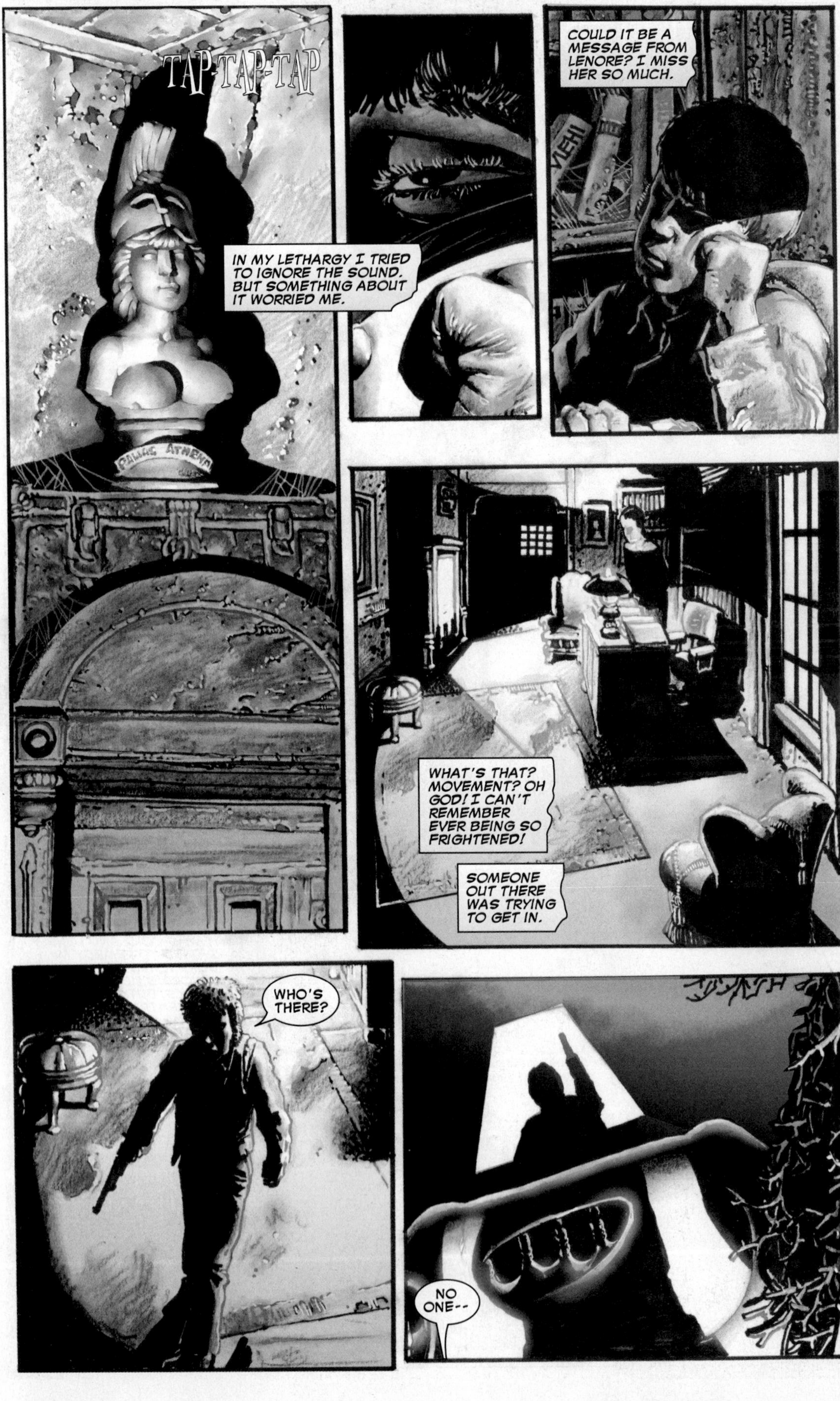

TAP-TAP-TAP
PALLAS ATHENA
IN MY LETHARGY I TRIED TO IGNORE THE SOUND. BUT SOMETHING ABOUT IT WORRIED ME.
COULD IT BE A MESSAGE FROM LENORE? I MISS HER SO MUCH.
WHAT'S THAT? MOVEMENT? OH GOD! I CAN'T REMEMBER EVER BEING SO FRIGHTENED!
SOMEONE OUT THERE WAS TRYING TO GET IN.
WHO'S THERE?
NO ONE--

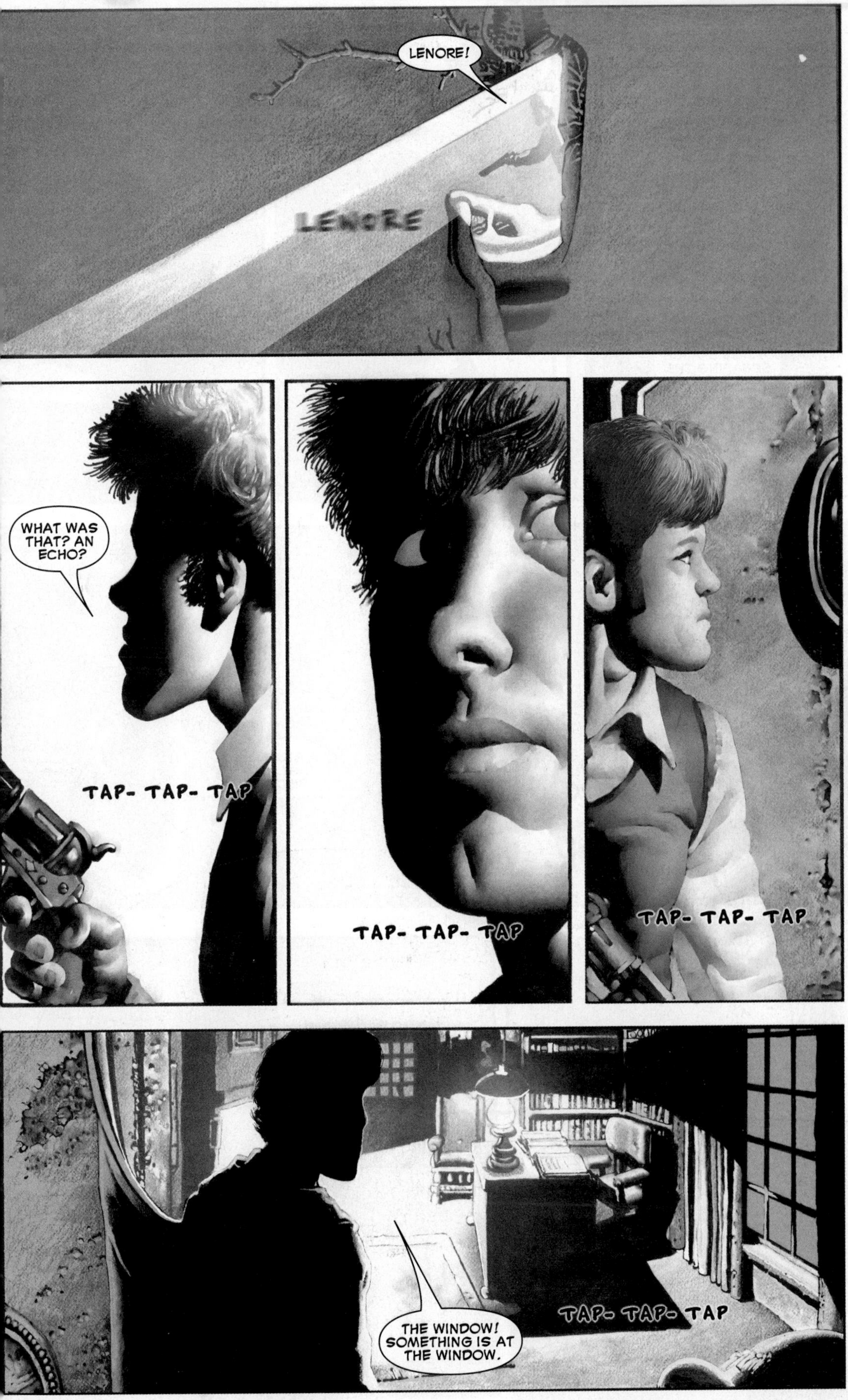
LENORE!
LENORE
WHAT WAS THAT? AN ECHO?
TAP- TAP- TAP
TAP- TAP- TAP
TAP- TAP- TAP
TAP- TAP- TAP
THE WINDOW! SOMETHING IS AT THE WINDOW.

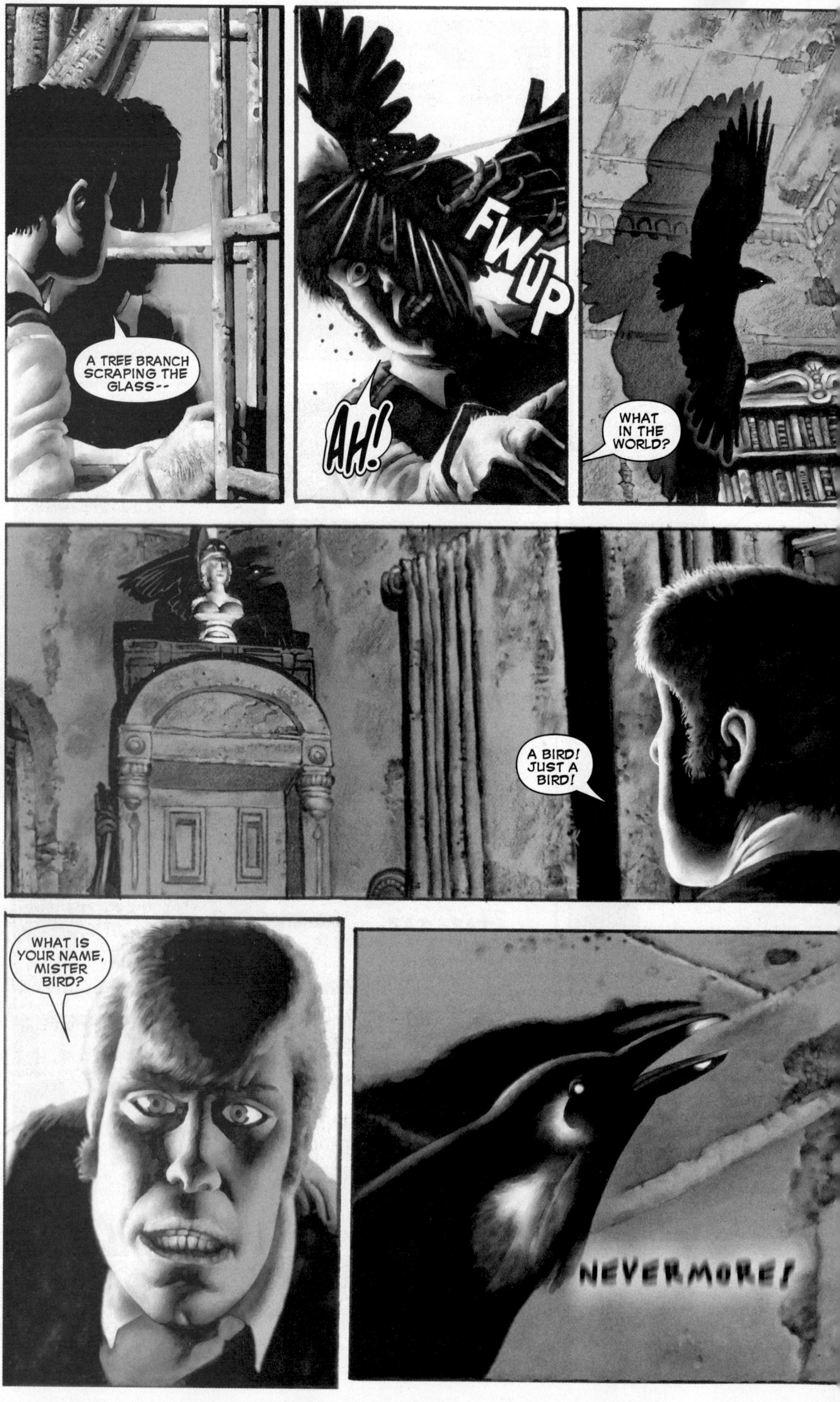
A TREE BRANCH SCRAPING THE GLASS--
FWUP
AH!
WHAT IN THE WORLD?
A BIRD! JUST A BIRD!
WHAT IS YOUR NAME, MISTER BIRD?
NEVERMORE!

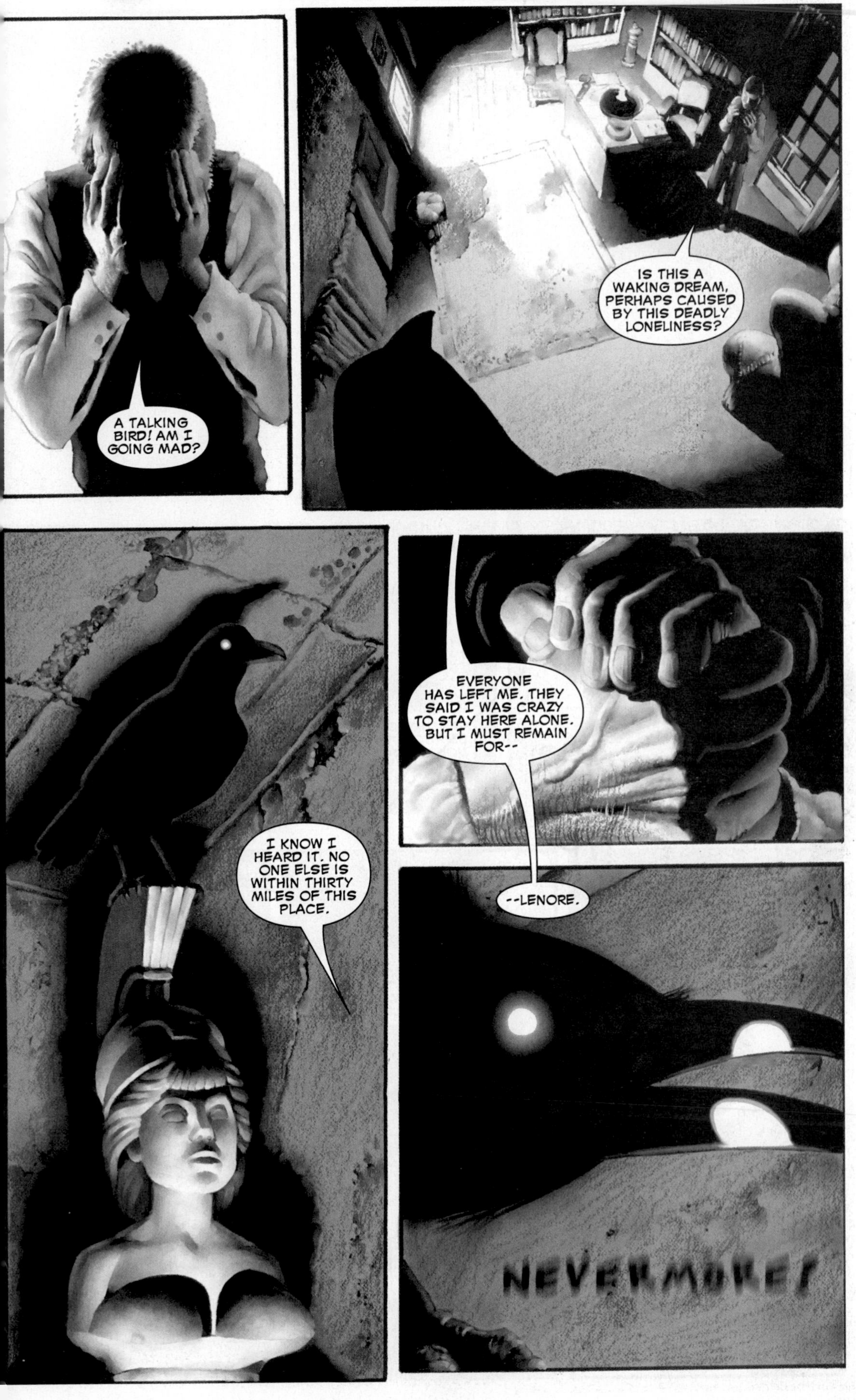
A TALKING BIRD! AM I GOING MAD?
IS THIS A WAKING DREAM, PERHAPS CAUSED BY THIS DEADLY LONELINESS?
I KNOW I HEARD IT. NO ONE ELSE IS WITHIN THIRTY MILES OF THIS PLACE.
EVERYONE HAS LEFT ME. THEY SAID I WAS CRAZY TO STAY HERE ALONE. BUT I MUST REMAIN FOR--
--LENORE.
NEVERMORE!

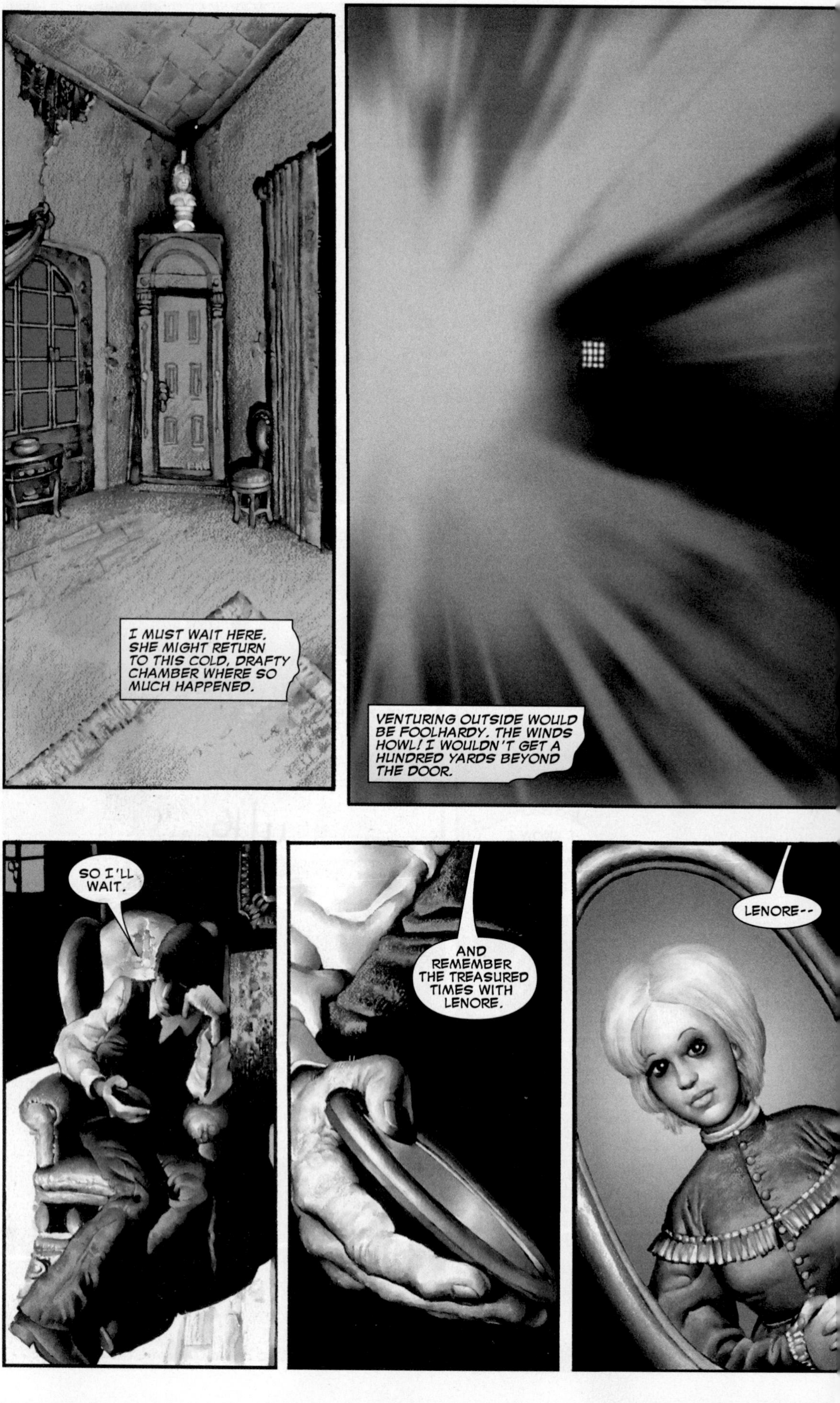
I MUST WAIT HERE. SHE MIGHT RETURN TO THIS COLD, DRAFTY CHAMBER WHERE SO MUCH HAPPENED.
VENTURING OUTSIDE WOULD BE FOOLHARDY. THE WINDS HOWL! I WOULDN'T GET A HUNDRED YARDS BEYOND THE DOOR.
SO I'LL WAIT.
AND REMEMBER THE TREASURED TIMES WITH LENORE.
LENORE--

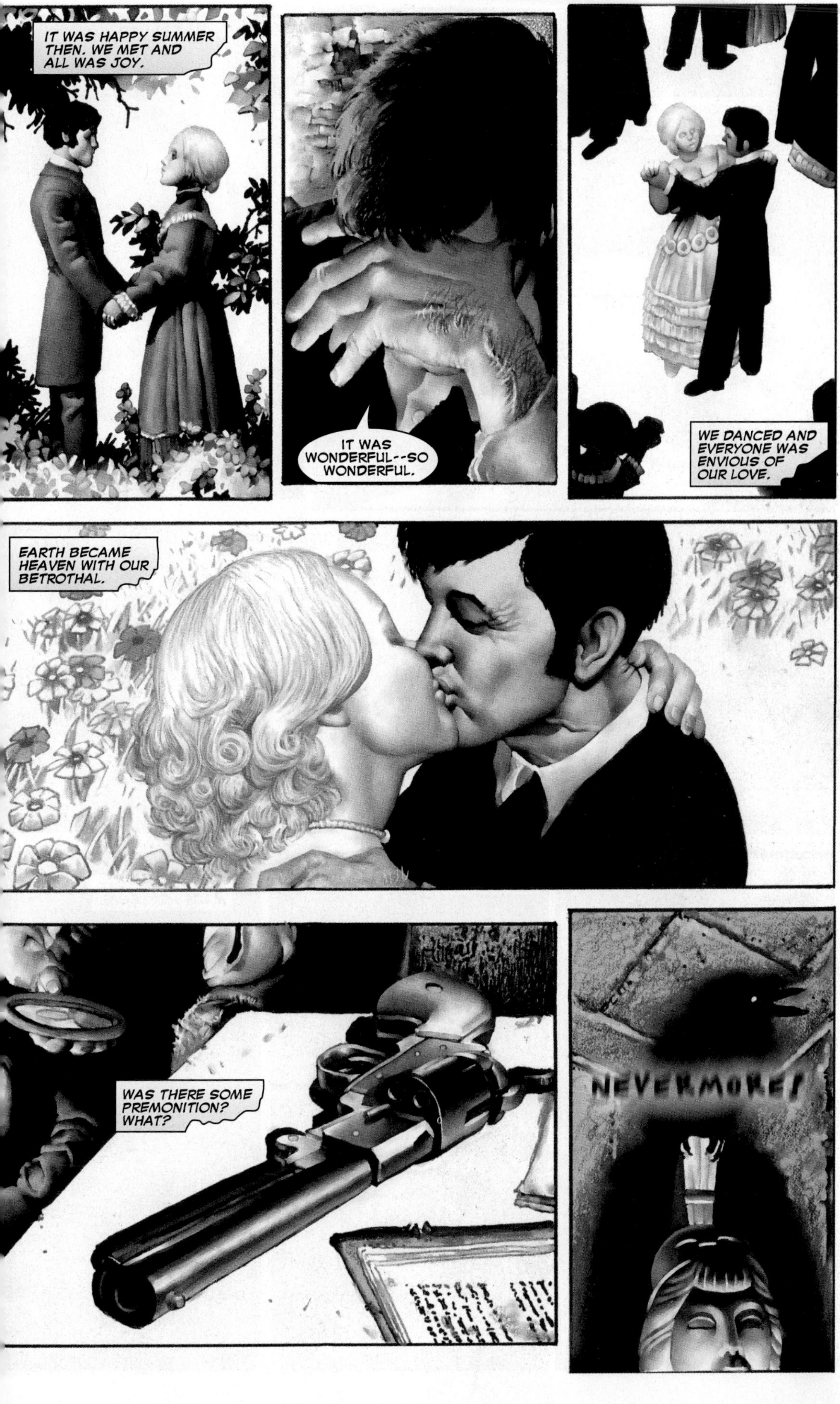
IT WAS HAPPY SUMMER THEN. WE MET AND ALL WAS JOY.
IT WAS WONDERFUL--SO WONDERFUL.
WE DANCED AND EVERYONE WAS ENVIOUS OF OUR LOVE.
EARTH BECAME HEAVEN WITH OUR BETROTHAL.
WAS THERE SOME PREMONITION? WHAT?
NEVERMORE!

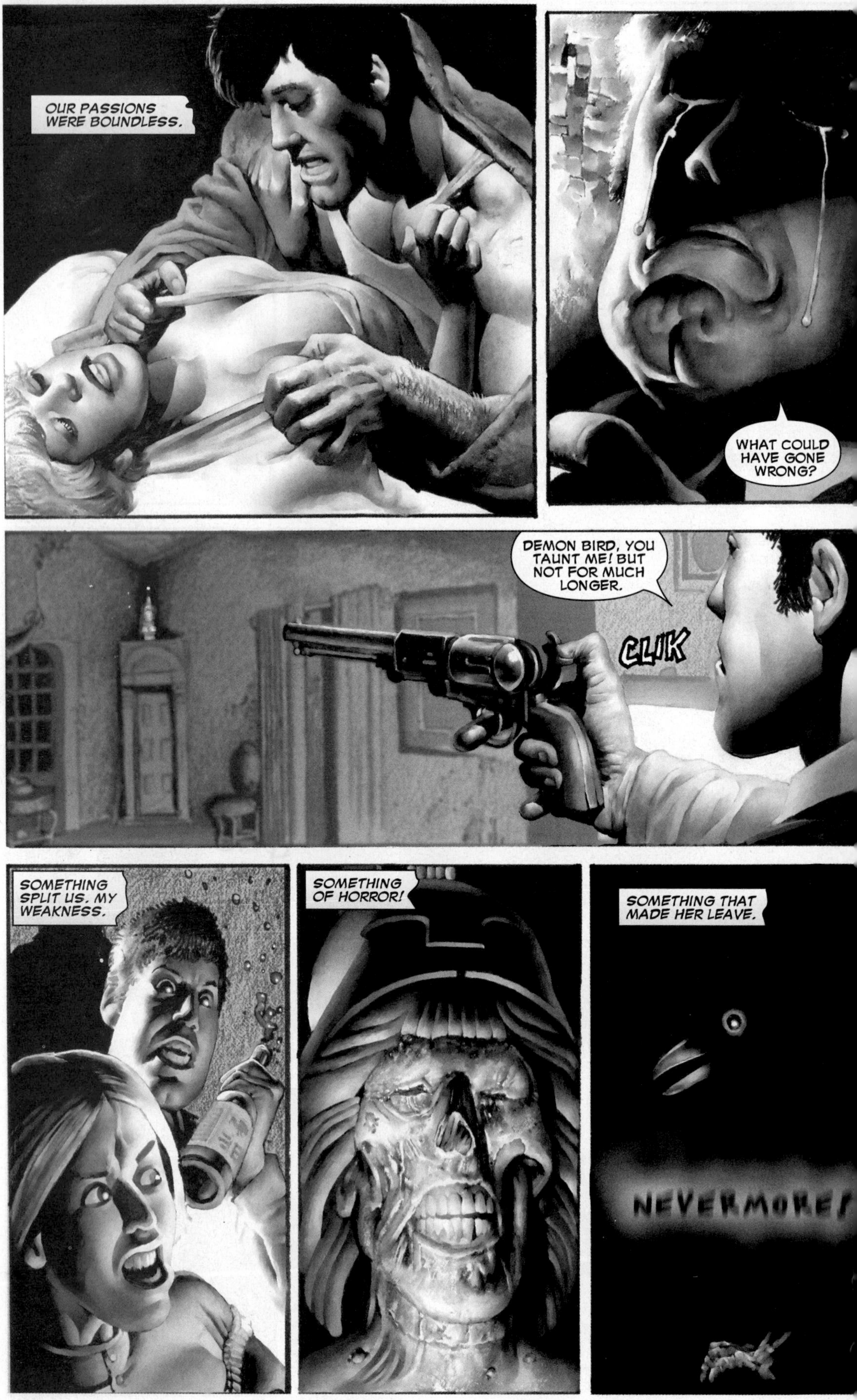
OUR PASSIONS WERE BOUNDLESS.
WHAT COULD HAVE GONE WRONG?
DEMON BIRD, YOU TAUNT ME! BUT NOT FOR MUCH LONGER.
CLIK
SOMETHING SPLIT US. MY WEAKNESS.
SOMETHING OF HORROR!
SOMETHING THAT MADE HER LEAVE.
NEVERMORE!

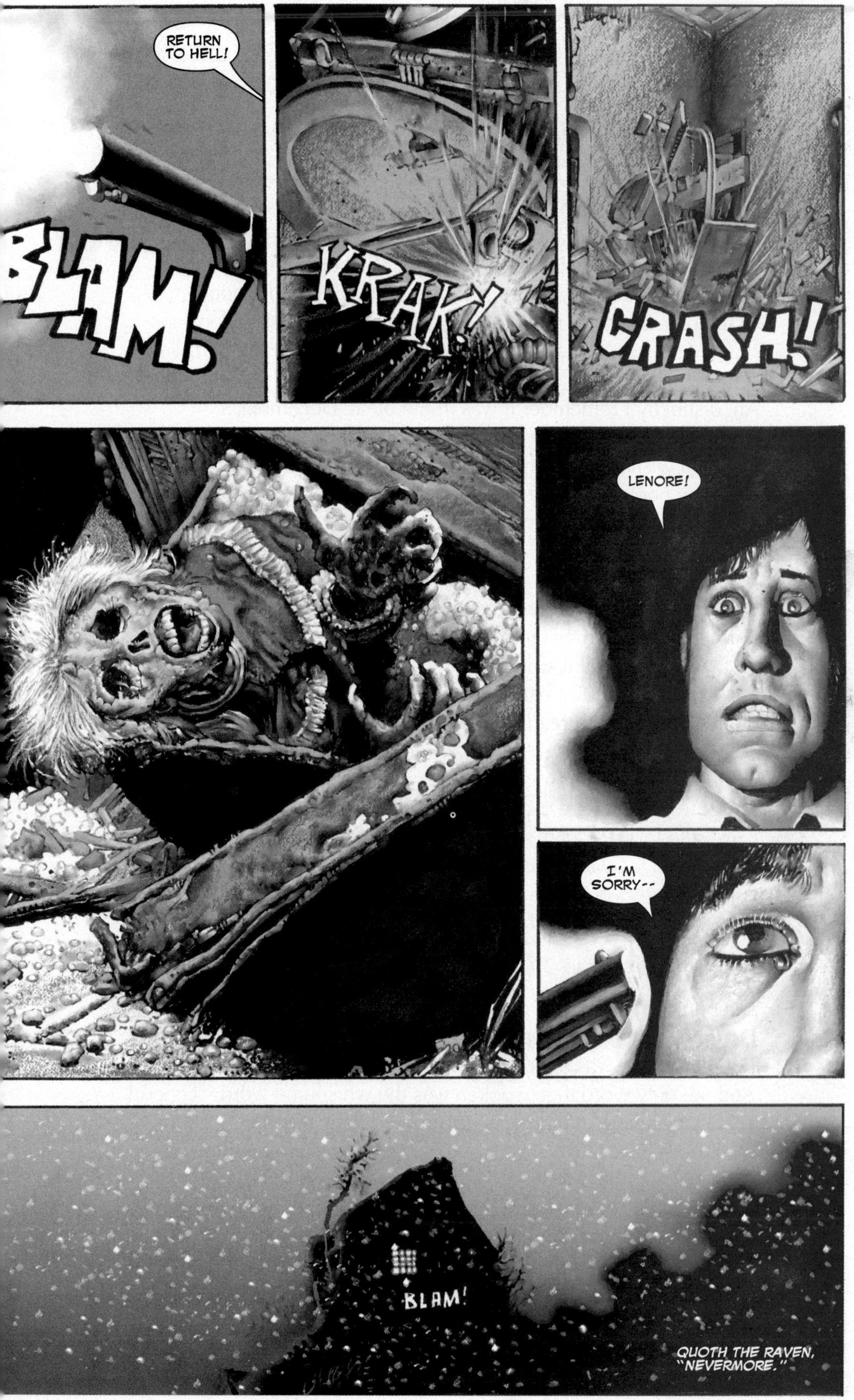
RETURN TO HELL!
BLAM!
KRAK!
CRASH!
LENORE!
I'M SORRY--
BLAM!
QUOTH THE RAVEN, "NEVERMORE."

# The Raven

Once upon a midnight dreary, while I pondered, weak and weary,
Over many a quaint and curious volume of forgotten lore—
While I nodded, nearly napping, suddenly there came a tapping,
As of someone gently rapping, rapping at my chamber door.
" 'Tis some visitor," I muttered, "tapping at my chamber door—
        Only this, and nothing more."

Ah, distinctly I remember it was in the bleak December,
And each separate dying ember wrought its ghost upon the floor.
Eagerly I wished the morrow;—vainly I had sought to borrow
From my books surcease of sorrow—sorrow for the lost Lenore—
For the rare and radiant maiden whom the angels name Lenore—
        Nameless here for evermore.

And the silken sad uncertain rustling of each purple curtain
Thrilled me—filled me with fantastic terrors never felt before;
So that now, to still the beating of my heart, I stood repeating:
" 'Tis some visitor entreating entrance at my chamber door—
Some late visitor entreating entrance at my chamber door;
        This it is and nothing more."

Presently my soul grew stronger; hesitating  then no longer,
"Sir," said I, "or Madam, truly your forgiveness I implore;
But the fact is I was napping, and so gently you came rapping,
And so faintly you came tapping, tapping at my chamber door,
That I scarce was sure I heard you,"—here I opened wide the door;—
        Darkness there and nothing more.

Deep into that darkness peering, long I stood there wondering, fearing,
Doubting, dreaming dreams no mortals ever dared to dream before;
But the silence was unbroken, and the stillness gave no token,
And the only word there spoken was the whispered word, "Lenore!"
This I whispered, and an echo murmured back the word, "Lenore!"—
        Merely this and nothing more.

Back into the chamber turning, all my soul within me burning,
Soon again I heard a tapping something louder than before.
"Surely," said I, "surely that is something at my window lattice;
Let me see, then, what thereat is, and this mystery explore—
Let my heart be still a moment, and this mystery explore;—
        'Tis the wind and nothing more."

Open here I flung the shutter, when, with many a flirt and flutter,
In there stepped a stately Raven of the saintly days of yore.
Not the least obeisance made he; not a minute stopped or stayed he,
But, with mien of lord or lady, perched above my chamber door—
Perched upon a bust of Pallas just above my chamber door—
                    Perched, and sat, and nothing more.

Then this ebony bird beguiling my sad fancy into smiling,
By the grave and stern decorum of the countenance it wore,
"Though thy crest be shorn and shaven, thou," I said, "art sure no craven,
Ghastly grim and ancient Raven wandering from the Nightly shore—
Tell me what thy lordly name is on the Night's Plutonian shore!"
                    Quoth the Raven, "Nevermore."

Much I marvelled this ungainly fowl to hear discourse so plainly,
Though its answer little meaning—little relevancy bore;
For we cannot help agreeing that no living human being
Ever yet was blessed with seeing bird above his chamber door—
Bird or beast upon the sculptured bust above his chamber door,
                    With such name as "Nevermore."

But the Raven, sitting lonely on that placid bust, spoke only
That one word, as if his soul in that one word he did outpour.
Nothing farther then he uttered; not a feather then he fluttered—
Till I scarcely more than muttered: "Other friends have flown before—
On the morrow *he* will leave me as my Hopes have flown before."
                    Then the bird said, "Nevermore."

Startled at the stillness broken by reply so aptly spoken,
"Doubtless," said I, "what it utters is its only stock and store,
Caught from some unhappy master whom unmerciful Disaster
Followed fast and followed faster till his songs one burden bore—
Till the dirges of his Hope that melancholy burden bore
                    Of 'Never—nevermore.'"

But the Raven still beguiling all my sad soul into smiling,
Straight I wheeled a cushioned seat in front of bird and bust and door;
Then, upon the velvet sinking, I betook myself to linking
Fancy unto fancy, thinking what this ominous bird of yore—
What this grim, ungainly, ghastly, gaunt, and ominous bird of yore
                    Meant in croaking "Nevermore."

This I sat engaged in guessing, but no syllable expressing
To the fowl whose fiery eyes now burned into my bosom's core;
This and more I sat divining, with my head at ease reclining
On the cushion's velvet lining that the lamp-light gloated o'er,
But whose velvet violet lining with the lamp-light gloating o'er
       *She* shall press, ah, nevermore!

Then, methought, the air grew denser, perfumed from an unseen censer
Swung by Seraphim whose foot-falls tinkled on the tufted floor.
"Wretch," I cried, "thy God hath lent thee—by these angels he hath sent thee
Respite—respite and nepenthe from thy memories of Lenore!
Quaff, oh quaff this kind nepenthe and forget this lost Lenore!"
       Quoth the Raven, "Nevermore."

"Prophet!" said I, "thing of evil!—prophet still, if bird or devil!—
Whether Tempter sent, or whether tempest tossed thee here ashore,
Desolate, yet all undaunted, on this desert land enchanted—
On this home by Horror haunted,—tell me truly, I implore—
Is there—*is* there balm in Gilead?—tell me—tell me, I implore!"
       Quoth the Raven, "Nevermore."

"Prophet!" said I, "thing of evil!—prophet still, if bird or devil!
By that heaven that bends above us—by that God we both adore—
Tell this soul with sorrow laden if, within the distant Aidenn,
It shall clasp a sainted maiden whom the angels name Lenore—
Clasp a rare and radiant maiden whom the angels name Lenore."
       Quoth the Raven, "Nevermore."

"Be that word our sign of parting, bird or fiend!" I shrieked, upstarting—
"Get thee back into the tempest and the Night's Plutonian shore!
Leave no black plume as a token of that lie thy soul hath spoken!
Leave my loneliness unbroken!—quit the bust above my door!
Take thy beak from out my heart, and take thy form from off my door!"
       Quoth the Raven, "Nevermore."

And the Raven, never flitting, still is sitting, still is sitting
On the pallid bust of Pallas just above my chamber door;
And his eyes have all the seeming of a demon's that is dreaming,
And the lamp-light o'er him streaming throws his shadow on the floor;
And my soul from out that shadow that lies floating on the floor
       Shall be lifted—nevermore!

      — Edgar Allan Poe

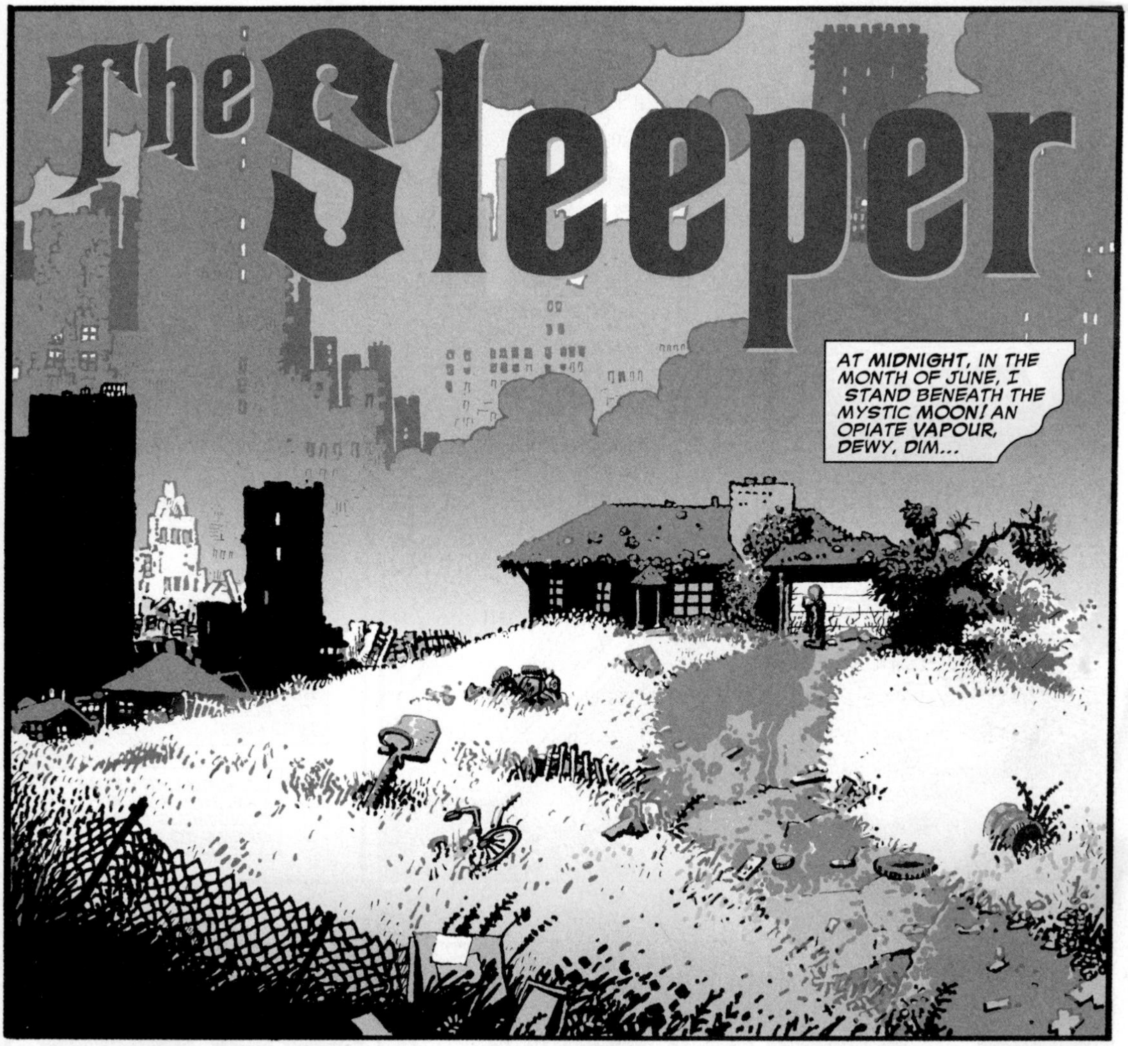
The Sleeper
AT MIDNIGHT, IN THE MONTH OF JUNE, I STAND BENEATH THE MYSTIC MOON! AN OPIATE VAPOUR, DEWY, DIM...

Exquisite **night terrors** brought to you by the **usual suspects:**

**POE, MARGOPOULOS, & CORBEN**

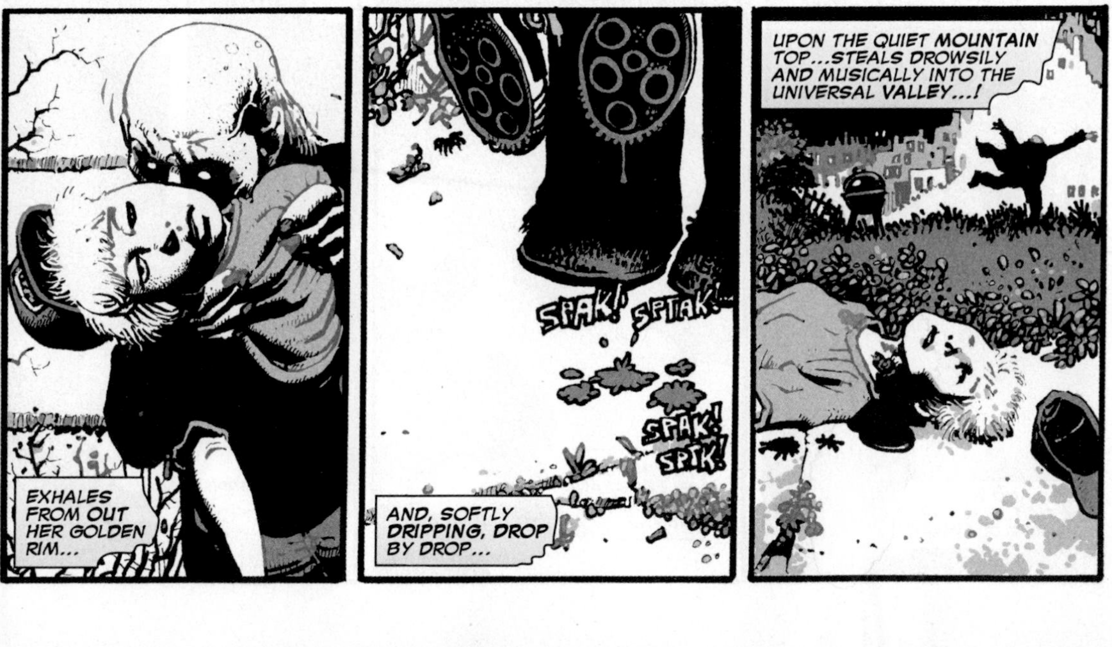
EXHALES FROM OUT HER GOLDEN RIM...
SPAK! SPTAK!
SPAK! SPTK!
AND, SOFTLY DRIPPING, DROP BY DROP...
UPON THE QUIET MOUNTAIN TOP...STEALS DROWSILY AND MUSICALLY INTO THE UNIVERSAL VALLEY...!

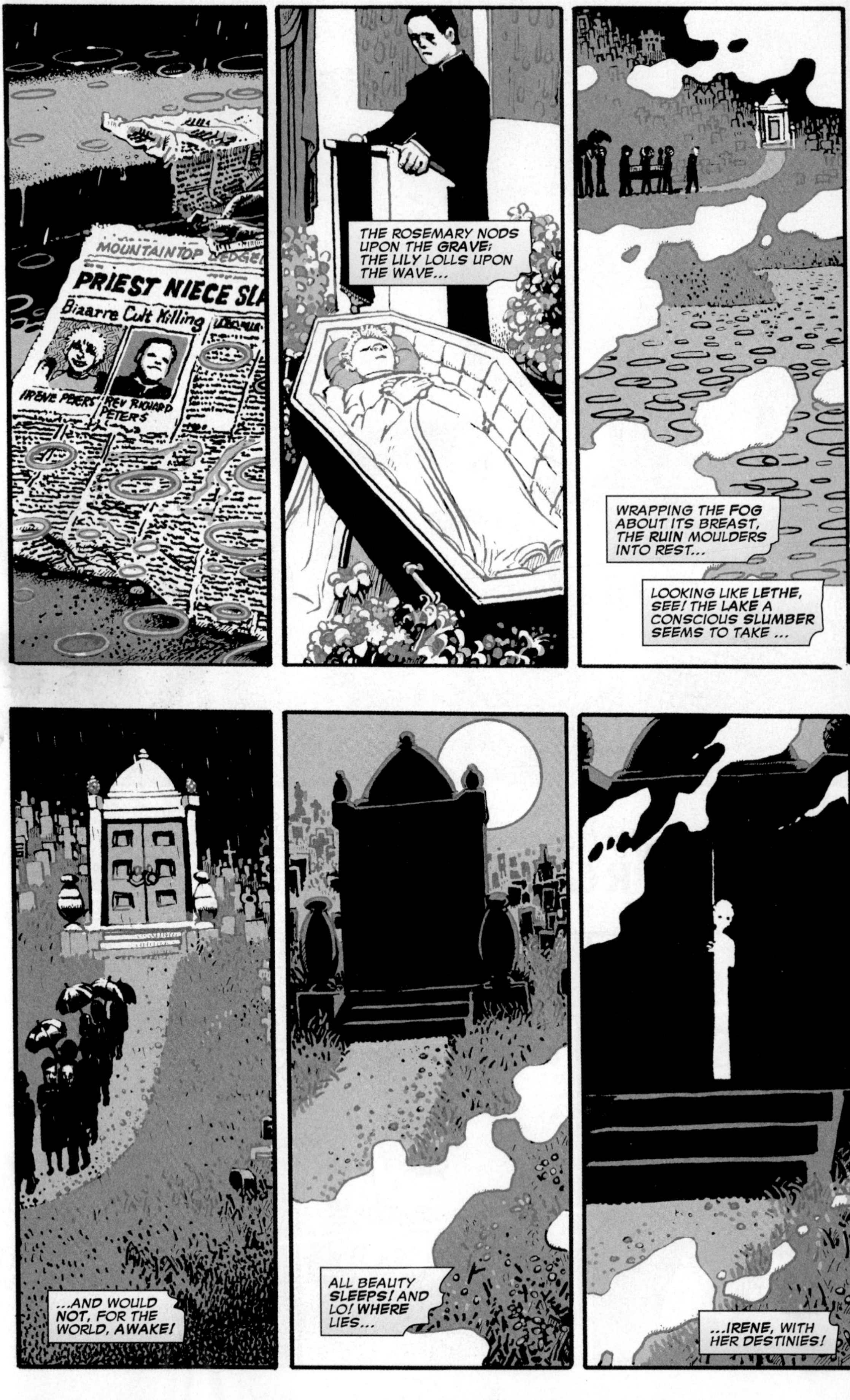
MOUNTAINTOP LEDGE
PRIEST NIECE SLA
Bizarre Cult Killing
IRENE PEERS
REV RICHARD PETERS
THE ROSEMARY NODS UPON THE GRAVE; THE LILY LOLLS UPON THE WAVE...
WRAPPING THE FOG ABOUT ITS BREAST, THE RUIN MOULDERS INTO REST...
LOOKING LIKE LETHE, SEE! THE LAKE A CONSCIOUS SLUMBER SEEMS TO TAKE ...
...AND WOULD NOT, FOR THE WORLD, AWAKE!
ALL BEAUTY SLEEPS! AND LO! WHERE LIES...
...IRENE, WITH HER DESTINIES!

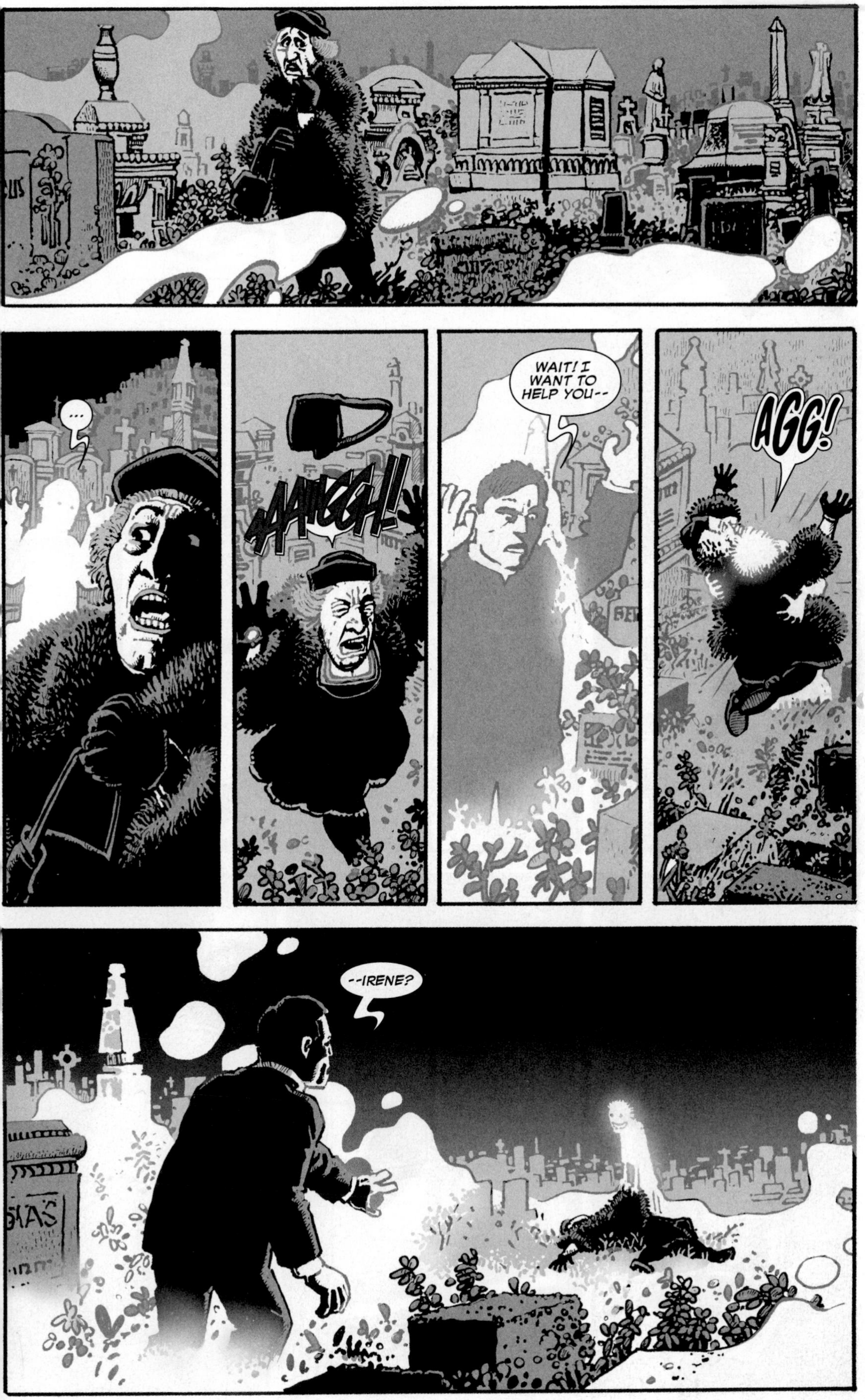

...
AAIIGGH!!
WAIT! I WANT TO HELP YOU--
AGG!
--IRENE?

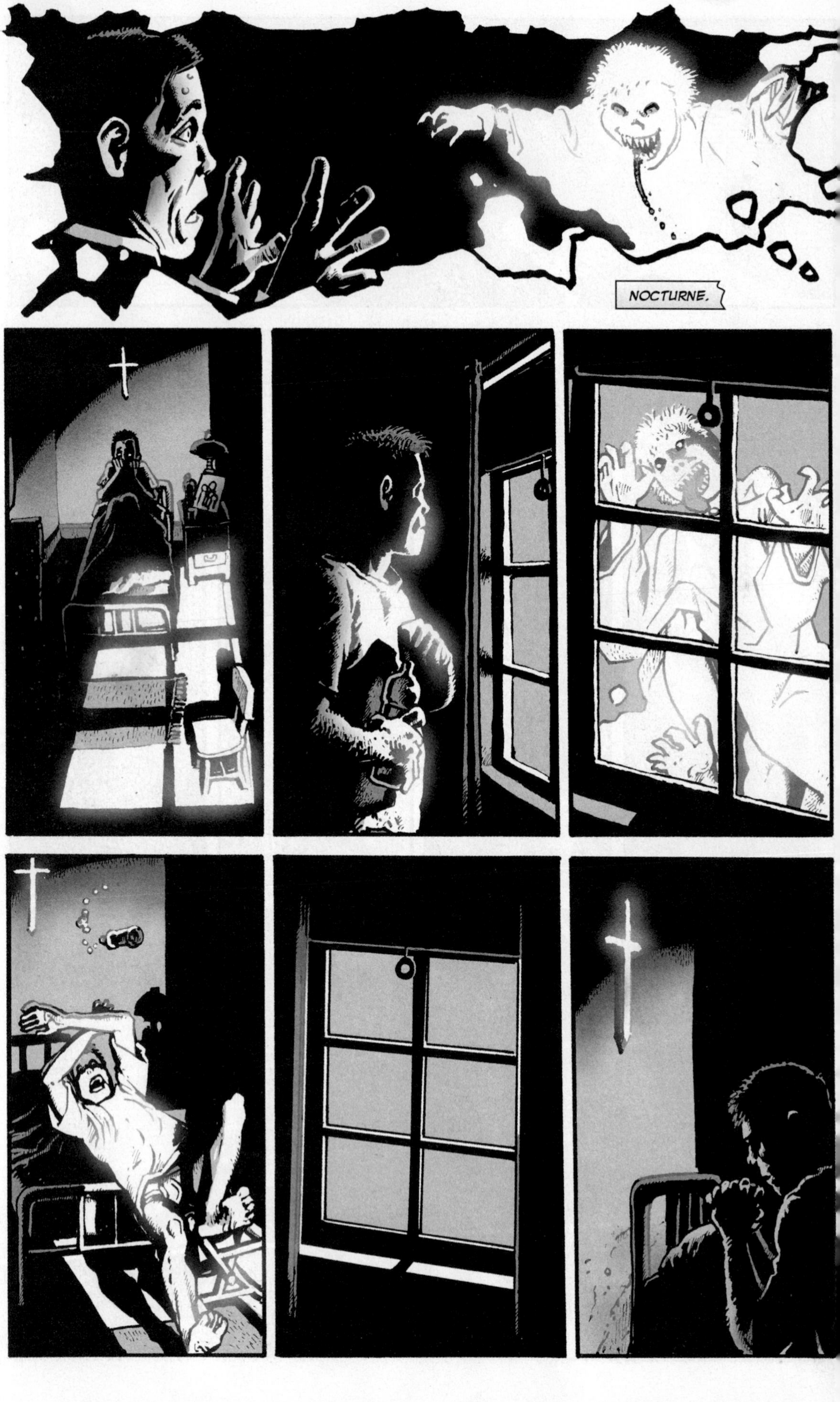
NOCTURNE.

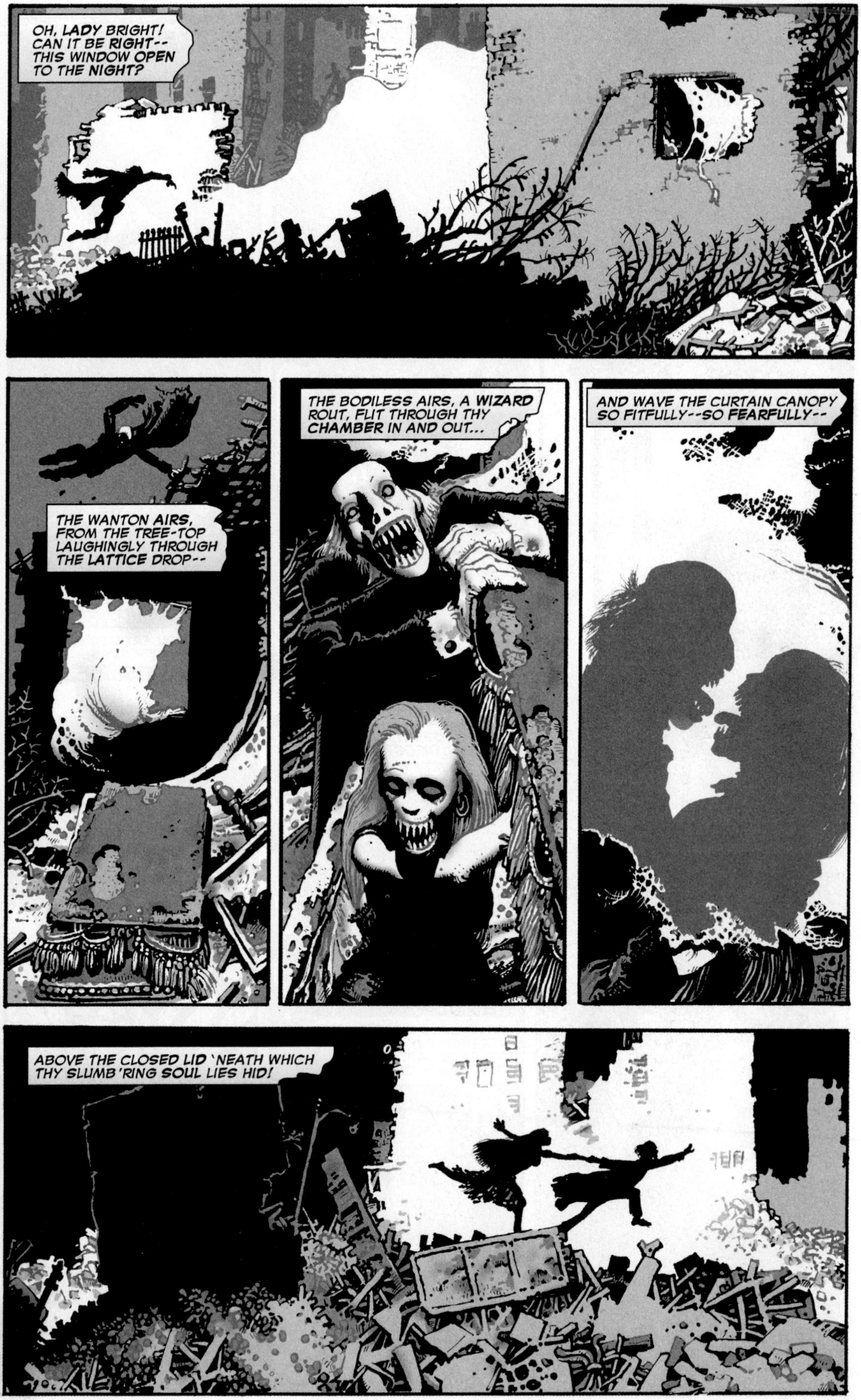
OH, LADY BRIGHT! CAN IT BE RIGHT-- THIS WINDOW OPEN TO THE NIGHT?
THE WANTON AIRS, FROM THE TREE-TOP LAUGHINGLY THROUGH THE LATTICE DROP--
THE BODILESS AIRS, A WIZARD ROUT, FLIT THROUGH THY CHAMBER IN AND OUT...
AND WAVE THE CURTAIN CANOPY SO FITFULLY--SO FEARFULLY--
ABOVE THE CLOSED LID 'NEATH WHICH THY SLUMB'RING SOUL LIES HID!

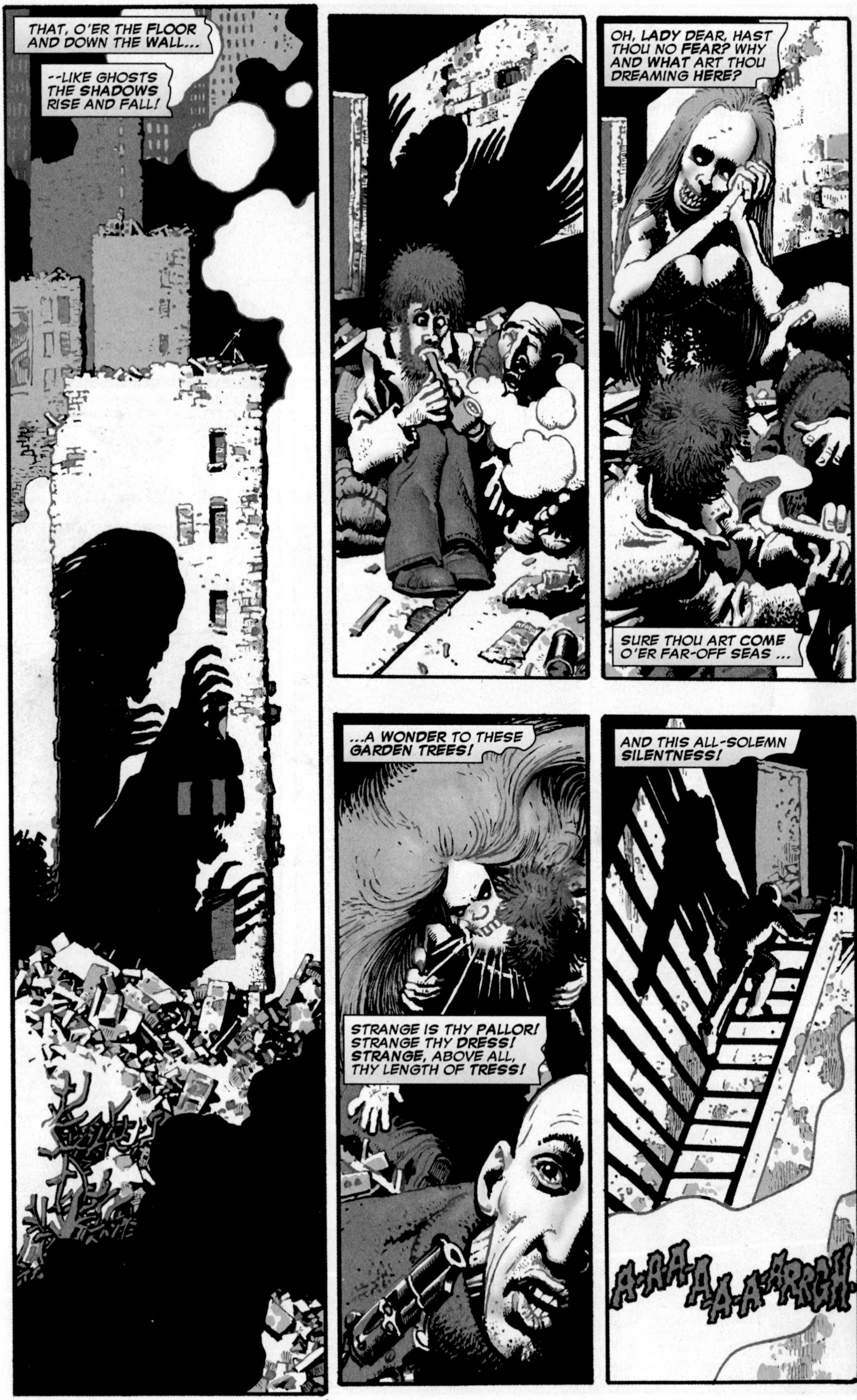
THAT, O'ER THE FLOOR AND DOWN THE WALL...
--LIKE GHOSTS THE SHADOWS RISE AND FALL!
OH, LADY DEAR, HAST THOU NO FEAR? WHY AND WHAT ART THOU DREAMING HERE?
SURE THOU ART COME O'ER FAR-OFF SEAS ...
...A WONDER TO THESE GARDEN TREES!
STRANGE IS THY PALLOR! STRANGE THY DRESS! STRANGE, ABOVE ALL, THY LENGTH OF TRESS!
AND THIS ALL-SOLEMN SILENTNESS!
A-A-A-A-A-A-ARRGH

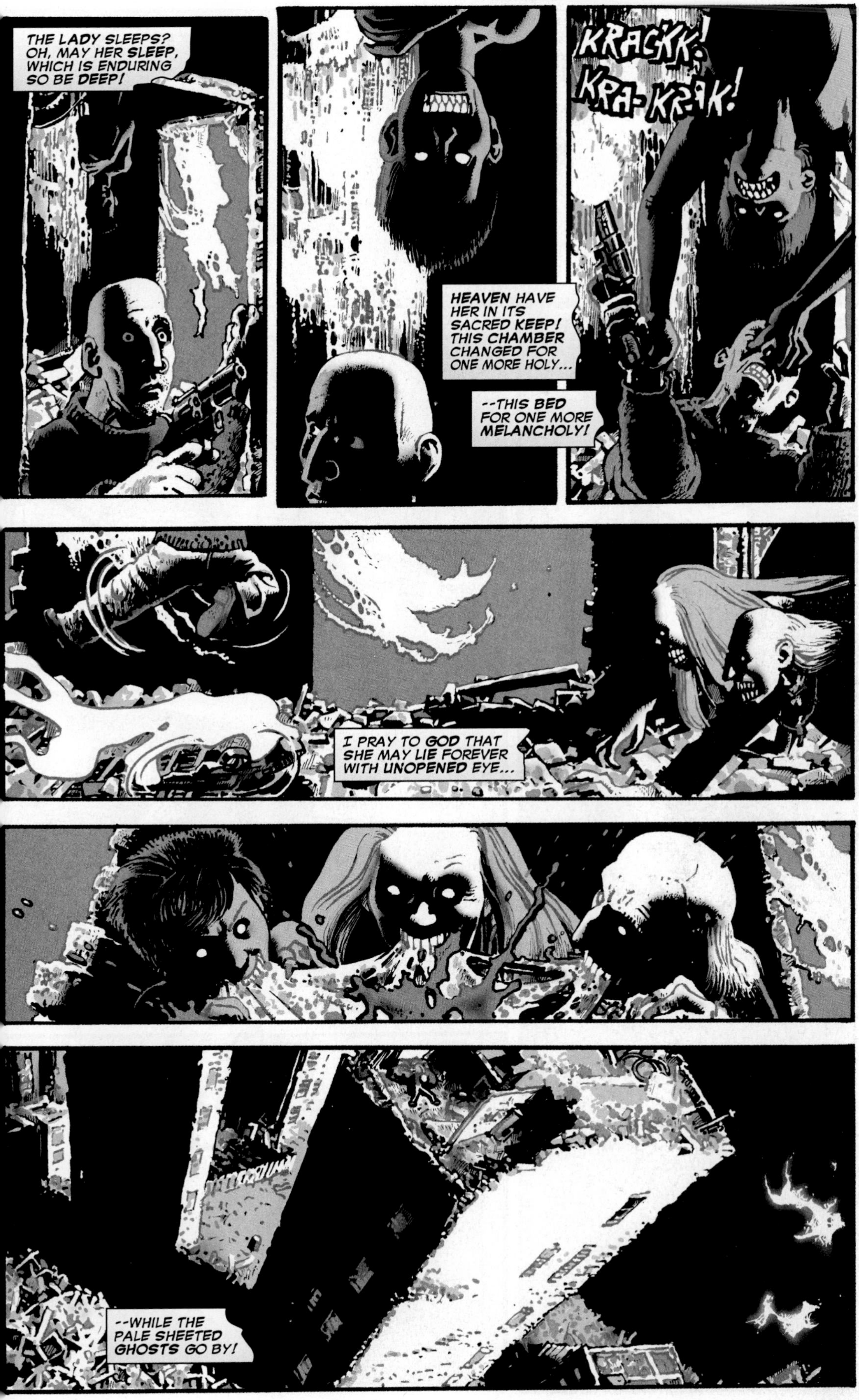
THE LADY SLEEPS? OH, MAY HER SLEEP, WHICH IS ENDURING SO BE DEEP!
HEAVEN HAVE HER IN ITS SACRED KEEP! THIS CHAMBER CHANGED FOR ONE MORE HOLY...
--THIS BED FOR ONE MORE MELANCHOLY!
KRACKK! KRA-KRAK!
I PRAY TO GOD THAT SHE MAY LIE FOREVER WITH UNOPENED EYE...
--WHILE THE PALE SHEETED GHOSTS GO BY!

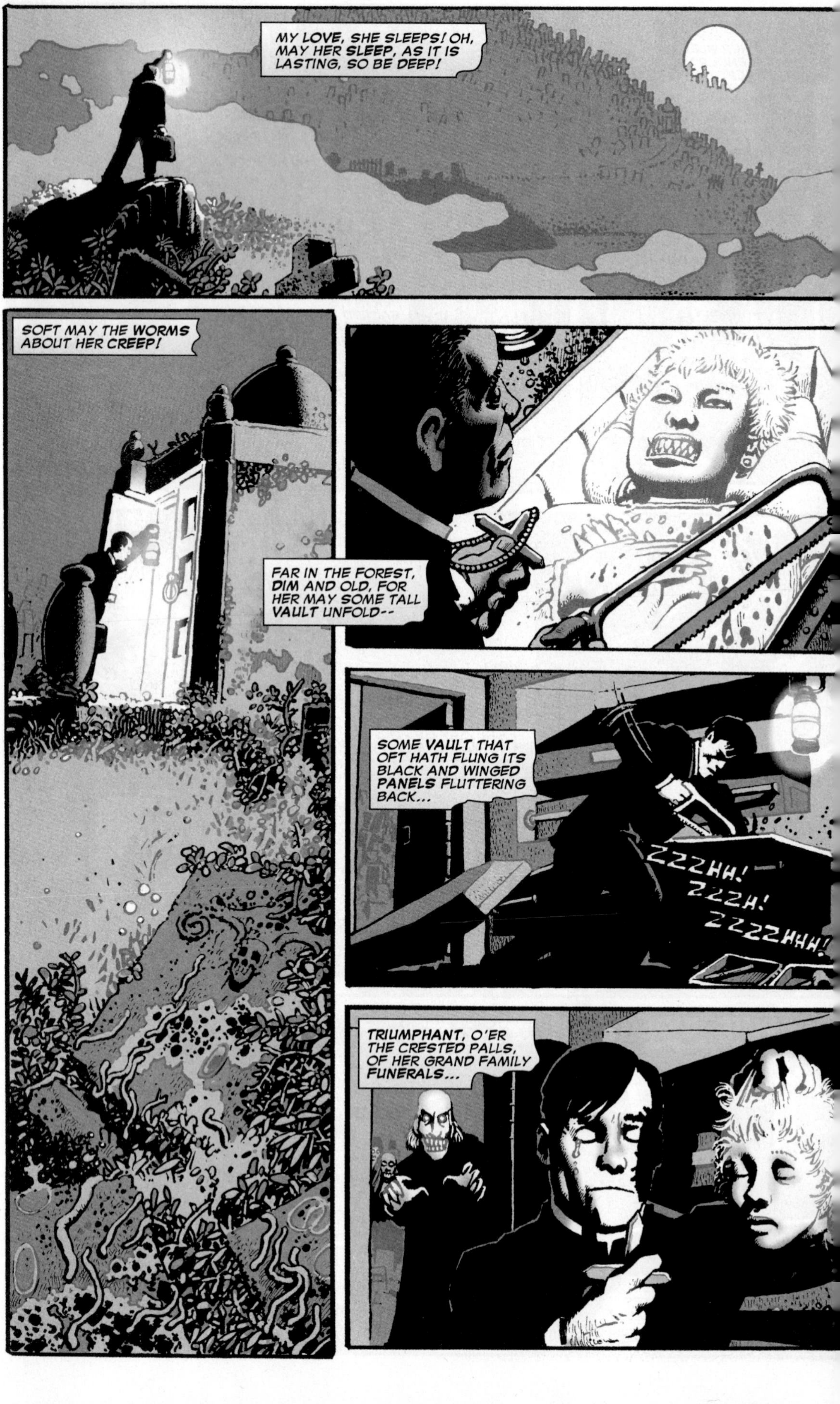
MY LOVE, SHE SLEEPS! OH, MAY HER SLEEP, AS IT IS LASTING, SO BE DEEP!
SOFT MAY THE WORMS ABOUT HER CREEP!
FAR IN THE FOREST, DIM AND OLD, FOR HER MAY SOME TALL VAULT UNFOLD--
SOME VAULT THAT OFT HATH FLUNG ITS BLACK AND WINGED PANELS FLUTTERING BACK...
ZZZHH!
ZZZH!
ZZZZHHH!
TRIUMPHANT, O'ER THE CRESTED PALLS, OF HER GRAND FAMILY FUNERALS...

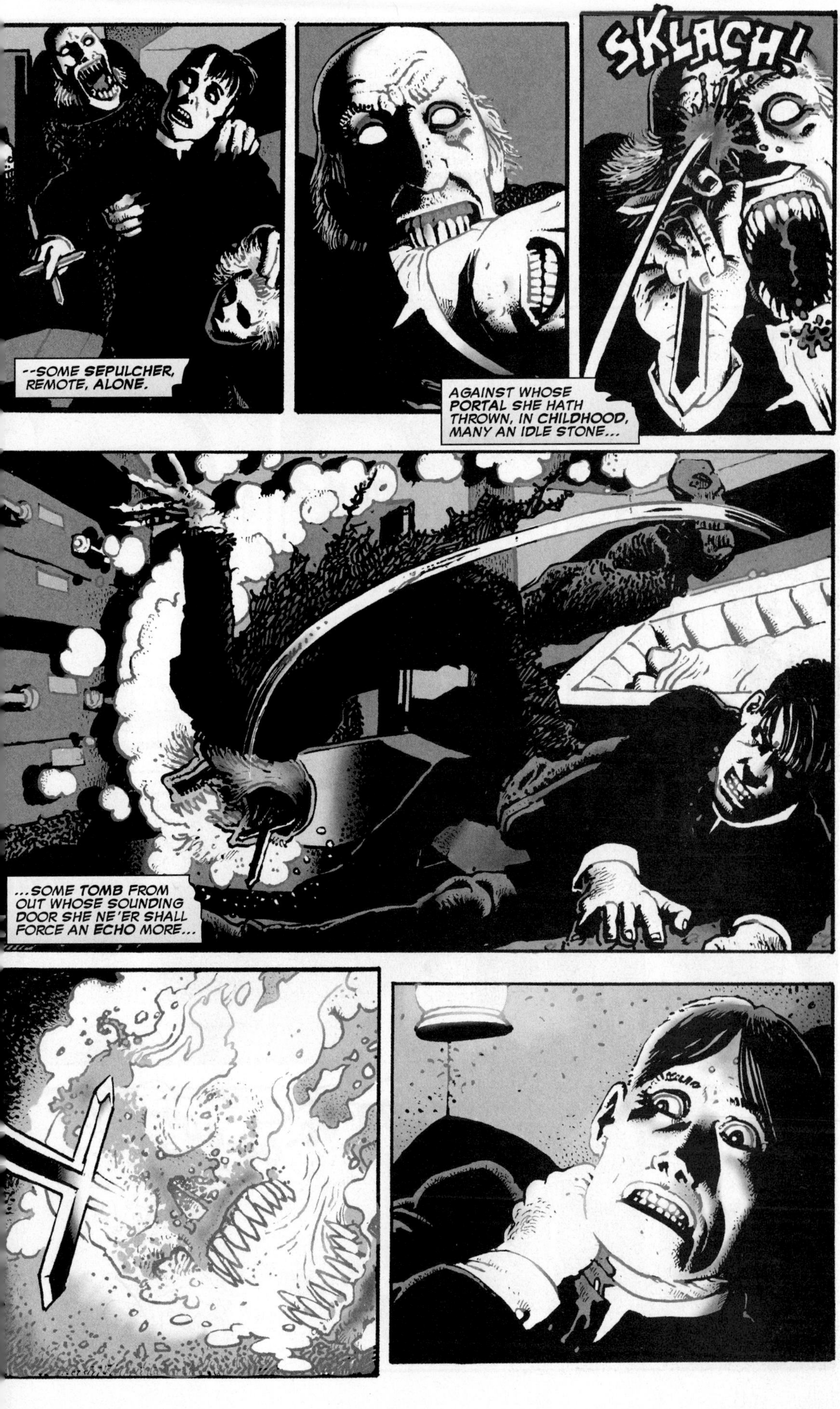
--SOME SEPULCHER, REMOTE, ALONE.
AGAINST WHOSE PORTAL SHE HATH THROWN, IN CHILDHOOD, MANY AN IDLE STONE...
SKLACH!
...SOME TOMB FROM OUT WHOSE SOUNDING DOOR SHE NE'ER SHALL FORCE AN ECHO MORE...

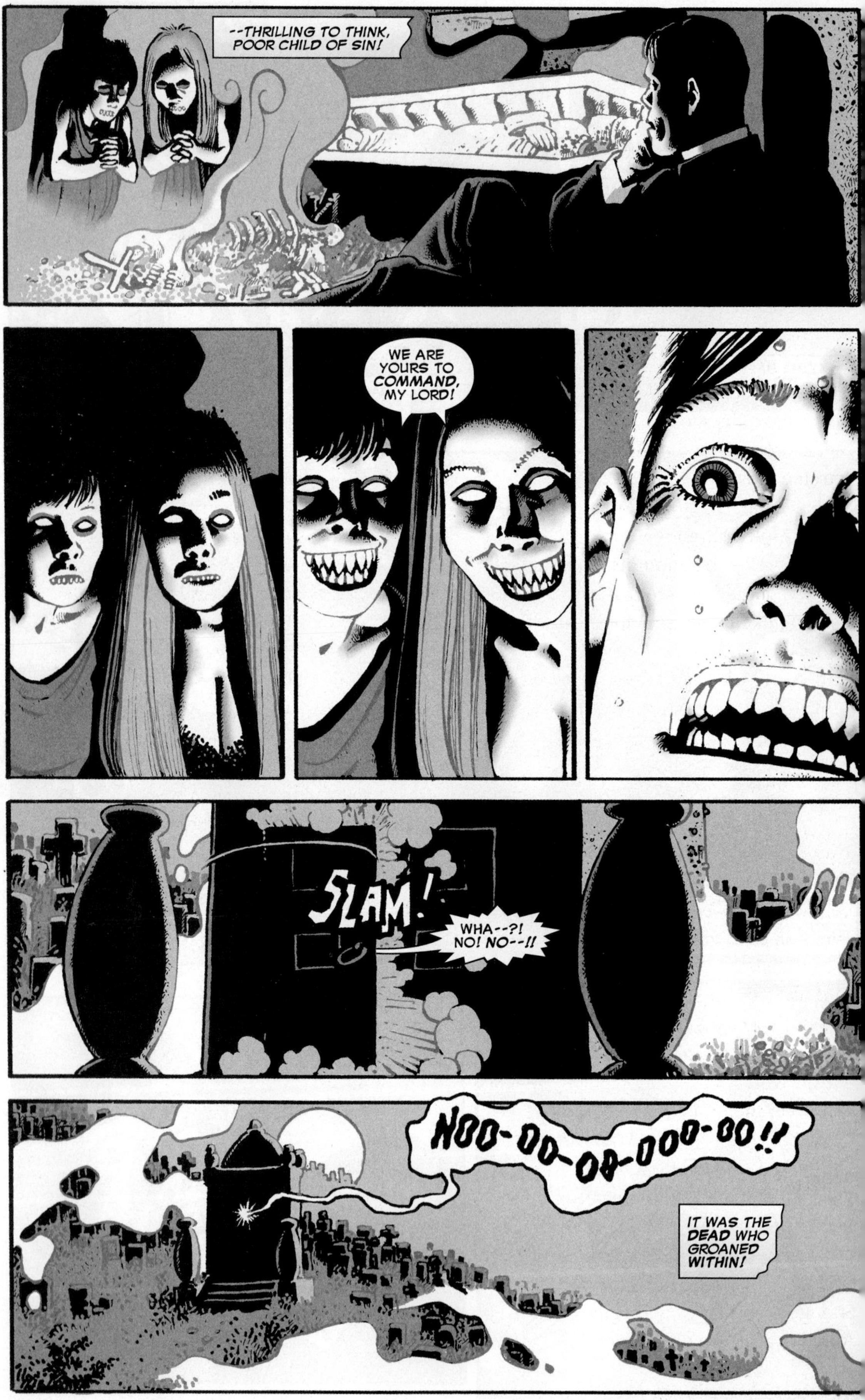
--THRILLING TO THINK, POOR CHILD OF SIN!
WE ARE YOURS TO COMMAND, MY LORD!
SLAM!
WHA--?! NO! NO--!!
NOO-OO-OO-OOO-OO!!
IT WAS THE DEAD WHO GROANED WITHIN!

# The Sleeper

At midnight, in the month of June,
I stand beneath the mystic moon.
An opiate vapor, dewy, dim,
Exhales from out her golden rim,
And, softly dripping, drop by drop,
Upon the quiet mountain top,
Steals drowsily and musically
Into the universal valley.
The rosemary nods upon the grave;
The lily lolls upon the wave;
Wrapping the fog about its breast,
The ruin moulders into rest;
Looking like Lethe, see! the lake
A conscious slumber seems to take,
And would not, for the world, awake.
All Beauty sleeps!—and lo! where lies
(Her casement open to the skies)
Irene, with her Destinies!

Oh, lady bright! can it be right—
This window open to the night?
The wanton airs, from the tree-top,
Laughingly through the lattice drop—
The bodiless airs, a wizard rout,
Flit through thy chamber in and out,
And wave the curtain canopy
So fitfully—so carefully—
Above the closed and fringed lid
'Neath which thy slumb'ring soul lies hid,
That, o'er the floor and down the wall,
Like ghosts the shadows rise and fall!
Oh, lady dear, hast thou no fear?
Why and what art thou dreaming here?
Sure thou art come o'er far-off seas,
A wonder to these garden trees!
Strange is thy pallor! strange thy dress!
Strange, above all, thy length of tress,
And this all solemn silentness!

The lady sleeps! Oh, may her sleep,
Which is enduring, so be deep!
Heaven have her in its sacred keep!
This chamber changed for one more holy,
This bed for one more melancholy,
I pray to God that she may lie
Forever with unopened eye,
While dim sheeted ghosts go by!

My love, she sleeps! Oh, may her sleep,
As it is lasting, so be deep!
Soft may the worms about her creep!
Far in the forest, dim and old,
For her may some tall vault unfold—
Some vault that oft hath flung its black
And winged panels fluttering back,
Triumphant, o'er the crested palls,
Of her grand family funerals—
Some sepulcher, remote, alone,
Against whose portal she hath thrown,
In childhood, many an idle stone—
Some tomb from out whose sounding door
She ne'er shall force an echo more,
Thrilling to think, poor child of sin!
It was the dead who groaned within.

— Edgar Allan Poe

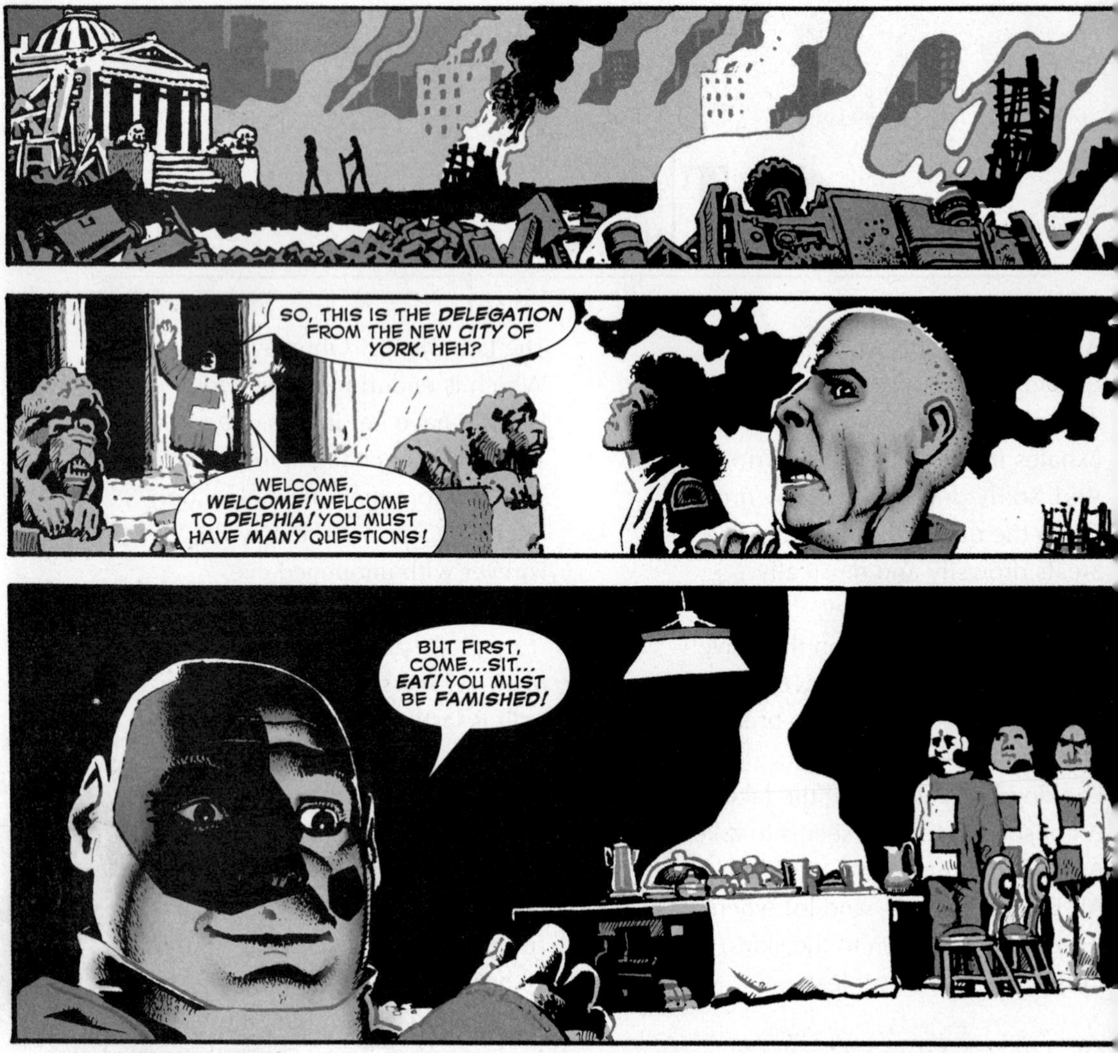
SO, THIS IS THE DELEGATION FROM THE NEW CITY OF YORK, HEH?
WELCOME, WELCOME! WELCOME TO DELPHIA! YOU MUST HAVE MANY QUESTIONS!
BUT FIRST, COME...SIT... EAT! YOU MUST BE FAMISHED!

# THE CONQUEROR WORM

INSPIRED BY A POEM PENNED BY EDGAR ALLAN POE

A RICK DAHL n' RICH CORBEN COLLABORATION

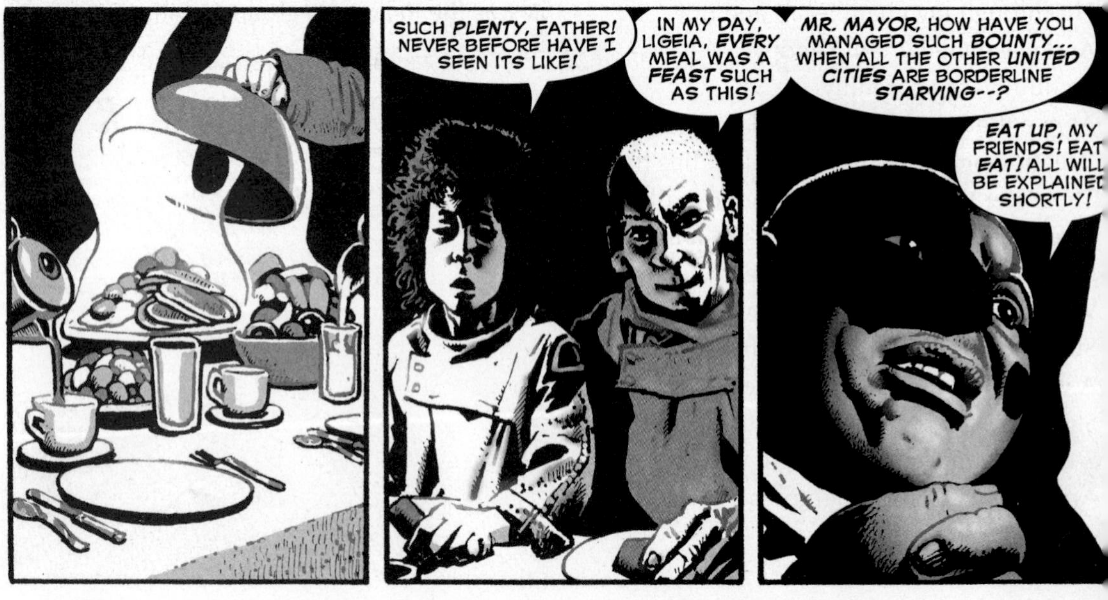
SUCH PLENTY, FATHER! NEVER BEFORE HAVE I SEEN ITS LIKE!
IN MY DAY, LIGEIA, EVERY MEAL WAS A FEAST SUCH AS THIS!
MR. MAYOR, HOW HAVE YOU MANAGED SUCH BOUNTY... WHEN ALL THE OTHER UNITED CITIES ARE BORDERLINE STARVING--?
EAT UP, MY FRIENDS! EAT EAT! ALL WILL BE EXPLAINED SHORTLY!

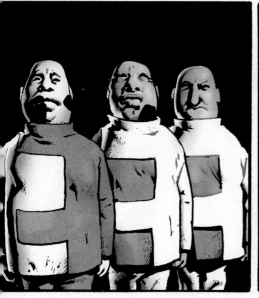

MILK! BUTTER! EGGS! MEAT, EVEN! THIS IS SCIENTIFICALLY IMPOSSIBLE--!

ALL *TRUE!* YOU ARE A MAN OF *SCIENCE,* THEN?

HERE, MY DEAR! TRY A WEDGE OF *CHEESE!* GOOD, NO?

YES, MR. MAYOR, A *SCIENTIST!* PROBABLY THE LAST ONE IN ALL OF *RE-NEW ENGLAND!*

I TAKE IT YOU WERE *ALIVE* DURING THE ALIEN *WORM* INVASION SOME 50 YEARS AGO, HM?

CORRECT! I EVEN PARTICIPATED IN *OPERATION FINAL PUSH* TO GET THEM *OFF* THE PLANET!

BUT NOT *SOON* ENOUGH, EH? THE *DAMAGE* THEY CAUSED--!

*HERE,* MY DEAR! TRY THESE JELLIED *EGGS!* PLEASE! I *INSIST!* EAT... EAT!

THE *DESTRUCTION* THEY CAUSED WAS *ABSOLUTE* AND *TOTAL!*

THE *WORM* TERRA-FORMING PROJECTS PLAYED HAVOC WITH THE *ENVIRONMENT,* STUNTING OUR *CROPS...!*

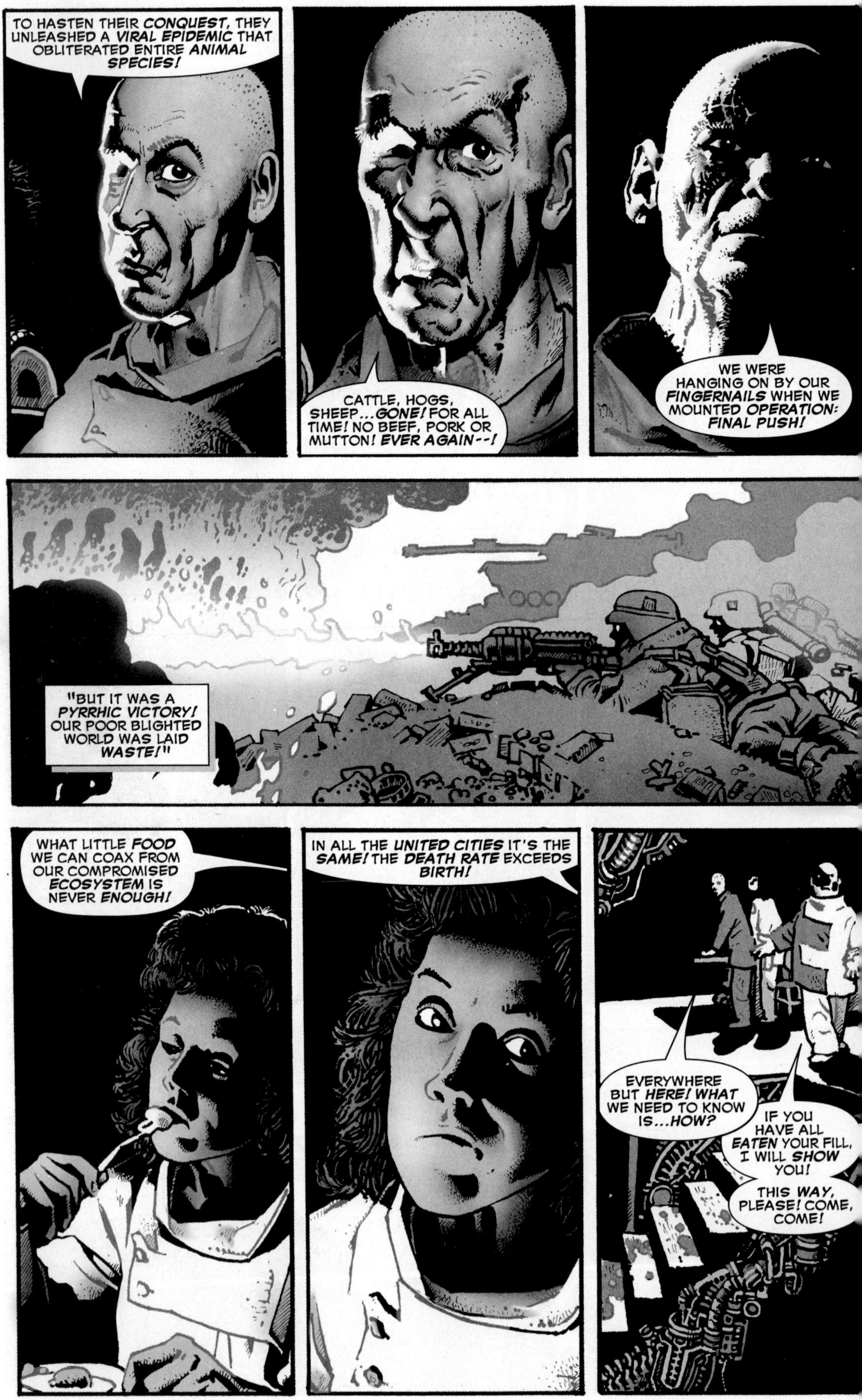
TO HASTEN THEIR CONQUEST, THEY UNLEASHED A VIRAL EPIDEMIC THAT OBLITERATED ENTIRE ANIMAL SPECIES!
CATTLE, HOGS, SHEEP...GONE! FOR ALL TIME! NO BEEF, PORK OR MUTTON! EVER AGAIN--!
WE WERE HANGING ON BY OUR FINGERNAILS WHEN WE MOUNTED OPERATION: FINAL PUSH!
"BUT IT WAS A PYRRHIC VICTORY! OUR POOR BLIGHTED WORLD WAS LAID WASTE!"
WHAT LITTLE FOOD WE CAN COAX FROM OUR COMPROMISED ECOSYSTEM IS NEVER ENOUGH!
IN ALL THE UNITED CITIES IT'S THE SAME! THE DEATH RATE EXCEEDS BIRTH!
EVERYWHERE BUT HERE! WHAT WE NEED TO KNOW IS...HOW?
IF YOU HAVE ALL EATEN YOUR FILL, I WILL SHOW YOU!
THIS WAY, PLEASE! COME, COME!

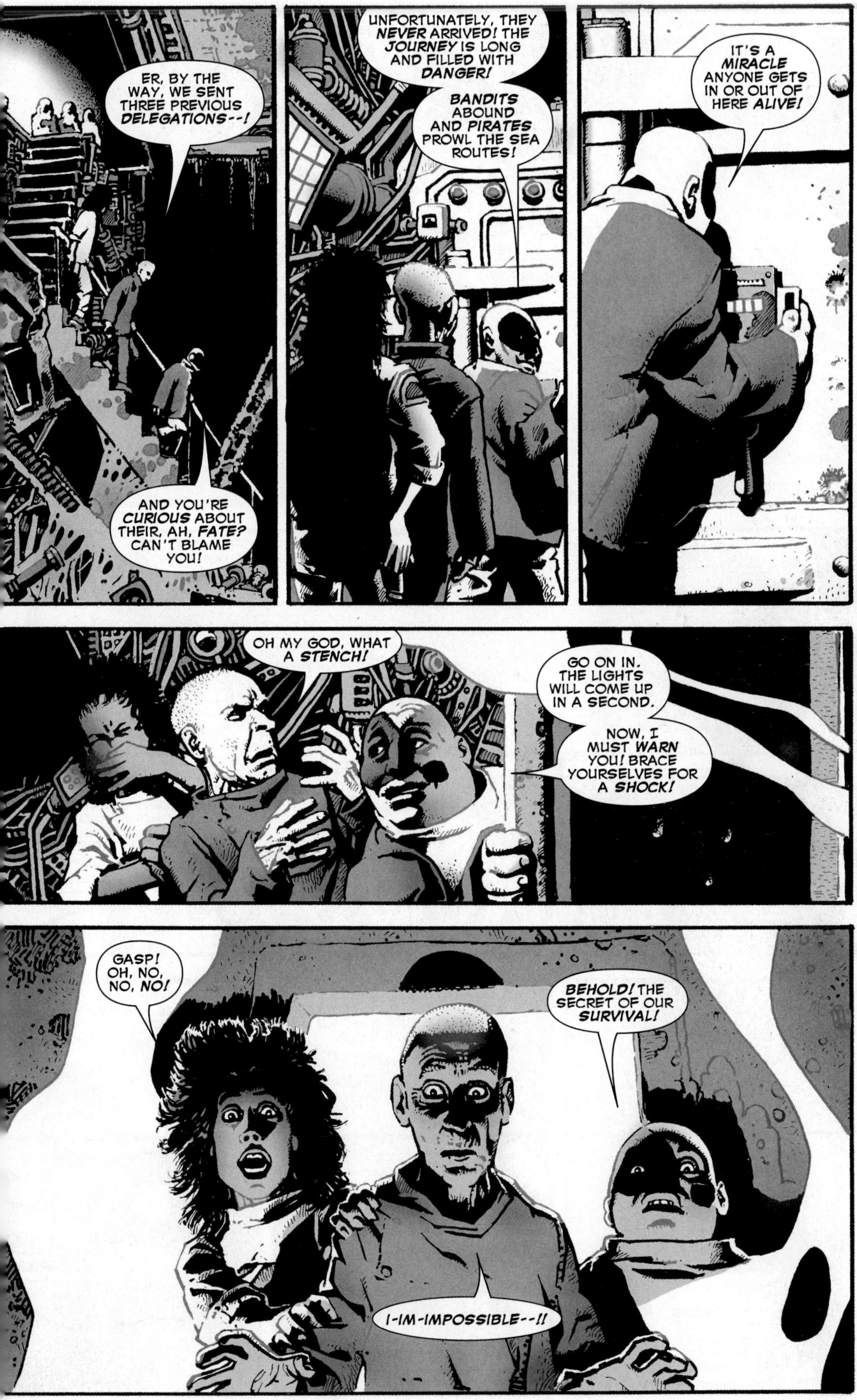
ER, BY THE WAY, WE SENT THREE PREVIOUS DELEGATIONS--!
AND YOU'RE CURIOUS ABOUT THEIR, AH, FATE? CAN'T BLAME YOU!
UNFORTUNATELY, THEY NEVER ARRIVED! THE JOURNEY IS LONG AND FILLED WITH DANGER!
BANDITS ABOUND AND PIRATES PROWL THE SEA ROUTES!
IT'S A MIRACLE ANYONE GETS IN OR OUT OF HERE ALIVE!
OH MY GOD, WHAT A STENCH!
GO ON IN. THE LIGHTS WILL COME UP IN A SECOND.
NOW, I MUST WARN YOU! BRACE YOURSELVES FOR A SHOCK!
GASP! OH, NO, NO, NO!
BEHOLD! THE SECRET OF OUR SURVIVAL!
I-IM-IMPOSSIBLE--!!

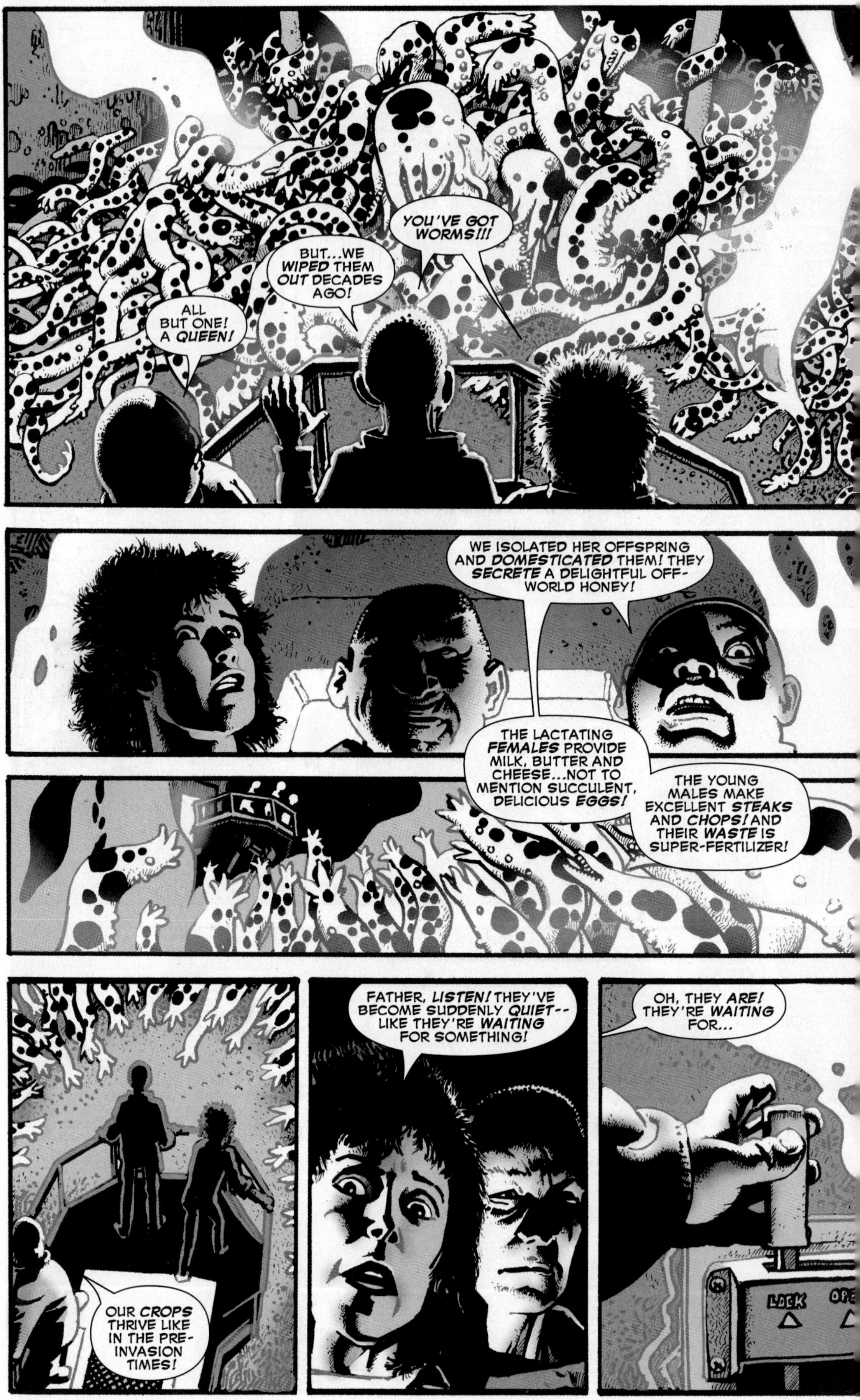
YOU'VE GOT WORMS!!!
BUT...WE WIPED THEM OUT DECADES AGO!
ALL BUT ONE! A QUEEN!
WE ISOLATED HER OFFSPRING AND DOMESTICATED THEM! THEY SECRETE A DELIGHTFUL OFF-WORLD HONEY!
THE LACTATING FEMALES PROVIDE MILK, BUTTER AND CHEESE...NOT TO MENTION SUCCULENT, DELICIOUS EGGS!
THE YOUNG MALES MAKE EXCELLENT STEAKS AND CHOPS! AND THEIR WASTE IS SUPER-FERTILIZER!
OUR CROPS THRIVE LIKE IN THE PRE-INVASION TIMES!
FATHER, LISTEN! THEY'VE BECOME SUDDENLY QUIET--LIKE THEY'RE WAITING FOR SOMETHING!
OH, THEY ARE! THEY'RE WAITING FOR...
LOCK

--YOU!!!

KA-THUNKK!

LCBK OPEN

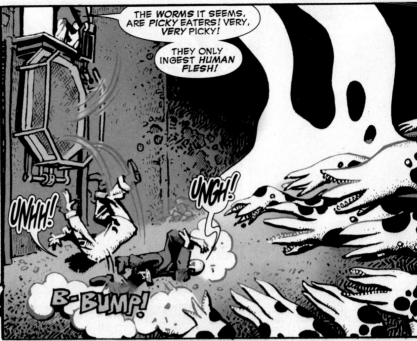

THE WORMS IT SEEMS, ARE PICKY EATERS! VERY, VERY PICKY!

THEY ONLY INGEST HUMAN FLESH!

UNHH!

UNGH!

B-BUMP!

AN OCCASIONAL PIRATE OR BANDIT ONLY GOES SO FAR! BUT A CITY DELEGATION--!

AHH, THAT CAN LAST THEM A WEEK!

LIGEIA! ARE YOU ALL RIGHT?

I DROPPED THE GUN!

WE EAT THEM-- NOW THEY EAT US!!

ERGH!! THEY'RE TOO STRONG!

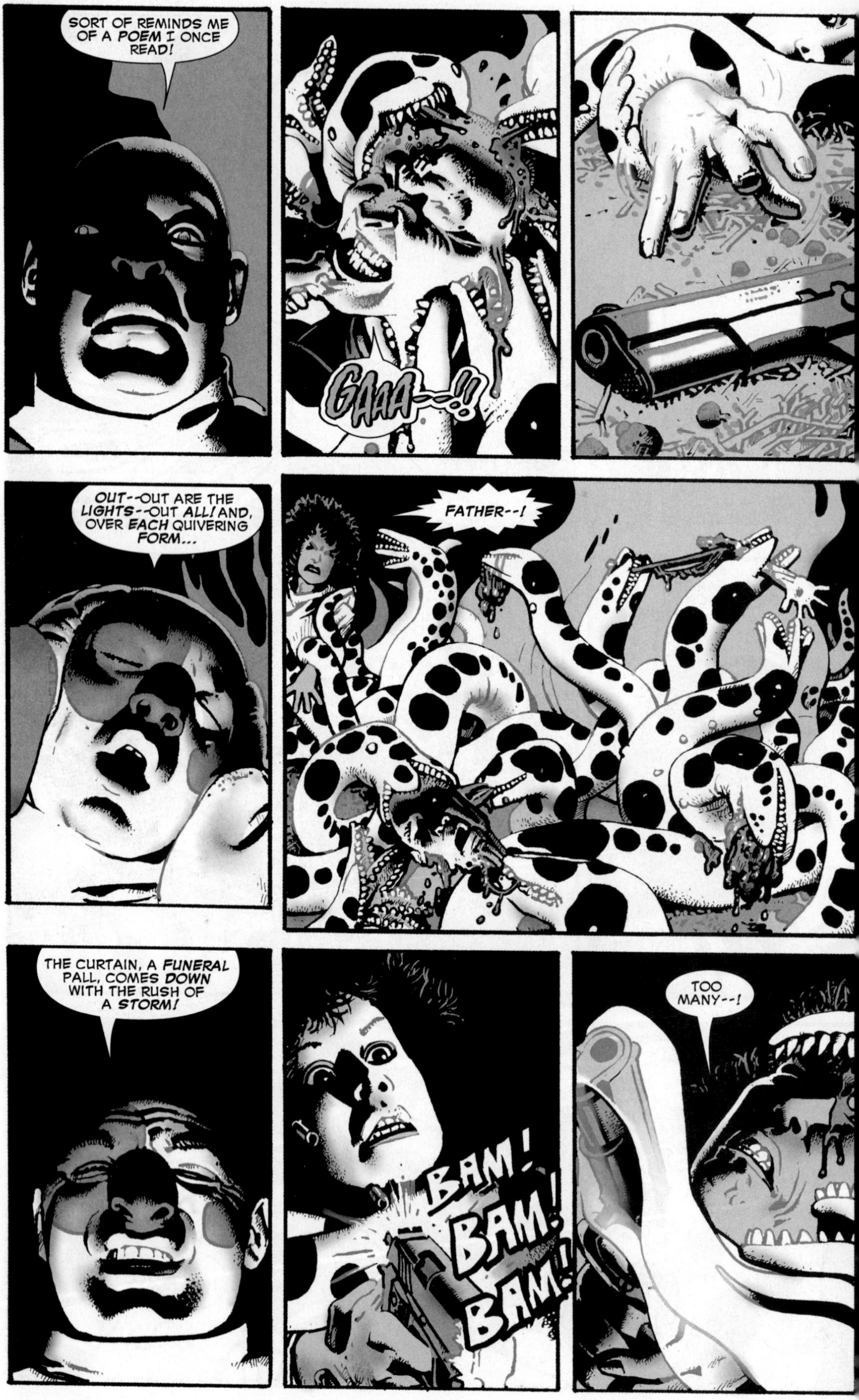
SORT OF REMINDS ME OF A POEM I ONCE READ!
GAAA--!!
OUT--OUT ARE THE LIGHTS--OUT ALL! AND, OVER EACH QUIVERING FORM...
FATHER--!
THE CURTAIN, A FUNERAL PALL, COMES DOWN WITH THE RUSH OF A STORM!
BAM! BAM! BAM!
TOO MANY--!

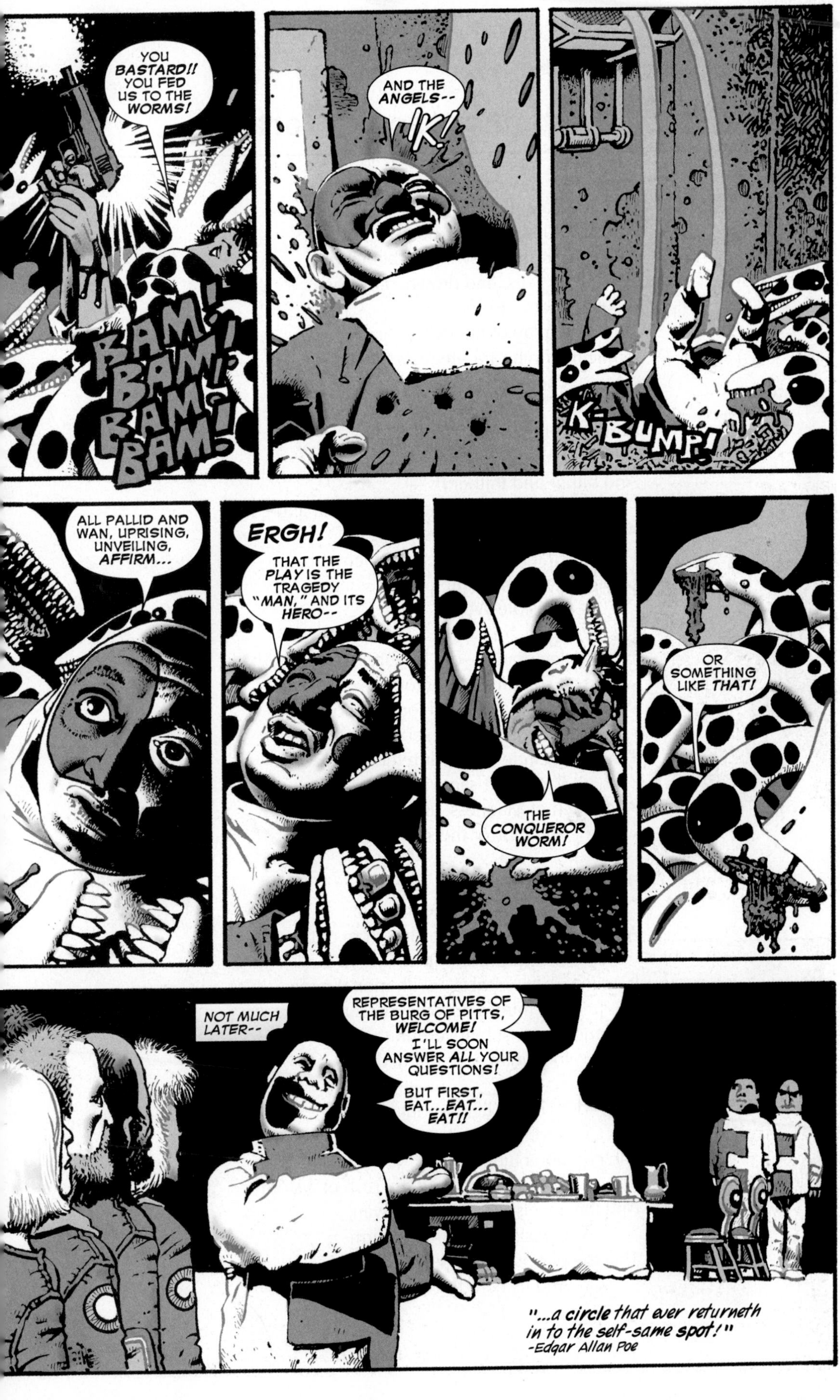
YOU BASTARD!! YOU FED US TO THE WORMS!
BAM! BAM! BAM! BAM!
AND THE ANGELS--
IK!
K-BUMP!
ALL PALLID AND WAN, UPRISING, UNVEILING, AFFIRM...
ERGH!
THAT THE PLAY IS THE TRAGEDY "MAN," AND ITS HERO--
THE CONQUEROR WORM!
OR SOMETHING LIKE THAT!
NOT MUCH LATER--
REPRESENTATIVES OF THE BURG OF PITTS, WELCOME!
I'LL SOON ANSWER ALL YOUR QUESTIONS!
BUT FIRST, EAT...EAT... EAT!!
"...a circle that ever returneth in to the self-same spot!"
-Edgar Allan Poe

# The Conqueror Worm

Lo! 'tis a gala night
    Within the lonesome latter years!
An angel throng, bewinged, bedight
    In veils, and drowned in tears,
Sit in a theatre, to see
    A play of hopes and fears,
While the orchestra breathes fitfully
    The music of the spheres.

Mimes, in the form of God on high,
    Mutter and mumble low,
And hither and thither fly—
    Mere puppets they, who come and go
At bidding of vast formless things
    That shift the scenery to and fro,
Flapping from out their Condor wings
    Invisible Woe!

That motley drama—oh, be sure
    It shall not be forgot!
With its Phantom chased for evermore,
    By a crowd that seize it not,
Through a circle that ever returneth in
    To the self-same spot,
And much of Madness, and more of Sin,
    And Horror the soul of the plot.

But see, amid the mimic rout
    A crawling shape intrude!
A blood-red thing that writhes from out
    The scenic solitude!
It writhes!—it writhes!—with mortal pangs
    The mimes become its food,
And the angels sob at vermin fangs
    In human gore imbued.

Out—out are the lights—out all!
    And, over each quivering form,
The curtain, a funeral pall,
    Comes down with the rush of a storm,
And the angels, all pallid and wan,
    Uprising, unveiling, affirm
That the play is the tragedy "Man,"
    And its hero the Conqueror Worm.

— Edgar Allan Poe

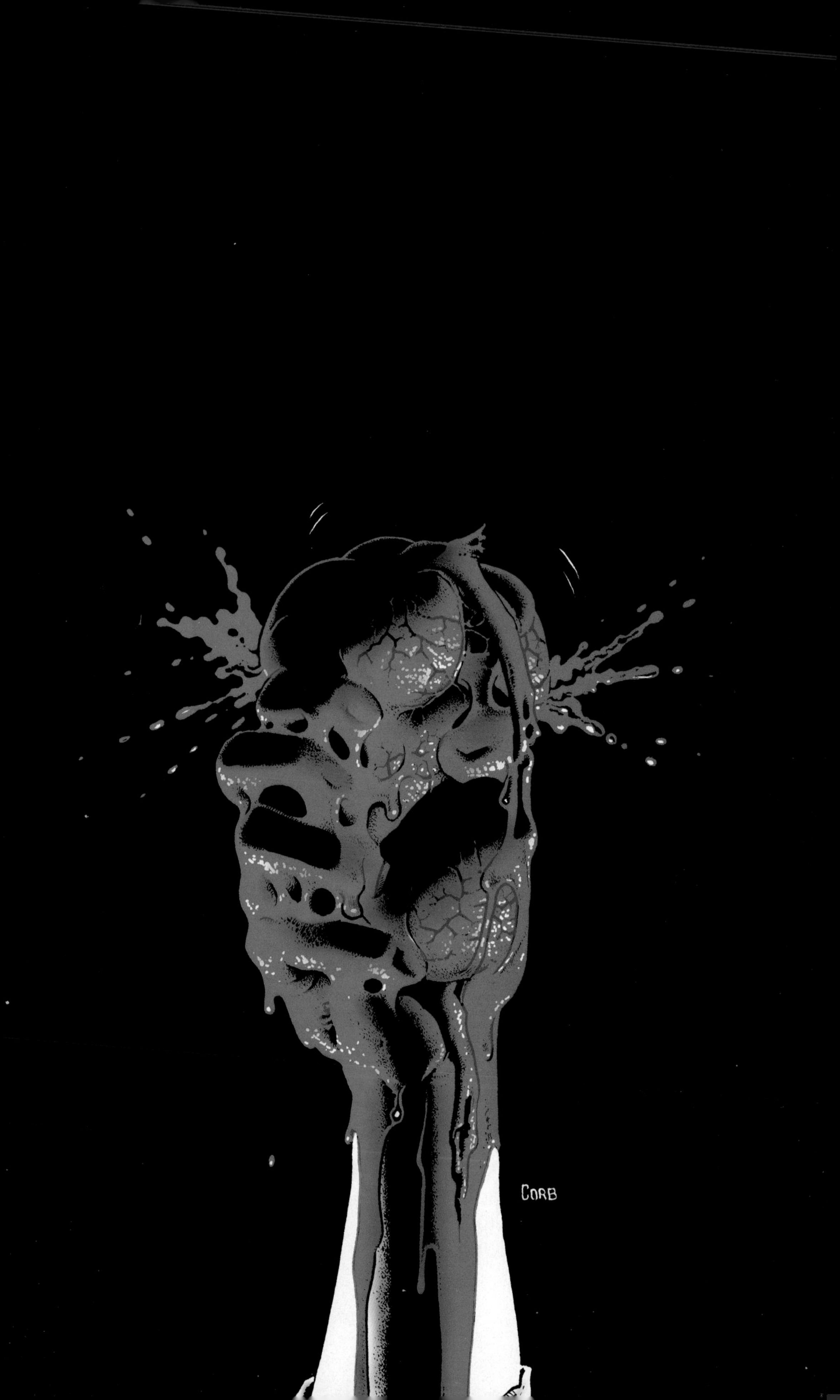
CORB

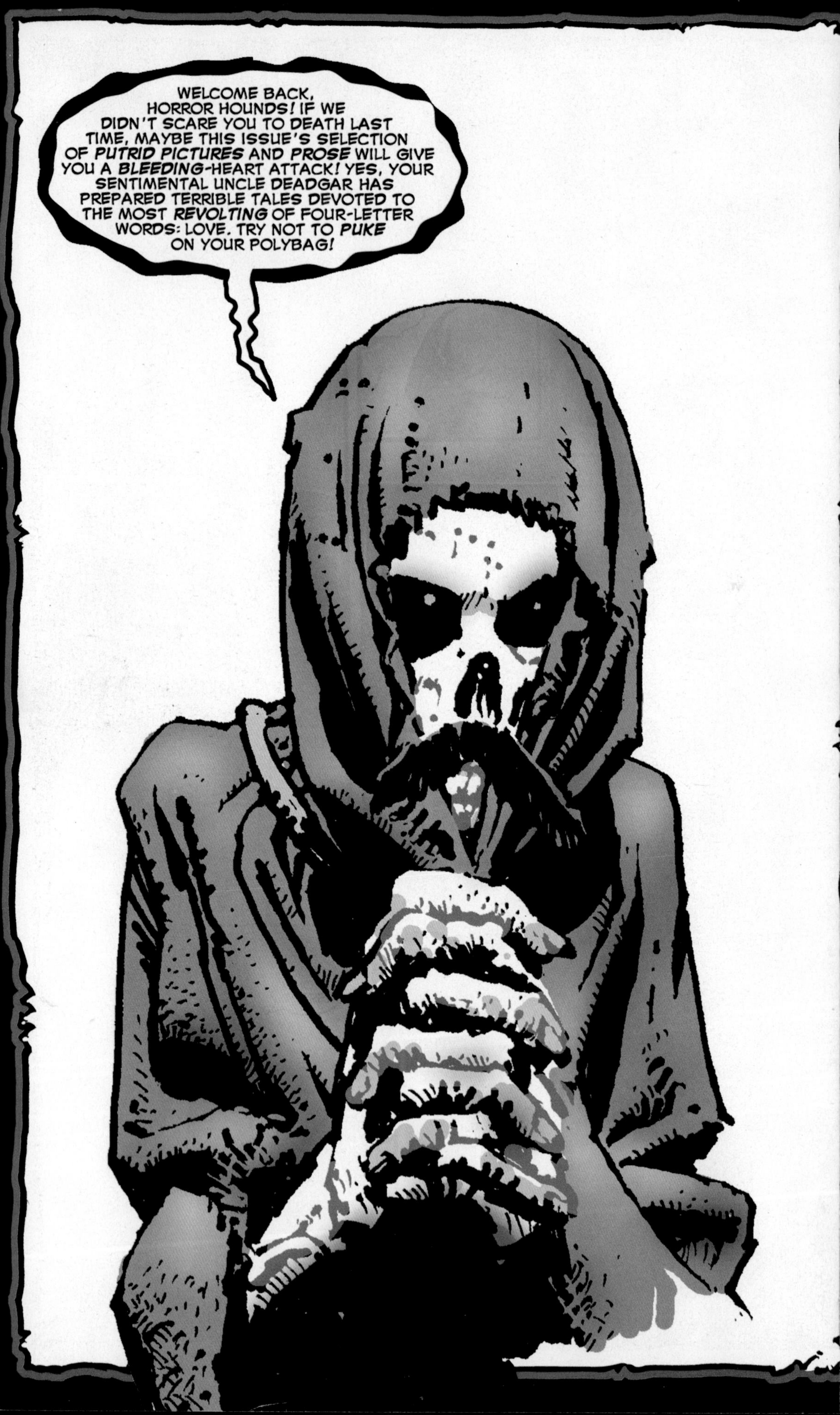
WELCOME BACK, HORROR HOUNDS! IF WE DIDN'T SCARE YOU TO DEATH LAST TIME, MAYBE THIS ISSUE'S SELECTION OF PUTRID PICTURES AND PROSE WILL GIVE YOU A BLEEDING-HEART ATTACK! YES, YOUR SENTIMENTAL UNCLE DEADGAR HAS PREPARED TERRIBLE TALES DEVOTED TO THE MOST REVOLTING OF FOUR-LETTER WORDS: LOVE. TRY NOT TO PUKE ON YOUR POLYBAG!

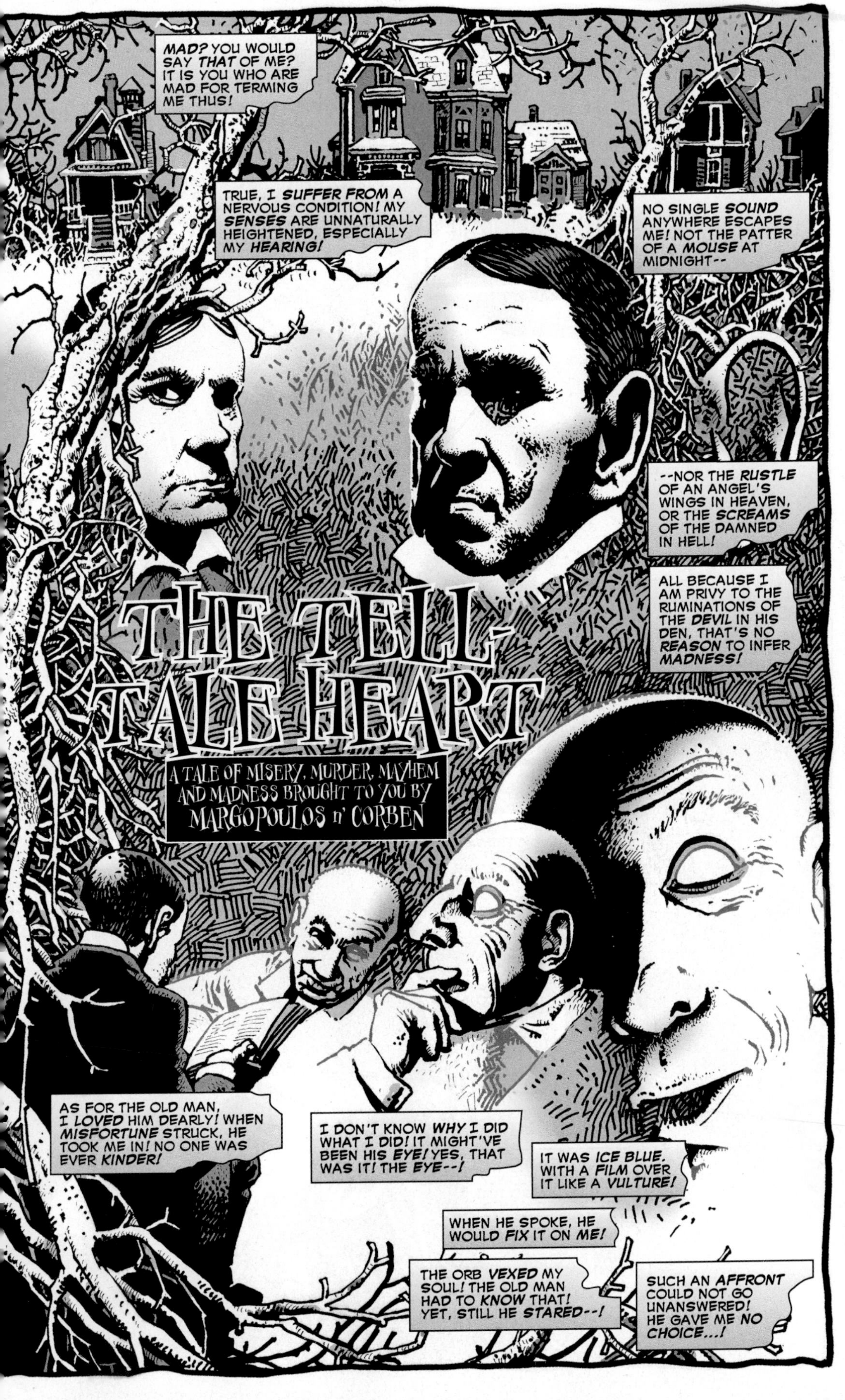
MAD? YOU WOULD SAY THAT OF ME? IT IS YOU WHO ARE MAD FOR TERMING ME THUS!
TRUE, I SUFFER FROM A NERVOUS CONDITION! MY SENSES ARE UNNATURALLY HEIGHTENED, ESPECIALLY MY HEARING!
NO SINGLE SOUND ANYWHERE ESCAPES ME! NOT THE PATTER OF A MOUSE AT MIDNIGHT--
--NOR THE RUSTLE OF AN ANGEL'S WINGS IN HEAVEN, OR THE SCREAMS OF THE DAMNED IN HELL!
ALL BECAUSE I AM PRIVY TO THE RUMINATIONS OF THE DEVIL IN HIS DEN, THAT'S NO REASON TO INFER MADNESS!
THE TELL-TALE HEART
A TALE OF MISERY, MURDER, MAYHEM AND MADNESS BROUGHT TO YOU BY MARGOPOULOS n' CORBEN
AS FOR THE OLD MAN, I LOVED HIM DEARLY! WHEN MISFORTUNE STRUCK, HE TOOK ME IN! NO ONE WAS EVER KINDER!
I DON'T KNOW WHY I DID WHAT I DID! IT MIGHT'VE BEEN HIS EYE! YES, THAT WAS IT! THE EYE--!
IT WAS ICE BLUE, WITH A FILM OVER IT LIKE A VULTURE!
WHEN HE SPOKE, HE WOULD FIX IT ON ME!
THE ORB VEXED MY SOUL! THE OLD MAN HAD TO KNOW THAT! YET, STILL HE STARED--!
SUCH AN AFFRONT COULD NOT GO UNANSWERED! HE GAVE ME NO CHOICE...!

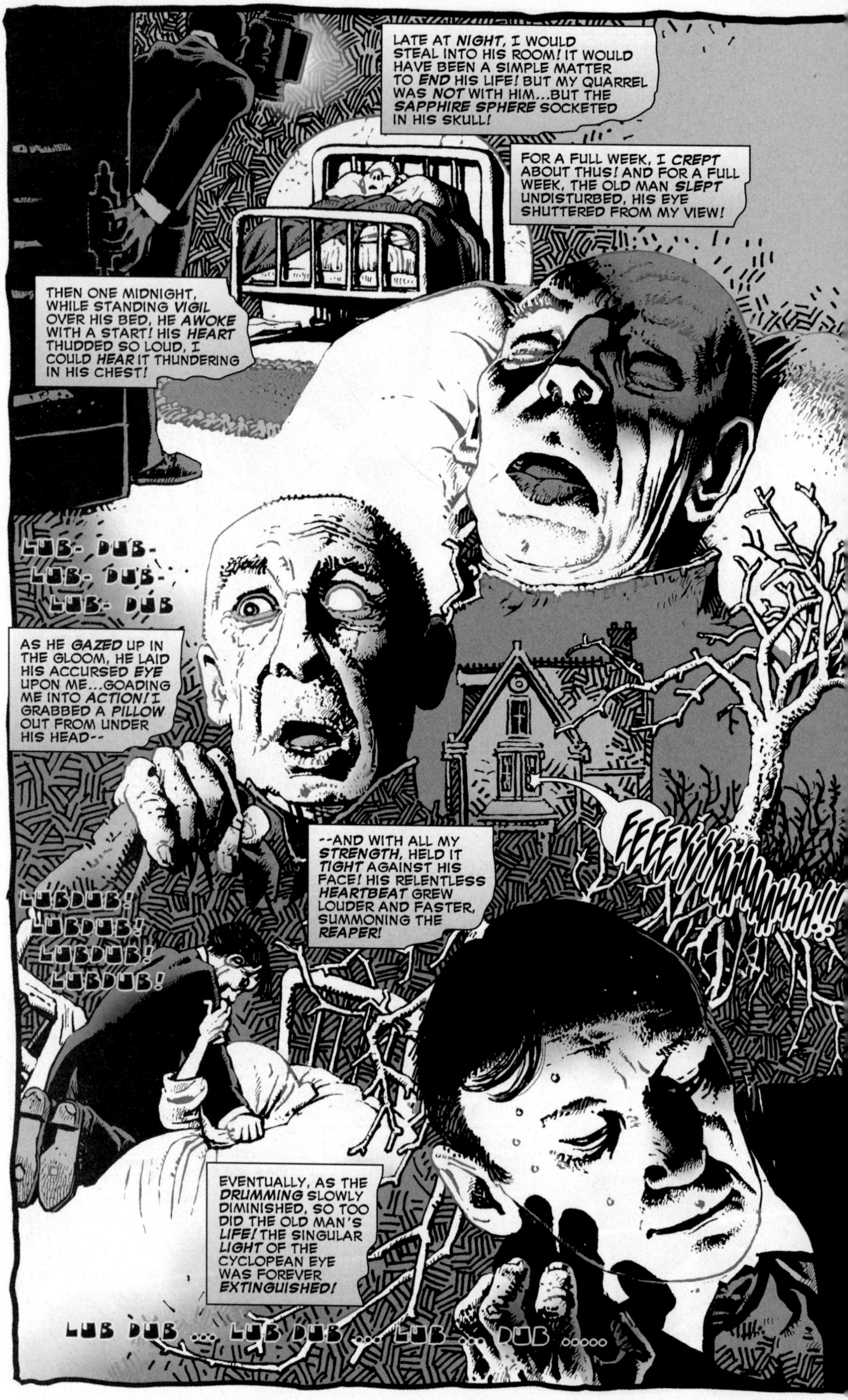
LATE AT NIGHT, I WOULD STEAL INTO HIS ROOM! IT WOULD HAVE BEEN A SIMPLE MATTER TO END HIS LIFE! BUT MY QUARREL WAS NOT WITH HIM...BUT THE SAPPHIRE SPHERE SOCKETED IN HIS SKULL!
FOR A FULL WEEK, I CREPT ABOUT THUS! AND FOR A FULL WEEK, THE OLD MAN SLEPT UNDISTURBED, HIS EYE SHUTTERED FROM MY VIEW!
THEN ONE MIDNIGHT, WHILE STANDING VIGIL OVER HIS BED, HE AWOKE WITH A START! HIS HEART THUDDED SO LOUD, I COULD HEAR IT THUNDERING IN HIS CHEST!
LUB- DUB- LUB- DUB- LUB- DUB
AS HE GAZED UP IN THE GLOOM, HE LAID HIS ACCURSED EYE UPON ME...GOADING ME INTO ACTION! I GRABBED A PILLOW OUT FROM UNDER HIS HEAD--
--AND WITH ALL MY STRENGTH, HELD IT TIGHT AGAINST HIS FACE! HIS RELENTLESS HEARTBEAT GREW LOUDER AND FASTER, SUMMONING THE REAPER!
EEEEYYYAAAAAHHH!!
LUBDUB! LUBDUB! LUBDUB! LUBDUB!
EVENTUALLY, AS THE DRUMMING SLOWLY DIMINISHED, SO TOO DID THE OLD MAN'S LIFE! THE SINGULAR LIGHT OF THE CYCLOPEAN EYE WAS FOREVER EXTINGUISHED!
LUB DUB ... LUB DUB ... LUB ... DUB ......

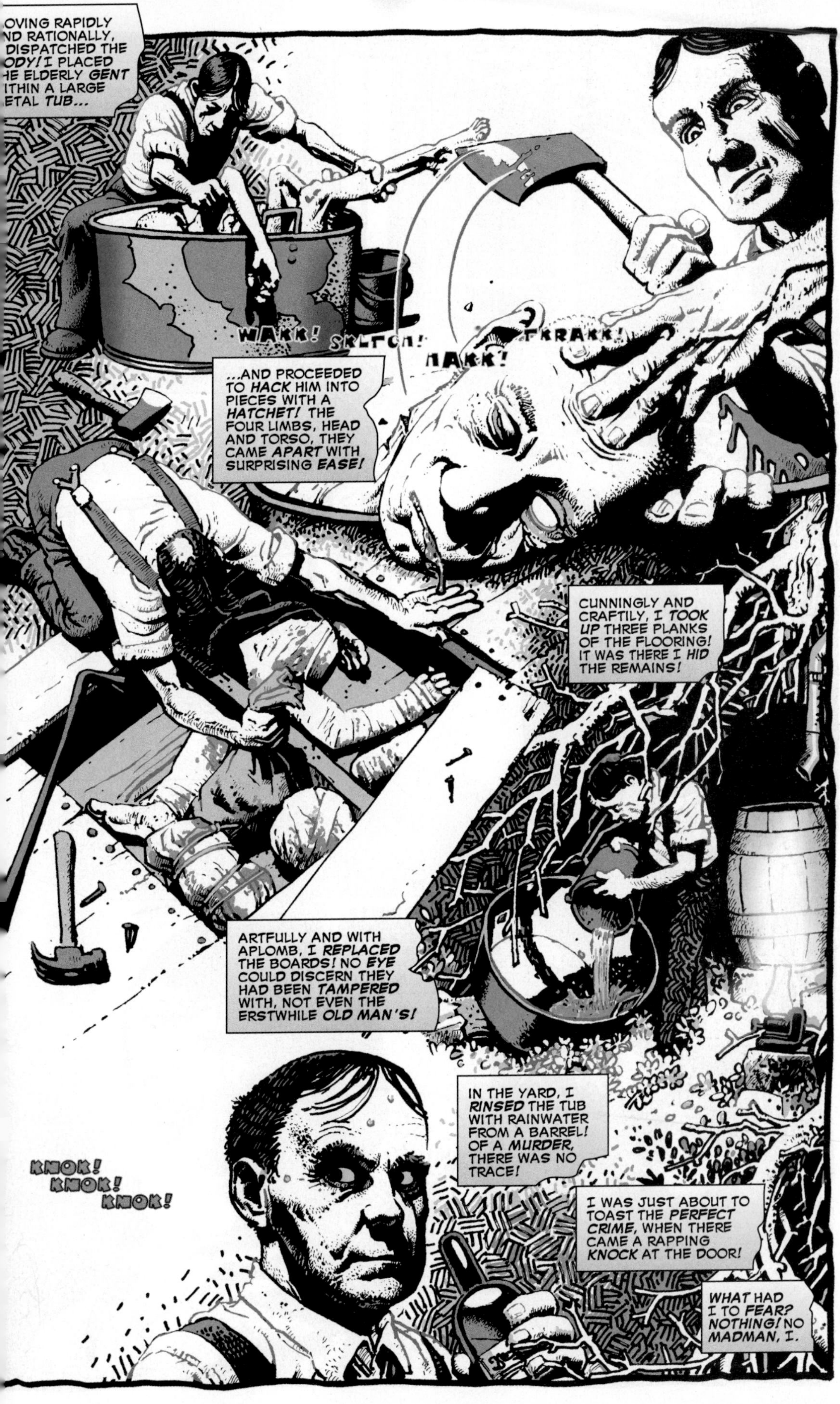
OVING RAPIDLY ND RATIONALLY, DISPATCHED THE ODY! I PLACED HE ELDERLY GENT ITHIN A LARGE ETAL TUB...
WAKK! SKLTCH! KRAKK! WAKK!
...AND PROCEEDED TO HACK HIM INTO PIECES WITH A HATCHET! THE FOUR LIMBS, HEAD AND TORSO, THEY CAME APART WITH SURPRISING EASE!
CUNNINGLY AND CRAFTILY, I TOOK UP THREE PLANKS OF THE FLOORING! IT WAS THERE I HID THE REMAINS!
ARTFULLY AND WITH APLOMB, I REPLACED THE BOARDS! NO EYE COULD DISCERN THEY HAD BEEN TAMPERED WITH, NOT EVEN THE ERSTWHILE OLD MAN'S!
IN THE YARD, I RINSED THE TUB WITH RAINWATER FROM A BARREL! OF A MURDER, THERE WAS NO TRACE!
I WAS JUST ABOUT TO TOAST THE PERFECT CRIME, WHEN THERE CAME A RAPPING KNOCK AT THE DOOR!
KNOK! KNOK! KNOK!
WHAT HAD I TO FEAR? NOTHING! NO MADMAN, I.

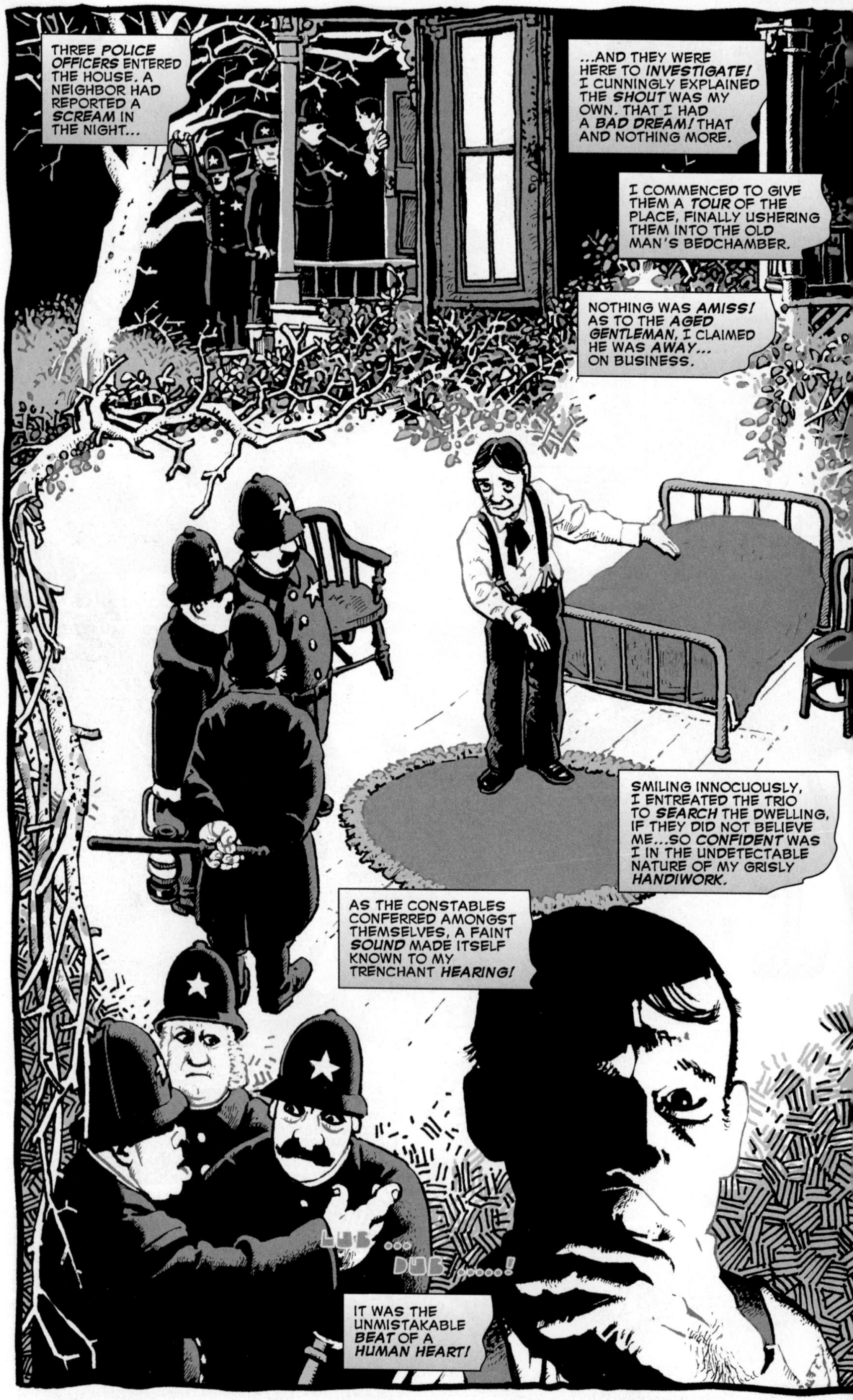
THREE POLICE OFFICERS ENTERED THE HOUSE. A NEIGHBOR HAD REPORTED A SCREAM IN THE NIGHT...
...AND THEY WERE HERE TO INVESTIGATE! I CUNNINGLY EXPLAINED THE SHOUT WAS MY OWN. THAT I HAD A BAD DREAM! THAT AND NOTHING MORE.
I COMMENCED TO GIVE THEM A TOUR OF THE PLACE, FINALLY USHERING THEM INTO THE OLD MAN'S BEDCHAMBER.
NOTHING WAS AMISS! AS TO THE AGED GENTLEMAN, I CLAIMED HE WAS AWAY... ON BUSINESS.
SMILING INNOCUOUSLY, I ENTREATED THE TRIO TO SEARCH THE DWELLING, IF THEY DID NOT BELIEVE ME...SO CONFIDENT WAS I IN THE UNDETECTABLE NATURE OF MY GRISLY HANDIWORK.
AS THE CONSTABLES CONFERRED AMONGST THEMSELVES, A FAINT SOUND MADE ITSELF KNOWN TO MY TRENCHANT HEARING!
LUB ...
DUB ......!
IT WAS THE UNMISTAKABLE BEAT OF A HUMAN HEART!

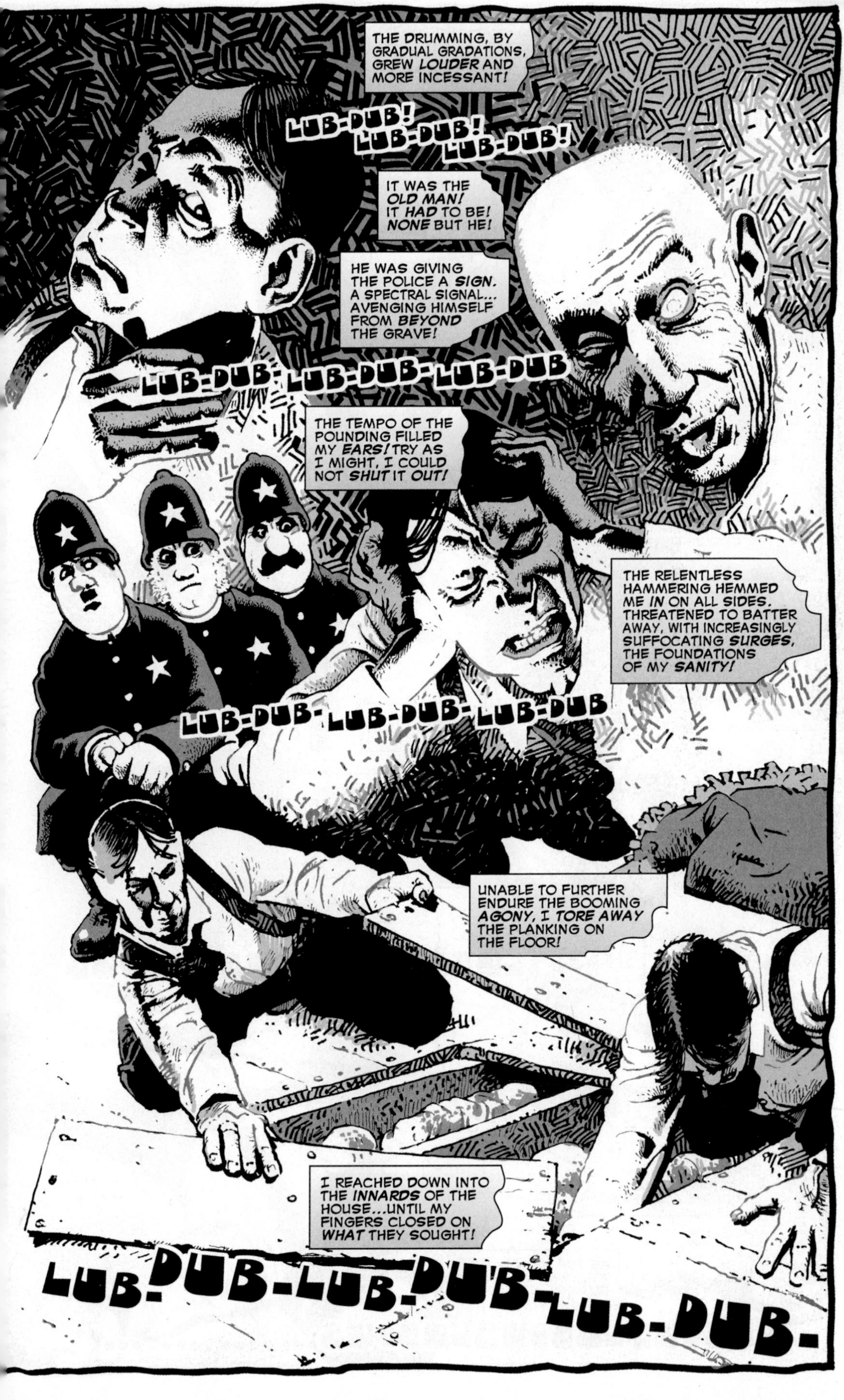
THE DRUMMING, BY GRADUAL GRADATIONS, GREW LOUDER AND MORE INCESSANT!
LUB-DUB! LUB-DUB! LUB-DUB!
IT WAS THE OLD MAN! IT HAD TO BE! NONE BUT HE!
HE WAS GIVING THE POLICE A SIGN. A SPECTRAL SIGNAL... AVENGING HIMSELF FROM BEYOND THE GRAVE!
LUB-DUB-LUB-DUB-LUB-DUB
THE TEMPO OF THE POUNDING FILLED MY EARS! TRY AS I MIGHT, I COULD NOT SHUT IT OUT!
THE RELENTLESS HAMMERING HEMMED ME IN ON ALL SIDES. THREATENED TO BATTER AWAY, WITH INCREASINGLY SUFFOCATING SURGES, THE FOUNDATIONS OF MY SANITY!
LUB-DUB-LUB-DUB-LUB-DUB
UNABLE TO FURTHER ENDURE THE BOOMING AGONY, I TORE AWAY THE PLANKING ON THE FLOOR!
I REACHED DOWN INTO THE INNARDS OF THE HOUSE...UNTIL MY FINGERS CLOSED ON WHAT THEY SOUGHT!
LUB-DUB-LUB-DUB-LUB-DUB-

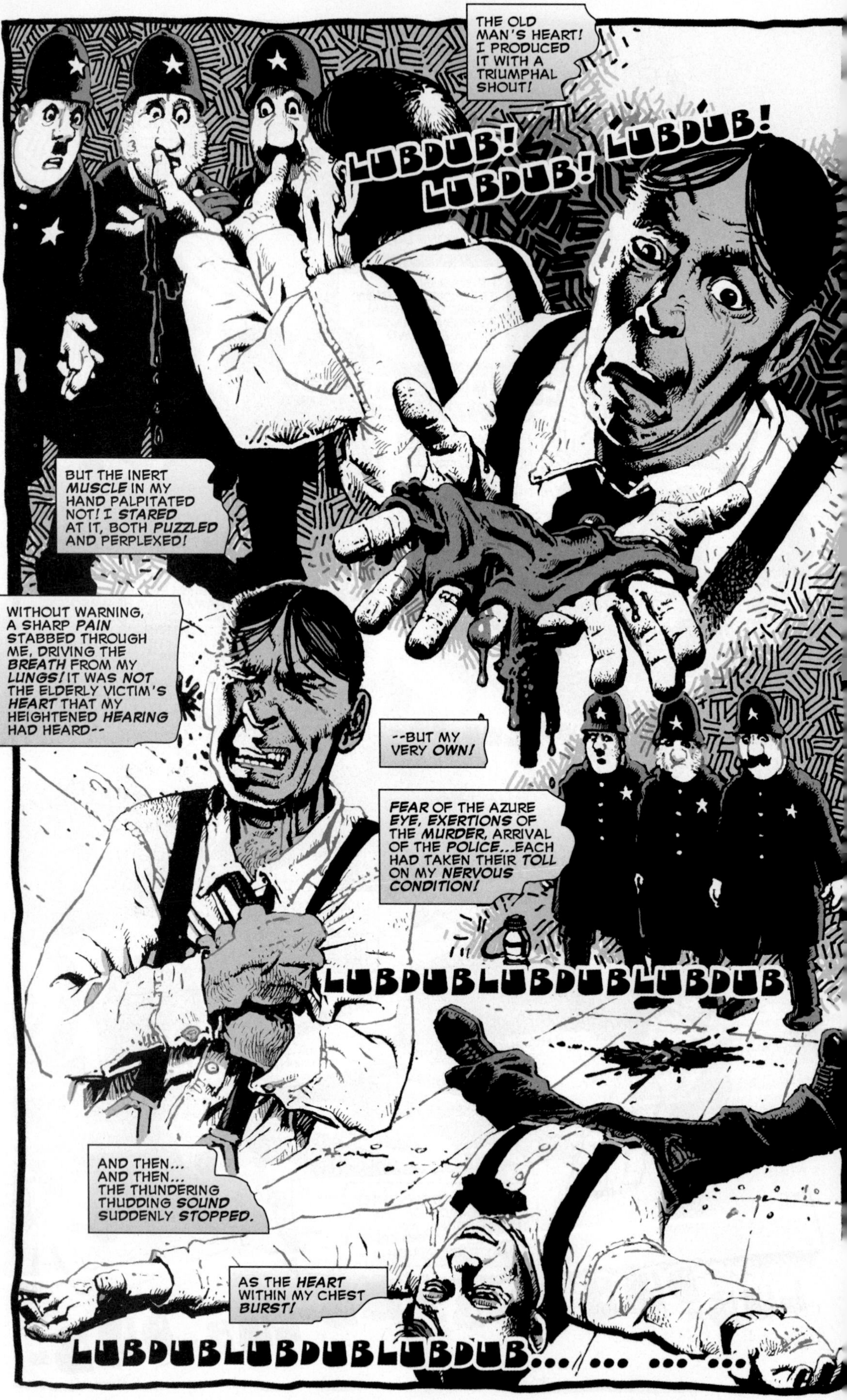
THE OLD MAN'S HEART! I PRODUCED IT WITH A TRIUMPHAL SHOUT!
LUBDUB! LUBDUB! LUBDUB!
BUT THE INERT MUSCLE IN MY HAND PALPITATED NOT! I STARED AT IT, BOTH PUZZLED AND PERPLEXED!
WITHOUT WARNING, A SHARP PAIN STABBED THROUGH ME, DRIVING THE BREATH FROM MY LUNGS! IT WAS NOT THE ELDERLY VICTIM'S HEART THAT MY HEIGHTENED HEARING HAD HEARD--
--BUT MY VERY OWN!
FEAR OF THE AZURE EYE, EXERTIONS OF THE MURDER, ARRIVAL OF THE POLICE...EACH HAD TAKEN THEIR TOLL ON MY NERVOUS CONDITION!
LUBDUBLUBDUBLUBDUB
AND THEN... AND THEN... THE THUNDERING THUDDING SOUND SUDDENLY STOPPED.
AS THE HEART WITHIN MY CHEST BURST!
LUBDUBLUBDUBLUBDUB... ... ... ...

TRUE!—nervous—very, very dreadfully nervous I had been and am; but why *will* you say that I am mad? The disease had sharpened my senses—not destroyed—not dulled them. Above all was the sense of hearing acute. I heard all things in the heaven and in the earth. I heard many things in hell. How, then, am I mad? Hearken! and observe how healthily—how calmly I can tell you the whole story.

It is impossible to say how first the idea entered my brain; but once conceived, it haunted me day and night. Object there was none. Passion there was none. I loved the old man. He had never wronged me. He had never given me insult. For his gold I had no desire. I think it was his eye! yes, it was this! One of his eyes resembled that of a vulture—a pale blue eye, with a film over it. Whenever it fell upon me, my blood ran cold; and so by degrees—very gradually—I made up my mind to take the life of the old man, and thus rid myself of the eye for ever.

Now this is the point. You fancy me mad. Madmen know nothing. But you should have seen *me*. You should have seen how wisely I proceeded—with what caution—with what foresight—with what dissimulation I went to work! I was never kinder to the old man than during the whole week before I killed him. And every night, about midnight, I turned the latch of his door and opened it—oh, so gently! And then, when I had made an opening sufficient for my head, I put in a dark lantern, all closed, closed, so that no light shone out, and then I thrust in my head. Oh, you would have laughed to see how cunningly I thrust it in! I moved it slowly—very, very slowly, so that I might not disturb the old man's sleep. It took me an hour to place my whole head within the opening so far that I could see him as he lay upon his bed. Ha!—would a madman have been so wise as this? And then, when my head was well in the room, I undid the lantern cautiously—oh, so cautiously—cautiously (for the hinges creaked)—I undid it just so much that a single thin ray fell upon the vulture eye. And this I did for seven long nights—every night just at midnight—but I found the eye always closed; and so it was impossible to do the work; for it was not the old man who vexed me, but his Evil Eye. And every morning, when the day broke, I went boldly into the chamber, and spoke courageously to him, calling him by name in a hearty tone, and inquiring how he has passed the night. So you see he would have been a very profound old man, indeed, to suspect that every night, just at twelve, I looked in upon him while he slept.

Upon the eighth night I was more than usually cautious in opening the door. A watch's minute hand moves more quickly than did mine. Never before that night had I *felt* the extent of my own powers—of my sagacity.

I could scarcely contain my feelings of triumph. To think that there I was, opening the door, little by little, and he not even to dream of my secret deeds or thoughts. I fairly chuckled at the idea; and perhaps he heard me; for he moved on the bed suddenly, as if startled. Now you may think that I drew back—but no. His room was as black as pitch with the thick darkness, (for the shutters were close fastened, through fear of robbers), and so I knew that he could not see the opening of the door, and I kept pushing it on steadily, steadily.

I had my head in, and was about to open the lantern, when my thumb slipped upon the tin fastening, and the old man sprang up in the bed, crying out—"Who's there?"

I kept quite still and said nothing. For a whole hour I did not move a muscle, and in the meantime I did not hear him lie down. He was still sitting up in the bed listening;—just as I have done, night after night, hearkening to the death watches in the wall.

Presently I heard a slight groan, and I knew it was the groan of mortal terror. It was not a groan of pain or of grief—oh, no!—it was the low stifled sound that arises from the bottom of the soul when overcharged with awe. I knew the sound well. Many a night, just at midnight, when all the world slept, it has welled up from my own bosom, deepening, with its dreadful echo, the terrors that distracted me. I say I knew it well. I knew what the old man felt, and pitied him, although I chuckled at heart. I knew that he had been lying awake ever since the first slight noise, when he had turned in the bed. His fears had been ever since growing upon him. He had been trying to fancy them causeless, but could not. He had been saying to himself—"It is nothing but the wind in the chimney—it is only a mouse crossing the floor," or "it is merely a cricket which has made a single chirp." Yes, he had been trying to comfort himself with these suppositions; but he had found all in vain. *All in vain*; because Death, in approaching him had stalked with his black shadow before him, and enveloped the victim. And it was the mournful influence of the unperceived shadow that caused him to *feel*—although he neither saw nor heard—to feel the presence of my head within the room.

When I had waited a long time, very patiently, without hearing him lie down, I resolved to open a little—a very, very little crevice in the lantern. So I opened it—you cannot imagine how stealthily, stealthily—until, at length, a simple dim ray, like the thread of the spider, shot from out the crevice and full upon the vulture eye.

It was open—wide, wide open—and I grew furious as I gazed upon it. I saw it with perfect distinctness—all a dull blue, with a hideous veil over it that chilled the very marrow in my bones; but I could see nothing else of the old man's face or person: for I had directed the ray as if by instinct, precisely upon the damned spot.

And now have I not told you that what you mistake for madness is but over-acuteness of the senses?—now, I say, there came to my ears a low, dull, quick sound, such as a watch makes when enveloped in cotton. I knew *that* sound well too. It was the beating of the old man's heart. It increased my fury, as the beating of a drum stimulates the soldier into courage.

But even yet I refrained and kept still. I scarcely breathed. I held the lantern motionless. I tried how steadily I could maintain the ray upon the eye. Meantime the hellish tattoo of the heart increased. It grew quicker and quicker, and louder and louder every instant. The old man's terror *must* have been extreme! It grew louder, I say, louder every moment!—do you mark me well? I have told you that I am nervous: so I am. And now at the dead hour of the night, amid the dreadful silence of that old house, so strange a noise as this excited me to uncontrollable terror. Yet, for some minutes longer I refrained and stood still. But the beating grew louder, louder! I thought the heart must burst. And now a new anxiety seized me—the sound would be heard by a neighbor! The old man's hour had come! With a loud yell, I threw open the lantern and leaped into the room. He shrieked once—once only. In an instant I dragged him to the floor, and pulled the heavy bed over him. I then smiled gaily, to find the deed so far done. But, for many minutes, the heart beat on with a muffled sound. This, however, did not vex me; it would not be heard through the wall. At length it ceased. The old man was dead. I removed the bed and examined the corpse. Yes, he was stone, stone dead. I placed my hand upon the heart and held it there many minutes. There was no pulsation. He was stone dead. His eye would trouble me no more.

If still you think me mad, you will think so no longer when I describe the wise precautions I took for the concealment of the body. The night waned, and I worked hastily, but in silence. First of all I dismembered the corpse. I cut off the head and the arms and the legs.

I then took up three planks from the flooring of the chamber, and deposited all between the scantlings. I then replaced the boards so cleverly, so cunningly, that no human eye—not even *his*—could have detected any thing wrong. There was nothing to wash out—no stain of any kind—no blood-spot whatever. I had been too wary for that. A tub had caught all—ha! ha!

When I had made an end of these labors, it was four o'clock—still dark as midnight. As the bell sounded the hour, there came a knocking at the street door. I went down to open it with a light heart,—for what had I *now* to fear? There entered three men, who introduced themselves, with perfect suavity, as officers of the police. A shriek had been heard by a neighbor during the night; suspicion of foul play had been aroused; information had been lodged at the police office, and they (the officers) had been deputed to search the premises.

I smiled,—for *what* had I to fear? I bade the gentlemen welcome. The shriek, I said, was my own in a dream. The old man, I mentioned, was absent in the country. I took my visitors all over the house. I bade them search—search *well*. I led them, at length, to *his* chamber. I showed them his treasures, secure, undisturbed. In the enthusiasm of my confidence, I brought chairs into the room, and desired them *here* to rest from their fatigues, while I myself, in the wild audacity of my perfect triumph, placed my own seat upon the very spot beneath which reposed the corpse of the victim.

The officers were satisfied. My *manner* had convinced them. I was singularly at ease. They sat, and while I answered cheerily, they chatted of familiar things. But, ere long, I felt myself getting pale and wished them gone. My head ached, and I fancied a ringing in my ears: but still they sat and still chatted. The ringing became more distinct:—it continued and became more distinct: I talked more freely to get rid of the feeling: but it continued and gained definitiveness—until, at length, I found that the noise was *not* within my ears.

No doubt I now grew *very* pale;—but I talked more fluently, and with a heightened voice. Yet the sound increased—and what could I do? It was *a low, dull, quick sound—much such a sound as a watch makes when enveloped in cotton*. I gasped for breath—and yet the officers heard it not. I talked more quickly—more vehemently; but the noise steadily increased. I arose and argued about trifles, in a high key and with violent gesticulations; but the noise steadily increased. Why *would* they not be gone? I paced the floor to and fro with heavy strides, as if excited to fury by the observation of the men—but the noise steadily increased. Oh God! what *could* I do? I foamed—I raved—I swore! I swung the chair upon which I had been sitting, and grated it upon the boards, but the noise arose over all and continually increased. It grew louder—louder—*louder*! And still the men chatted pleasantly, and smiled. Was it possible they heard not? Almighty God!—no, no! They heard!—they suspected!—they *knew*!—they were making a mockery of my horror!—this I thought, and this I think. But any thing was better than this agony! Anything was more tolerable than this derision! I could bear those hypocritical smiles no longer! I felt that I must scream or die!—and now—again!—hark! louder! louder! louder! *louder*!—

"Villains!" I shrieked, "dissemble no more! I admit the deed!—tear up the planks!—here, here!—it is the beating of his hideous heart!"

— *Edgar Allan Poe*

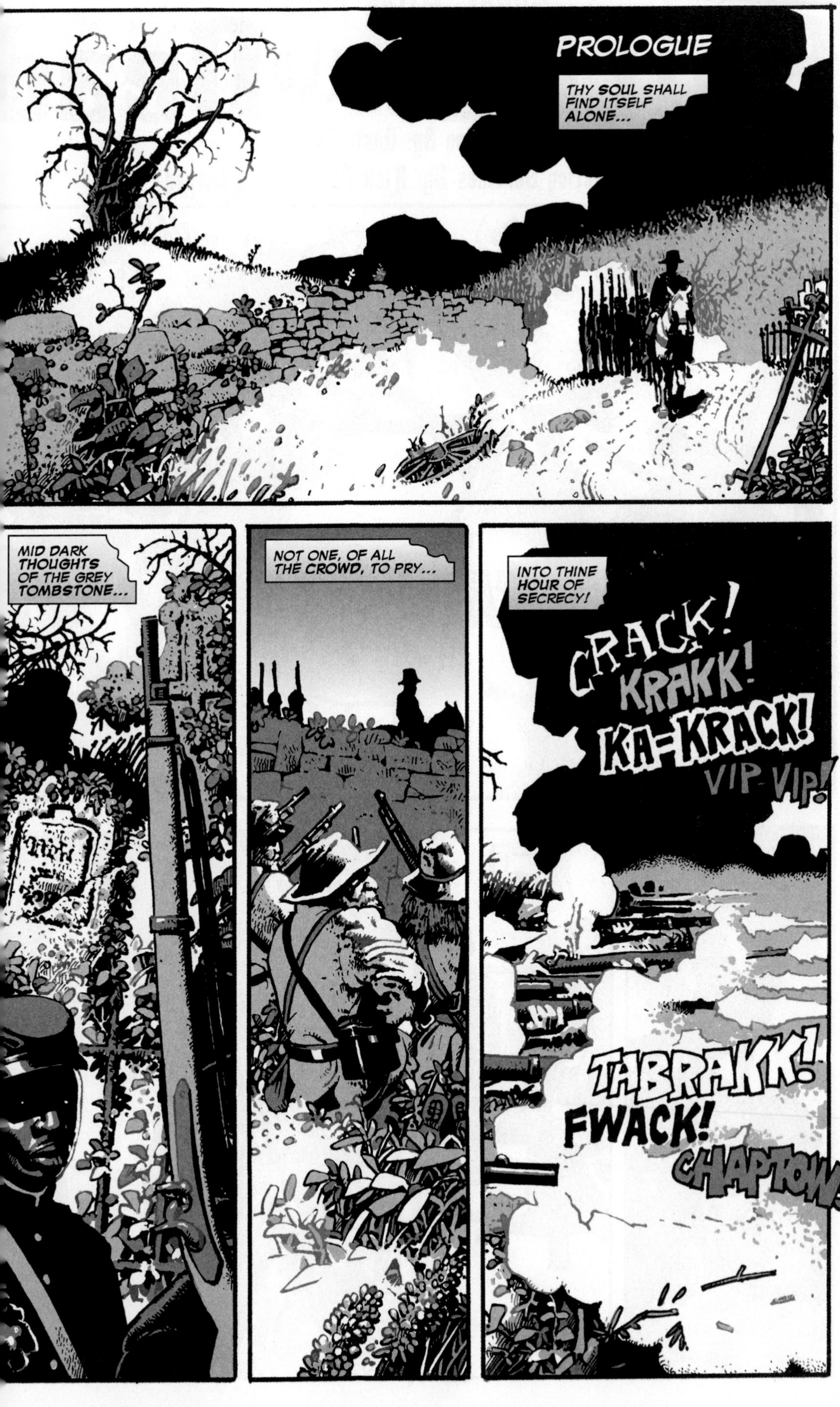
PROLOGUE
THY SOUL SHALL FIND ITSELF ALONE...
MID DARK THOUGHTS OF THE GREY TOMBSTONE...
NOT ONE, OF ALL THE CROWD, TO PRY...
INTO THINE HOUR OF SECRECY!
CRACK!
KRAKK!
KA-KRACK!
VIP VIP!
TABRAKK!
FWACK!
CHAPTOW!

Edgar Allan Poe's

# Spirits of the Dead

Inspiration By: Uncle Edgar

Resurrection Services By: Rick Dahl and Rich Corben

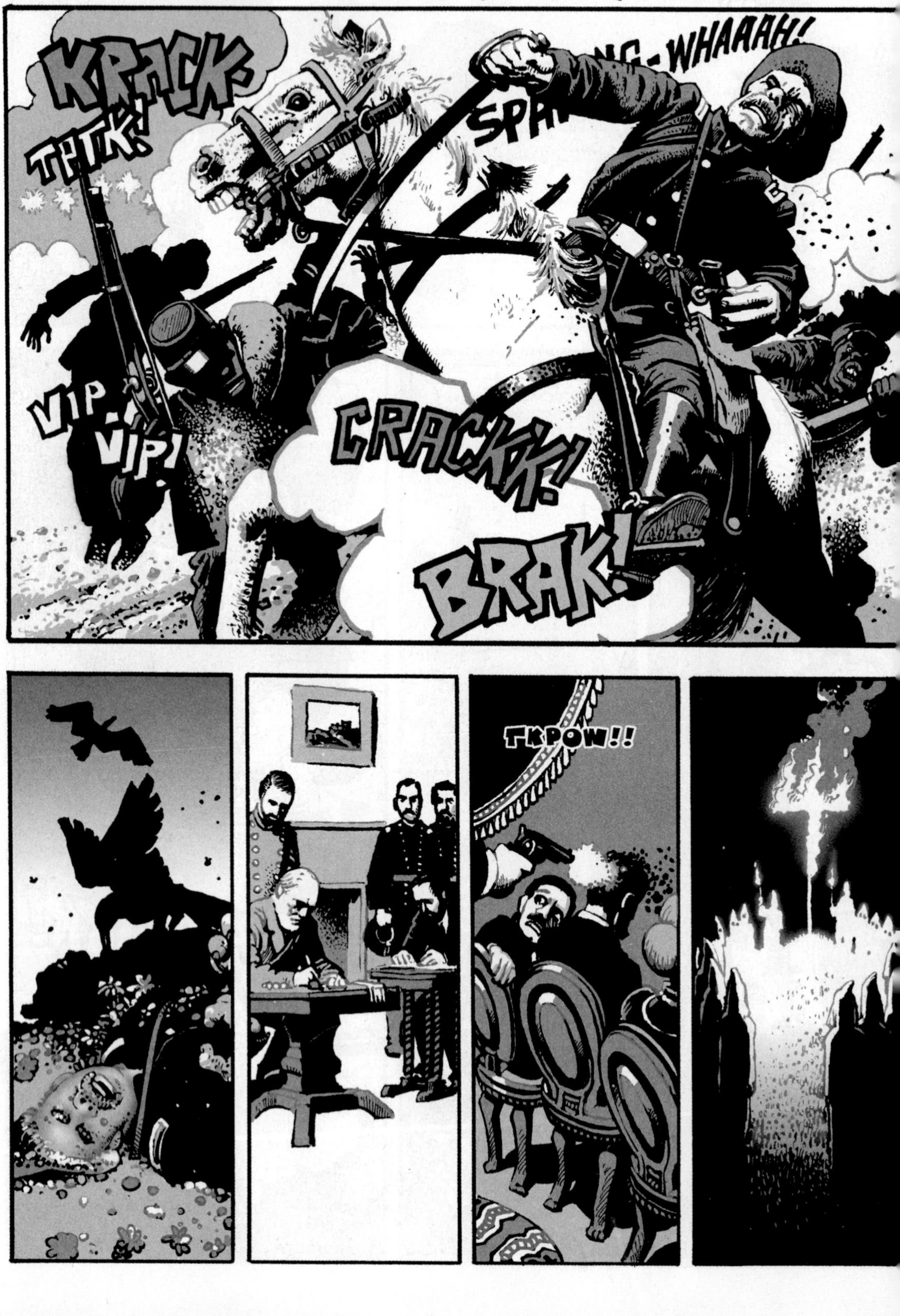
KRACK-
T-TK!
SPA...NG-WHAAAH!
VIP
VIP!
CRACKK!
BRAK!
TKPOW!!

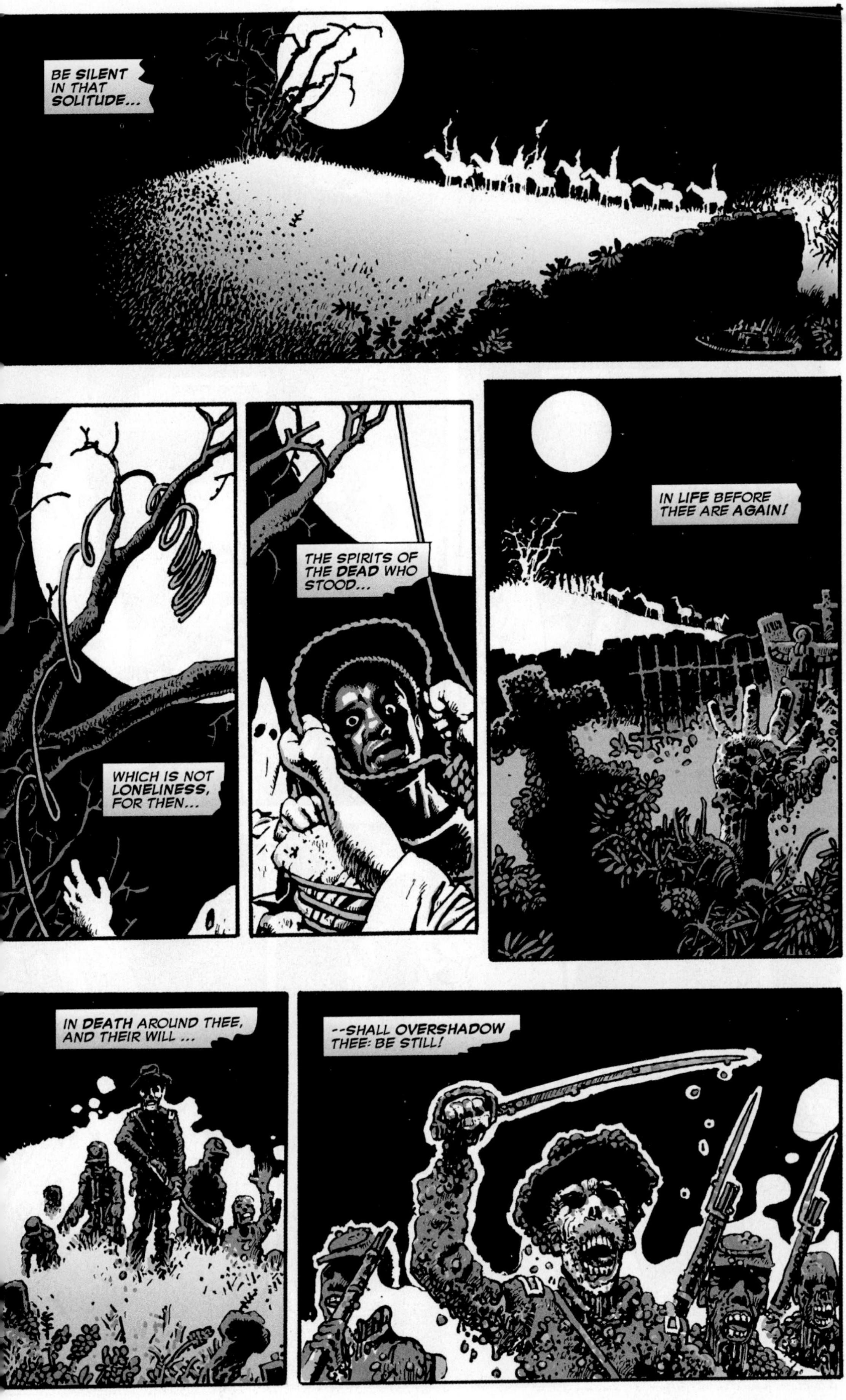
BE SILENT IN THAT SOLITUDE...
WHICH IS NOT LONELINESS, FOR THEN...
THE SPIRITS OF THE DEAD WHO STOOD...
IN LIFE BEFORE THEE ARE AGAIN!
IN DEATH AROUND THEE, AND THEIR WILL ...
--SHALL OVERSHADOW THEE: BE STILL!

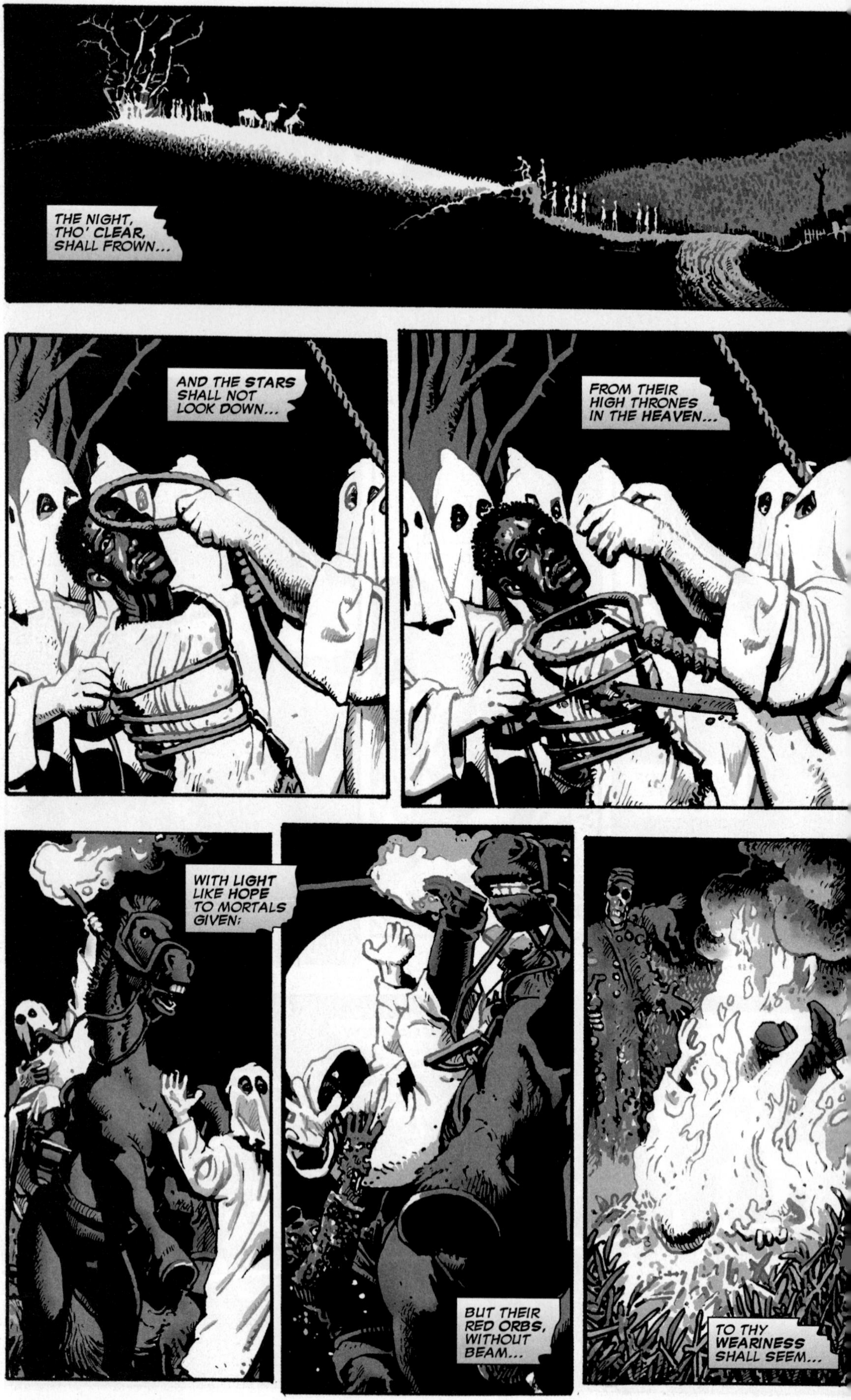
THE NIGHT, THO' CLEAR, SHALL FROWN...
AND THE STARS SHALL NOT LOOK DOWN...
FROM THEIR HIGH THRONES IN THE HEAVEN...
WITH LIGHT LIKE HOPE TO MORTALS GIVEN;
BUT THEIR RED ORBS, WITHOUT BEAM...
TO THY WEARINESS SHALL SEEM...

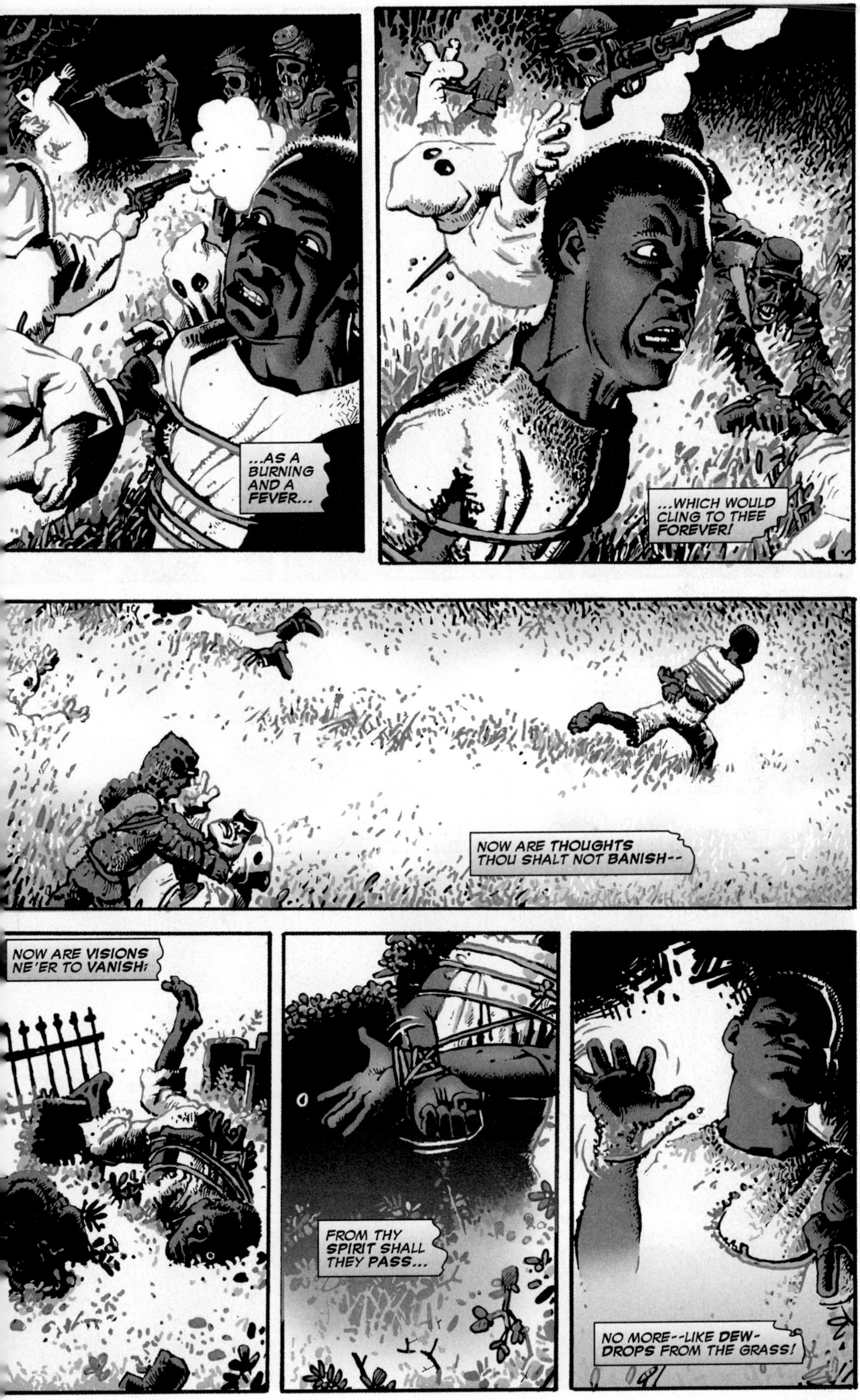
...AS A BURNING AND A FEVER...
...WHICH WOULD CLING TO THEE FOREVER!
NOW ARE THOUGHTS THOU SHALT NOT BANISH--
NOW ARE VISIONS NE'ER TO VANISH;
FROM THY SPIRIT SHALL THEY PASS...
NO MORE--LIKE DEW-DROPS FROM THE GRASS!

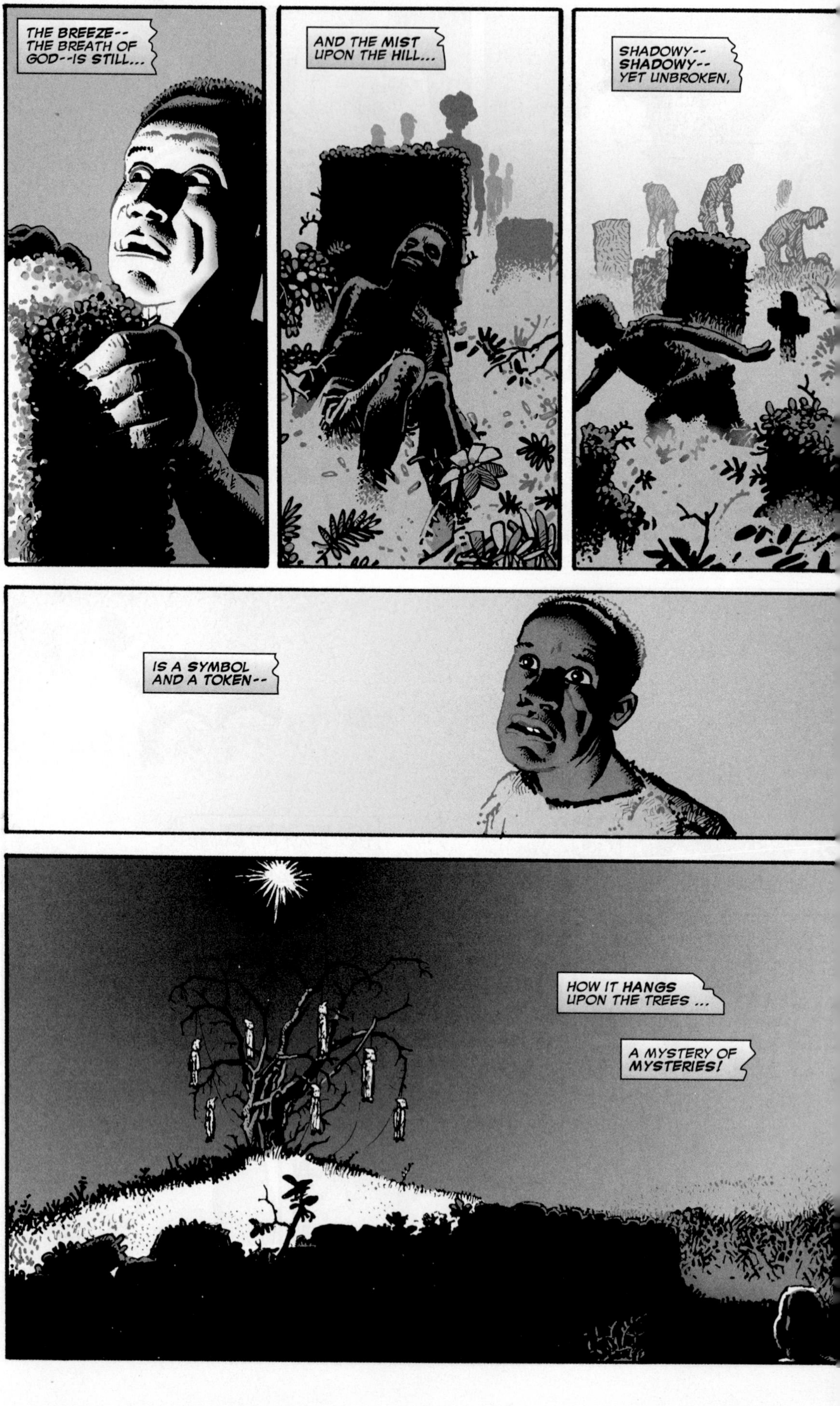
THE BREEZE-- THE BREATH OF GOD--IS STILL...
AND THE MIST UPON THE HILL...
SHADOWY-- SHADOWY-- YET UNBROKEN,
IS A SYMBOL AND A TOKEN--
HOW IT HANGS UPON THE TREES ...
A MYSTERY OF MYSTERIES!

# Spirits of the Dead

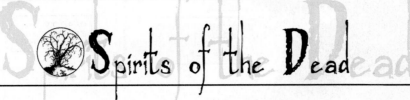

Thy soul shall find itself alone
'Mid dark thoughts of the gray tombstone—
Not one, of all the crowd, to pry
Into thine hour of secrecy.

Be silent in that solitude
   Which is not loneliness, for then
The spirits of the dead who stood
   In life before thee are again
In death around thee, and their will
Shall overshadow thee: be still.

The night, tho' clear, shall frown,
And the stars shall not look down
From their high thrones in the Heaven
With light like Hope to mortals given;
But their red orbs, without beam,
To thy weariness shall seem

As a burning and a fever
Which would cling to thee forever.
Now are thoughts thou shalt not banish—
Now are visions ne'er to vanish;
From thy spirit shall they pass
No more—like dew-drops from the grass.

The breeze—the breath of God—is still,
And the mist upon the hill
Shadowy—shadowy—yet unbroken,
Is a symbol and a token,—
How it hangs upon the trees,
A mystery of mysteries!

— Edgar Allan Poe

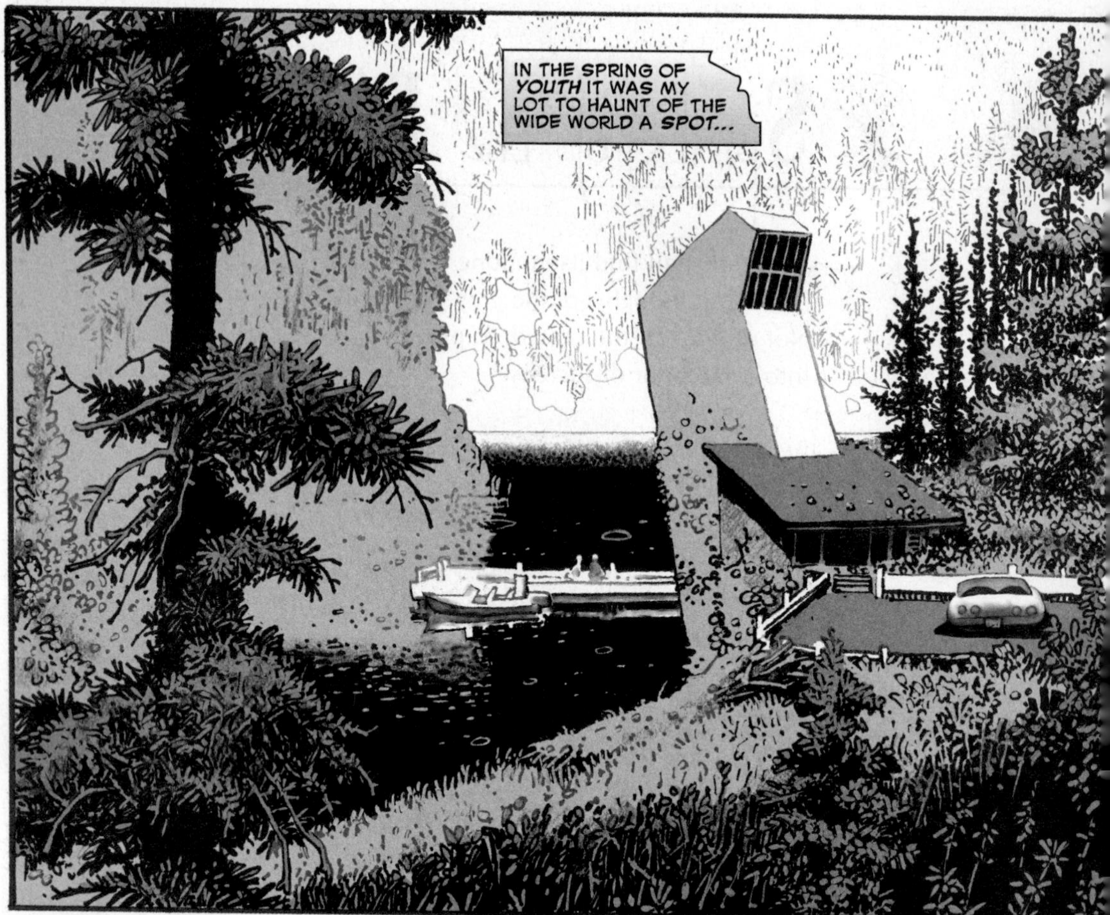
IN THE SPRING OF YOUTH IT WAS MY LOT TO HAUNT OF THE WIDE WORLD A SPOT...

# THE LAKE

INSANITY PROVIDED BY EDGAR ALLAN POE
INCOHERENTLY RANTED BY RICH MARGOPOULOS
DRAWN IN BLOOD BY RICH CORBEN

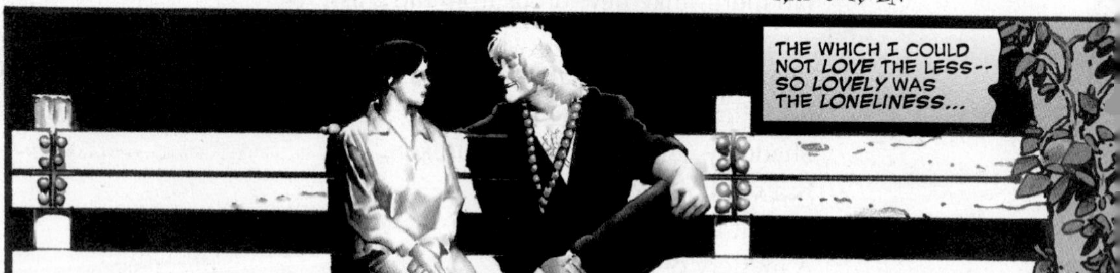
THE WHICH I COULD NOT LOVE THE LESS-- SO LOVELY WAS THE LONELINESS...

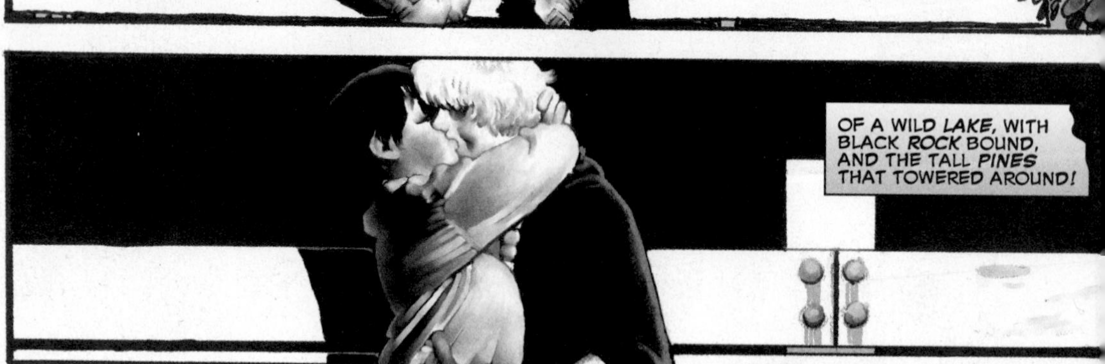
OF A WILD LAKE, WITH BLACK ROCK BOUND, AND THE TALL PINES THAT TOWERED AROUND!

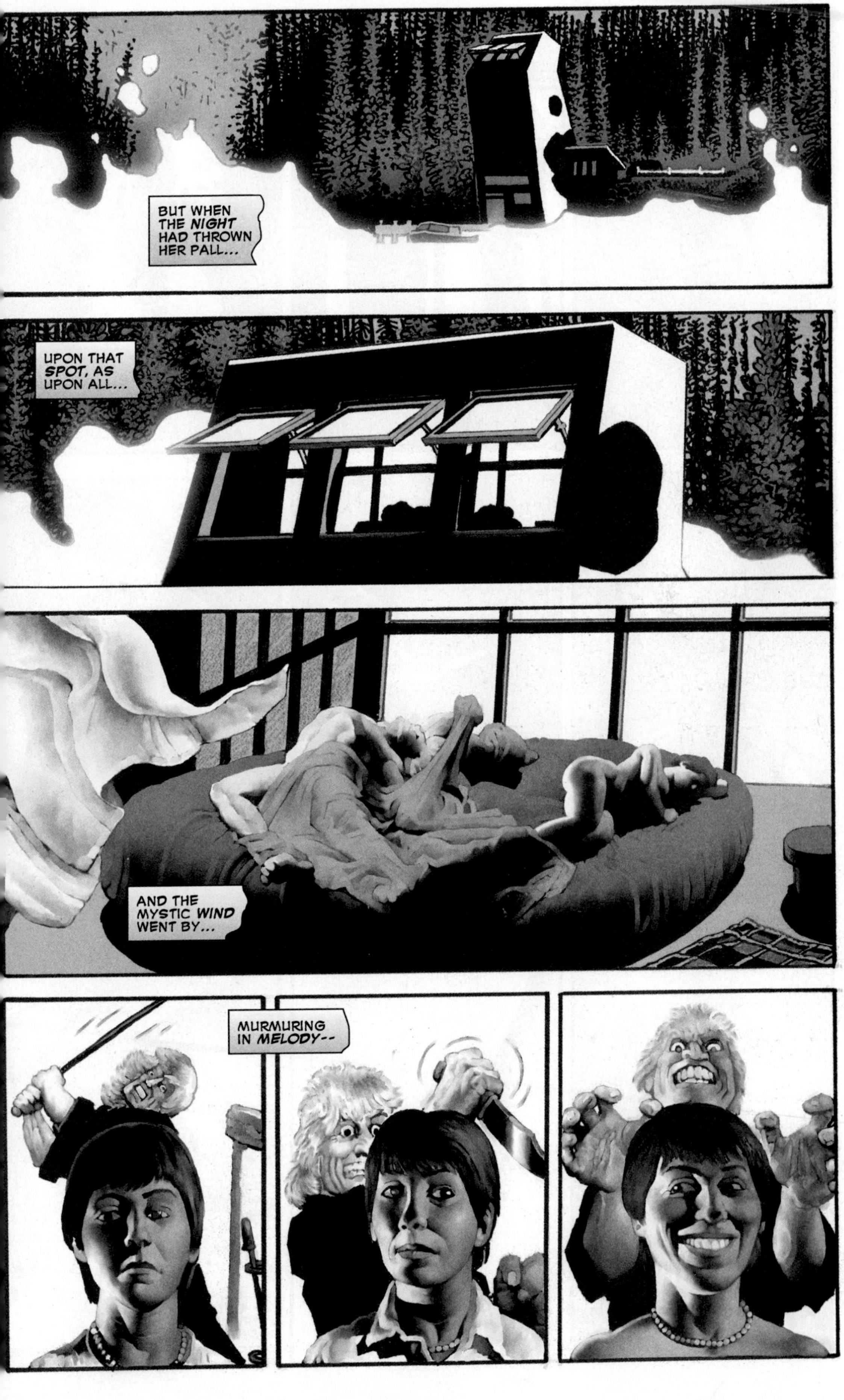
BUT WHEN THE NIGHT HAD THROWN HER PALL...
UPON THAT SPOT, AS UPON ALL...
AND THE MYSTIC WIND WENT BY...
MURMURING IN MELODY--

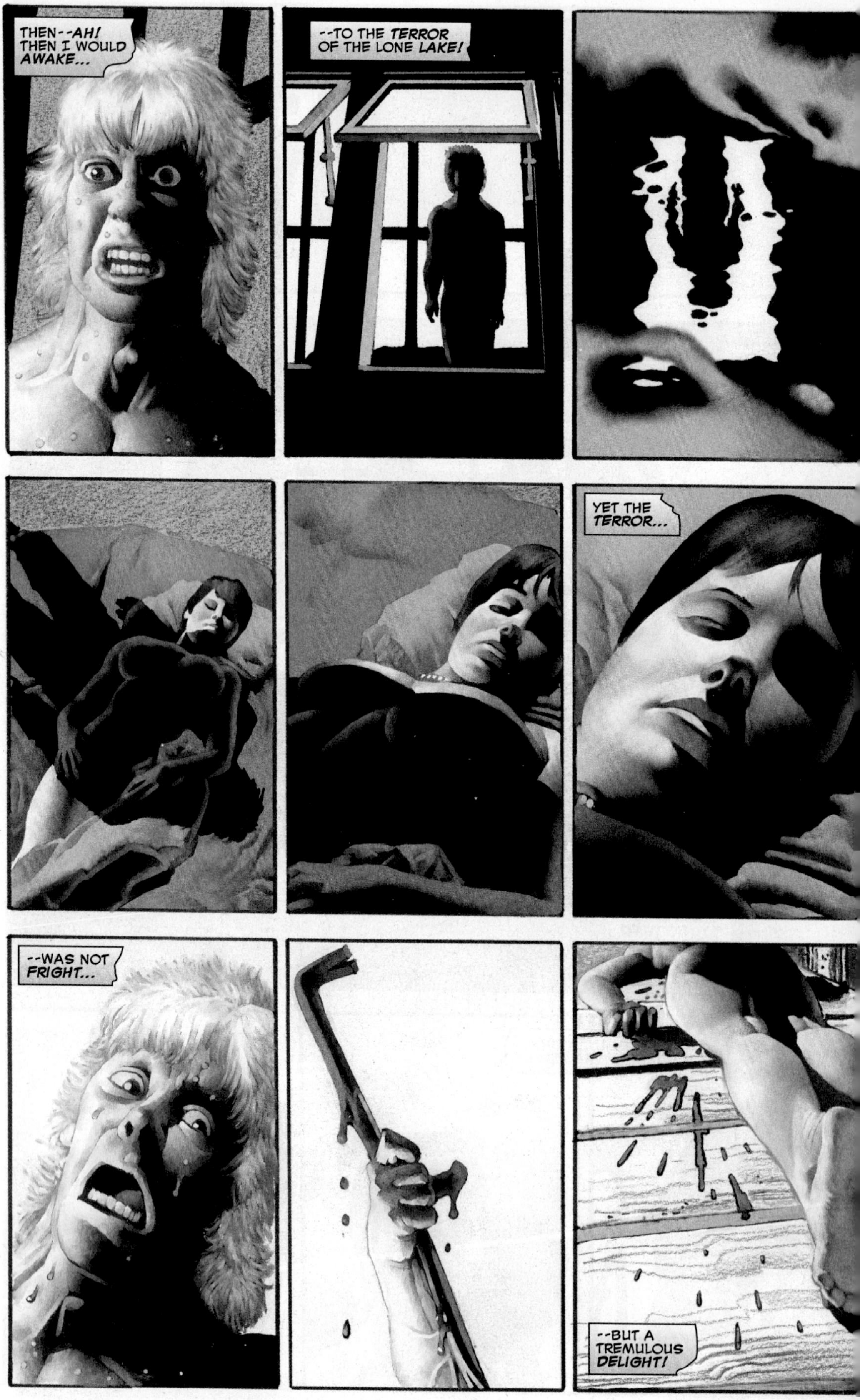
THEN--AH! THEN I WOULD AWAKE...
--TO THE TERROR OF THE LONE LAKE!
YET THE TERROR...
--WAS NOT FRIGHT...
--BUT A TREMULOUS DELIGHT!

A FEELING NOT THE JEWELED MINE...

SPLUK!

COULD TEACH...

OR BRIBE ME TO DEFINE...

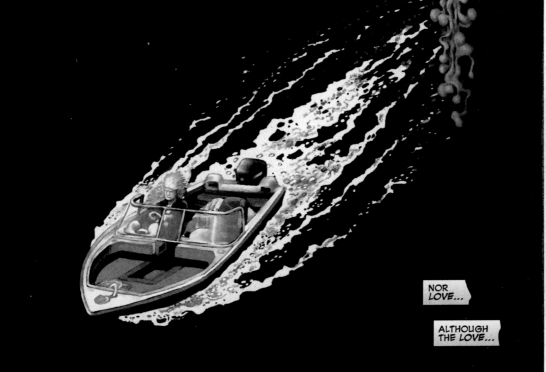

NOR LOVE...

ALTHOUGH THE LOVE...

--WERE THINE!

--FOR HIM WHO THENCE COULD *SOLACE* BRING...

...TO HIS *LONE* IMAGINING!

WHOSE SOLITARY *SOUL* COULD MAKE...

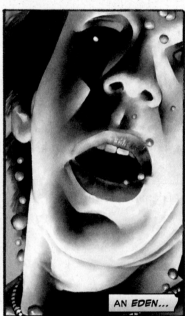

AN *EDEN*...

...OF THAT *DIM LAKE!*

THE PINEWOOD BUGLE

**DEADLY MYSTERY**
MAN FOUND IN BED
**DROWNED!**

# The Lake - to ——

In spring of youth it was my lot
To haunt of the wide world a spot
The which I could not love the less—
So lovely was the loneliness
Of a wild lake, with black rock bound,
And the tall pines that towered around.

But when the Night had thrown her pall
Upon that spot, as upon all,
And the mystic wind went by
Murmuring in melody—
Then—ah! then I would awake
To the terror of the lone lake.

Yet that terror was not fright,
But a tremulous delight—
A feeling not the jeweled mine
Could teach or bribe me to define—
Nor Love—although the Love were thine.

Death was in that poisonous wave,
And in its gulf a fitting grave
For him who thence could solace bring
To his lone imagining—
Whose solitary soul could make
An Eden of that dim lake.

— Edgar Allan Poe

I dwelt alone...
...in a world of moan!

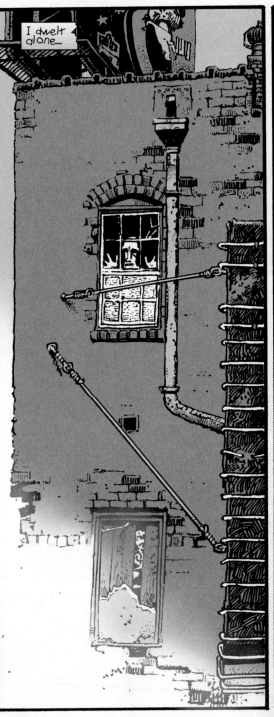

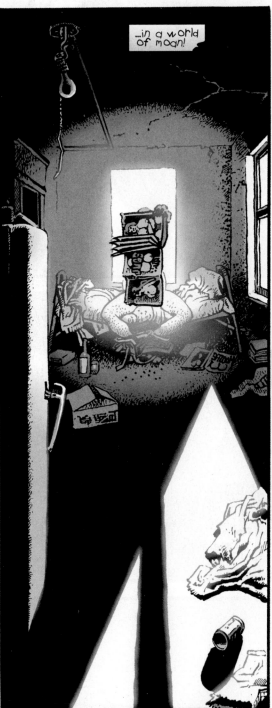

# EULALIE

Transcribed By: **Richard Dahl**   Visually Executed By: **Rich Corben**

Note: This Ain't Exactly your Daddy's Edgar Allan Poe--!

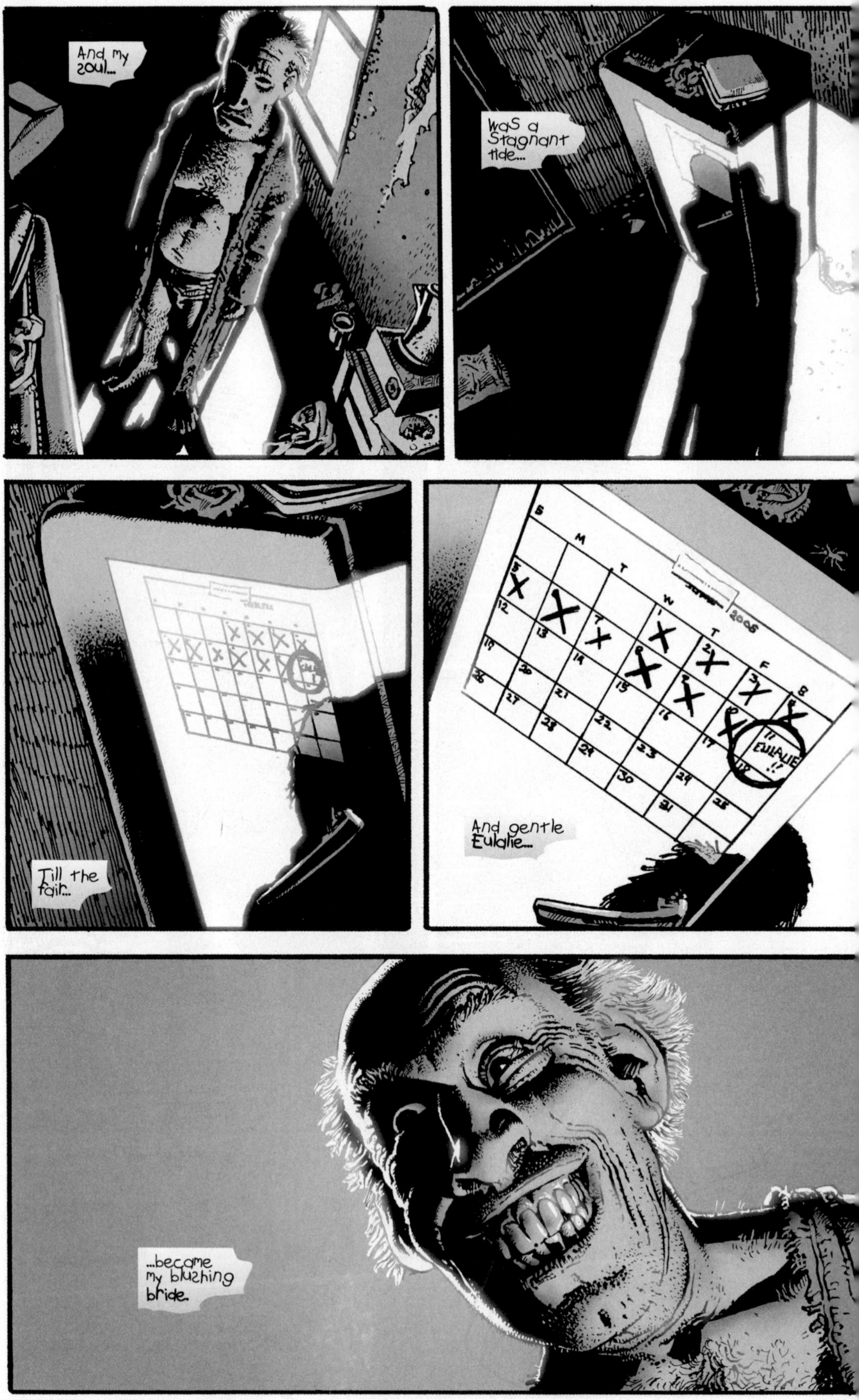
And my soul...
Was a Stagnant tide...
Till the fair...
EULALIE !!
And gentle Eulalie...
...became my blushing bride.

Till the yellow-haired young Eulalie...

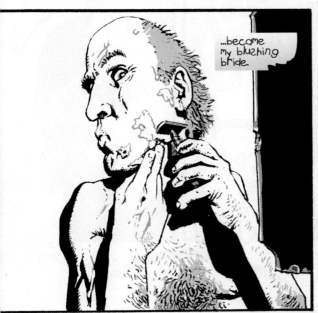

...became my blushing bride.

Ah, less...

...less bright...

The stars of the night...

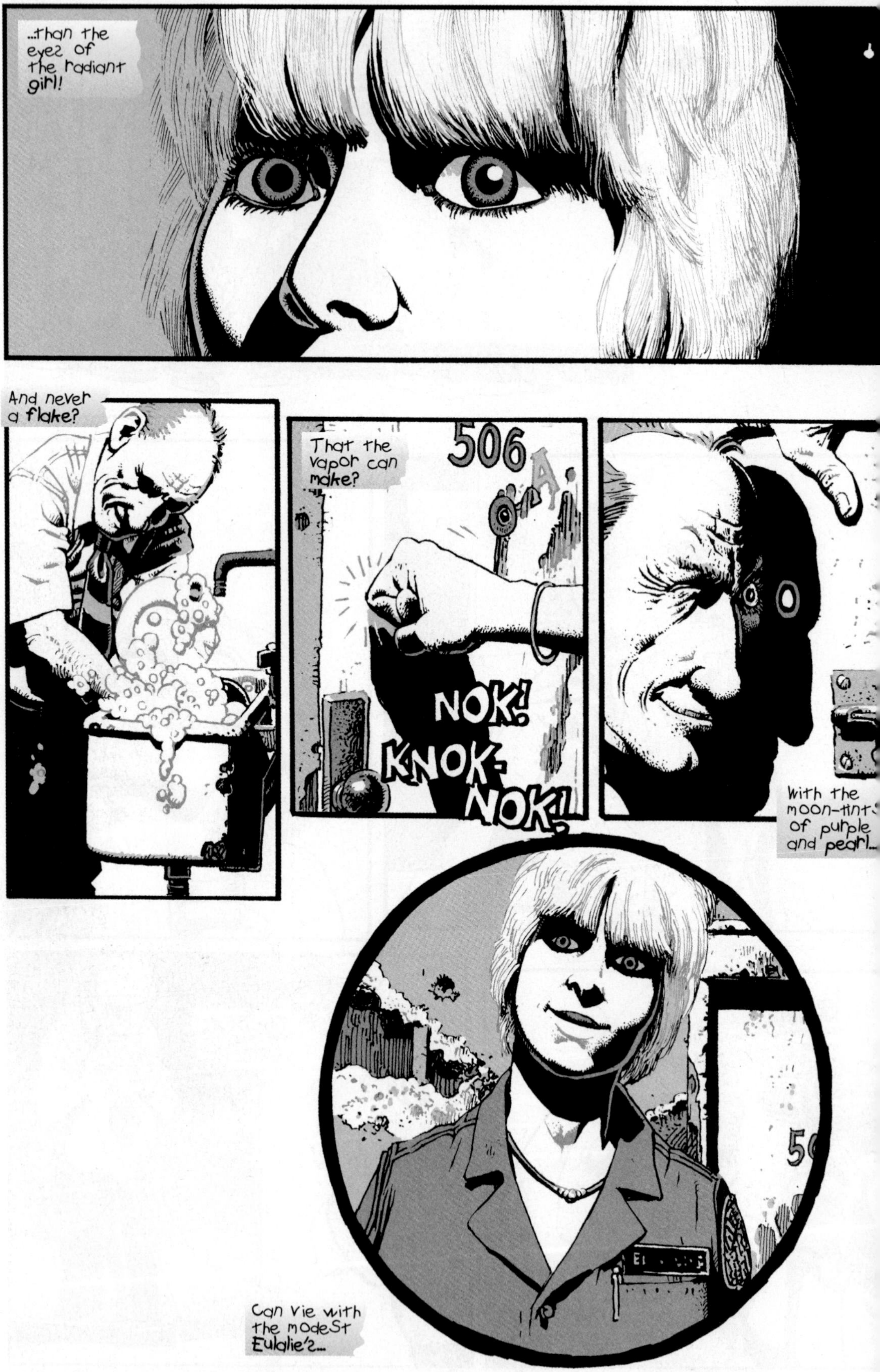
...than the eyes of the radiant girl!
And never a flake?
That the vapor can make?
506
NOK!
KNOK-NOK!
With the moon-tints of purple and pearl...
Can vie with the modest Eulalie's...

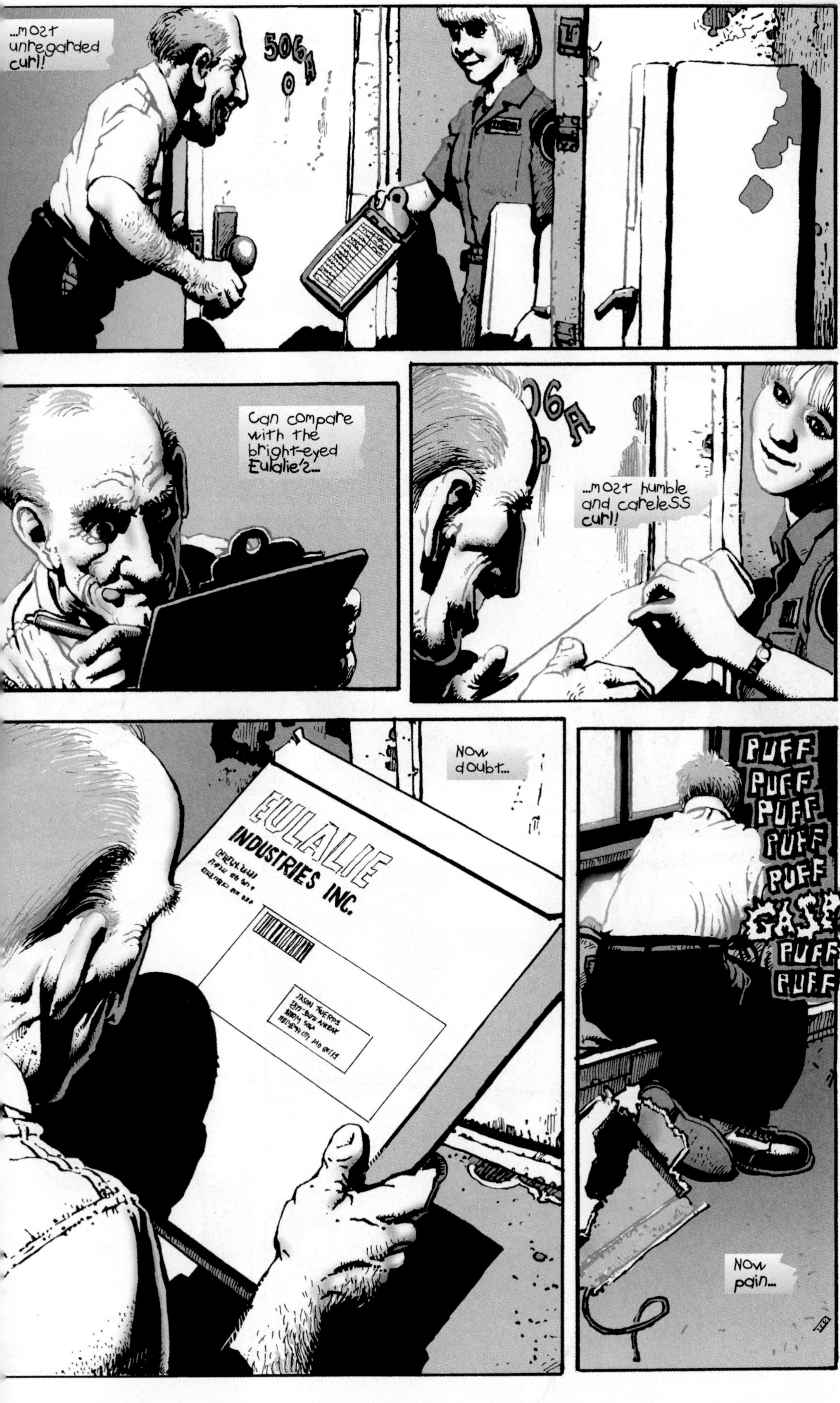
...most unregarded curl!
506A
Can compare with the bright-eyed Eulalie's...
06A
...most humble and careless curl!
EULALIE
INDUSTRIES INC.
Now doubt...
PUFF
PUFF
PUFF
PUFF
PUFF
GASP!
PUFF
PUFF
Now pain...

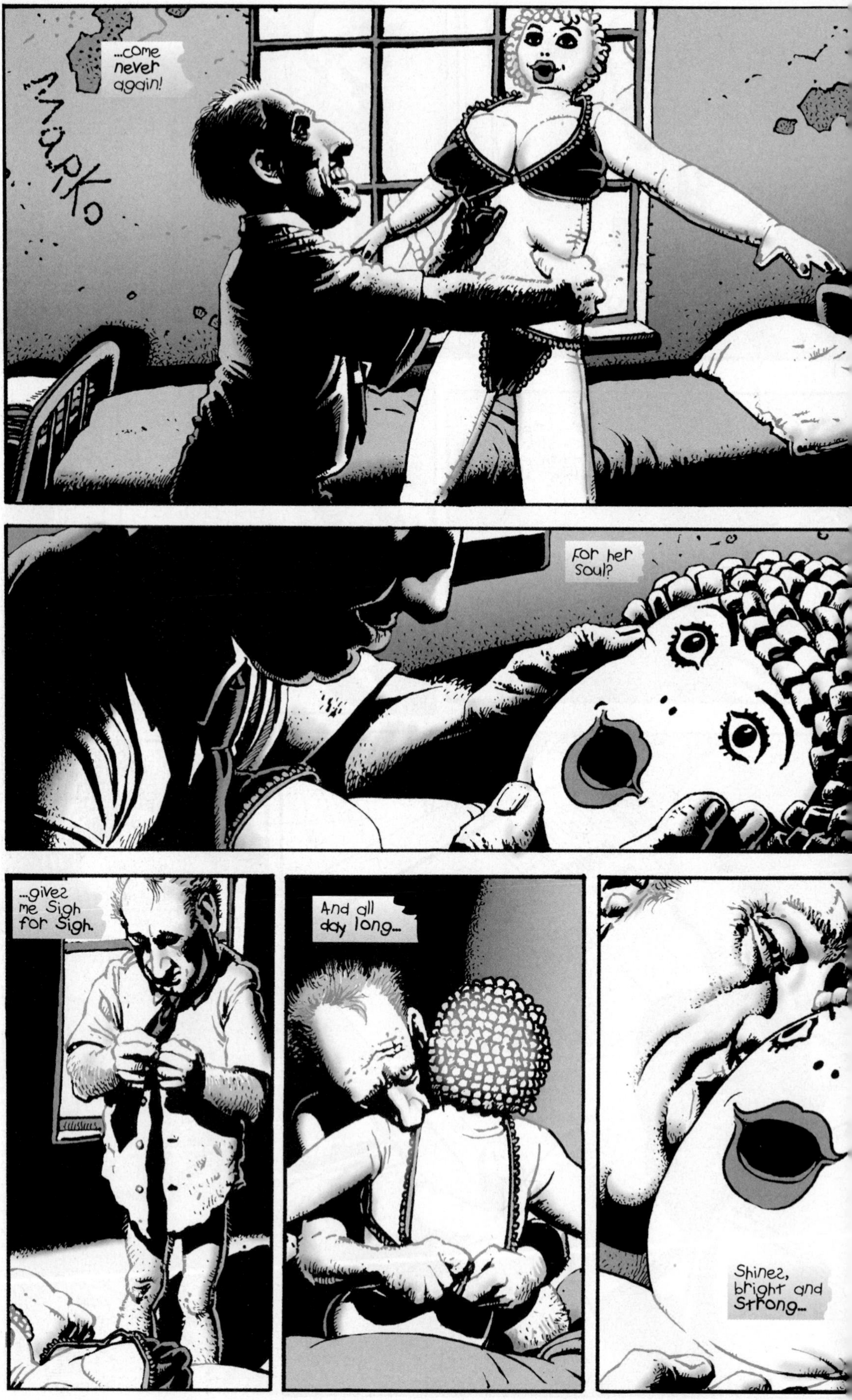
...come never again!
MAPKO
For her soul?
...gives me sigh for sigh.
And all day long...
Shines, bright and strong...

A Starte within the sky.

THUMP!
THUMP!
THUMP!
THUMP!
THUMP!

While ever to her dear Eulalie?

BRAG!

..upturns her matron eye.

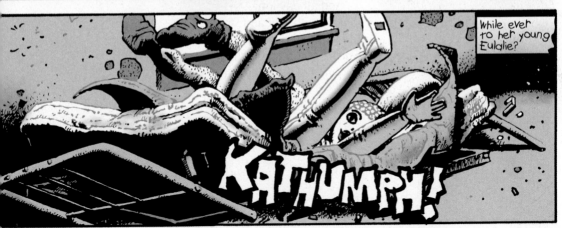

While ever to her young Eulalie?

KATHUMPH!

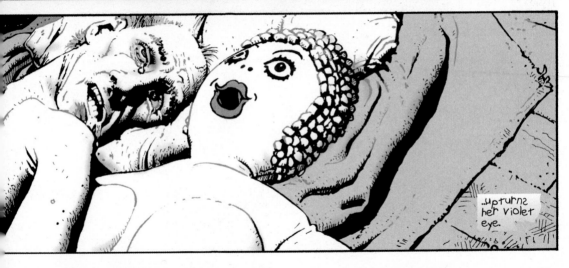

..upturns her violet eye.

# Eulalie

I dwelt alone
In a world of moan,
And my soul was a stagnant tide,
Till the fair and gentle Eulalie became my blushing bride—
Till the yellow-haired young Eulalie became my smiling bride.

Ah, less—less bright
The stars of the night
Than the eyes of the radiant girl!
And never a flake
That the vapor can make
With the moon-tints of purple and pearl,
Can vie with the modest Eulalie's most unregarded curl—
Can compare with the bright-eyed Eulalie's most humble and careless
curl.

Now Doubt—now Pain
Come never again,
For her soul gives me sigh for sigh,
And all day long
Shines, bright and strong,
Astarté within the sky,
While ever to her dear Eulalie upturns her matron eye—
While ever to her young Eulalie upturns her violet eye.

— Edgar Allan Poe

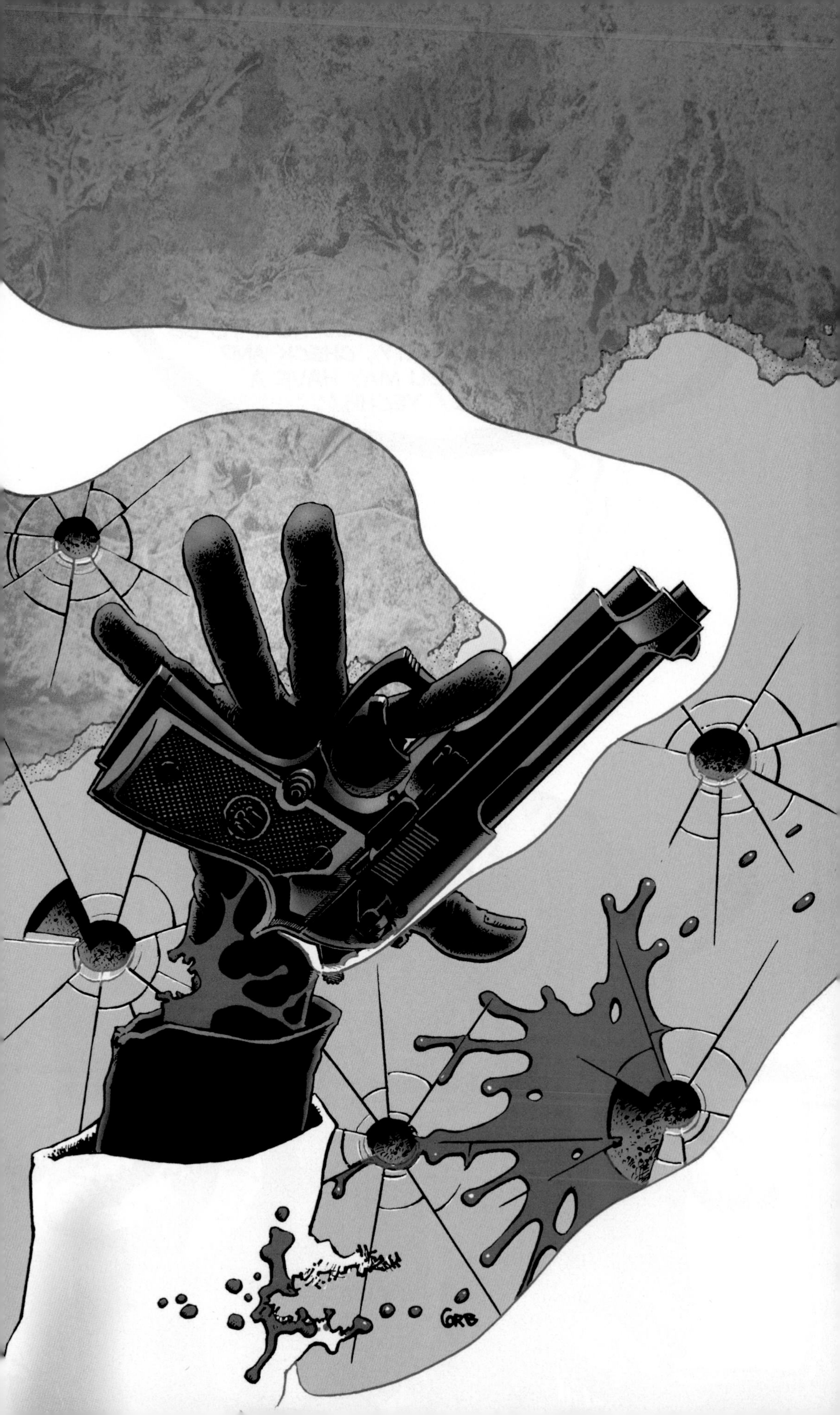

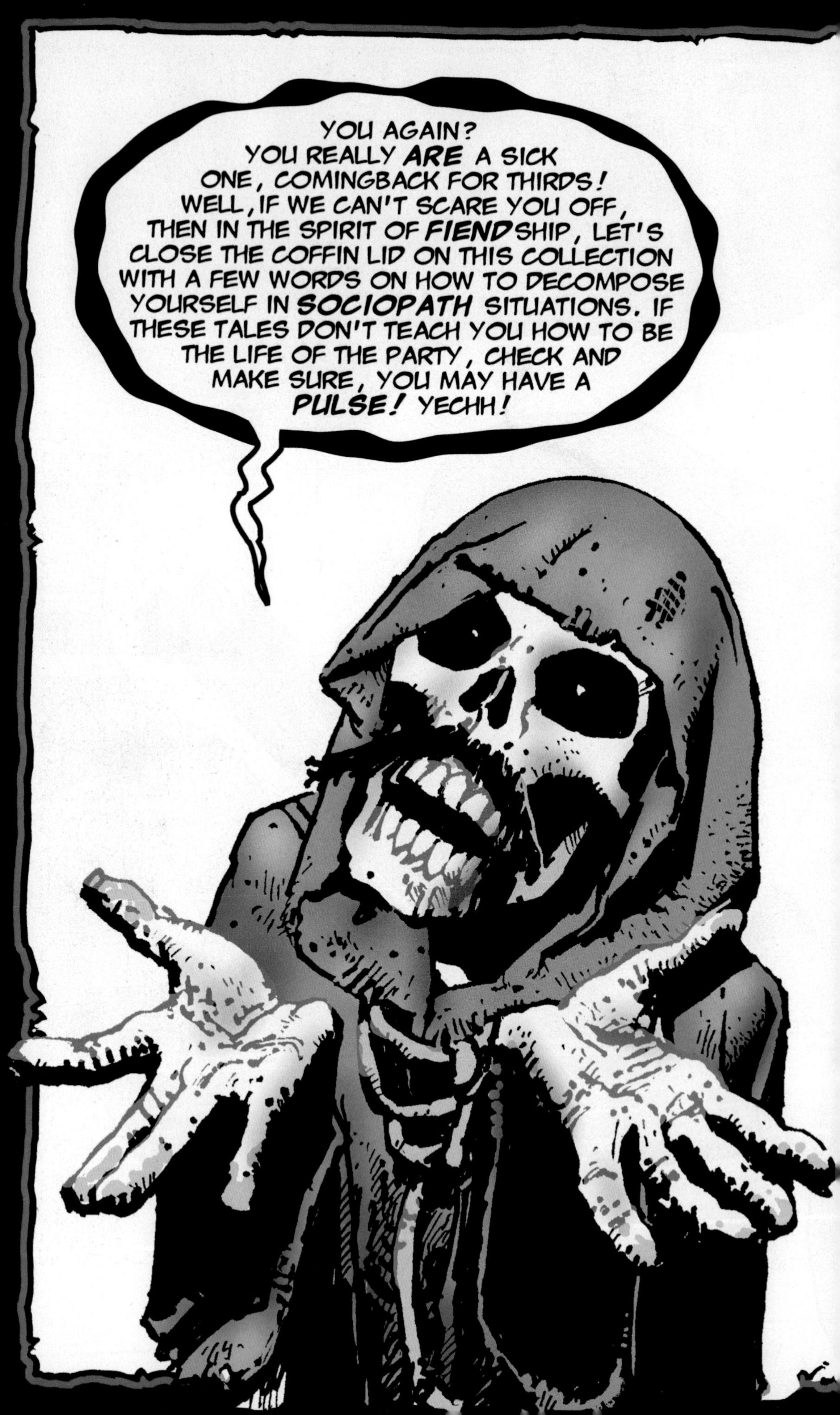
YOU AGAIN? YOU REALLY ARE A SICK ONE, COMINGBACK FOR THIRDS! WELL, IF WE CAN'T SCARE YOU OFF, THEN IN THE SPIRIT OF FIENDSHIP, LET'S CLOSE THE COFFIN LID ON THIS COLLECTION WITH A FEW WORDS ON HOW TO DECOMPOSE YOURSELF IN SOCIOPATH SITUATIONS. IF THESE TALES DON'T TEACH YOU HOW TO BE THE LIFE OF THE PARTY, CHECK AND MAKE SURE, YOU MAY HAVE A PULSE! YECHH!

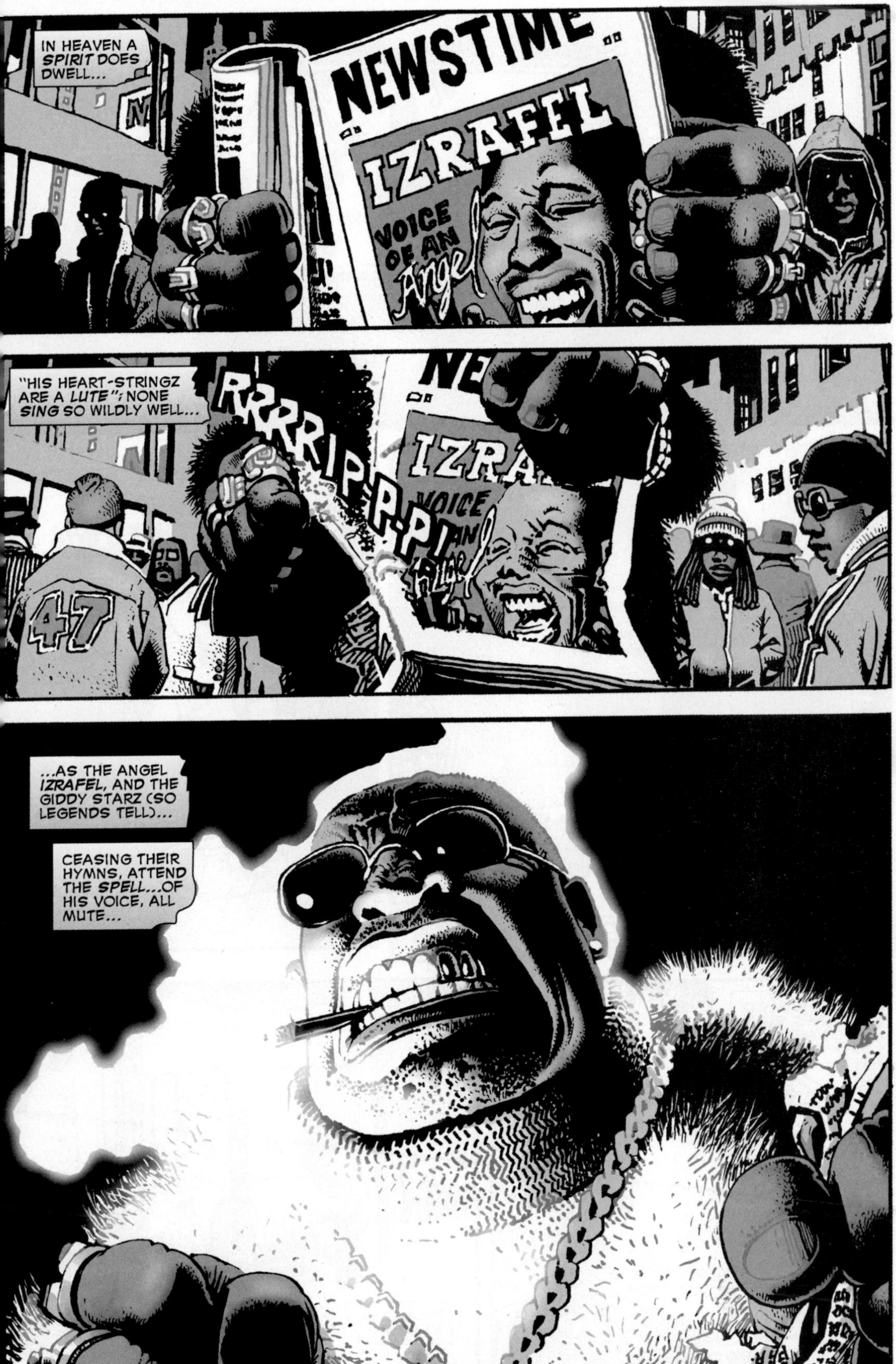
IN HEAVEN A SPIRIT DOES DWELL...
NEWSTIME
IZRAFEL
IZRAFEL
VOICE OF AN Angel
"HIS HEART-STRINGZ ARE A LUTE"; NONE SING SO WILDLY WELL...
RRRRIP-P-P!
...AS THE ANGEL IZRAFEL, AND THE GIDDY STARZ (SO LEGENDS TELL)...
CEASING THEIR HYMNS, ATTEND THE SPELL...OF HIS VOICE, ALL MUTE...

# IZRAFEL

KREDITZ:
WORDS BY EDGAR ALLAN "PO' BOY" POE   REMIX BY RICH "RICH-E-RICH" MARGOPOULOS
PICTURES BY RICH "KRA-Z KRAYONZ" CORBEN

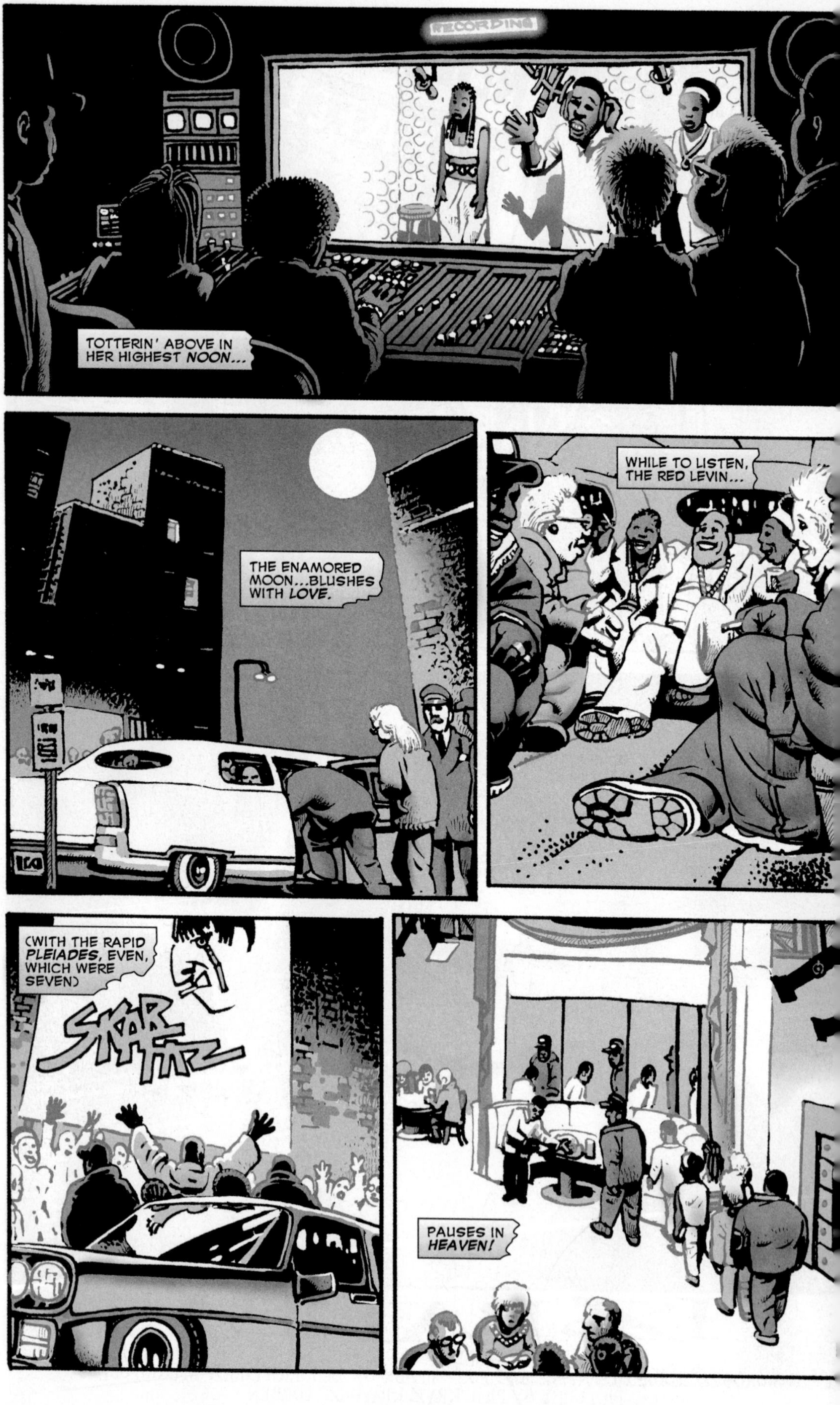
RECORDING
TOTTERIN' ABOVE IN HER HIGHEST NOON...
THE ENAMORED MOON...BLUSHES WITH LOVE.
WHILE TO LISTEN, THE RED LEVIN...
(WITH THE RAPID PLEIADES, EVEN, WHICH WERE SEVEN)
SKAR FITZ
PAUSES IN HEAVEN!

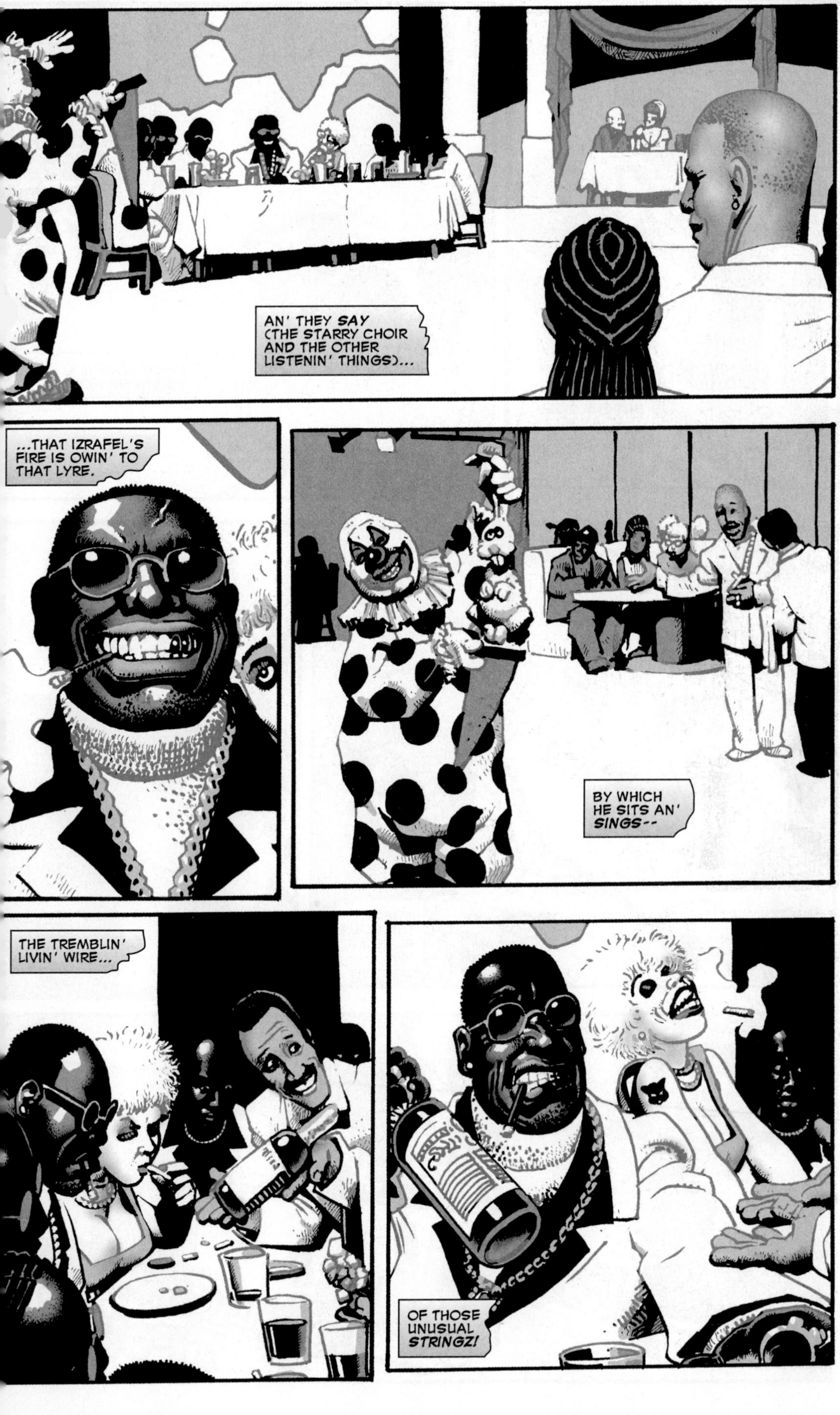
AN' THEY SAY (THE STARRY CHOIR AND THE OTHER LISTENIN' THINGS)...
...THAT IZRAFEL'S FIRE IS OWIN' TO THAT LYRE.
BY WHICH HE SITS AN' SINGS--
THE TREMBLIN' LIVIN' WIRE...
OF THOSE UNUSUAL STRINGZ!

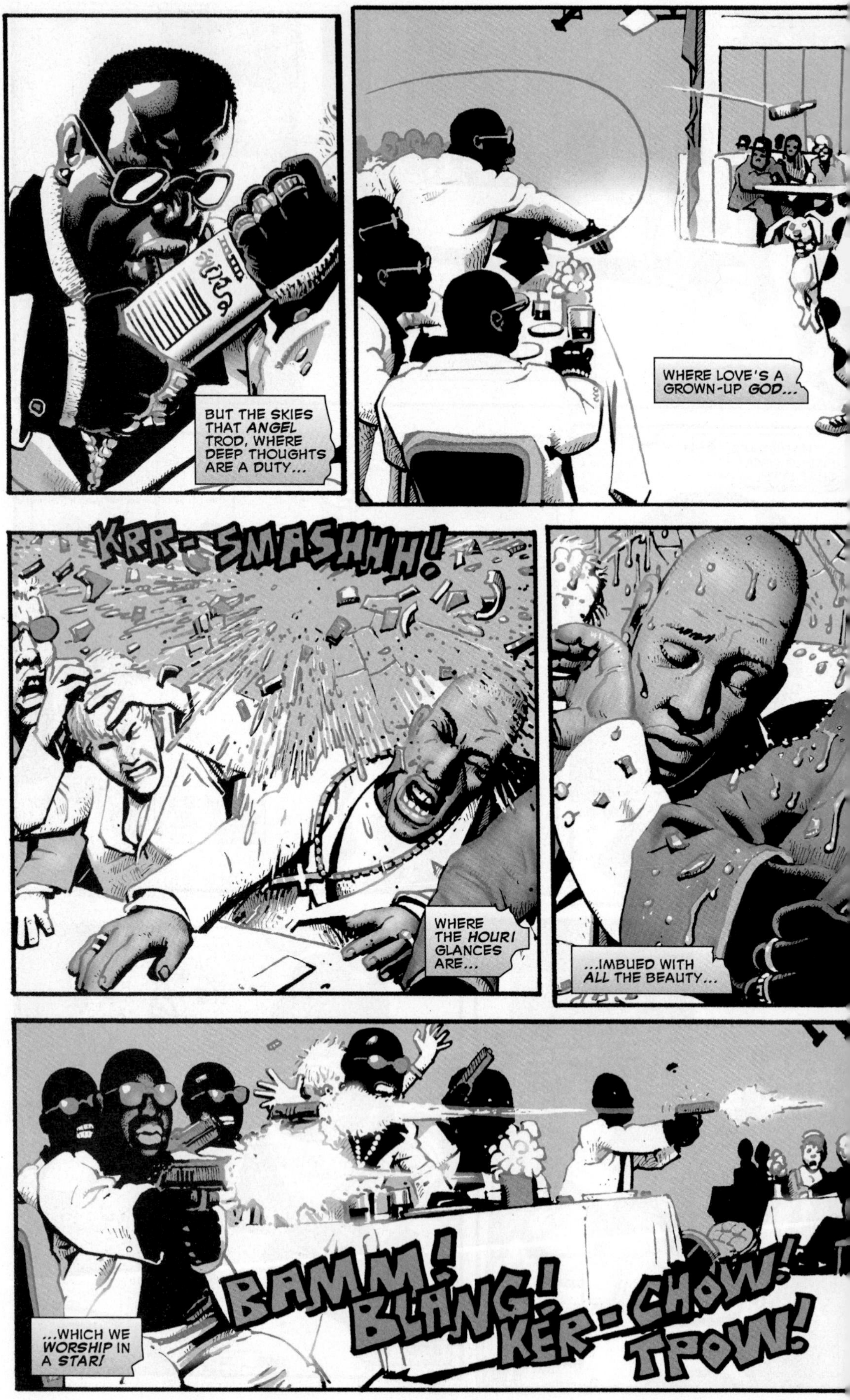
BUT THE SKIES THAT ANGEL TROD, WHERE DEEP THOUGHTS ARE A DUTY...
WHERE LOVE'S A GROWN-UP GOD...
KRR-SMASHHH!
WHERE THE HOURI GLANCES ARE...
...IMBUED WITH ALL THE BEAUTY...
...WHICH WE WORSHIP IN A STAR!
BAMM! BLANG! KER-CHOW! TPOW!

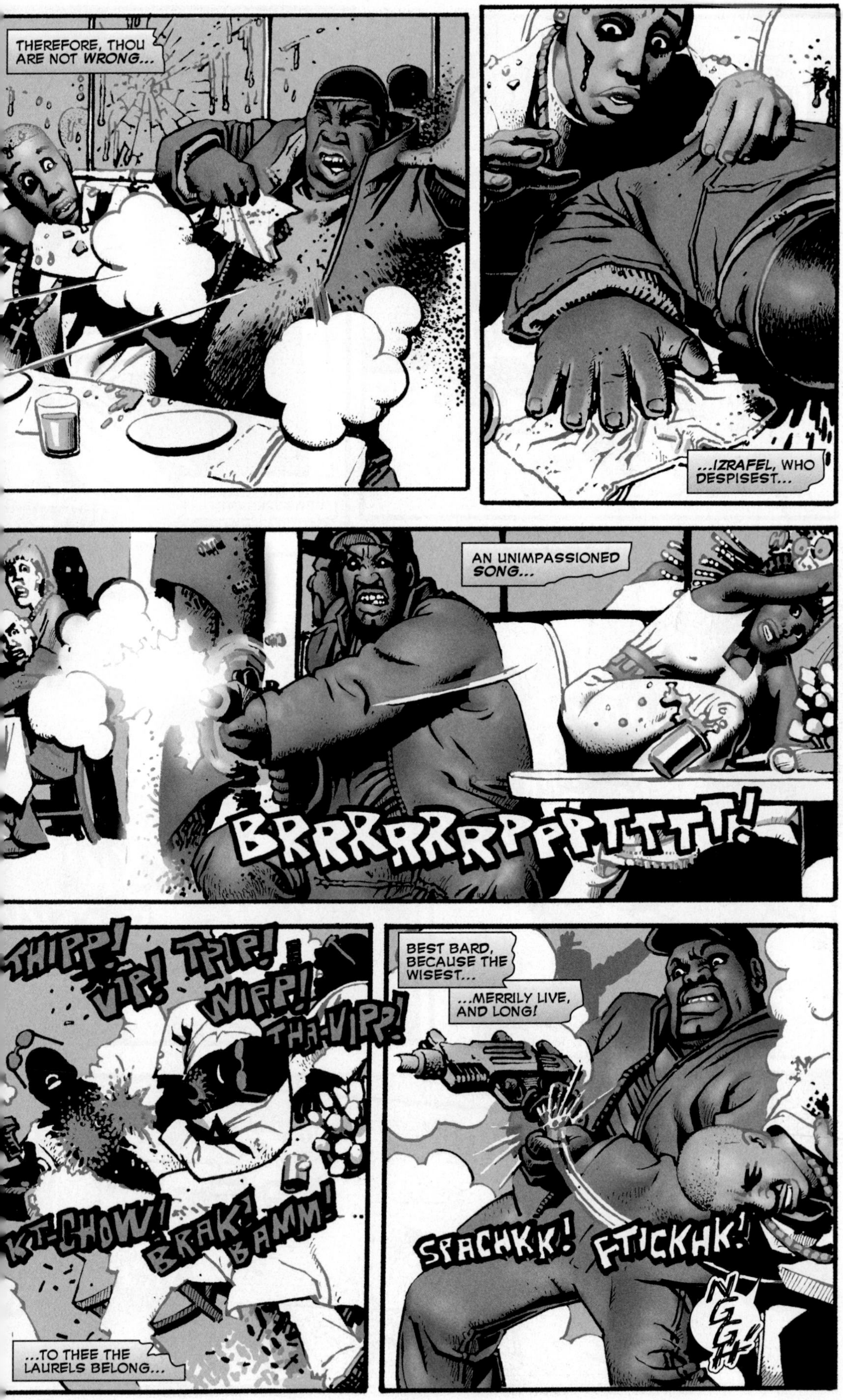
THEREFORE, THOU ARE NOT WRONG...
...IZRAFEL, WHO DESPISEST...
AN UNIMPASSIONED SONG...
BRRRRRRRPPPTTTTT!
THIPP! VIP! TPIP! WIPP! THA-VIPP!
KT-CHOW! BRAK! BAMM!
...TO THEE THE LAURELS BELONG...
BEST BARD, BECAUSE THE WISEST...
...MERRILY LIVE, AND LONG!
SPACHKK! FTICKHK!
NGGH!

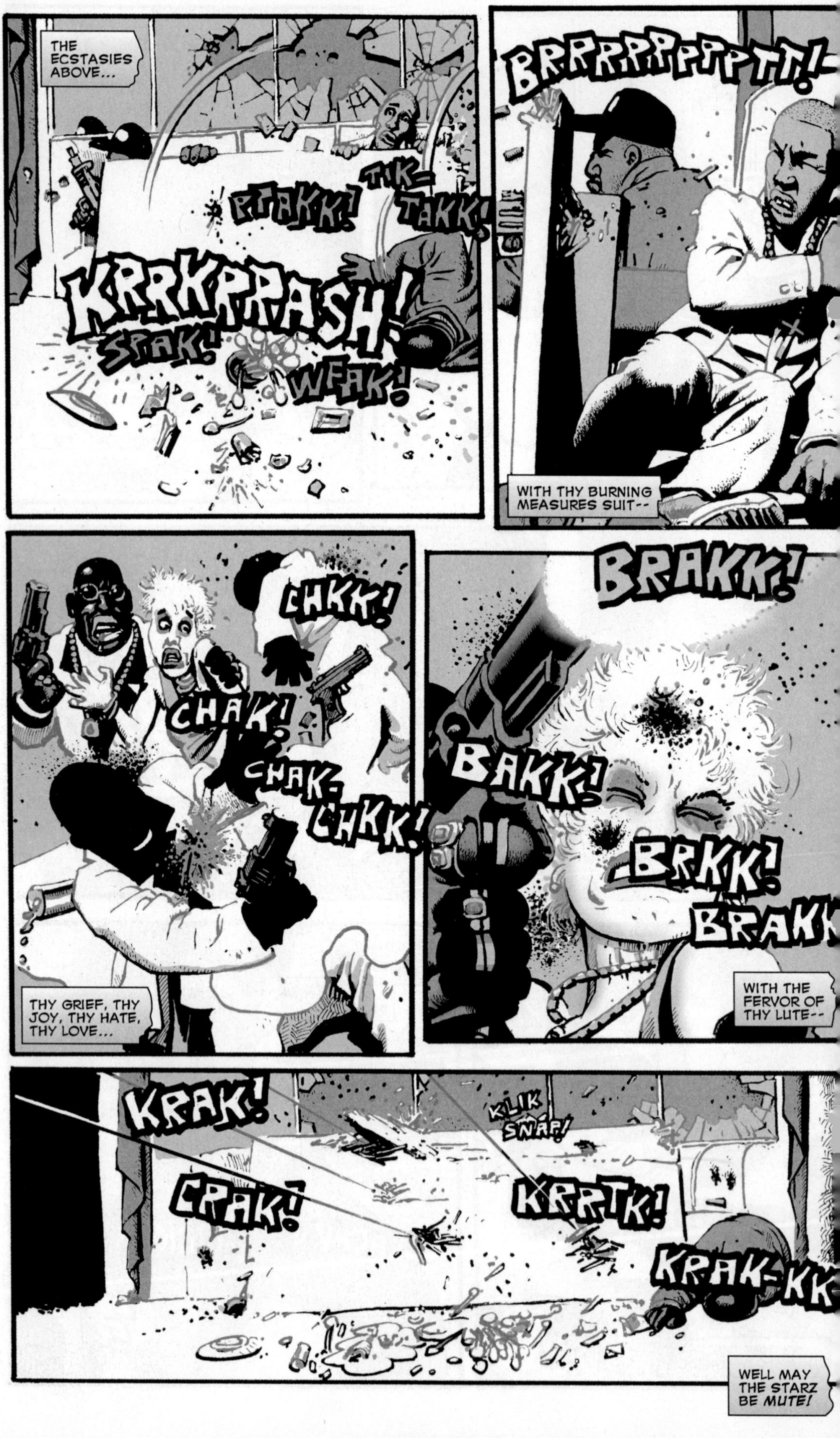
THE ECSTASIES ABOVE...
PTAKK!
TAK-TAKK!
KRRKPPASH!
SPAK!
WFAK!
BRRRPPPPPTT!
WITH THY BURNING MEASURES SUIT--
CHKK!
CHAK!
CHAK-CHKK!
THY GRIEF, THY JOY, THY HATE, THY LOVE...
BRAKK!
BAKK!
BRKK!
BRAKK
WITH THE FERVOR OF THY LUTE--
KRAK!
KLIK SNAP!
CRAK!
KRRTK!
KRAK-KK
WELL MAY THE STARZ BE *MUTE!*

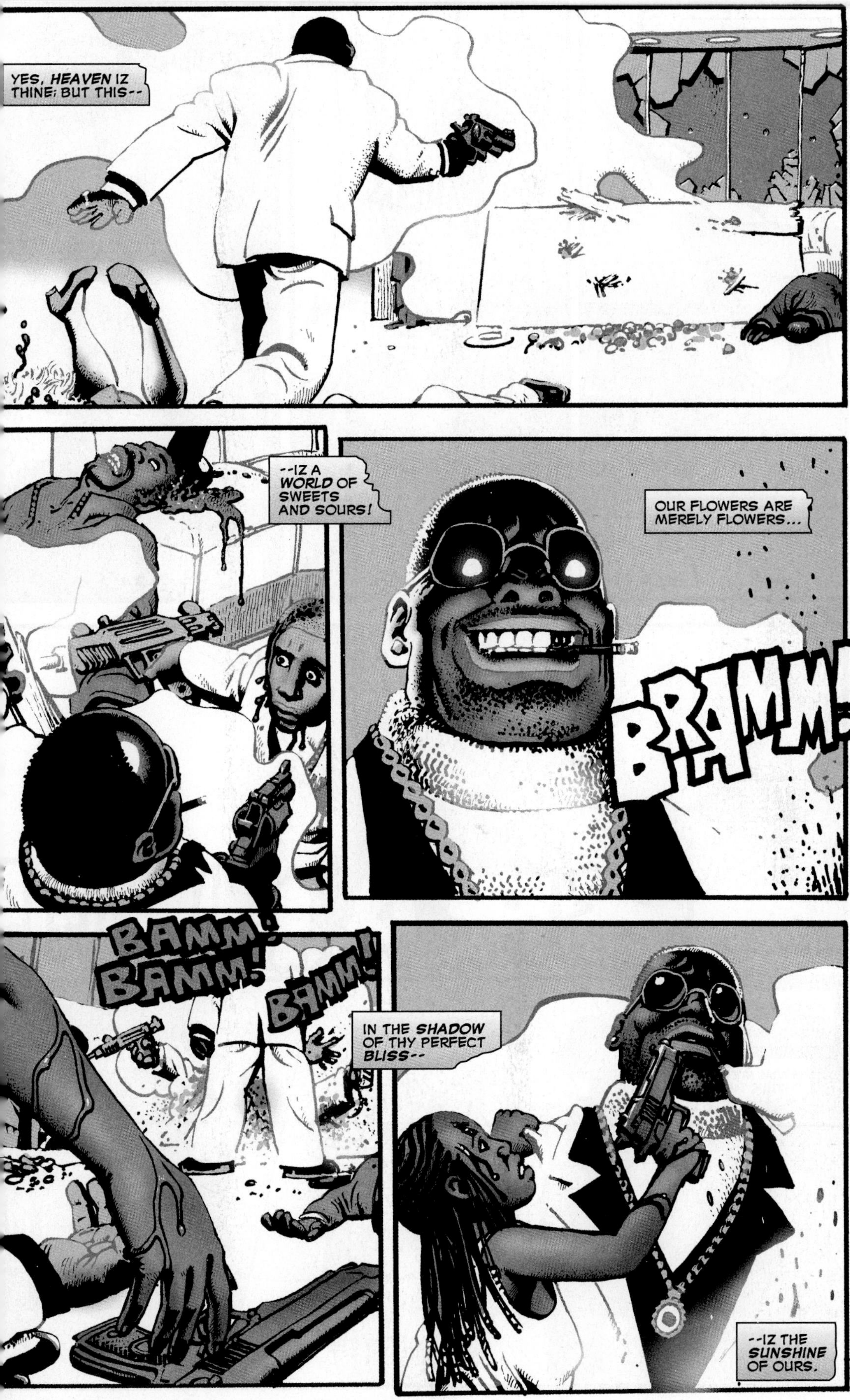
YES, *HEAVEN* IZ THINE; BUT THIS--
--IZ A *WORLD* OF SWEETS AND SOURS!
OUR FLOWERS ARE MERELY FLOWERS...
BRAMM!
BAMM! BAMM!
BAMM!
IN THE *SHADOW* OF THY PERFECT *BLISS*--
--IZ THE *SUNSHINE* OF OURS.

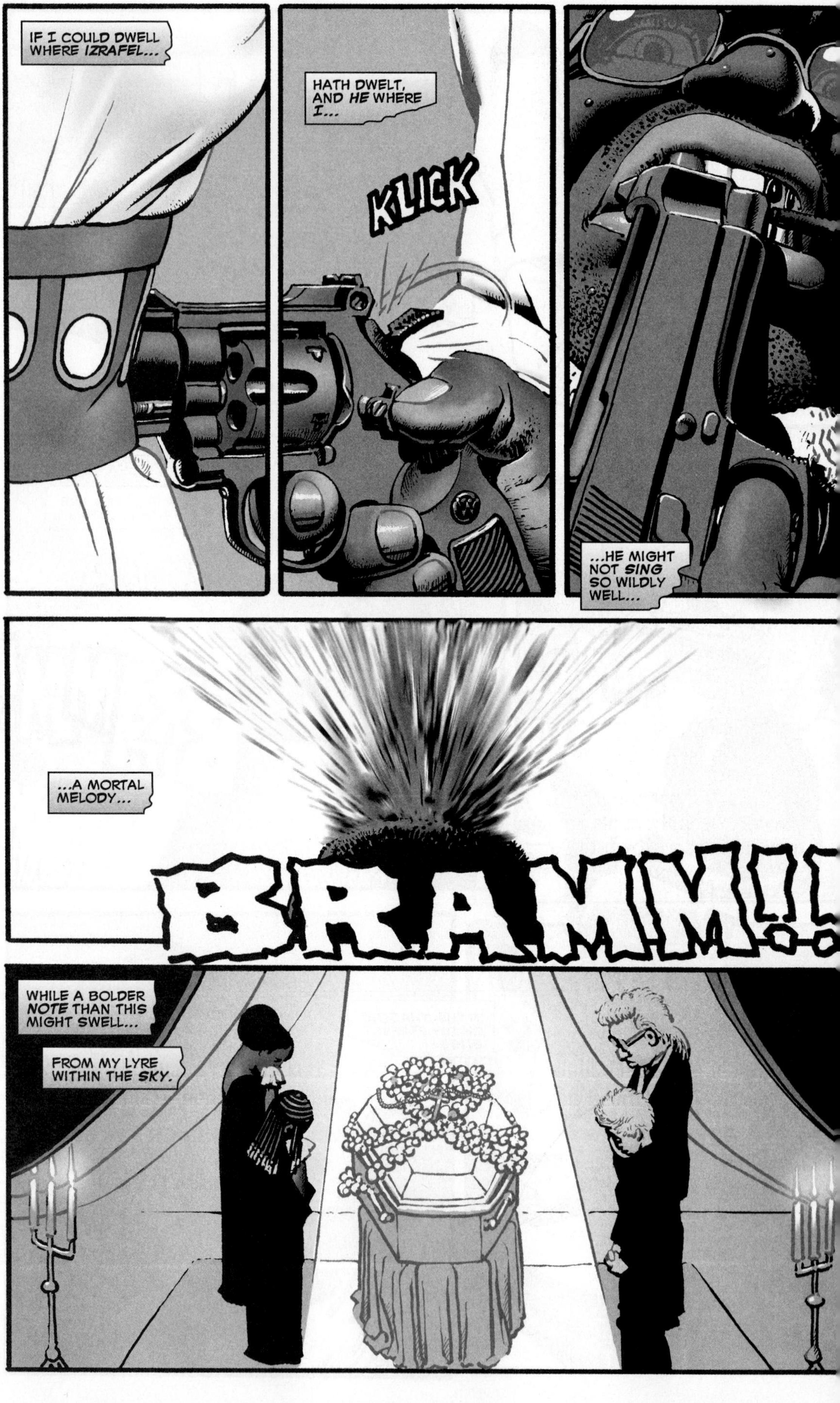
IF I COULD DWELL WHERE IZRAFEL...
HATH DWELT, AND HE WHERE I...
KLICK
...HE MIGHT NOT SING SO WILDLY WELL...
...A MORTAL MELODY...
BRAMM!!
WHILE A BOLDER NOTE THAN THIS MIGHT SWELL...
FROM MY LYRE WITHIN THE SKY.

#  Israfel

In Heaven a spirit doth dwell
"Whose heart-strings are a lute";
None sing so wildly well
As the angel Israfel,
And the giddy stars (so legends tell)
Ceasing their hymns, attend the spell
  Of his voice, all mute.

Tottering above
  In her highest noon,
  The enamored moon
Blushes with love,
  While, to listen, the red levin
  (With the rapid Pleiads, even,
  Which were seven)
  Pauses in Heaven.

And they say (the starry choir
  And the other listening things)
That Israfeli's fire
Is owing to that lyre
  By which he sits and sings—
The trembling living wire
  Of those unusual strings.

But the skies that angel trod,
  Where deep thoughts are a duty—
Where Love's a grown-up God—
  Where the Houri glances are
Imbued with all the beauty
  Which we worship in a star.

Therefore, thou art not wrong,
  Israfeli, who despisest
An unimpassioned song;
To thee the laurels belong,
Best bard, because the wisest!
Merrily live, and long!

The ecstasies above
  With thy burning measures suit—
Thy grief, thy joy, thy hate, thy love,
  With the fervor of thy lute—
  Well may the stars be mute!

Yes, Heaven is thine; but this
  Is a world of sweets and sours;
  Our flowers are merely—flowers,
And the shadow of thy perfect bliss
  Is the sunshine of ours.

If I could dwell
Where Israfel
  Hath dwelt, and he where I,
He might not sing so wildly well
  A mortal melody,
While a bolder note than this might swell
  From my lyre within the sky.

— Edgar Allan Poe

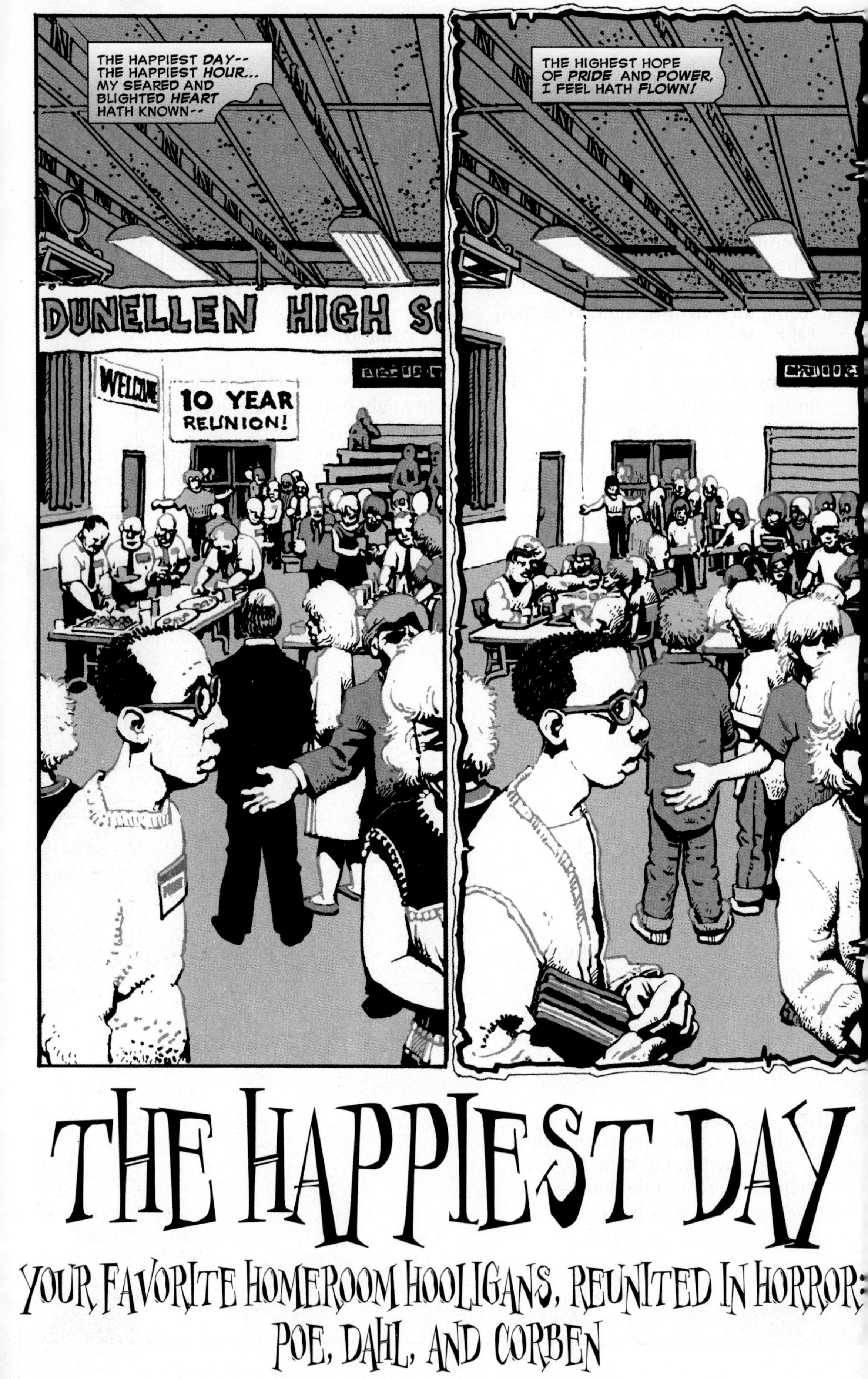
THE HAPPIEST DAY-- THE HAPPIEST HOUR... MY SEARED AND BLIGHTED HEART HATH KNOWN--
DUNELLEN HIGH S
WELCOME
10 YEAR REUNION!
THE HIGHEST HOPE OF PRIDE AND POWER, I FEEL HATH FLOWN!

# THE HAPPIEST DAY

## YOUR FAVORITE HOMEROOM HOOLIGANS, REUNITED IN HORROR: POE, DAHL, AND CORBEN

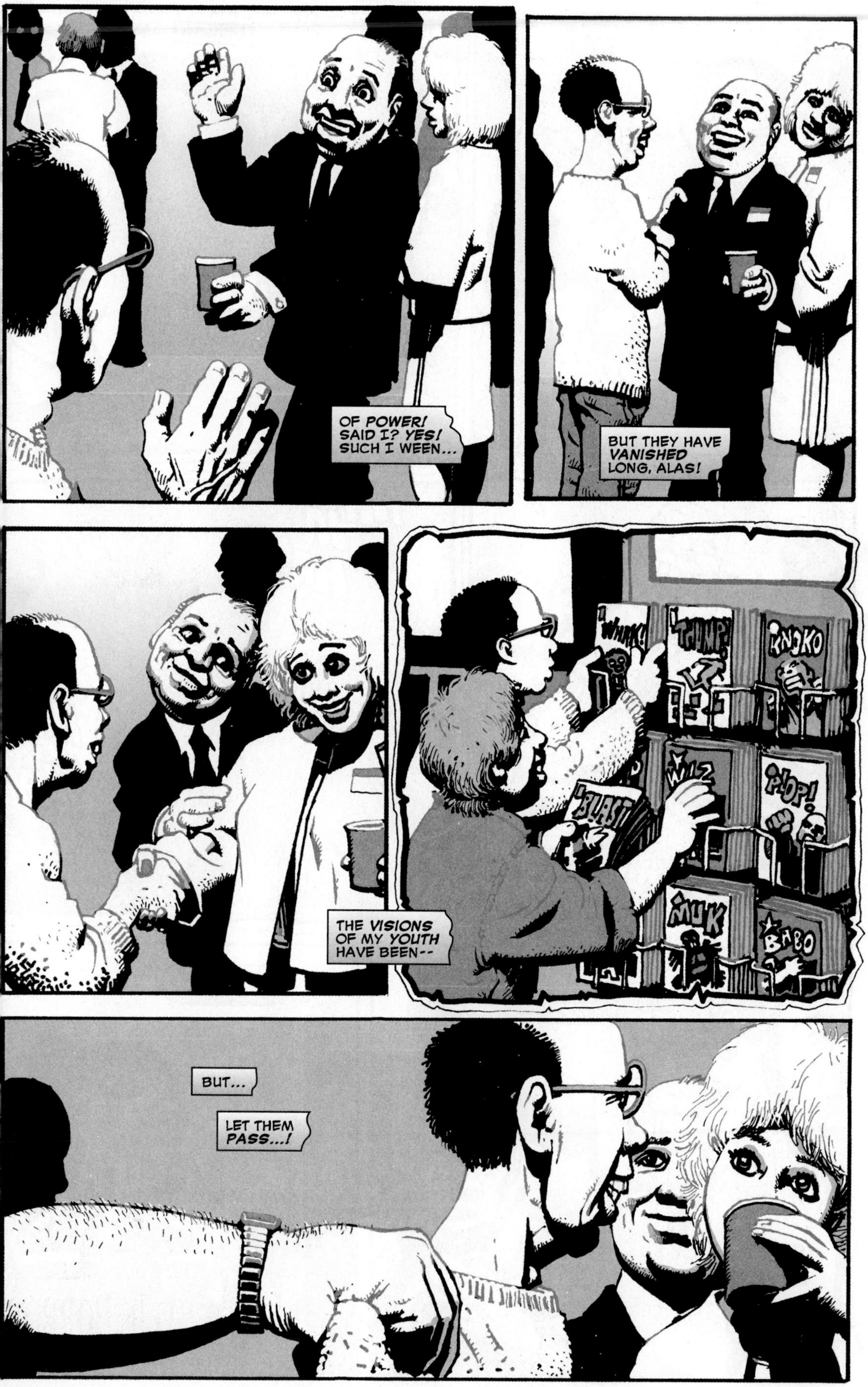
OF POWER! SAID I? YES! SUCH I WEEN...
BUT THEY HAVE VANISHED LONG, ALAS!
THE VISIONS OF MY YOUTH HAVE BEEN--
WHAK!
THUMP!
KNOKO
WIZ
PLOP!
BLAST
MUK
BABO
BUT...
LET THEM PASS...!

AND *PRIDE,* WHAT HAVE I NOW WITH THEE?

SHOWER

HA HA!

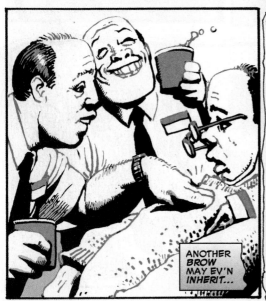

ANOTHER BROW MAY EV'N INHERIT...

HA HA HA!

HA HA HA

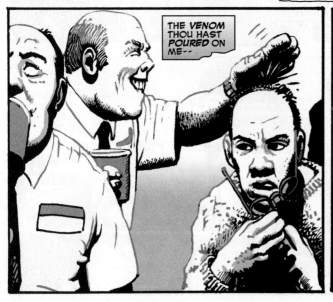

THE *VENOM* THOU HAST *POURED* ON ME--

BE *STILL* MY SPIRIT--!!

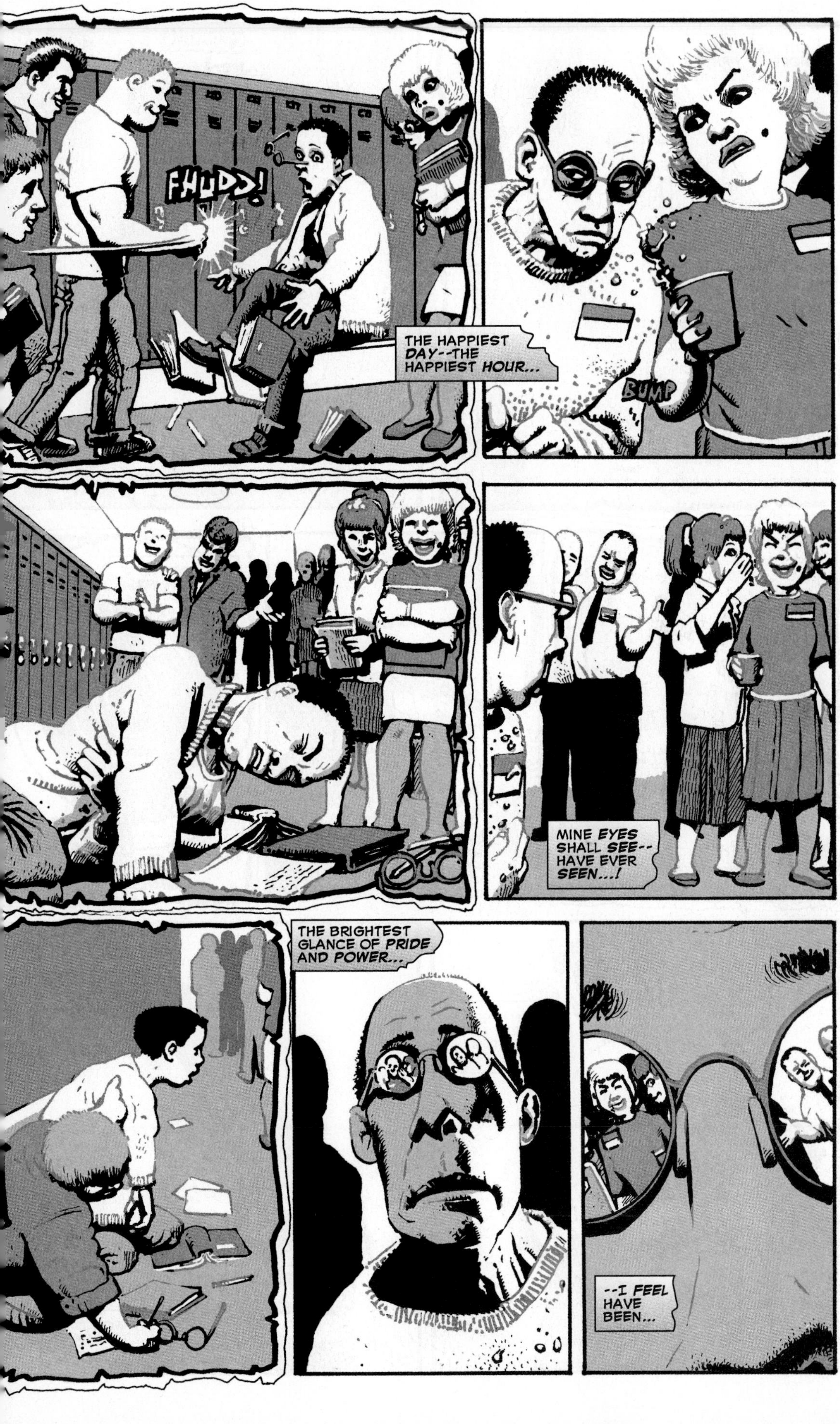
FHUDD!
THE HAPPIEST DAY--THE HAPPIEST HOUR...
BUMP
MINE EYES SHALL SEE--HAVE EVER SEEN...!
THE BRIGHTEST GLANCE OF PRIDE AND POWER...
--I FEEL HAVE BEEN...

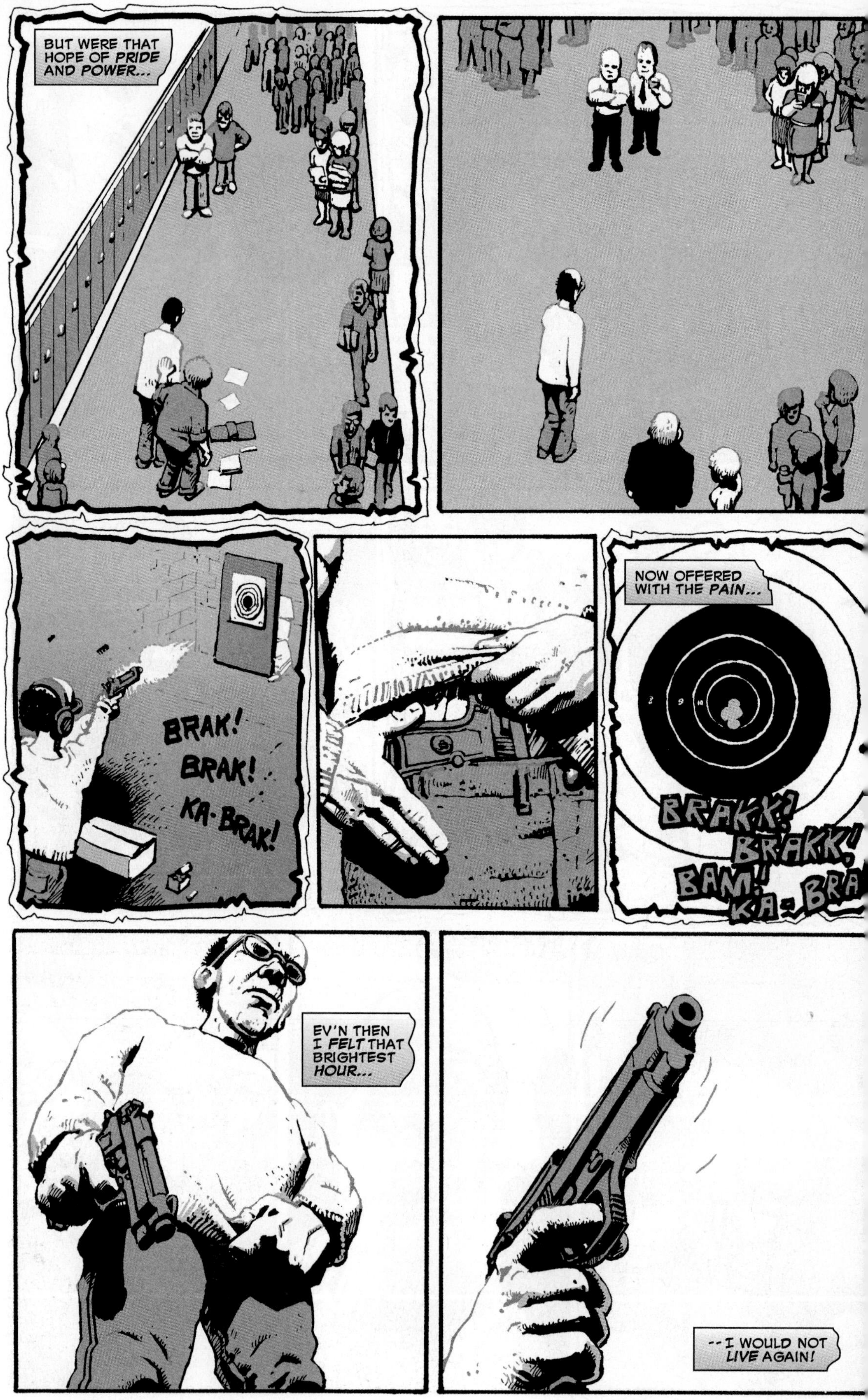
BUT WERE THAT HOPE OF PRIDE AND POWER...
BRAK!
BRAK!
KA-BRAK!
NOW OFFERED WITH THE PAIN...
BRAKK!
BRAKK!
BAM!
EV'N THEN I FELT THAT BRIGHTEST HOUR...
--I WOULD NOT LIVE AGAIN!

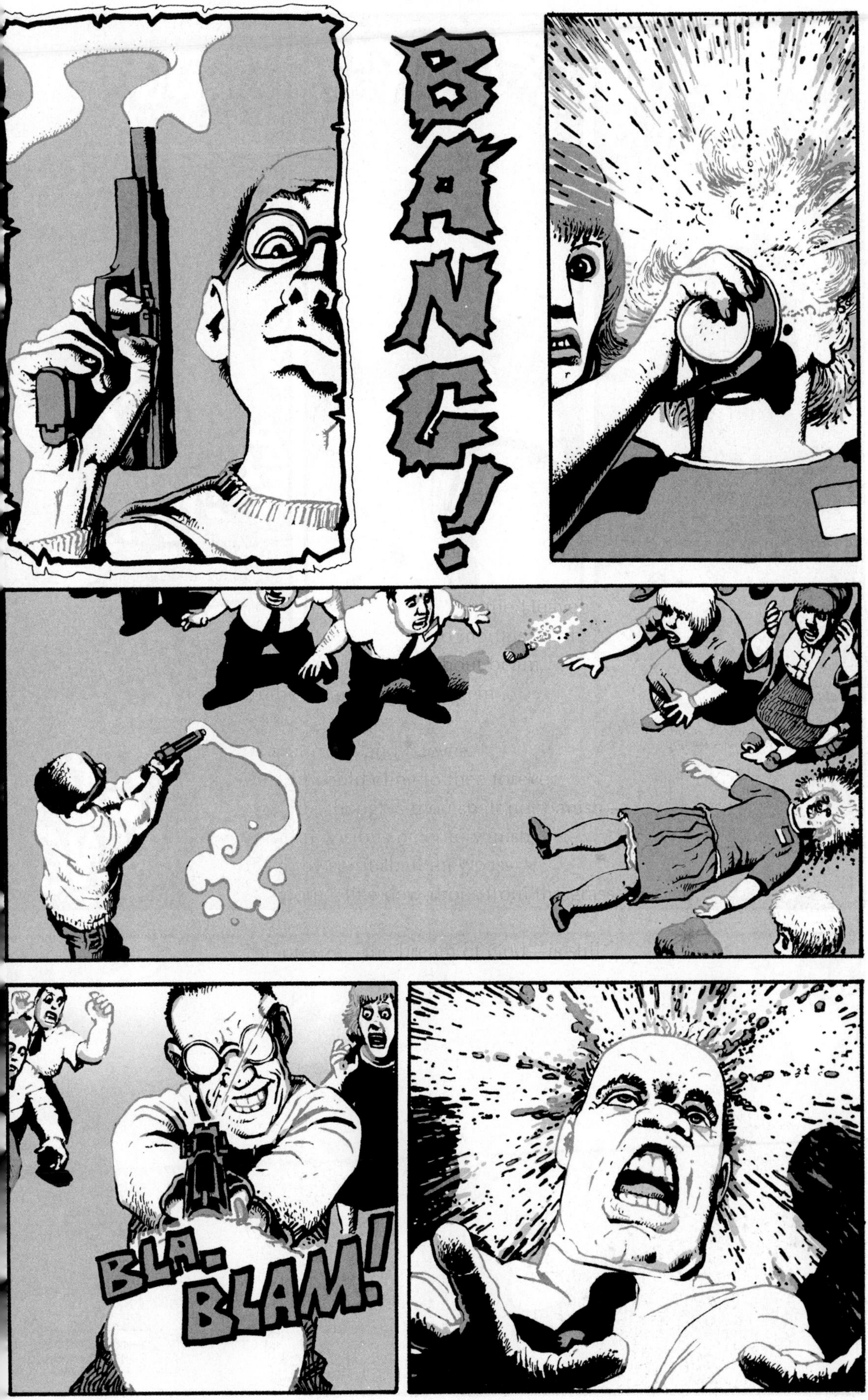
BANG!
BLA-
BLAM!

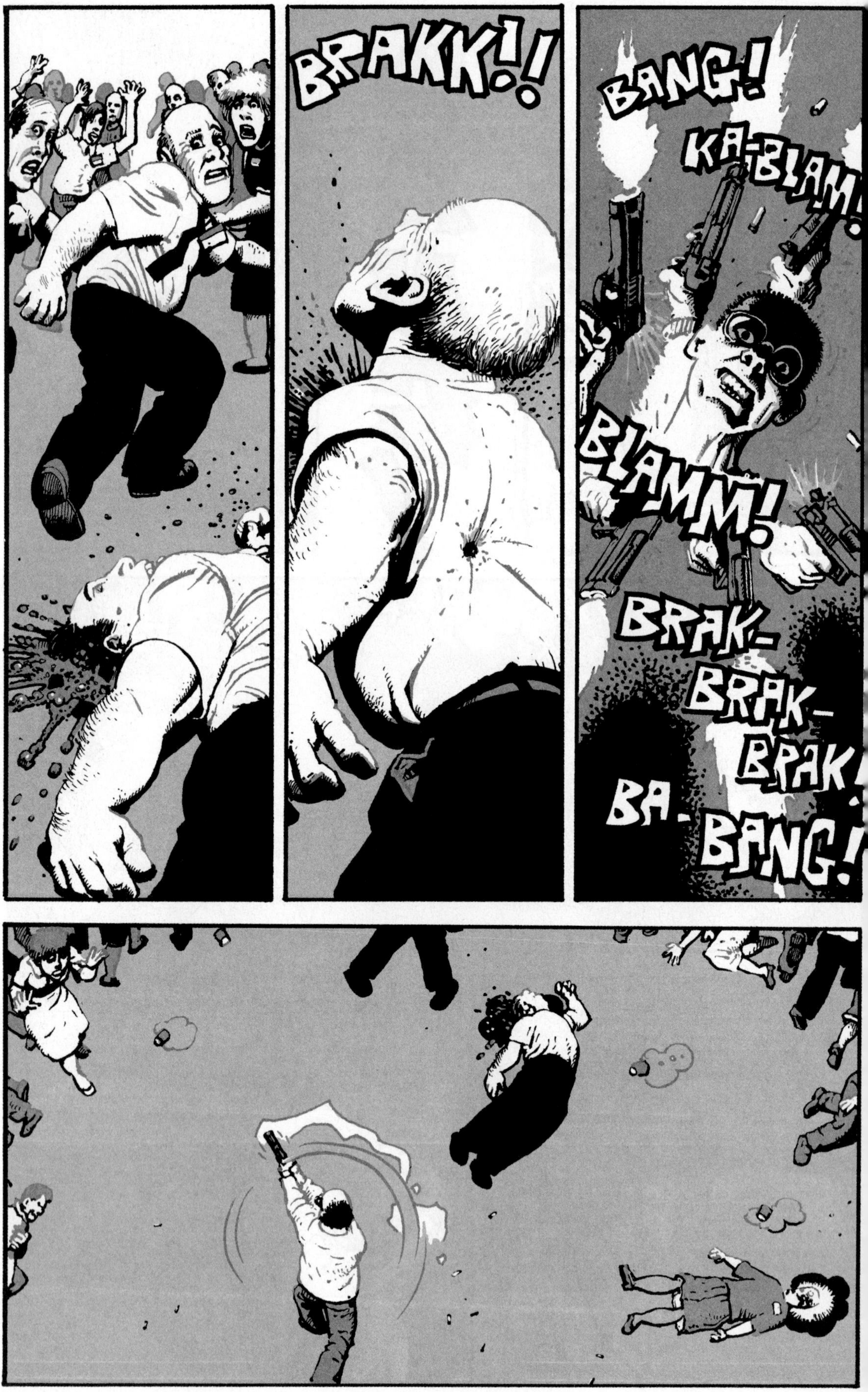
BRAKK!!
BANG!
KA-BLAM!
BLAMM!
BRAK-
BRAK-
BRAK-
BA-BANG!

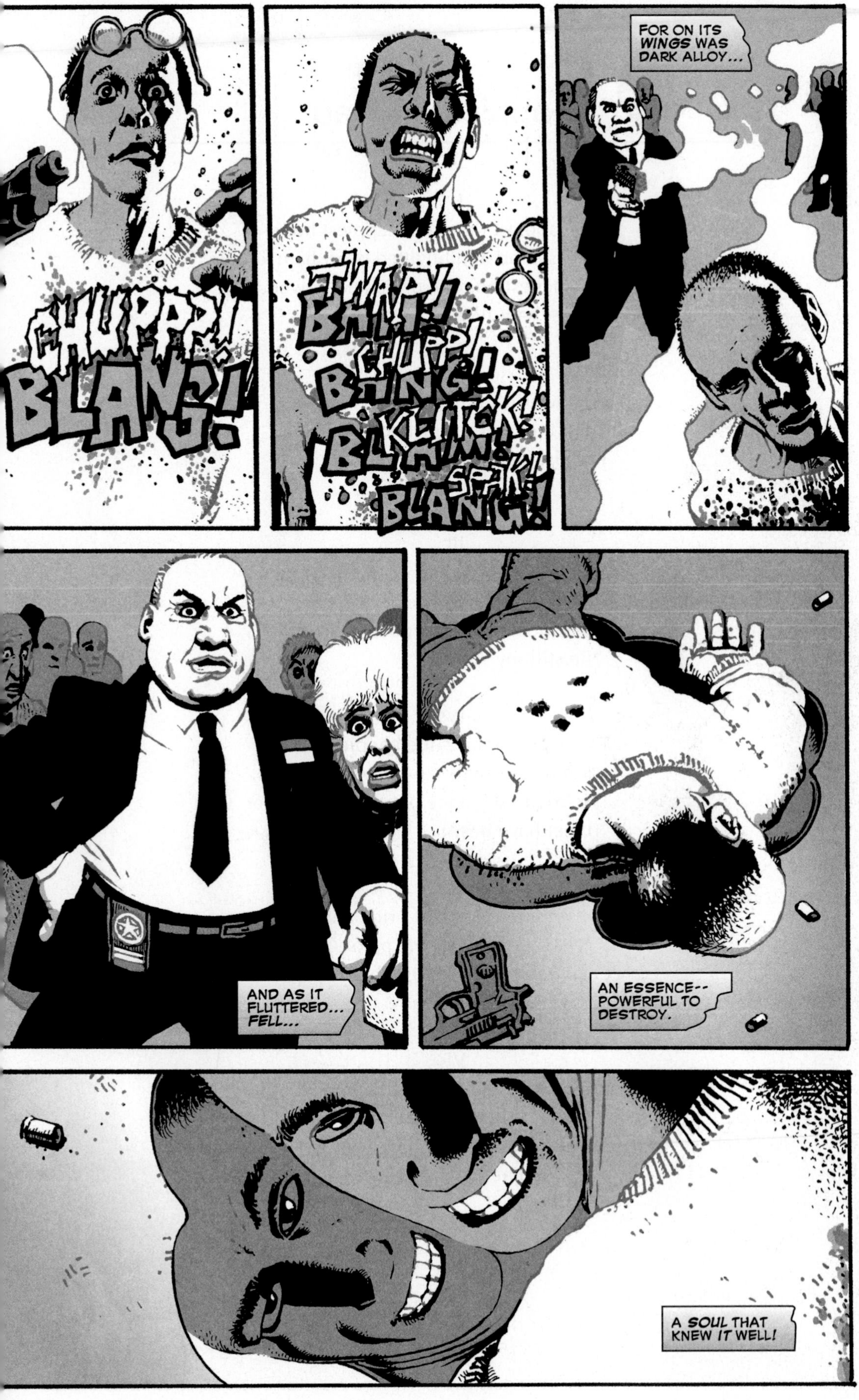
CHUPPP!
BLANG!
TWAP!
CHUPP!
BANG!
KLITCK!
SPAK!
BLANG!
FOR ON ITS *WINGS* WAS DARK ALLOY...
AND AS IT FLUTTERED... *FELL...*
AN ESSENCE-- POWERFUL TO DESTROY.
A *SOUL* THAT KNEW *IT* WELL!

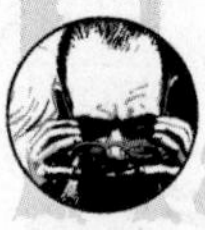

# Happiest Day

I

The happiest day—the happiest hour
My seared and blighted heart hath known,
The highest hope of pride and power,
I feel hath flown.

II

Of power! said I? Yes! such I ween
But they have vanished long, alas!
The visions of my youth have been—
But let them pass.

III

And, pride, what have I now with thee?
Another brow may ev'n inherit
The venom thou hast poured on me—
Be still my spirit!

IV

The happiest day—the happiest hour
Mine eyes shall see—have ever seen
The brightest glance of pride and power
I feel have been:

V

But were that hope of pride and power
Now offered with the pain
Ev'n *then* I felt—that brightest hour
I would not live again:

VI

For on its wings was dark alloy
And as it fluttered—fell
An essence—powerful to destroy
A soul that knew it well.

– Edgar Allan Poe

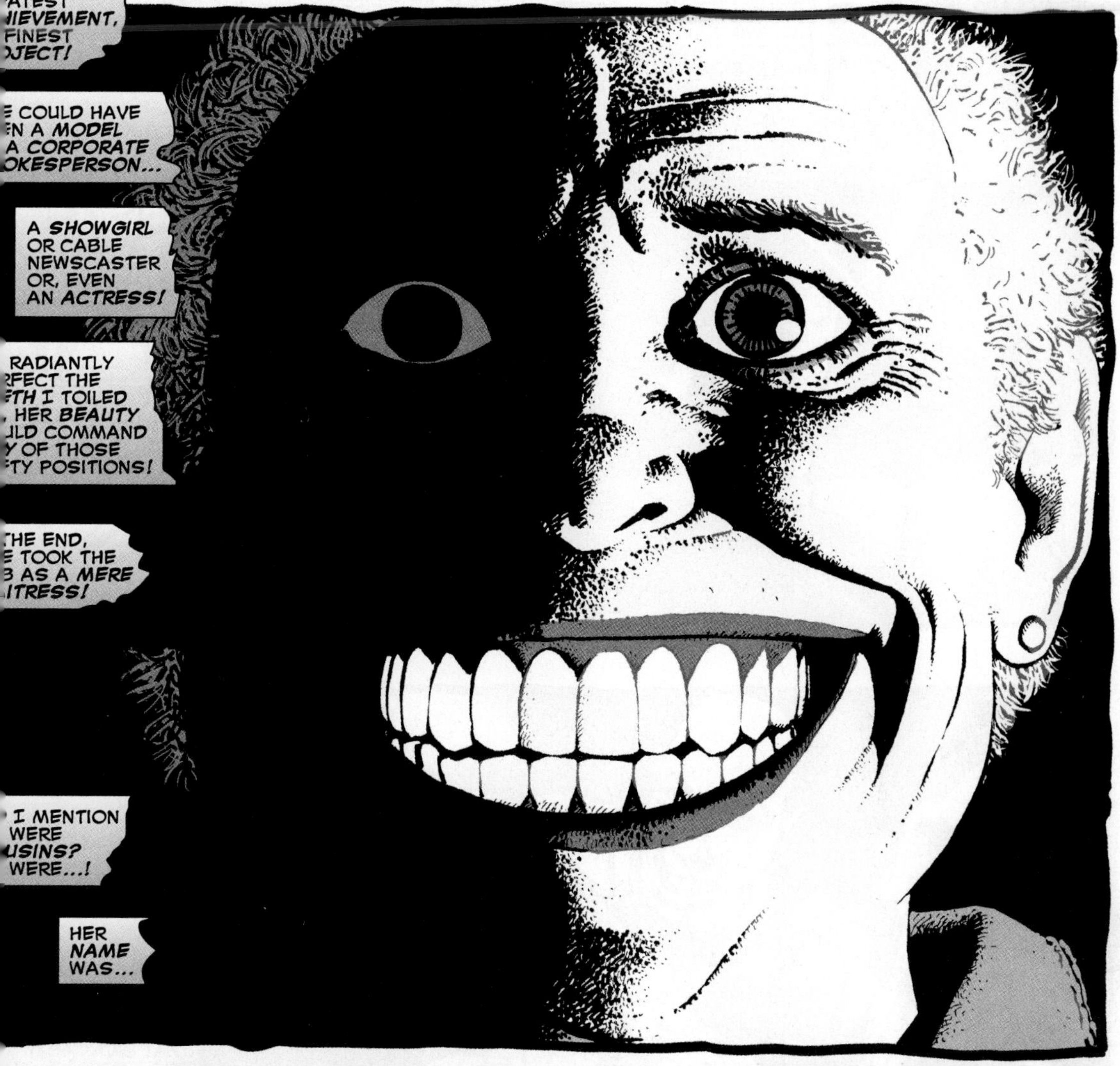
E WAS MY ATEST IEVEMENT, FINEST OJECT!
E COULD HAVE N A MODEL A CORPORATE OKESPERSON...
A SHOWGIRL OR CABLE NEWSCASTER OR, EVEN AN ACTRESS!
RADIANTLY RFECT THE TH I TOILED , HER BEAUTY ULD COMMAND Y OF THOSE TY POSITIONS!
THE END, E TOOK THE B AS A MERE ITRESS!
I MENTION WERE USINS? WERE...!
HER NAME WAS...

# BERENICE

SUBLIME HORROR BROUGHT TO YOU BY

POE, MARGOPOULOS AND CORBEN

HERE'S A TALE YOU CAN SINK YOUR TEETH INTO! GUARANTEED YOU'LL BE SALIVATING FOR MORE...!

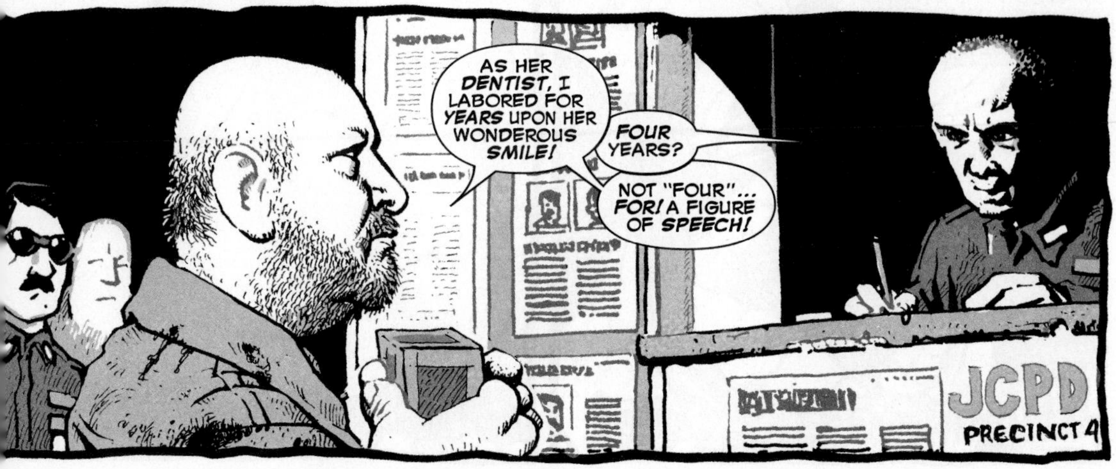
AS HER DENTIST, I LABORED FOR YEARS UPON HER WONDEROUS SMILE!
FOUR YEARS?
NOT "FOUR"... FOR! A FIGURE OF SPEECH!
JCPD
PRECINCT 4

I WAS THE WILLING *SLAVE* TO HER MOLARS, INCISORS AND BICUSPIDS! A DENTAL *KNIGHT-ERRANT...*

PROTECTING THE *DAMSEL* FROM THE TWIN RAVAGING *DRAGONS* GINGIVITIS AND PERIODONTITIS!

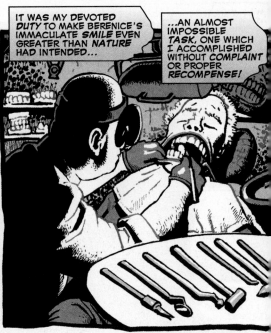

IT WAS MY DEVOTED *DUTY* TO MAKE BERENICE'S IMMACULATE *SMILE* EVEN GREATER THAN *NATURE* HAD INTENDED...

...AN ALMOST IMPOSSIBLE *TASK*, ONE WHICH I ACCOMPLISHED WITHOUT *COMPLAINT* OR PROPER *RECOMPENSE!*

THEN SOMETHING OCCURRED, A *HAPPENSTANCE* THAT INVARIABLY PROVED TO BE MY PERSONAL *DOWNFALL!*

I *SUDDENLY* REALIZED THAT, WHILE COMPLETELY ABSORBED IN THE CAVERNOUS EXPANSE OF HER GAPING *ORIFICE*--

MY *ELBOW* HAD STRAYED AND WAS NOW RESTING UPON THE AMPLE ORB OF ONE *BREAST!*

WHRTPREEEEEEEEEE!

RATHER THAN *REMOVE* THE OFFENDING ARM, I *PRESSED* ON...BARELY ABLE TO CONTAIN THE NEWFOUND *EXCITEMENT* DERIVED FROM THE *LABOR* I SO DEARLY LOVED!

GHRRRRRRRZZRRRWNN

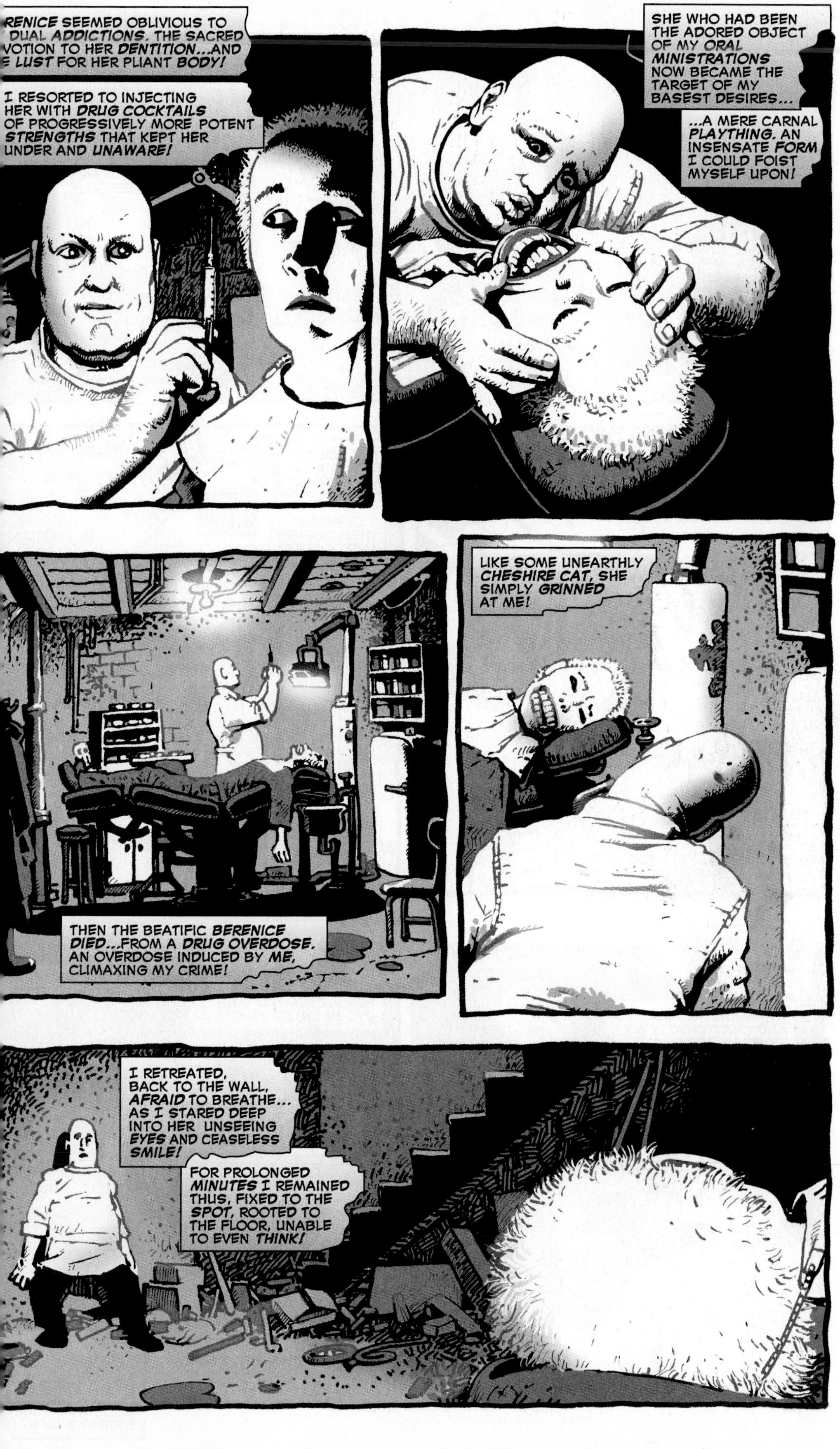
RENICE SEEMED OBLIVIOUS TO DUAL ADDICTIONS. THE SACRED VOTION TO HER DENTITION...AND LUST FOR HER PLIANT BODY!
I RESORTED TO INJECTING HER WITH DRUG COCKTAILS OF PROGRESSIVELY MORE POTENT STRENGTHS THAT KEPT HER UNDER AND UNAWARE!
SHE WHO HAD BEEN THE ADORED OBJECT OF MY ORAL MINISTRATIONS NOW BECAME THE TARGET OF MY BASEST DESIRES...
...A MERE CARNAL PLAYTHING. AN INSENSATE FORM I COULD FOIST MYSELF UPON!
THEN THE BEATIFIC BERENICE DIED...FROM A DRUG OVERDOSE. AN OVERDOSE INDUCED BY ME, CLIMAXING MY CRIME!
LIKE SOME UNEARTHLY CHESHIRE CAT, SHE SIMPLY GRINNED AT ME!
I RETREATED, BACK TO THE WALL, AFRAID TO BREATHE... AS I STARED DEEP INTO HER UNSEEING EYES AND CEASELESS SMILE!
FOR PROLONGED MINUTES I REMAINED THUS, FIXED TO THE SPOT, ROOTED TO THE FLOOR, UNABLE TO EVEN THINK!

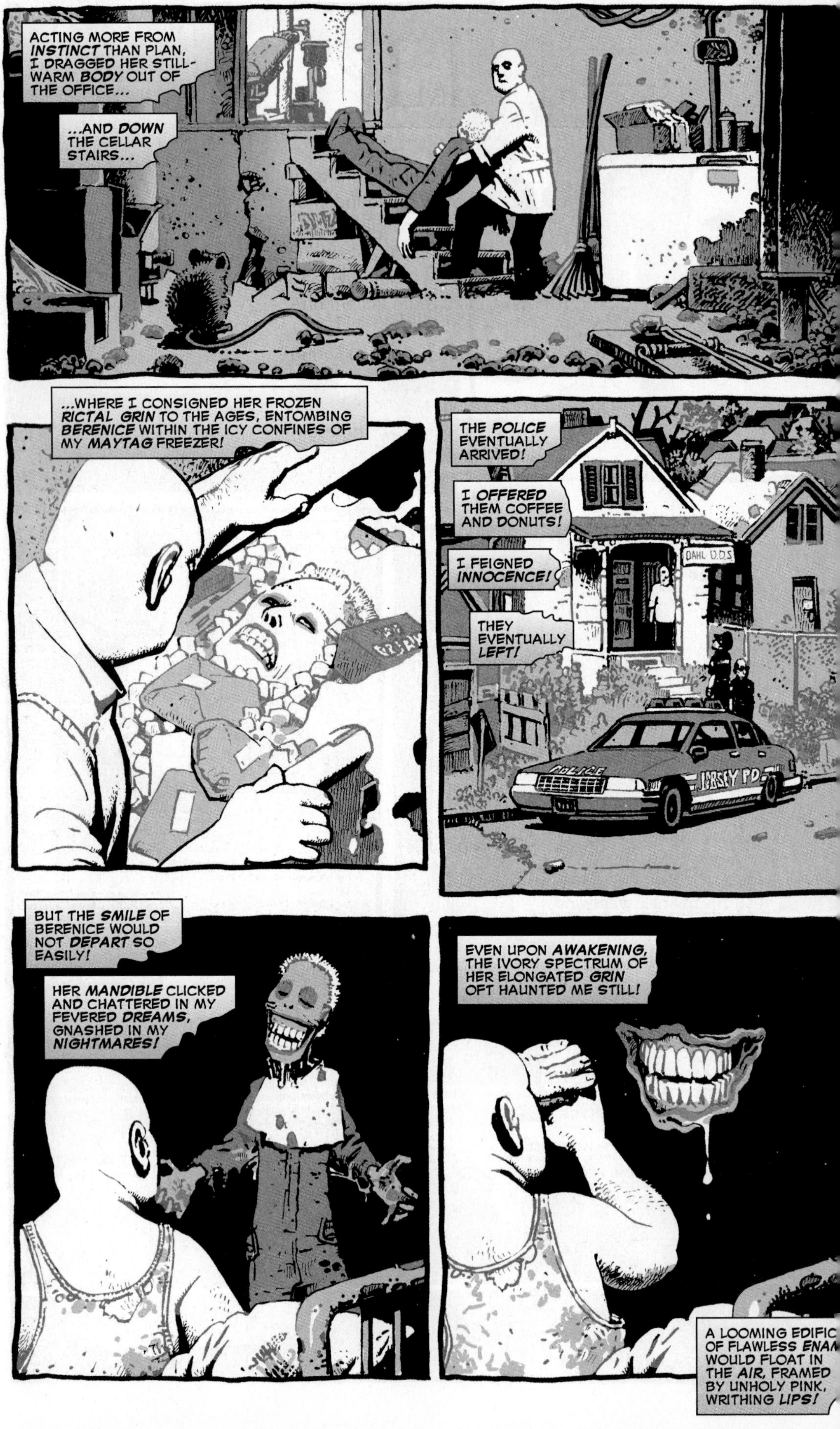

ACTING MORE FROM INSTINCT THAN PLAN, I DRAGGED HER STILL-WARM BODY OUT OF THE OFFICE...
...AND DOWN THE CELLAR STAIRS...
...WHERE I CONSIGNED HER FROZEN RICTAL GRIN TO THE AGES, ENTOMBING BERENICE WITHIN THE ICY CONFINES OF MY MAYTAG FREEZER!
THE POLICE EVENTUALLY ARRIVED!
I OFFERED THEM COFFEE AND DONUTS!
I FEIGNED INNOCENCE!
THEY EVENTUALLY LEFT!
DAHL D.D.S.
POLICE
JERSEY PD
BUT THE SMILE OF BERENICE WOULD NOT DEPART SO EASILY!
HER MANDIBLE CLICKED AND CHATTERED IN MY FEVERED DREAMS, GNASHED IN MY NIGHTMARES!
EVEN UPON AWAKENING, THE IVORY SPECTRUM OF HER ELONGATED GRIN OFT HAUNTED ME STILL!
A LOOMING EDIFIC OF FLAWLESS ENAM WOULD FLOAT IN THE AIR, FRAMED BY UNHOLY PINK, WRITHING LIPS!

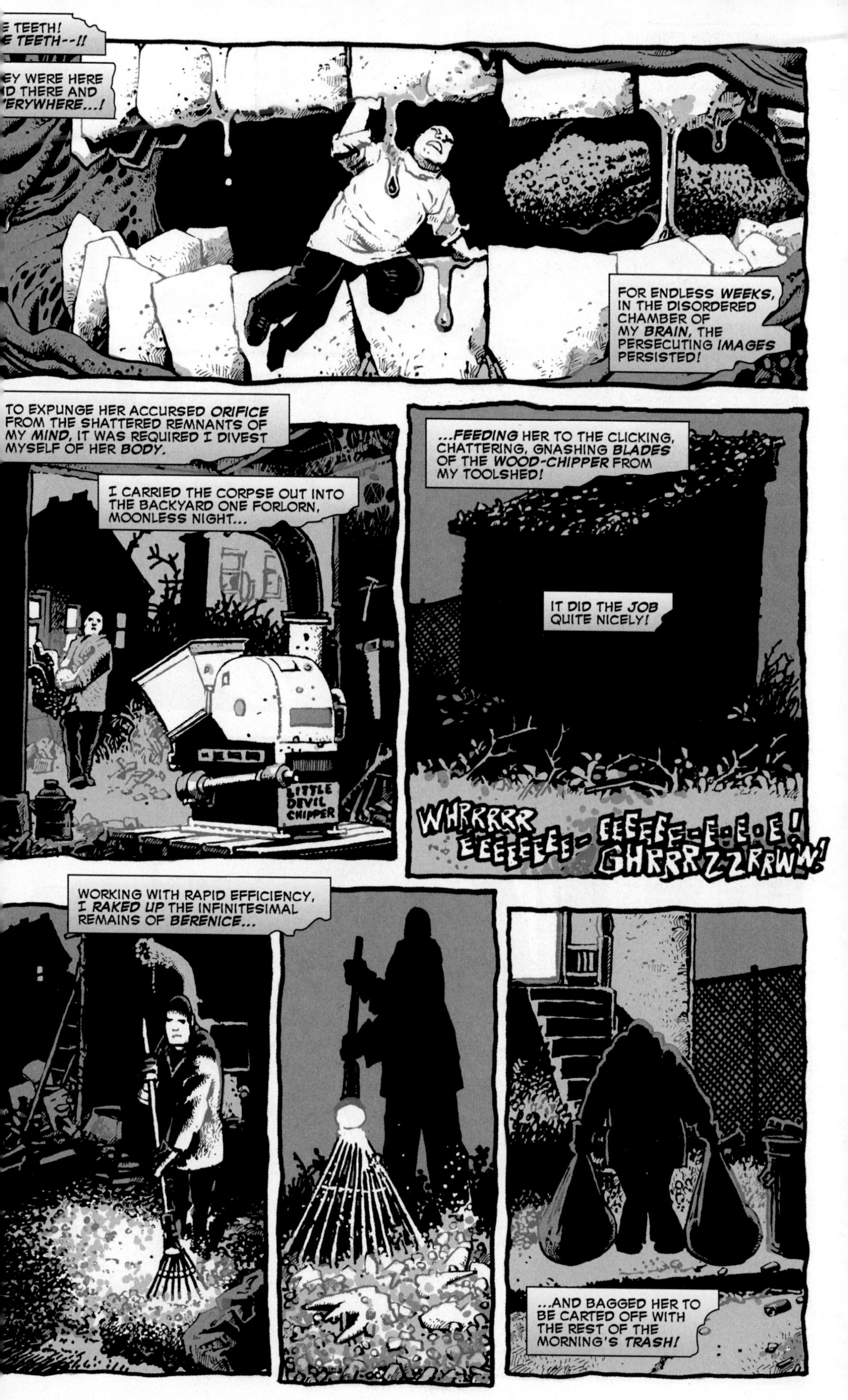
E TEETH! E TEETH--!!
EY WERE HERE D THERE AND ERYWHERE...!
FOR ENDLESS WEEKS, IN THE DISORDERED CHAMBER OF MY BRAIN, THE PERSECUTING IMAGES PERSISTED!
TO EXPUNGE HER ACCURSED ORIFICE FROM THE SHATTERED REMNANTS OF MY MIND, IT WAS REQUIRED I DIVEST MYSELF OF HER BODY.
I CARRIED THE CORPSE OUT INTO THE BACKYARD ONE FORLORN, MOONLESS NIGHT...
LITTLE DEVIL CHIPPER
...FEEDING HER TO THE CLICKING, CHATTERING, GNASHING BLADES OF THE WOOD-CHIPPER FROM MY TOOLSHED!
IT DID THE JOB QUITE NICELY!
WHRRRRR EEEEEEEE- EEEEEE-E-E-E! GHRRRZZRRWW!
WORKING WITH RAPID EFFICIENCY, I RAKED UP THE INFINITESIMAL REMAINS OF BERENICE...
...AND BAGGED HER TO BE CARTED OFF WITH THE REST OF THE MORNING'S TRASH!

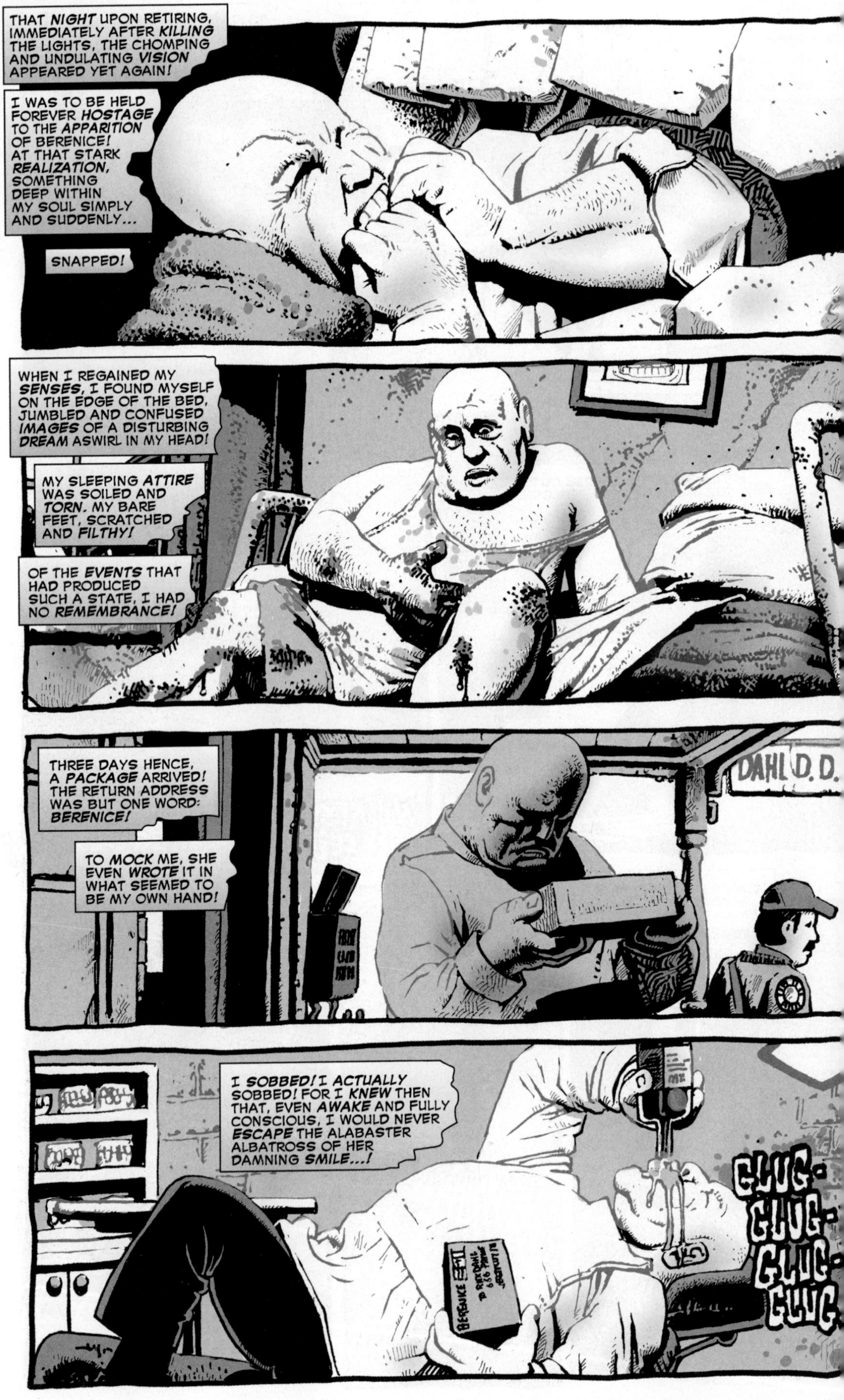
THAT NIGHT UPON RETIRING, IMMEDIATELY AFTER KILLING THE LIGHTS, THE CHOMPING AND UNDULATING VISION APPEARED YET AGAIN!
I WAS TO BE HELD FOREVER HOSTAGE TO THE APPARITION OF BERENICE! AT THAT STARK REALIZATION, SOMETHING DEEP WITHIN MY SOUL SIMPLY AND SUDDENLY...
SNAPPED!
WHEN I REGAINED MY SENSES, I FOUND MYSELF ON THE EDGE OF THE BED, JUMBLED AND CONFUSED IMAGES OF A DISTURBING DREAM ASWIRL IN MY HEAD!
MY SLEEPING ATTIRE WAS SOILED AND TORN. MY BARE FEET, SCRATCHED AND FILTHY!
OF THE EVENTS THAT HAD PRODUCED SUCH A STATE, I HAD NO REMEMBRANCE!
THREE DAYS HENCE, A PACKAGE ARRIVED! THE RETURN ADDRESS WAS BUT ONE WORD: BERENICE!
TO MOCK ME, SHE EVEN WROTE IT IN WHAT SEEMED TO BE MY OWN HAND!
DAHL D.D.
I SOBBED! I ACTUALLY SOBBED! FOR I KNEW THEN THAT, EVEN AWAKE AND FULLY CONSCIOUS, I WOULD NEVER ESCAPE THE ALABASTER ALBATROSS OF HER DAMNING SMILE...!
BERENICE
GLUG-GLUG-GLUG-GLUG

I TOOK TO ALCOHOL!

I DRANK!

I DRANK A LOT!

EXCESSIVELY BEYOND EXCESS!

I LOST MY *VOCATION*, THE *HOME* WHICH HOUSED MY *OFFICE*, AND WHAT LITTLE WAS LEFT OF MY *SANITY!*

SOMEWHERE FAR-OFF, OH, HOW MY ABJECT MISERY MUST HAVE MADE MY COUSIN SMILE!

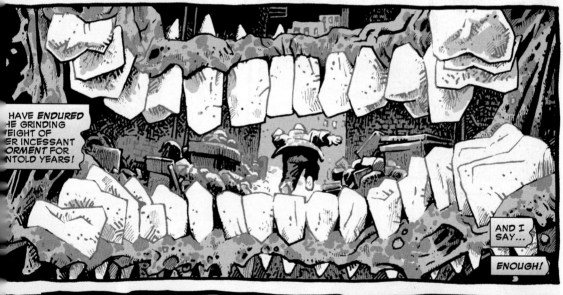

I HAVE *ENDURED* THE GRINDING WEIGHT OF HER *INCESSANT* TORMENT FOR UNTOLD YEARS!

AND I SAY...

ENOUGH!

I CONFESS!!

I KILLED BERENICE--!!

JCPD

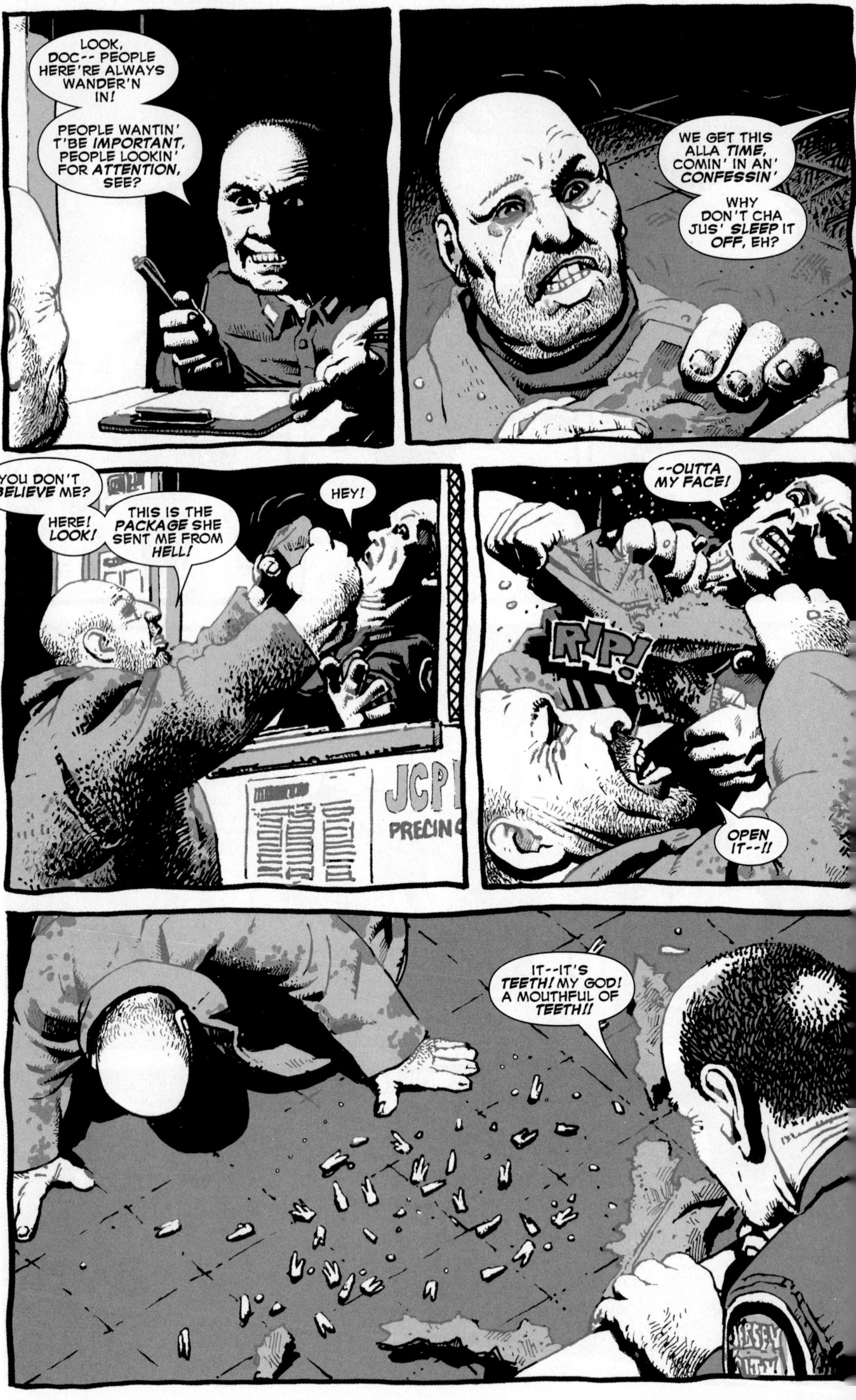
LOOK, DOC-- PEOPLE HERE'RE ALWAYS WANDER'N IN!
PEOPLE WANTIN' T'BE IMPORTANT, PEOPLE LOOKIN' FOR ATTENTION, SEE?
WE GET THIS ALLA TIME, COMIN' IN AN' CONFESSIN'
WHY DON'T CHA JUS' SLEEP IT OFF, EH?
YOU DON'T BELIEVE ME?
HERE! LOOK!
THIS IS THE PACKAGE SHE SENT ME FROM HELL!
HEY!
JCP
PRECIN
--OUTTA MY FACE!
RIP!
OPEN IT--!!
IT--IT'S TEETH! MY GOD! A MOUTHFUL OF TEETH!!

# Berenice

*Dicebant mihi sodales, si sepulchrum amicæ visitarem, curas meas aliquantulum fore levatas.*
—EBN ZAIAT

MISERY IS MANIFOLD. The wretchedness of earth is multiform. Overreaching the wide horizon as the rainbow, its hues are as various as the hues of that arch—as distinct too, yet as intimately blended. Overreaching the wide horizon as the rainbow! How is it that from beauty I have derived a type of unloveliness?—from the covenant of peace a simile of sorrow? But, as in ethics, evil is a consequence of good, so, in fact, out of joy is sorrow born. Either the memory of past bliss is the anguish of to-day, or the agonies which *are* have their origin in the ecstasies which *might have been*.

My baptismal name is Egæus; that of my family I will not mention. Yet there are no towers in the land more time-honored than my gloomy, gray, hereditary halls. Our line has been called a race of visionaries; and in many striking particulars—in the character of the family mansion—in the frescos of the chief saloon—in the tapestries of the dormitories—in the chiselling of some buttresses in the armory—but more especially in the gallery of antique paintings—in the fashion of the library chamber—and, lastly, in the very peculiar nature of the library's contents—there is more than sufficient evidence to warrant the belief.

The recollections of my earliest years are connected with that chamber, and with its volumes—of which latter I will say no more. Here died my mother. Herein was I born. But it is mere idleness to say that I had not lived before—that the soul has no previous existence. You deny it?—let us not argue the matter. Convinced myself, I seek not to convince. There is, however, a remembrance of aërial forms—of spiritual and meaning eyes—of sounds, musical yet sad; a remembrance which will not be excluded; a memory like a shadow—vague, variable, indefinite, unsteady; and like a shadow, too, in the impossibility of my getting rid of it while the sunlight of my reason shall exist.

In that chamber was I born. Thus awaking from the long night of what seemed, but was not, nonentity, at once into the very regions of fairy land—into a palace of imagination—into the wild dominions of monastic thought and erudition—it is not singular that I gazed around me with a startled and ardent eye—that I loitered away my boyhood in books, and dissipated my youth in reverie; but it *is* singular, that as years rolled away, and the noon of manhood found me still in the mansion of my fathers—it is wonderful what a stagnation there fell upon the springs of my life—wonderful how total an inversion took place in the character of my commonest thought. The realities of the world affected me as visions, and as visions only, while the wild ideas of the land of dreams became, in turn, not the material of my every-day existence, but in very deed that existence utterly and solely in itself.

\*     \*     \*

BERENICE AND I were cousins, and we grew up together in my paternal halls. Yet differently we grew—I, ill of health, and buried in gloom—she, agile, graceful, and overflowing with energy; hers the ramble on the hillside—mine, the studies of the cloister; I, living within my own heart, and addicted, body and soul, to the most intense and painful meditation—she, roaming carelessly through life, with no thought of the shadows in her path, or the silent flight of the raven-winged hours. Berenice!—I call upon her name—Berenice!—and from the gray ruins of memory a thousand tumultuous recollections are startled at the sound! Ah, vividly is her image before me now, as in the early days of her light-heartedness and joy! Oh, gorgeous yet fantastic beauty! Oh, sylph amid the shrubberies of Arnheim!—Oh, Naiad among its fountains! And then—then all is mystery and terror, and a tale which should not be told. Disease—a fatal disease, fell like the simoon upon her frame; and even, while I gazed upon her, the spirit of change swept over her, pervading her mind, her habits, and her character, and, in a manner the most subtle and terrible, disturbing even the identity of her person! Alas! the destroyer came and went!—and the victim—where is she? I knew her not—or knew her no longer as Berenice!

Among the numerous train of maladies superinduced by that fatal and primary one which effected a revolution of so horrible a kind in the moral and physical being of my cousin, may be mentioned as the most distressing and obstinate in its nature, a species of epilepsy not unfrequently terminating in *trance* itself—trance very nearly resembling positive dissolution, and from which her manner of recovery was, in most instances, startlingly abrupt. In the meantime, my own disease—for I have been told that I should call it by no other appellation—my own disease, then, grew rapidly upon me, and assumed finally a monomaniac character of a novel and extraordinary form—hourly and momently gaining vigor—and at length obtaining over me the most incomprehensible ascendancy. This monomania, if I must so term it, consisted in a morbid irritability of those properties of the mind in metaphysical science termed the *attentive*. It is more than probable that I am not understood; but I fear, indeed, that it is in no manner possible to convey to the mind of the merely general reader, an adequate idea of that nervous *intensity of interest* with which, in my case, the powers of meditation (not to speak technically) busied and buried themselves, in the contemplation of even the most ordinary objects of the universe.

To muse for long unwearied hours, with my attention riveted to some frivolous device on the margin, or in the topography of a book; to become absorbed, for the better part of a summer's day, in a quaint shadow falling aslant upon the tapestry or upon the floor; to lose myself, for an entire night, in watching the steady flame of a lamp, or the embers of a fire; to dream away whole days over the perfume of a flower; to repeat, monotonously, some common word, until the sound, by dint of frequent repetition, ceased to convey any idea whatever to the mind; to lose all sense of motion or physical existence, by means of absolute bodily quiescence long and obstinately persevered in: such were a few of the most common and least pernicious vagaries induced by a condition of the mental faculties, not, indeed, altogether unparalleled, but certainly bidding defiance to any thing like analysis or explanation.

Yet let me not be misapprehended. The undue, earnest, and morbid attention thus excited by objects in their own nature frivolous, must not be confounded in character with that ruminating propensity common to all mankind, and more especially indulged in by persons of ardent imagination. It was not even, as might be at first supposed, an extreme condition, or exaggeration of such propensity, but primarily and essentially distinct and different. In the one instance, the dreamer, or enthusiast, being interested by an object usually *not* frivolous, imperceptibly loses sight of this object in a wilderness of deductions and suggestions issuing therefrom, until, at the conclusion of a day-dream *often replete with luxury*, he finds the *incitamentum*, or first cause of his musings, entirely vanished and forgotten. In my case, the primary object was *invariably frivolous*, although assuming, through the medium of my distempered vision, a refracted and unreal importance. Few deductions, if any, were made; and those few pertinaciously returning in upon the original object as a centre. The meditations were *never* pleasurable; and at the termination of the reverie, the first cause, so far from being out of sight, had attained that supernaturally exaggerated interest which was the prevailing feature of the disease. In a word, the powers of mind more particularly exercised were, with me, as I have said before, the *attentive*, and are, with the day-dreamer, the *speculative*.

My books, at this epoch, if they did not actually serve to irritate the disorder, partook, it will be perceived, largely, in their imaginative and inconsequential nature, of the characteristic qualities of the disorder itself. I well remember, among others, the treatise of the noble Italian, Coelius Secundus Curio, "De Amplitudine Beati Regni Dei"; St. Austin's great work, "The City of God"; and Tertullian's "De Carne Christi," in which the paradoxical sentence, "Mortuus est Dei filius; credibile est quia ineptum est; et sepultus resurrexit; certum est quia impossible est," occupied my undivided time, for many weeks of laborious and fruitless investigation.

Thus it will appear that, shaken from its balance only by trivial things, my reason bore resemblance to that ocean-crag spoken of by Ptolemy Hephestion, which steadily resisting the attacks of human violence, and the fiercer fury of the waters and the winds, trembled only to the touch of the flower called Asphodel. And although, to a careless thinker, it might appear a matter beyond doubt, that the alteration produced by her unhappy malady, in the *moral* condition of Berenice, would afford me many objects for the exercise of that intense and abnormal meditation whose nature I have been at some trouble in explaining, yet such was not in any degree the case. In the lucid intervals of my infirmity, her calamity, indeed, gave me pain, and, taking deeply to heart that total wreck of her fair and gentle life, I did not fail to ponder, frequently and bitterly, upon the wonder-working means by which so strange a revolution had been so suddenly brought to pass. But these reflections partook not of the idiosyncrasy of my disease, and were such as would have occurred, under similar circumstances, to the ordinary mass of mankind. True to its own character, my disorder revelled in the less important but more startling changes wrought in the *physical* frame of Berenice—in the singular and most appalling distortion of her personal identity.

During the brightest days of her unparalleled beauty, most surely I had never loved her. In the strange anomaly of my existence, feelings with me, *had never been* of the heart, and my passions *always were* of the mind. Through the gray of the early morning—among the trellised shadows of the forest at noonday—and in the silence of my library at night—she had flitted by my eyes, and I had seen her—not as the living and breathing Berenice, but as the Berenice of a dream; not as a being of the earth, earthy, but as the abstraction of such a being; not as a thing to admire, but to analyze; not as an object of love, but as the theme of the most abstruse although desultory speculation. And *now*—now I shuddered in her presence, and grew pale at her approach; yet, bitterly lamenting her fallen and desolate condition, I called to mind that she had loved me long, and, in an evil moment, I spoke to her of marriage.

And at length the period of our nuptials was approaching, when, upon an afternoon in the winter of the year—one of those unseasonably warm, calm, and misty days which are the nurse of the beautiful Halcyon[1],—I sat, (and sat, as I thought, alone,) in the inner apartment of the library. But, uplifting my eyes, I saw that Berenice stood before me.

Was it my own excited imagination—or the misty influence of the atmosphere—or the uncertain twilight of the chamber—or the gray draperies which fell around her figure—that caused in it so vacillating and indistinct an outline? I could not tell. She spoke no word; and I—not for worlds could I have uttered a syllable. An icy chill ran through my frame; a sense of insufferable anxiety oppressed me; a consuming curiosity pervaded my soul; and, sinking back upon the chair, I remained for some time breathless and motionless, with my eyes riveted upon her person. Alas! its emaciation was excessive, and not one vestige of the former being lurked in any single line of the contour. My burning glances at length fell upon the face.

---

For as love, during the winter season, gives twice seven days of warmth, men have called this clement and temperate time the nurse of the beautiful Halcyon. —Simonides.

The forehead was high, and very pale, and singularly placid; and the once jetty hair fell partially over it, and overshadowed the hollow temples with innumerable ringlets, now of a vivid yellow, and jarring discordantly, in their fantastic character, with the reigning melancholy of the countenance. The eyes were lifeless, and lustreless, and seemingly pupilless, and I shrank involuntarily from their glassy stare to the contemplation of the thin and shrunken lips. They parted; and in a smile of peculiar meaning, *the teeth* of the changed Berenice disclosed themselves slowly to my view. Would to God that I had never beheld them, or that, having done so, I had died!

*      *      *

THE SHUTTING OF A DOOR disturbed me, and looking up, I found that my cousin had departed from the chamber. But from the disordered chamber of my brain, had not, alas! departed, and would not be driven away, the white and ghastly *spectrum* of the teeth. Not a speck on their surface—not a shade on their enamel—not an indenture in their edges—but what that brief period of her smile had sufficed to brand in upon my memory. I saw them *now* even more unequivocally than I beheld them *then*. The teeth!—the teeth!—they were here, and there, and everywhere, and visibly and palpably before me; long, narrow, and excessively white, with the pale lips writhing about them, as in the very moment of their first terrible development. Then came the full fury of my *monomania*, and I struggled in vain against its strange and irresistible influence. In the multiplied objects of the external world I had no thoughts but for the teeth. For these I longed with a frenzied desire. All other matters and all different interests became absorbed in their single contemplation. They—they alone were present to the mental eye, and they, in their sole individuality, became the essence of my mental life. I held them in every light. I turned them in every attitude. I surveyed their characteristics. I dwelt upon their peculiarities. I pondered upon their conformation. I mused upon the alteration in their nature. I shuddered as I assigned to them, in imagination, a sensitive and sentient power, and, even when unassisted by the lips, a capability of moral expression. Of Mademoiselle Salle it has been well said: *"Que tous ses pas étaient des sentiments,"* and of Berenice I more seriously believed *que tous ses dents étaient des idées. Des idées!*—ah, *therefore* was the idiotic thought that destroyed me! Des idées!—ah, therefore it was that I coveted them so madly! I felt that their possession could alone ever restore me to peace, in giving me back to reason.

And the evening closed in upon me thus—and then the darkness came, and tarried, and went—and the day again dawned—and the mists of a second night were now gathering around—and still I sat motionless in that solitary room—and still I sat buried in meditation—and still the *phantasma* of the teeth maintained its terrible ascendancy, as, with the most vivid hideous distinctness, it floated about amid the changing lights and shadows of the chamber. At length there broke in upon my dreams a cry as of horror and dismay; and thereunto, after a pause, succeeded the sound of troubled voices, intermingled with many low moanings of sorrow or of pain. I arose from my seat, and throwing open one of the doors of the library, saw standing out in the antechamber a servant maiden, all in tears, who told me that Berenice was—no more! She had been seized with epilepsy in the early morning, and now, at the closing in of the night, the grave was ready for its tenant, and all the preparations for the burial were completed.

*      *      *

I FOUND MYSELF SITTING in the library, and again sitting there alone. It seemed to me that I had newly awakened from a confused and exciting dream. I knew that it was now midnight, and I was well aware, that since the setting of the sun, Berenice had been interred. But of that dreary period which intervened I had no positive, at least no definite, comprehension. Yet its memory was replete with horror—horror more horrible from being vague, and terror more terrible from ambiguity. It was a fearful page in the record my existence, written all over with dim, and hideous, and unintelligible recollections. I strived to decipher them, but in vain; while ever and anon, like the spirit of a departed sound, the shrill and piercing shriek of a female voice seemed to be ringing in my ears. I had done a deed—what was it? I asked myself the question aloud, and the whispering echoes of the chamber answered me—*"What was it?"*

On the table beside me burned a lamp, and near it lay a little box. It was of no remarkable character, and I had seen it frequently before, for it was the property of the family physician; but how came it *there*, upon my table, and why did I shudder in regarding it? These things were in no manner to be accounted for, and my eyes at length dropped to the open pages of a book, and to a sentence underscored therein. The words were the singular but simple ones of the poet Ebn Zaiat:—*"Dicebant mihi sodales si sepulchrum amicæ visitarem, curas meas aliquantulum fore levatas."* Why then, as I perused them, did the hairs of my head erect themselves on end, and the blood of my body become congealed within my veins?

There came a light tap at the library door—and, pale as the tenant of a tomb, a menial entered upon tiptoe. His looks were wild with terror, and he spoke to me in a voice tremulous, husky, and very low. What said he?—some broken sentences I heard. He told of a wild cry disturbing the silence of the night—of the gathering together of the household—of a search in the direction of the sound; and then his tones grew thrillingly distinct as he whispered me of a violated grave—of a disfigured body enshrouded, yet still breathing—still palpitating—*still alive!*

He pointed to garments; they were muddy and clotted with gore. I spoke not, and he took me gently by the hand: it was indented with the impress of human nails. He directed my attention to some object against the wall. I looked at it for some minutes: it was a spade. With a shriek I bounded to the table, and grasped the box that lay upon it. But I could not force it open; and, in my tremor, it slipped from my hands, and fell heavily, and burst into pieces; and from it, with a rattling sound, there rolled out some instruments of dental surgery, intermingled with thirty-two small, white, and ivory-looking substances that were scattered to and fro about the floor.

— Edgar Allan Poe

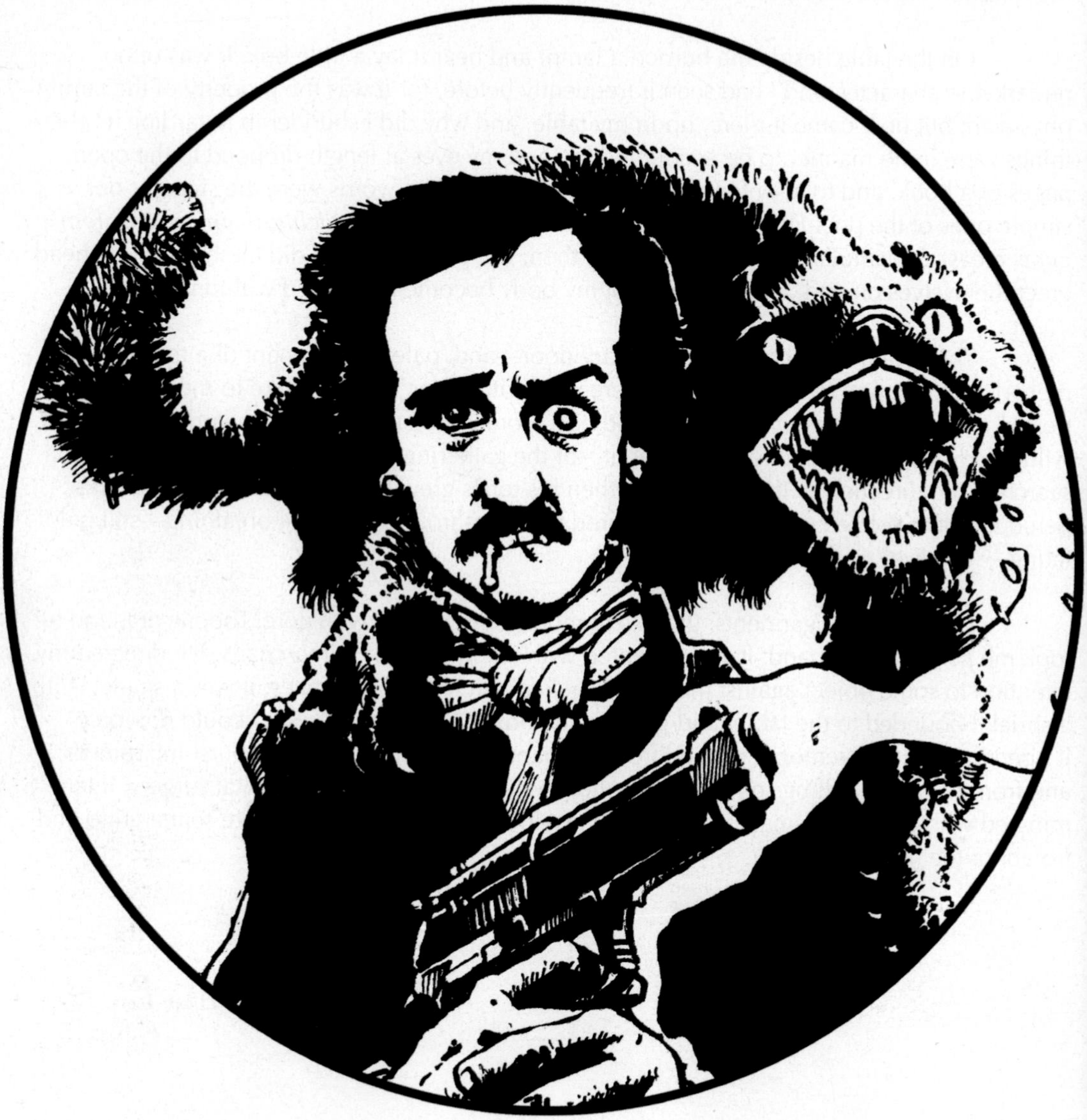

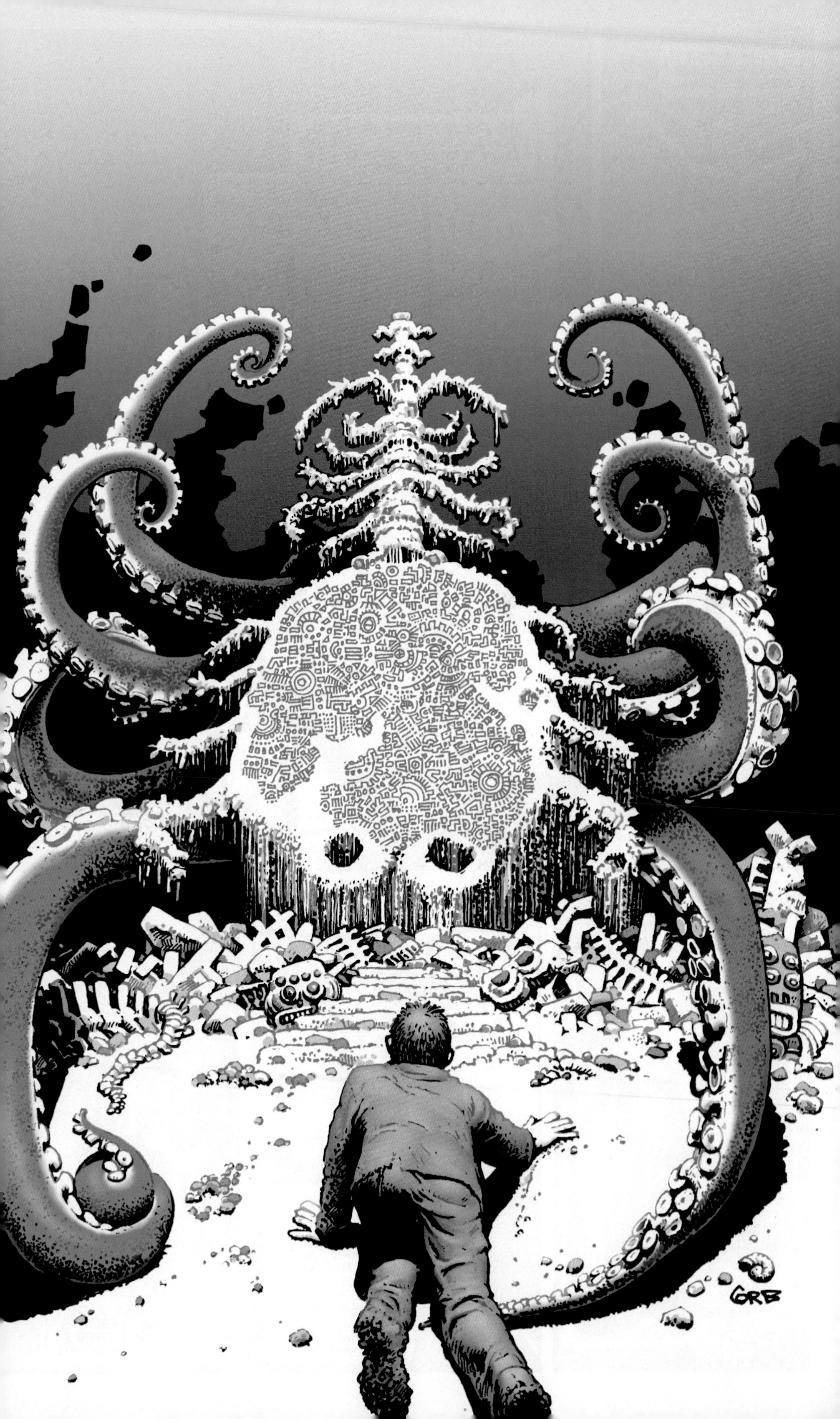

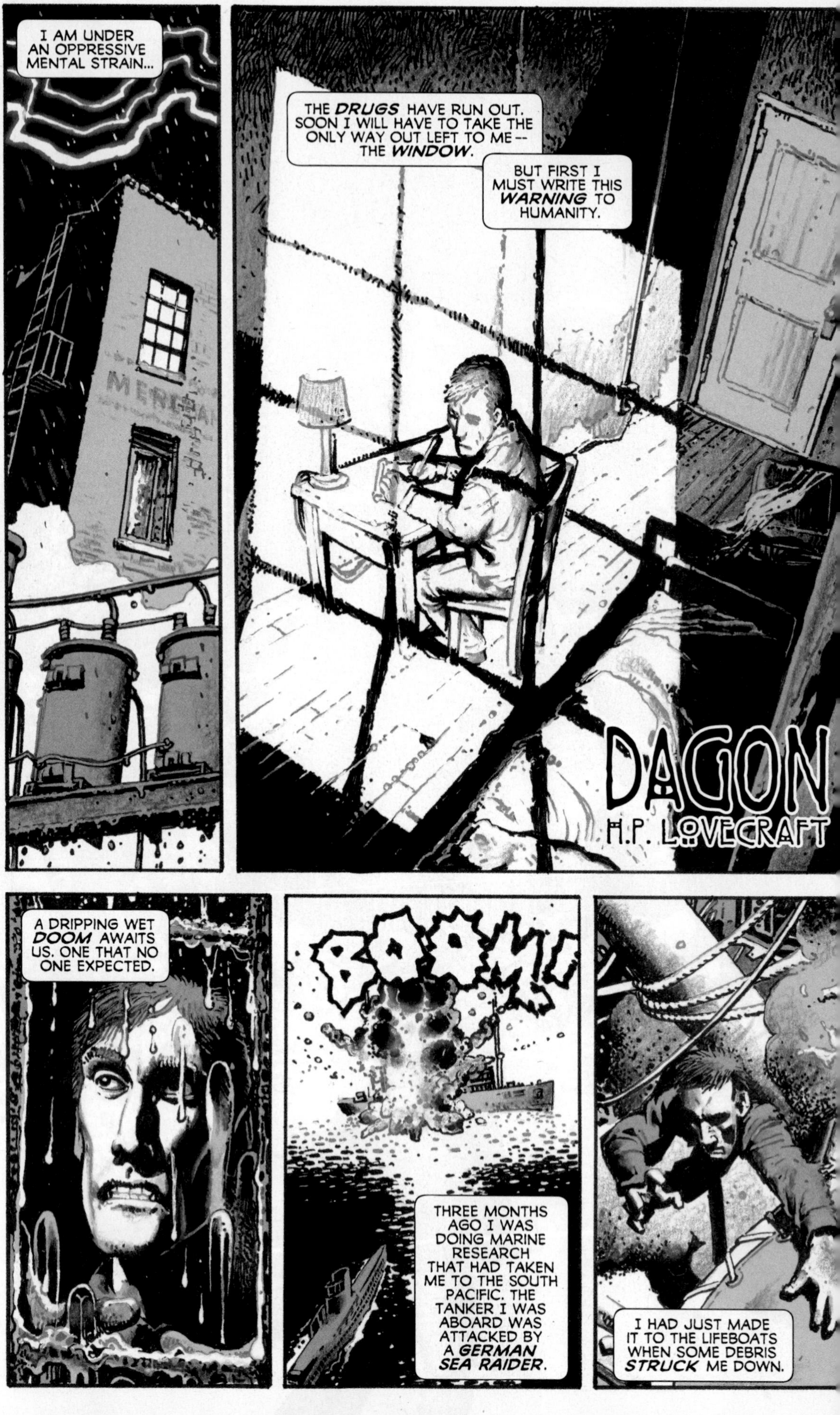

I AM UNDER AN OPPRESSIVE MENTAL STRAIN...
THE DRUGS HAVE RUN OUT. SOON I WILL HAVE TO TAKE THE ONLY WAY OUT LEFT TO ME -- THE WINDOW.
BUT FIRST I MUST WRITE THIS WARNING TO HUMANITY.
DAGON
H.P. LOVECRAFT
A DRIPPING WET DOOM AWAITS US. ONE THAT NO ONE EXPECTED.
BOOM!!
THREE MONTHS AGO I WAS DOING MARINE RESEARCH THAT HAD TAKEN ME TO THE SOUTH PACIFIC. THE TANKER I WAS ABOARD WAS ATTACKED BY A GERMAN SEA RAIDER.
I HAD JUST MADE IT TO THE LIFEBOATS WHEN SOME DEBRIS STRUCK ME DOWN.

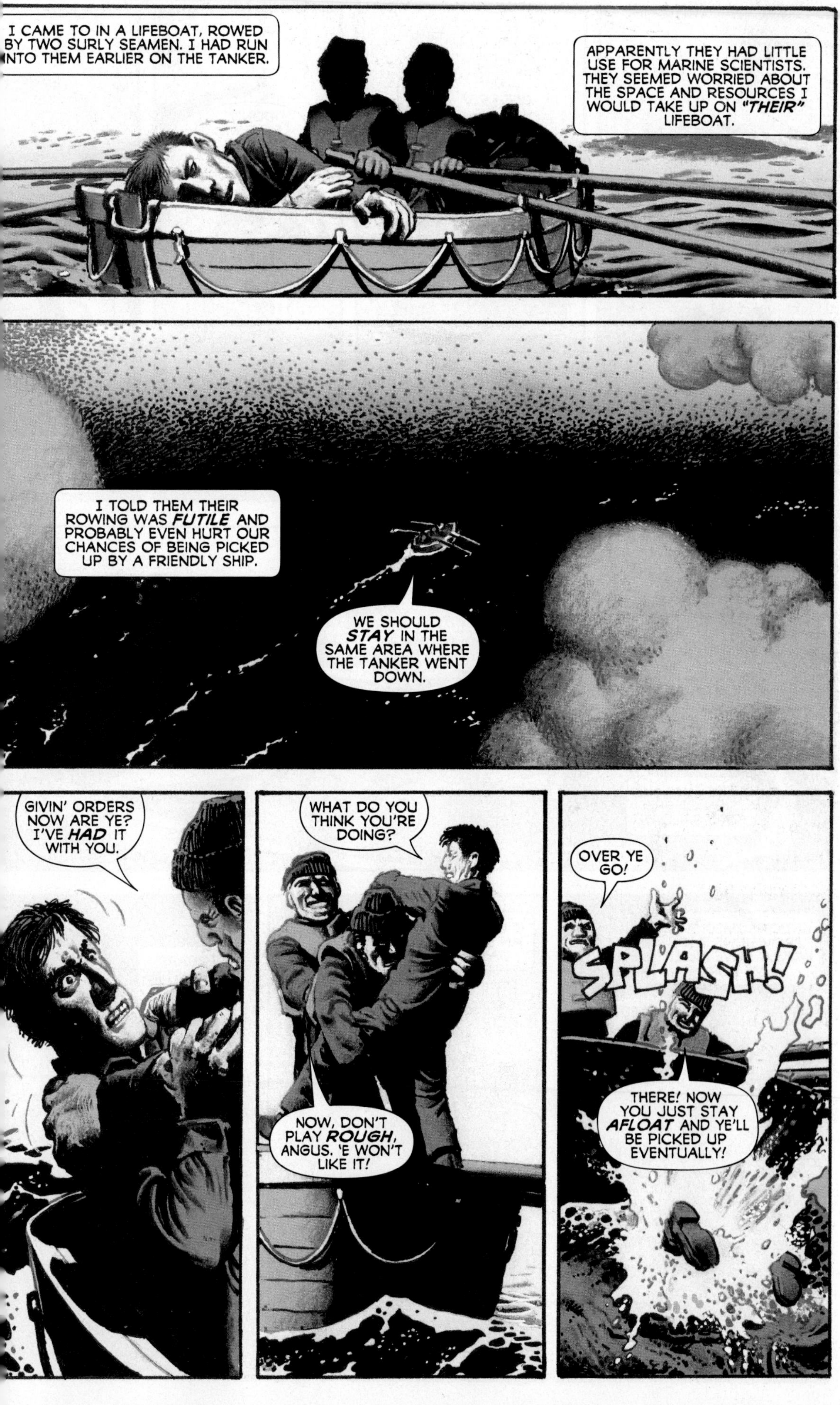
I CAME TO IN A LIFEBOAT, ROWED BY TWO SURLY SEAMEN. I HAD RUN INTO THEM EARLIER ON THE TANKER.
APPARENTLY THEY HAD LITTLE USE FOR MARINE SCIENTISTS. THEY SEEMED WORRIED ABOUT THE SPACE AND RESOURCES I WOULD TAKE UP ON "THEIR" LIFEBOAT.
I TOLD THEM THEIR ROWING WAS FUTILE AND PROBABLY EVEN HURT OUR CHANCES OF BEING PICKED UP BY A FRIENDLY SHIP.
WE SHOULD STAY IN THE SAME AREA WHERE THE TANKER WENT DOWN.
GIVIN' ORDERS NOW ARE YE? I'VE HAD IT WITH YOU.
WHAT DO YOU THINK YOU'RE DOING?
NOW, DON'T PLAY ROUGH, ANGUS. 'E WON'T LIKE IT!
OVER YE GO!
SPLASH!
THERE! NOW YOU JUST STAY AFLOAT AND YE'LL BE PICKED UP EVENTUALLY!

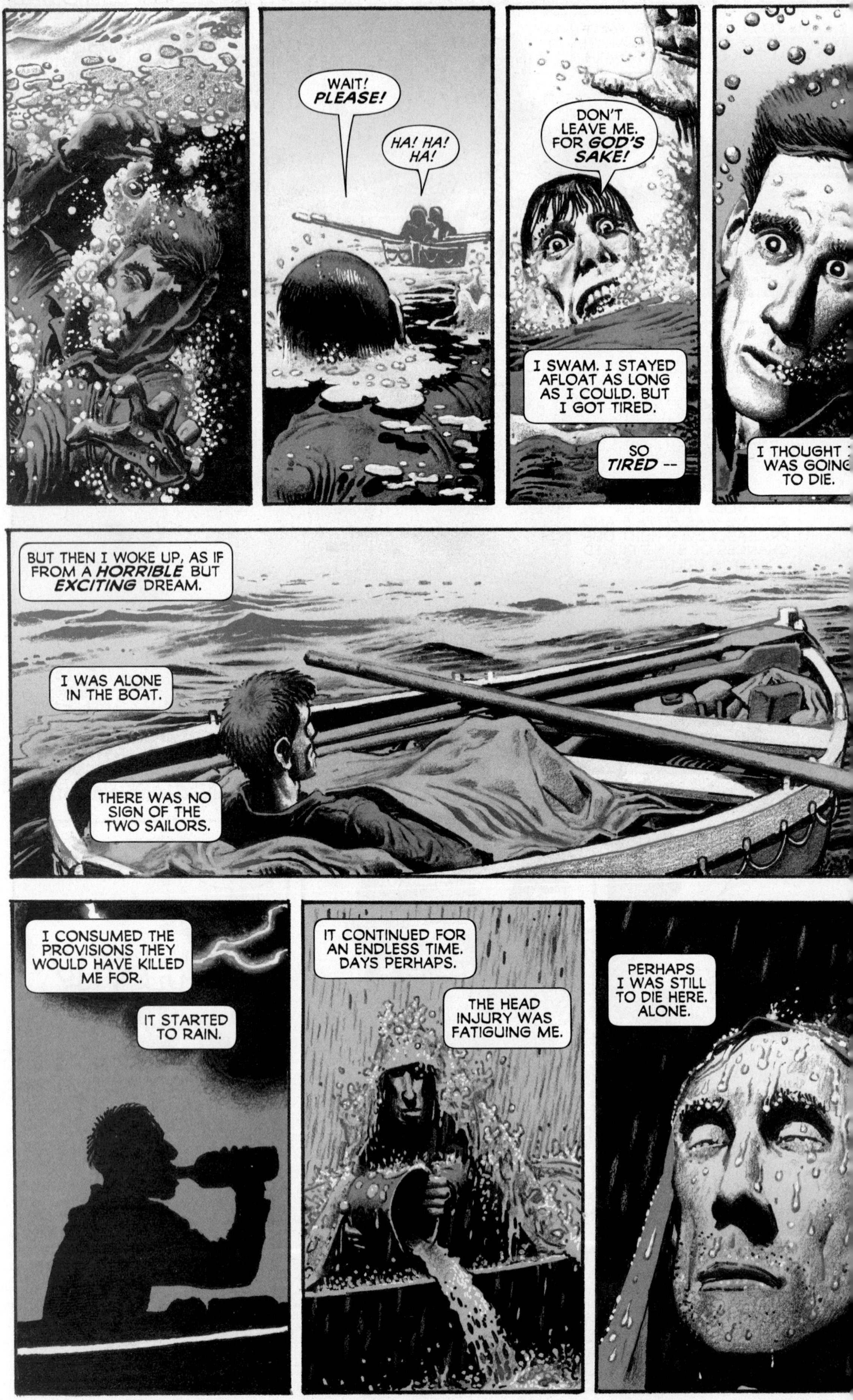

WAIT! PLEASE!
HA! HA! HA!
DON'T LEAVE ME. FOR GOD'S SAKE!
I SWAM. I STAYED AFLOAT AS LONG AS I COULD. BUT I GOT TIRED.
SO TIRED --
I THOUGHT I WAS GOING TO DIE.
BUT THEN I WOKE UP, AS IF FROM A HORRIBLE BUT EXCITING DREAM.
I WAS ALONE IN THE BOAT.
THERE WAS NO SIGN OF THE TWO SAILORS.
I CONSUMED THE PROVISIONS THEY WOULD HAVE KILLED ME FOR.
IT STARTED TO RAIN.
IT CONTINUED FOR AN ENDLESS TIME. DAYS PERHAPS.
THE HEAD INJURY WAS FATIGUING ME.
PERHAPS I WAS STILL TO DIE HERE. ALONE.

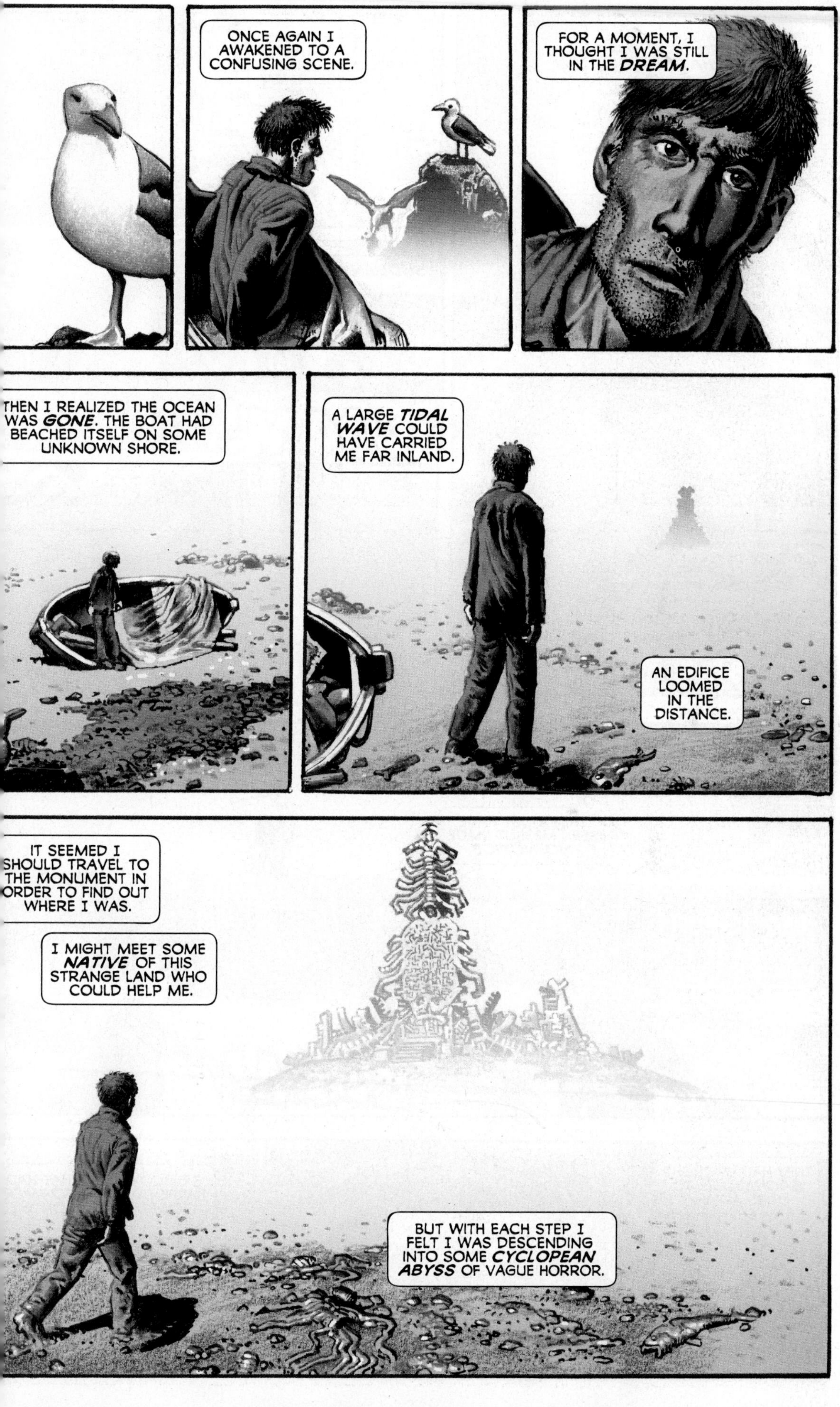
ONCE AGAIN I AWAKENED TO A CONFUSING SCENE.
FOR A MOMENT, I THOUGHT I WAS STILL IN THE DREAM.
THEN I REALIZED THE OCEAN WAS GONE. THE BOAT HAD BEACHED ITSELF ON SOME UNKNOWN SHORE.
A LARGE TIDAL WAVE COULD HAVE CARRIED ME FAR INLAND.
AN EDIFICE LOOMED IN THE DISTANCE.
IT SEEMED I SHOULD TRAVEL TO THE MONUMENT IN ORDER TO FIND OUT WHERE I WAS.
I MIGHT MEET SOME NATIVE OF THIS STRANGE LAND WHO COULD HELP ME.
BUT WITH EACH STEP I FELT I WAS DESCENDING INTO SOME CYCLOPEAN ABYSS OF VAGUE HORROR.

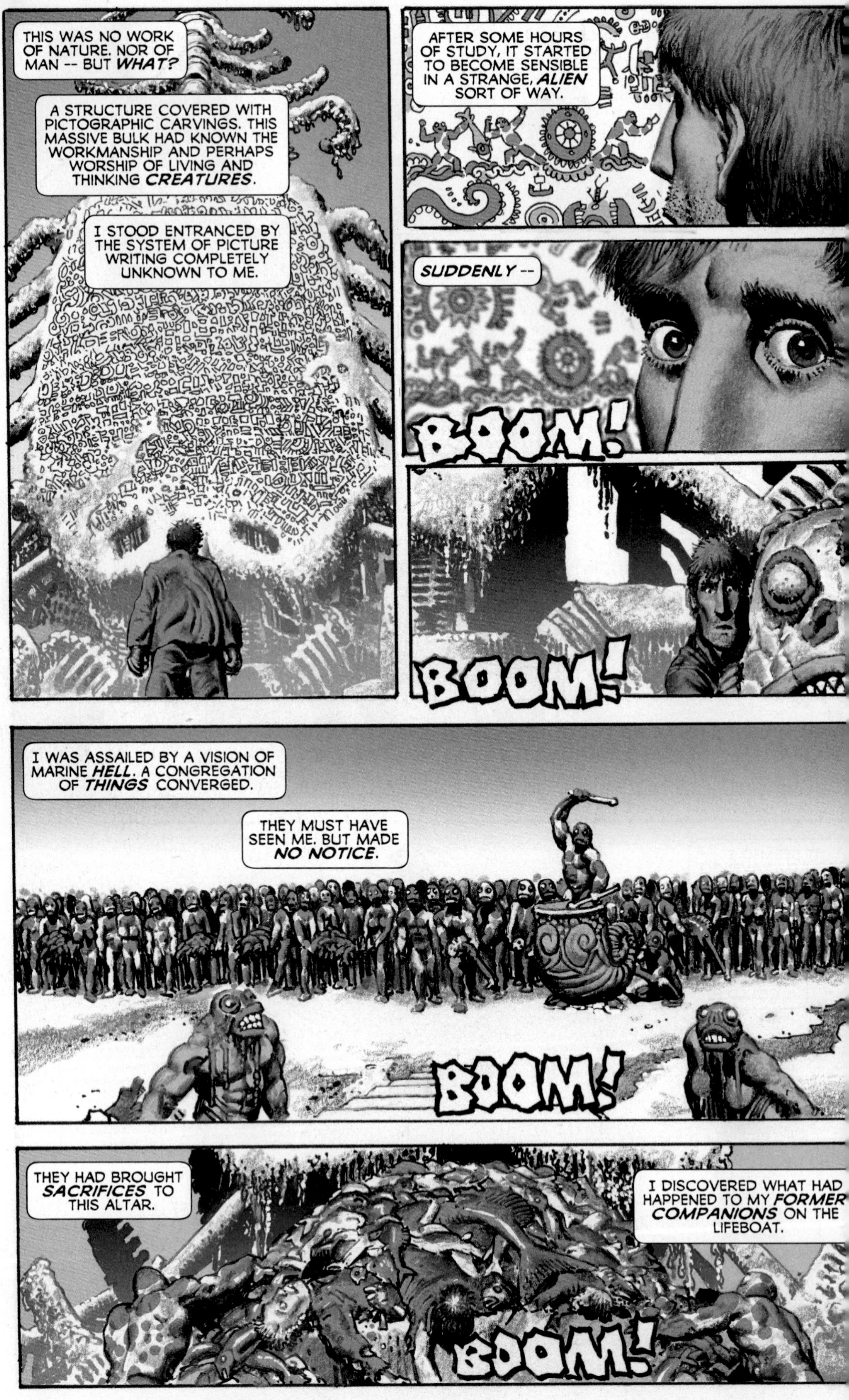
THIS WAS NO WORK OF NATURE. NOR OF MAN -- BUT *WHAT?*
A STRUCTURE COVERED WITH PICTOGRAPHIC CARVINGS. THIS MASSIVE BULK HAD KNOWN THE WORKMANSHIP AND PERHAPS WORSHIP OF LIVING AND THINKING *CREATURES*.
I STOOD ENTRANCED BY THE SYSTEM OF PICTURE WRITING COMPLETELY UNKNOWN TO ME.
AFTER SOME HOURS OF STUDY, IT STARTED TO BECOME SENSIBLE IN A STRANGE, *ALIEN* SORT OF WAY.
*SUDDENLY* --
BOOM!
BOOM!
I WAS ASSAILED BY A VISION OF MARINE *HELL*. A CONGREGATION OF *THINGS* CONVERGED.
THEY MUST HAVE SEEN ME. BUT MADE *NO NOTICE*.
BOOM!
THEY HAD BROUGHT *SACRIFICES* TO THIS ALTAR.
I DISCOVERED WHAT HAD HAPPENED TO MY *FORMER COMPANIONS* ON THE LIFEBOAT.
BOOM!

THEY WERE *DAMNABLY* SEMI-HUMAN. BUT WITH FISH-LIKE AND AMPHIBIAN-LIKE DEGRADATIONS.

AND THEY *DANCED!* FLIPPING, FLAPPING, FLOPPING, SLITHERING SLIMY, UNDULATIONS.

IT WAS *DISGUSTING* HORROR BEYOND IMAGINATION. I THINK I WENT *INSANE* THEN.

JUST WHEN I WAS ABOUT TO *RETCH*, ALL MOVEMENT STOPPED.

I FOLLOWED THEIR GAZE.

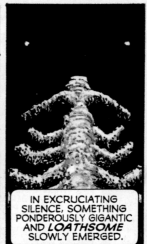

IN EXCRUCIATING SILENCE, SOMETHING PONDEROUSLY GIGANTIC AND *LOATHSOME* SLOWLY EMERGED.

TORRENTIAL RAINS COMMENCED AS THE SEA GOD TOOK ITS SACRIFICES AND *ATE* THEM.

AAAGGGGGGG!!

I WAS BEYOND CARING ABOUT DISCOVERY. IN A PANIC, I RAN!

I GIBBERED *MINDLESSLY*. SOMETIMES CRYING, SOMETIMES LAUGHING INSANELY.

NOTHING IS CLEAR FROM THEN. I MUST HAVE REACHED THE BOAT.

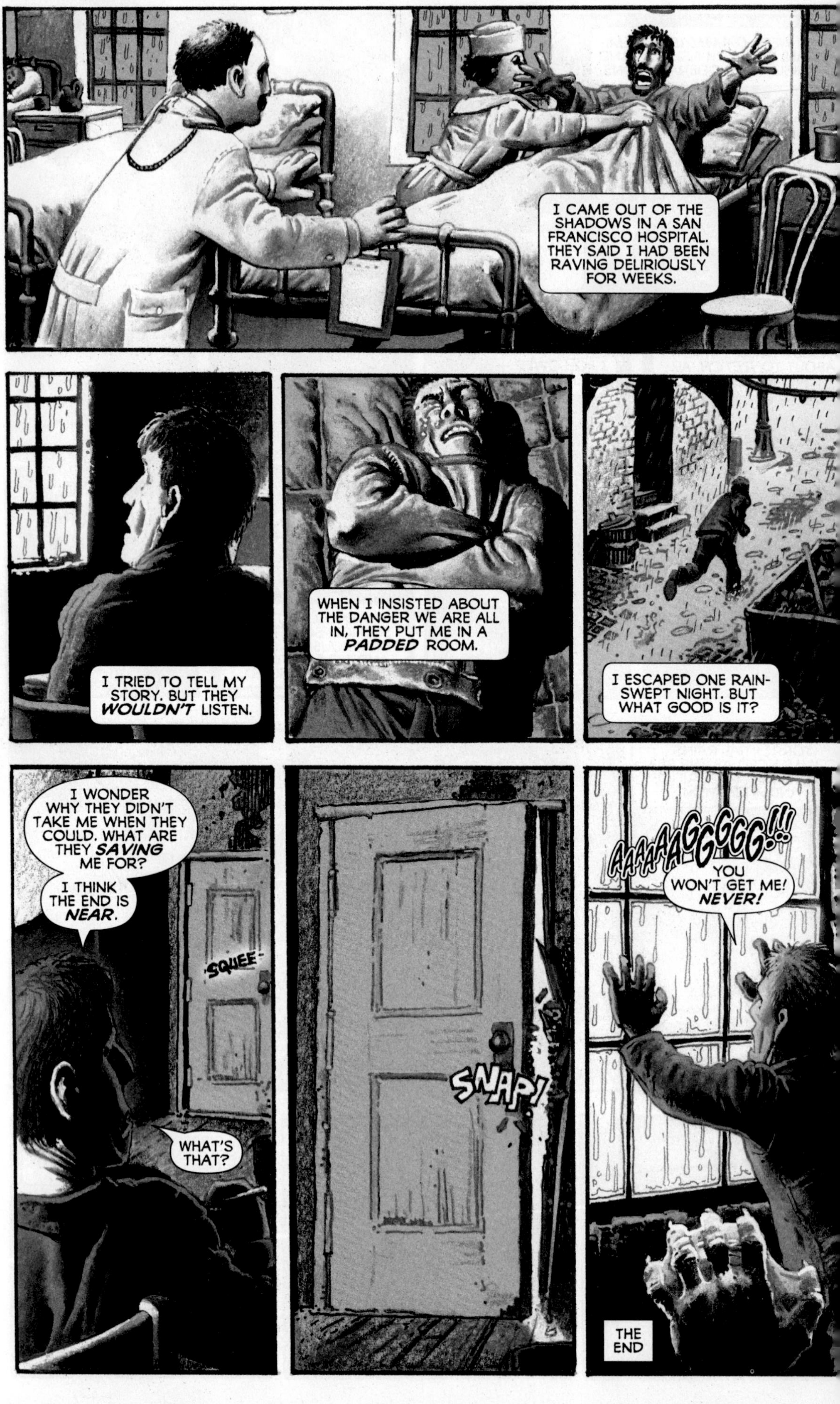
I CAME OUT OF THE SHADOWS IN A SAN FRANCISCO HOSPITAL. THEY SAID I HAD BEEN RAVING DELIRIOUSLY FOR WEEKS.
I TRIED TO TELL MY STORY. BUT THEY WOULDN'T LISTEN.
WHEN I INSISTED ABOUT THE DANGER WE ARE ALL IN, THEY PUT ME IN A PADDED ROOM.
I ESCAPED ONE RAIN-SWEPT NIGHT. BUT WHAT GOOD IS IT?
I WONDER WHY THEY DIDN'T TAKE ME WHEN THEY COULD. WHAT ARE THEY SAVING ME FOR?
I THINK THE END IS NEAR.
SQUEE
WHAT'S THAT?
SNAP!
AAAAAAGGGGG!!!
YOU WON'T GET ME! NEVER!
THE END

# Dagon

I am writing this under an appreciable mental strain, since by tonight I shall be no more. Penniless, and at the end of my supply of the drug which alone makes life endurable, I can bear the torture no longer; and shall cast myself from this garret window into the squalid street below. Do not think from my slavery to morphine that I am a weakling or a degenerate. When you have read these hastily scrawled pages you may guess, though never fully realise, why it is that I must have forgetfulness or death.

It was in one of the most open and least frequented parts of the broad Pacific that the packet of which I was supercargo fell a victim to the German sea-raider. The great war was then at its very beginning, and the ocean forces of the Hun had not completely sunk to their later degradation; so that our vessel was made a legitimate prize, whilst we of her crew were treated with all the fairness and consideration due us as naval prisoners. So liberal, indeed, was the discipline of our captors, that five days after we were taken I managed to escape alone in a small boat with water and provisions for a good length of time.

When I finally found myself adrift and free, I had but little idea of my surroundings. Never a competent navigator, I could only guess vaguely by the sun and stars that I was somewhat south of the equator. Of the longitude I knew nothing, and no island or coastline was in sight. The weather kept fair, and for uncounted days I drifted aimlessly beneath the scorching sun; waiting either for some passing ship, or to be cast on the shores of some habitable land. But neither ship nor land appeared, and I began to despair in my solitude upon the heaving vastness of unbroken blue.

The change happened whilst I slept. Its details I shall never know; for my slumber, though troubled and dream-infested, was continuous. When at last I awakened, it was to discover myself half sucked into a slimy expanse of hellish black mire which extended about me in monotonous undulations as far as I could see, and in which my boat lay grounded some distance away.

Though one might well imagine that my first sensation would be of wonder at so prodigious and unexpected a transformation of scenery, I was in reality more horrified than astonished; for there was in the air and in the rotting soil a sinister quality which chilled me to the very core. The region was putrid with the carcasses of decaying fish, and of other less describable things which I saw protruding from the nasty mud of the unending plain. Perhaps I should not hope to convey in mere words the unutterable *hideousness that can dwell in absolute silence and barren immensity. There was nothing within hearing, and nothing in sight save a vast reach of black slime; yet the very completeness of the stillness and the homogeneity of the landscape oppressed me with a nauseating fear.*

*The sun was blazing down from a sky which seemed to me almost black in its cloudless cruelty; as though reflecting the inky marsh beneath my feet. As I crawled into the stranded boat I realised that only one theory could explain my position. Through some unprecedented volcanic upheaval, a portion of the ocean floor must have been thrown to the surface, exposing regions which for innumerable millions of years had lain hidden under unfathomable watery depths. So great was the extent of the new land which had risen beneath me, that I could not detect the faintest noise of the surging ocean, strain my ears as I might. Nor were there any sea-fowl to prey upon the dead things.*

*For several hours I sat thinking or brooding in the boat, which lay upon its side and afforded a slight shade as the sun moved across the heavens. As the day progressed, the ground lost some of its stickiness, and seemed likely to dry sufficiently for travelling purposes in a short time. That night I slept but little, and the next day I made for myself a pack containing food and water, preparatory to an overland journey in search of the vanished sea and possible rescue.*

*On the third morning I found the soil dry enough to walk upon with ease. The odour of the fish was maddening; but I was too much concerned with graver things to mind so slight an evil, and set out boldly for an unknown goal. All day I forged steadily westward, guided by a far-away hummock which rose higher than any other elevation on the rolling desert. That night I encamped, and on the following day still travelled toward the hummock, though that object seemed scarcely nearer than when I had first espied it. By the fourth evening I attained the base of the mound, which turned out to be much higher than it had appeared from a distance; an intervening valley setting it out in sharper relief from the general surface. Too weary to ascend, I slept in the shadow of the hill.*

*I know not why my dreams were so wild that night; but ere the waning and fantastically gibbous moon had risen far above the eastern plain, I was awake in a cold perspiration, determined to sleep no more. Such visions as I had experienced were too much for me to endure again. And in the glow of the moon I saw how unwise I had been to travel by day. Without the glare of the parching sun, my journey would have cost me less energy; indeed, I now felt quite able to perform the ascent which had deterred me at sunset. Picking up my pack, I started for the crest of the eminence.*

I have said that the unbroken monotony of the rolling plain was a source of vague horror to me; but I think my horror was greater when I gained the summit of the mound and looked down the other side into an immeasurable pit or canyon, whose black recesses the moon had not yet soared high enough to illumine. I felt myself on the edge of the world, peering over the rim into a fathomless chaos of eternal night. Through my terror ran curious reminiscences of Paradise Lost, and Satan's hideous climb through the unfashioned realms of darkness.

As the moon climbed higher in the sky, I began to see that the slopes of the valley were not quite so perpendicular as I had imagined. Ledges and outcroppings of rock afforded fairly easy footholds for a descent, whilst after a drop of a few hundred feet, the declivity became very gradual. Urged on by an impulse which I cannot definitely analyse, I scrambled with difficulty down the rocks and stood on the gentler slope beneath, gazing into the Stygian deeps where no light had yet penetrated.

All at once my attention was captured by a vast and singular object on the opposite slope, which rose steeply about a hundred yards ahead of me; an object that gleamed whitely in the newly bestowed rays of the ascending moon. That it was merely a gigantic piece of stone, I soon assured myself; but I was conscious of a distinct impression that its contour and position were not altogether the work of Nature. A closer scrutiny filled me with sensations I cannot express; for despite its enormous magnitude, and its position in an abyss which had yawned at the bottom of the sea since the world was young, I perceived beyond a doubt that the strange object was a well-shaped monolith whose massive bulk had known the workmanship and perhaps the worship of living and thinking creatures.

Dazed and frightened, yet not without a certain thrill of the scientist's or archaeologist's delight, I examined my surroundings more closely. The moon, now near the zenith, shone weirdly and vividly above the towering steeps that hemmed in the chasm, and revealed the fact that a far-flung body of water flowed at the bottom, winding out of sight in both directions, and almost lapping my feet as I stood on the slope. Across the chasm, the wavelets washed the base of the Cyclopean monolith, on whose surface I could now trace both inscriptions and crude sculptures. The writing was in a system of hieroglyphics unknown to me, and unlike anything I had ever seen in books, consisting for the most part of conventionalised aquatic symbols such as fishes, eels, octopi, crustaceans, molluscs, whales and the like. Several characters obviously represented marine things which are unknown to the modern world, but whose decomposing forms I had observed on the ocean-risen plain.

It was the pictorial carving, however, that did most to hold me spell-bound. Plainly visible across the intervening water on account of their enormous size was an array of bas-reliefs whose subjects would have excited the envy of a Doré. I think that these things were supposed to depict men -- at least, a certain sort of men; though the creatures were shown disporting like fishes in the waters of some marine grotto, or paying homage at some monolithic shrine which appeared to be under the waves as well. Of their faces and forms I dare not speak in detail, for the mere remembrance makes me grow faint. Grotesque beyond the imagination of a Poe or a Bulwer, they were damnably human in general outline despite webbed hands and feet, shockingly wide and flabby lips, glassy, bulging eyes, and other features less pleasant to recall. Curiously enough, they seemed to have been chiselled badly out of proportion with their scenic background; for one of the creatures was shown in the act of killing a whale represented as but little larger than himself. I remarked, as I say, their grotesqueness and strange size; but in a moment decided that they were merely the imaginary gods of some primitive fishing or seafaring tribe; some tribe whose last descendant had perished eras before the first ancestor of the Piltdown or Neanderthal Man was born. Awestruck at this unexpected glimpse into a past beyond the conception of the most daring anthropologist, I stood musing whilst the moon cast queer reflections on the silent channel before me.

Then suddenly I saw it. With only a slight churning to mark its rise to the surface, the thing slid into view above the dark waters. Vast, Polyphemus-like, and loathsome, it darted like a stupendous monster of nightmares to the monolith, about which it flung its gigantic scaly arms, the while it bowed its hideous head and gave vent to certain measured sounds. I think I went mad then.

Of my frantic ascent of the slope and cliff, and of my delirious journey back to the stranded boat, I remember little. I believe I sang a great deal, and laughed oddly when I was unable to sing. I have indistinct recollections of a great storm some time after I reached the boat; at any rate, I knew that I heard peals of thunder and other tones which Nature utters only in her wildest moods.

When I came out of the shadows I was in a San Francisco hospital; brought thither by the captain of the American ship which had picked up my boat in mid-ocean. In my delirium I had said much, but found that my words had been given scant attention. Of any land upheaval in the Pacific, my rescuers knew nothing; nor did I deem it necessary to insist upon a thing which I knew they could not believe. Once I sought out a celebrated ethnologist, and amused him with peculiar questions regarding the ancient Philistine legend of Dagon, the Fish-God; but soon perceiving that he was hopelessly conventional, I did not press my inquiries.

It is at night, especially when the moon is gibbous and waning, that I see the
ing. I tried morphine; but the drug has given only transient surcease, and has
awn me into its clutches as a hopeless slave. So now I am to end it all, having
ritten a full account for the information or the contemptuous amusement of
y fellow-men. Often I ask myself if it could not all have been a pure phantasm
a mere freak of fever as I lay sun-stricken and raving in the open boat after my
cape from the German man-of-war. This I ask myself, but ever does there come
efore me a hideously vivid vision in reply. I cannot think of the deep sea with-
ut shuddering at the nameless things that may at this very moment be crawl-
g and floundering on its slimy bed, worshipping their ancient stone idols and
arving their own detestable likenesses on submarine obelisks of water-soaked
anite. I dream of a day when they may rise above the billows to drag down
their reeking talons the remnants of puny, war-exhausted mankind -- of a day
hen the land shall sink, and the dark ocean floor shall ascend amidst universal
andemonium.

The end is near. I hear a noise at the door, as of some immense slippery body
mbering against it. It shall not find me. God, that hand! The window! The
indow!

– H. P. Lovecraft

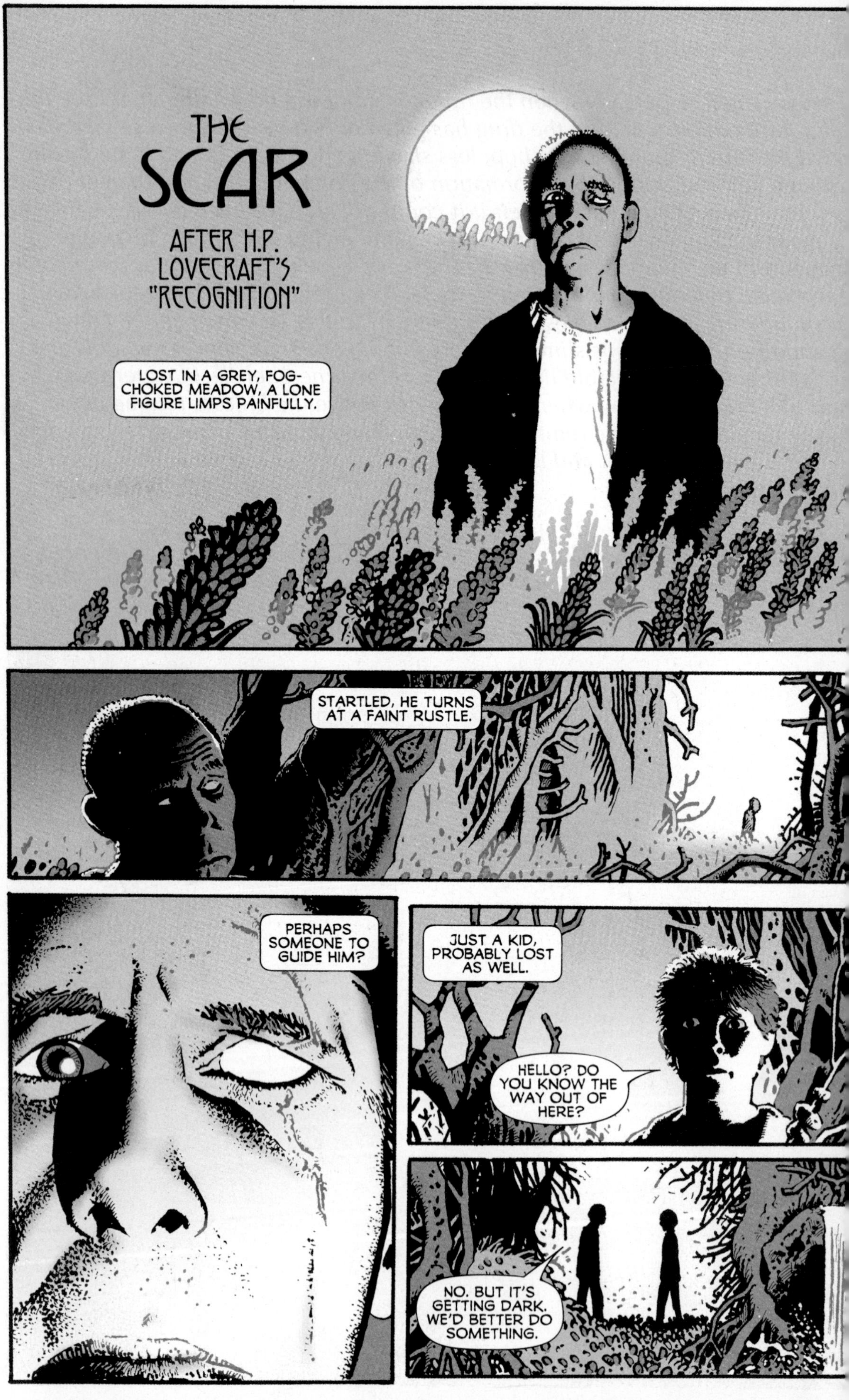
THE SCAR
AFTER H.P. LOVECRAFT'S "RECOGNITION"
LOST IN A GREY, FOG-CHOKED MEADOW, A LONE FIGURE LIMPS PAINFULLY.
STARTLED, HE TURNS AT A FAINT RUSTLE.
PERHAPS SOMEONE TO GUIDE HIM?
JUST A KID, PROBABLY LOST AS WELL.
HELLO? DO YOU KNOW THE WAY OUT OF HERE?
NO. BUT IT'S GETTING DARK. WE'D BETTER DO SOMETHING.

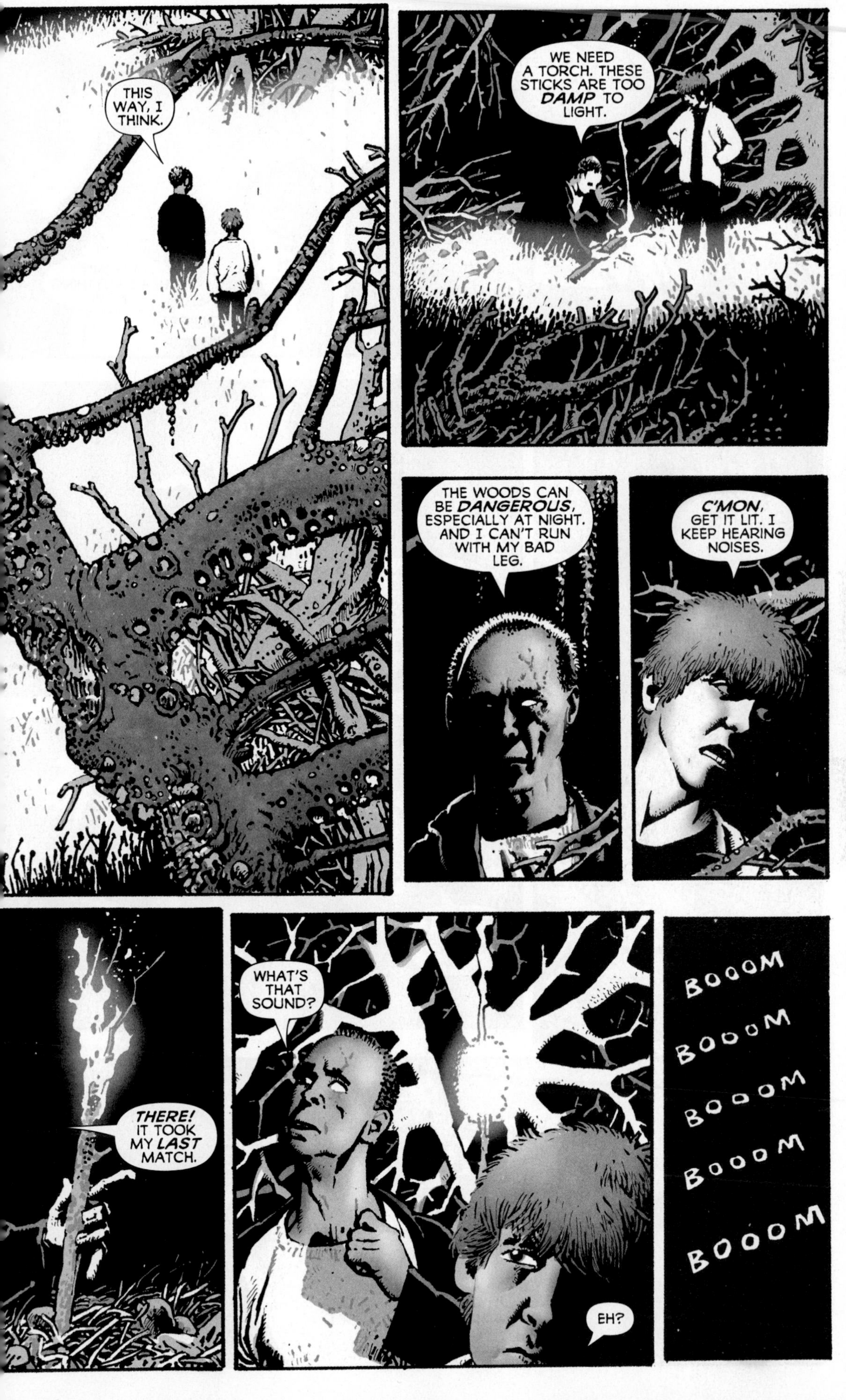
THIS WAY, I THINK.
WE NEED A TORCH. THESE STICKS ARE TOO DAMP TO LIGHT.
THE WOODS CAN BE DANGEROUS, ESPECIALLY AT NIGHT. AND I CAN'T RUN WITH MY BAD LEG.
C'MON, GET IT LIT. I KEEP HEARING NOISES.
THERE! IT TOOK MY LAST MATCH.
WHAT'S THAT SOUND?
EH?
BOOOM
BOOOM
BOOOM
BOOOM
BOOOM

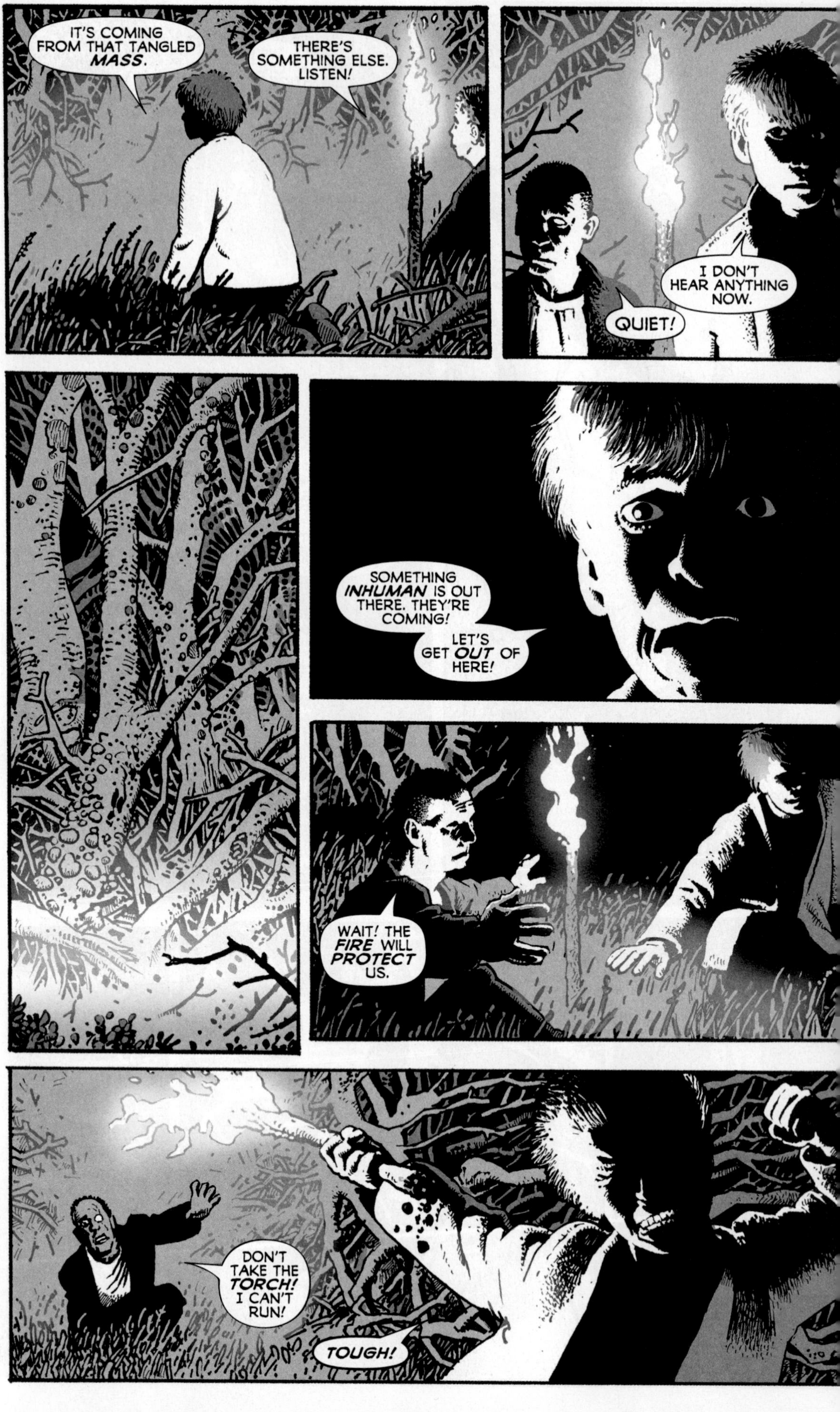
IT'S COMING FROM THAT TANGLED *MASS*.
THERE'S SOMETHING ELSE. LISTEN!
I DON'T HEAR ANYTHING NOW.
QUIET!
SOMETHING *INHUMAN* IS OUT THERE. THEY'RE COMING!
LET'S GET *OUT* OF HERE!
WAIT! THE *FIRE* WILL *PROTECT* US.
DON'T TAKE THE *TORCH!* I CAN'T RUN!
*TOUGH!*

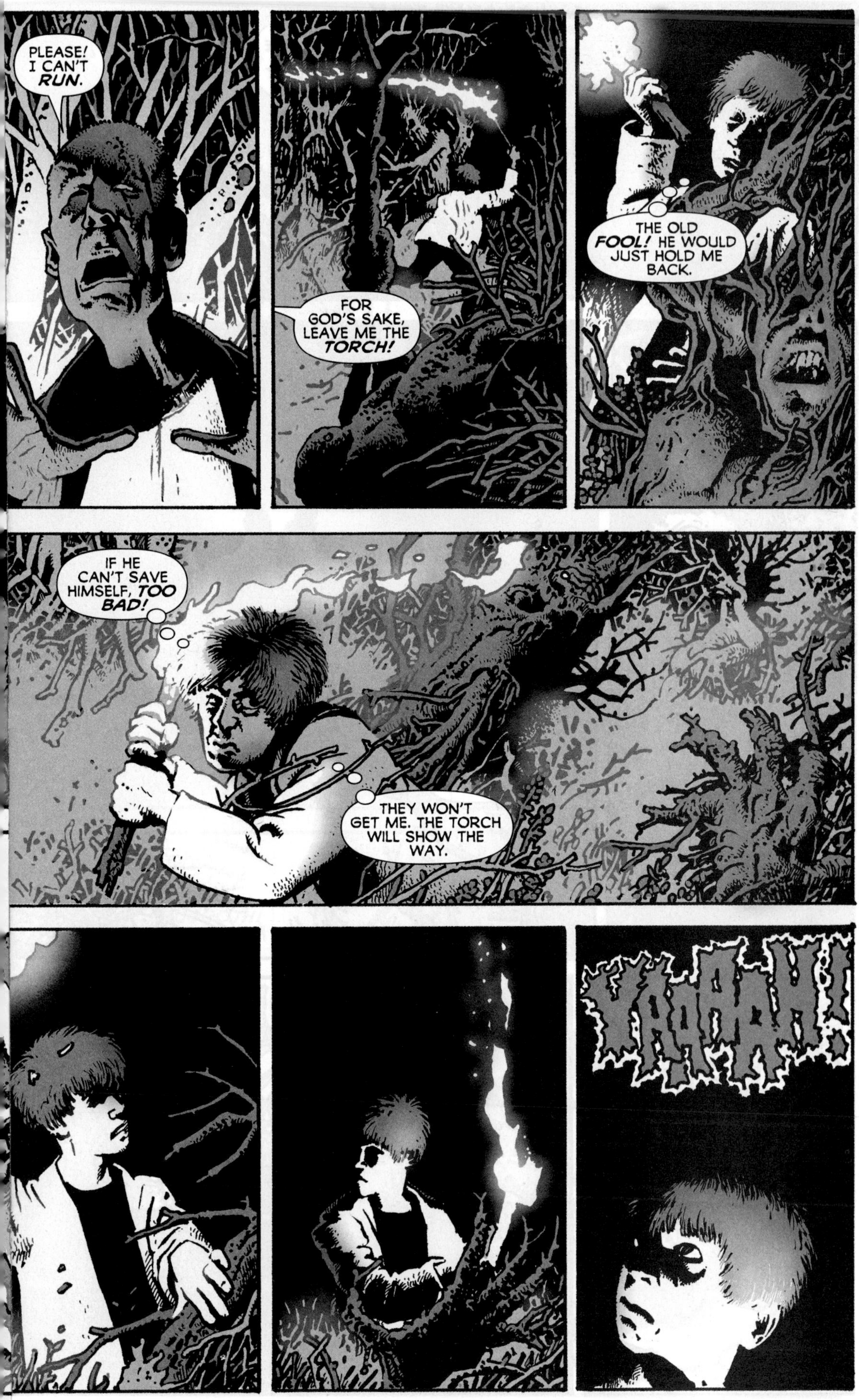
PLEASE! I CAN'T *RUN*.
FOR GOD'S SAKE, LEAVE ME THE *TORCH!*
THE OLD *FOOL!* HE WOULD JUST HOLD ME BACK.
IF HE CAN'T SAVE HIMSELF, *TOO BAD!*
THEY WON'T GET ME. THE TORCH WILL SHOW THE WAY.
YAAAAH!!

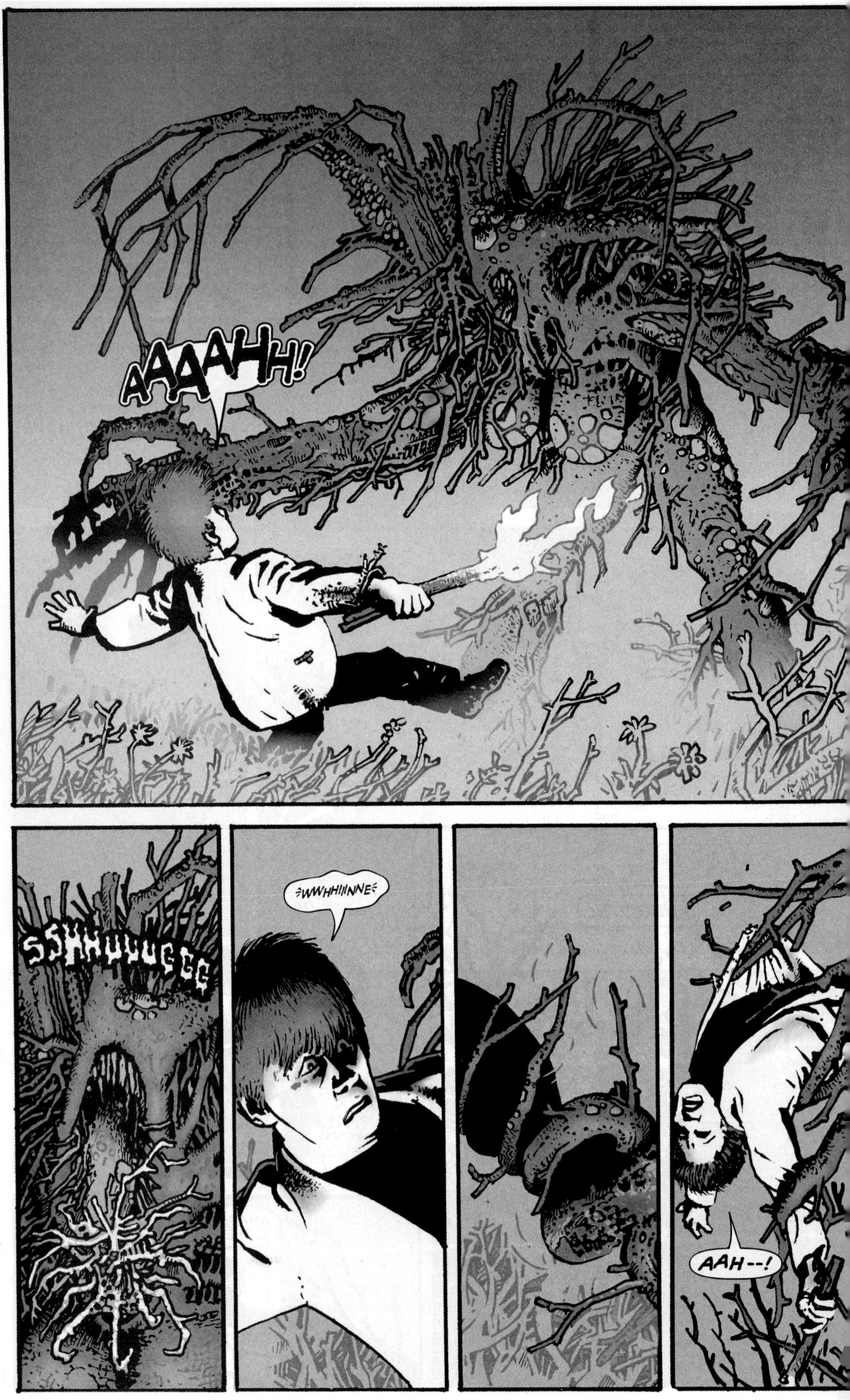
AAAAHH!
SSHHUUUGGG
WWHHIIINNE
AAH--!

THE CREATURE PULLED THE BOY CLOSER, SEEKING FOOD.

BUT WHEN THE CEREMONY COMMENCED...

*BOOM BOOM BOOM BOOM*

THE CREATURE PAUSED...

*BOOM BOOM BOOM BOOM*

AND DROPPED ITS PREY.

HUMP!

STAY AWAY!

*§SHRREEEEEEEEEEEE!*

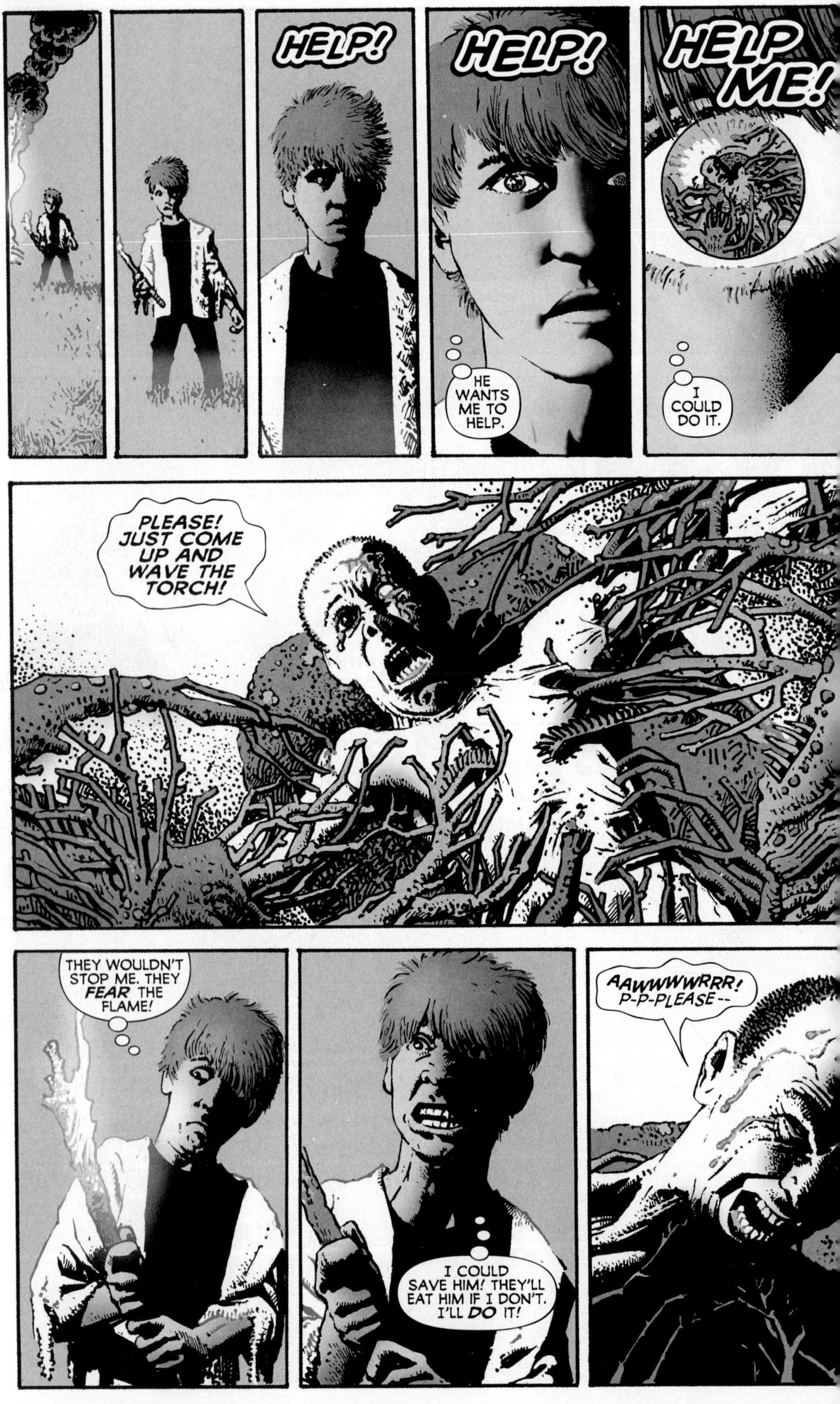
HELP!
HELP!
HE WANTS ME TO HELP.
HELP ME!
I COULD DO IT.
PLEASE! JUST COME UP AND WAVE THE TORCH!
THEY WOULDN'T STOP ME. THEY FEAR THE FLAME!
I COULD SAVE HIM! THEY'LL EAT HIM IF I DON'T. I'LL DO IT!
AAWWWWRRR! P-P-PLEASE--

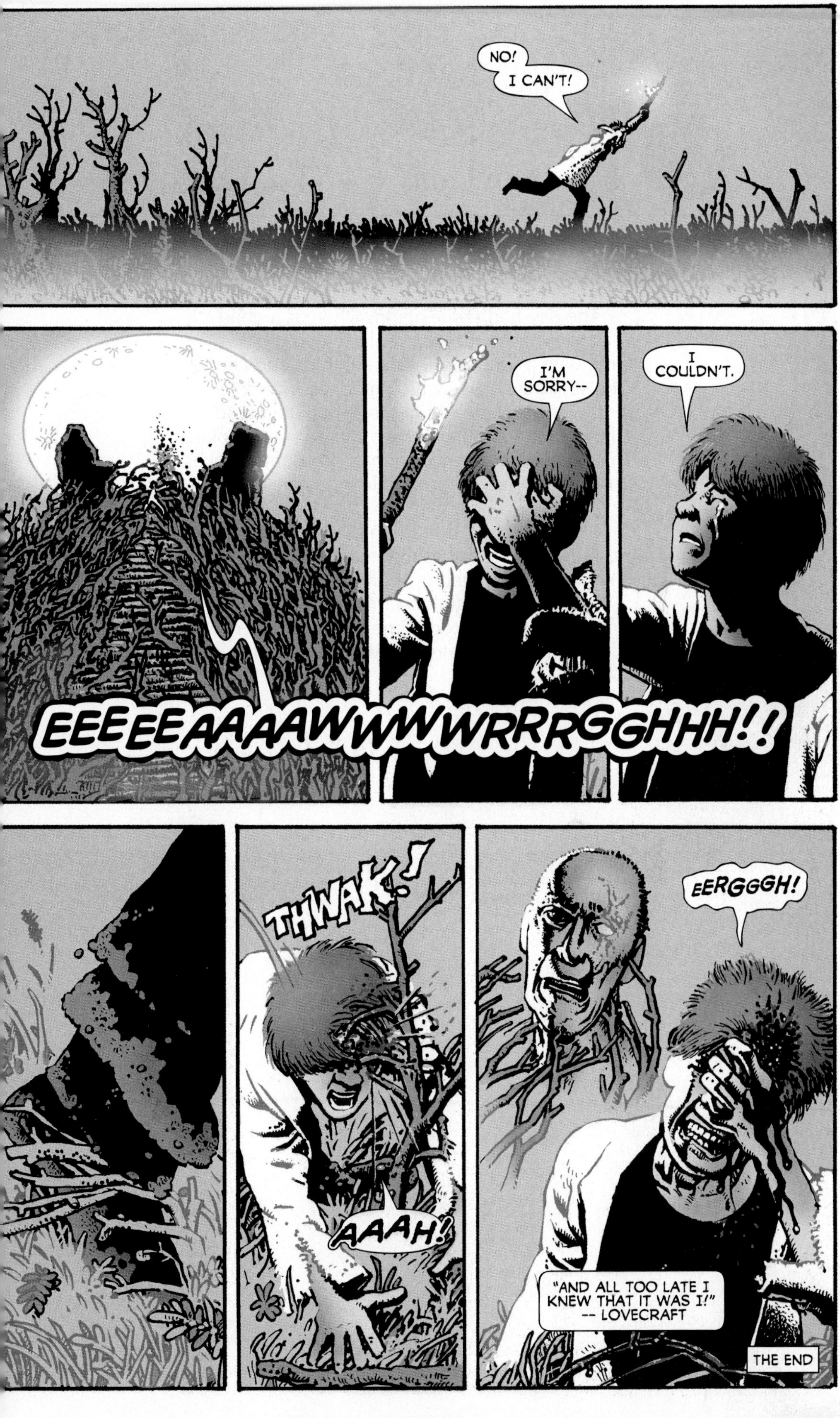
NO! I CAN'T!
I'M SORRY--
I COULDN'T.
EEEEEAAAAWWWWRRRRGGHHH!!
THWAK!
AAAH!
EERGGGH!
"AND ALL TOO LATE I KNEW THAT IT WAS I!" -- LOVECRAFT
THE END

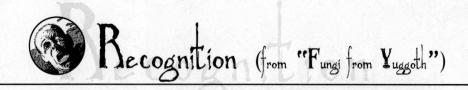

# Recognition (from "Fungi from Yuggoth")

The day had come again, when as a child
I saw- just once- that hollow of old oaks,
Grey with a ground-mist that enfolds and chokes
The slinking shapes which madness has defiled.
It was the same- an herbage rank and wild
Clings round an altar whose carved sign invokes
That Nameless One to whom a thousand smokes
Rose, aeons gone, from unclean towers up-piled.

I saw the body spread on that dank stone,
And I knew those things that feasted were not men;
I knew this strange grey world was not my own,
But Yuggoth, past the starry voids- and then
The body shrieked at me with a dead cry,
And all too late I knew that it was I!

— H. P. Lovecraft

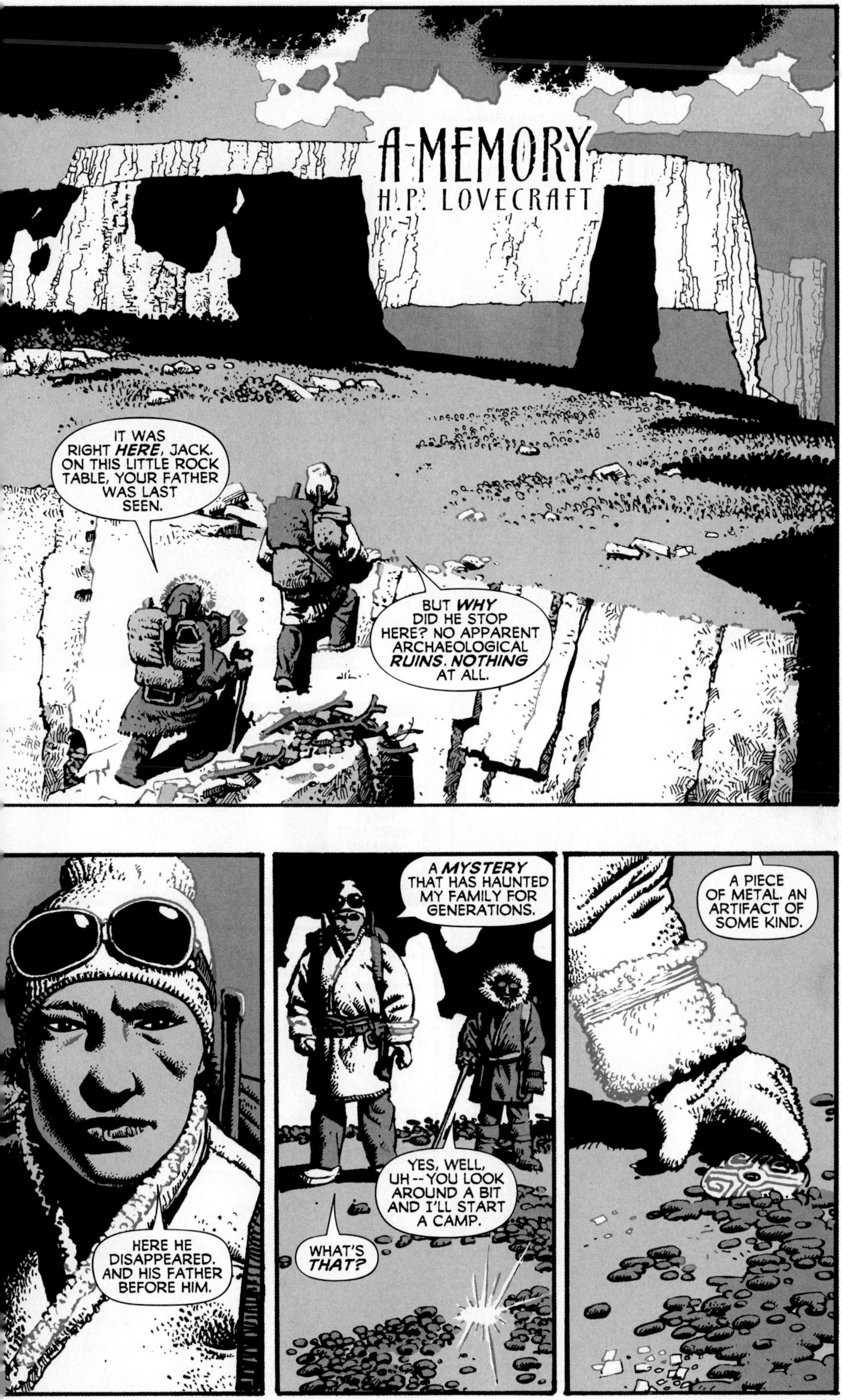
A MEMORY
H.P. LOVECRAFT
IT WAS RIGHT HERE, JACK. ON THIS LITTLE ROCK TABLE, YOUR FATHER WAS LAST SEEN.
BUT WHY DID HE STOP HERE? NO APPARENT ARCHAEOLOGICAL RUINS. NOTHING AT ALL.
HERE HE DISAPPEARED. AND HIS FATHER BEFORE HIM.
A MYSTERY THAT HAS HAUNTED MY FAMILY FOR GENERATIONS.
YES, WELL, UH -- YOU LOOK AROUND A BIT AND I'LL START A CAMP.
WHAT'S THAT?
A PIECE OF METAL. AN ARTIFACT OF SOME KIND.

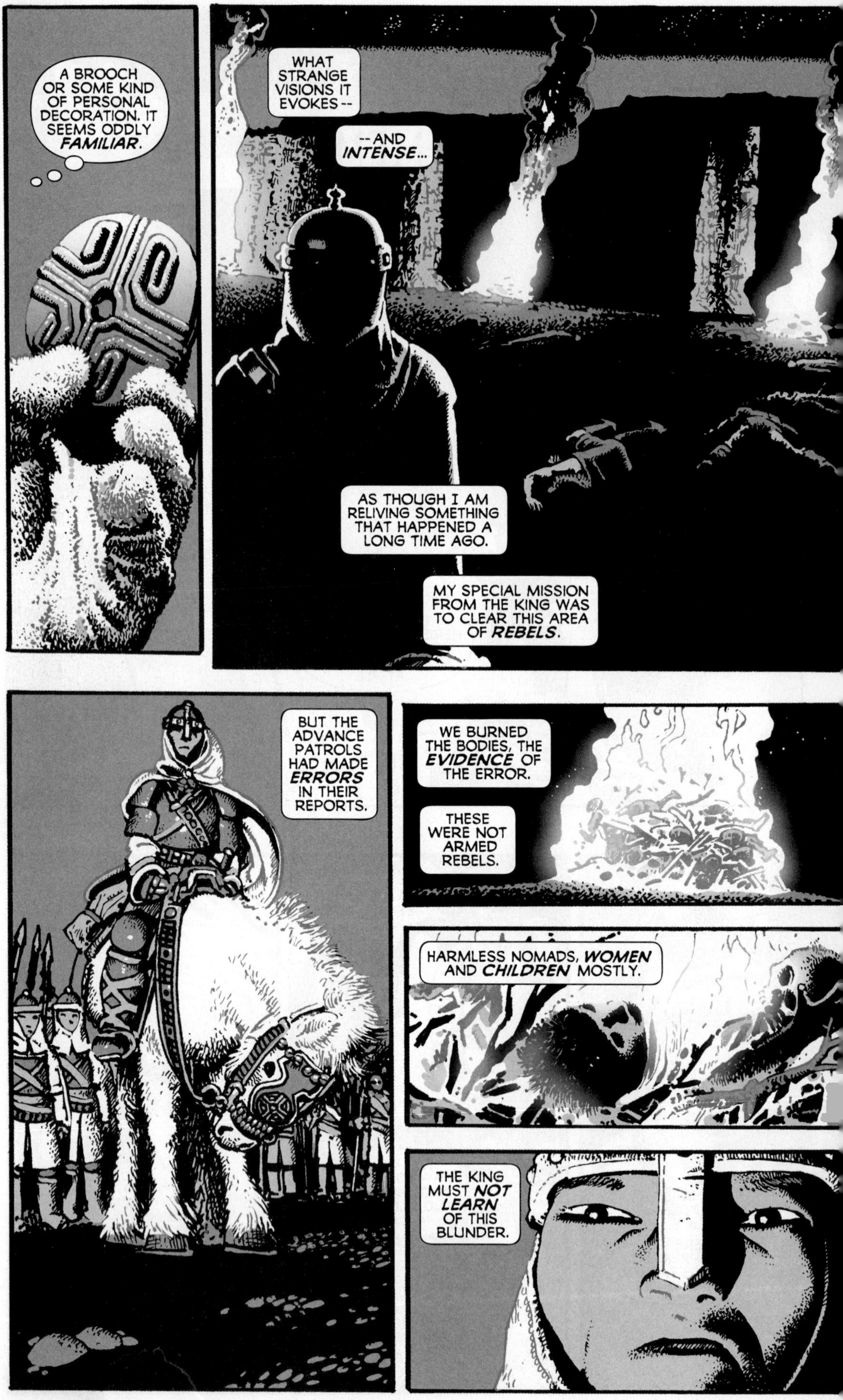

A BROOCH OR SOME KIND OF PERSONAL DECORATION. IT SEEMS ODDLY *FAMILIAR*.
WHAT STRANGE VISIONS IT EVOKES --
-- AND *INTENSE*...
AS THOUGH I AM RELIVING SOMETHING THAT HAPPENED A LONG TIME AGO.
MY SPECIAL MISSION FROM THE KING WAS TO CLEAR THIS AREA OF *REBELS*.
BUT THE ADVANCE PATROLS HAD MADE *ERRORS* IN THEIR REPORTS.
WE BURNED THE BODIES, THE *EVIDENCE* OF THE ERROR.
THESE WERE NOT ARMED REBELS.
HARMLESS NOMADS, *WOMEN* AND *CHILDREN* MOSTLY.
THE KING MUST *NOT LEARN* OF THIS BLUNDER.

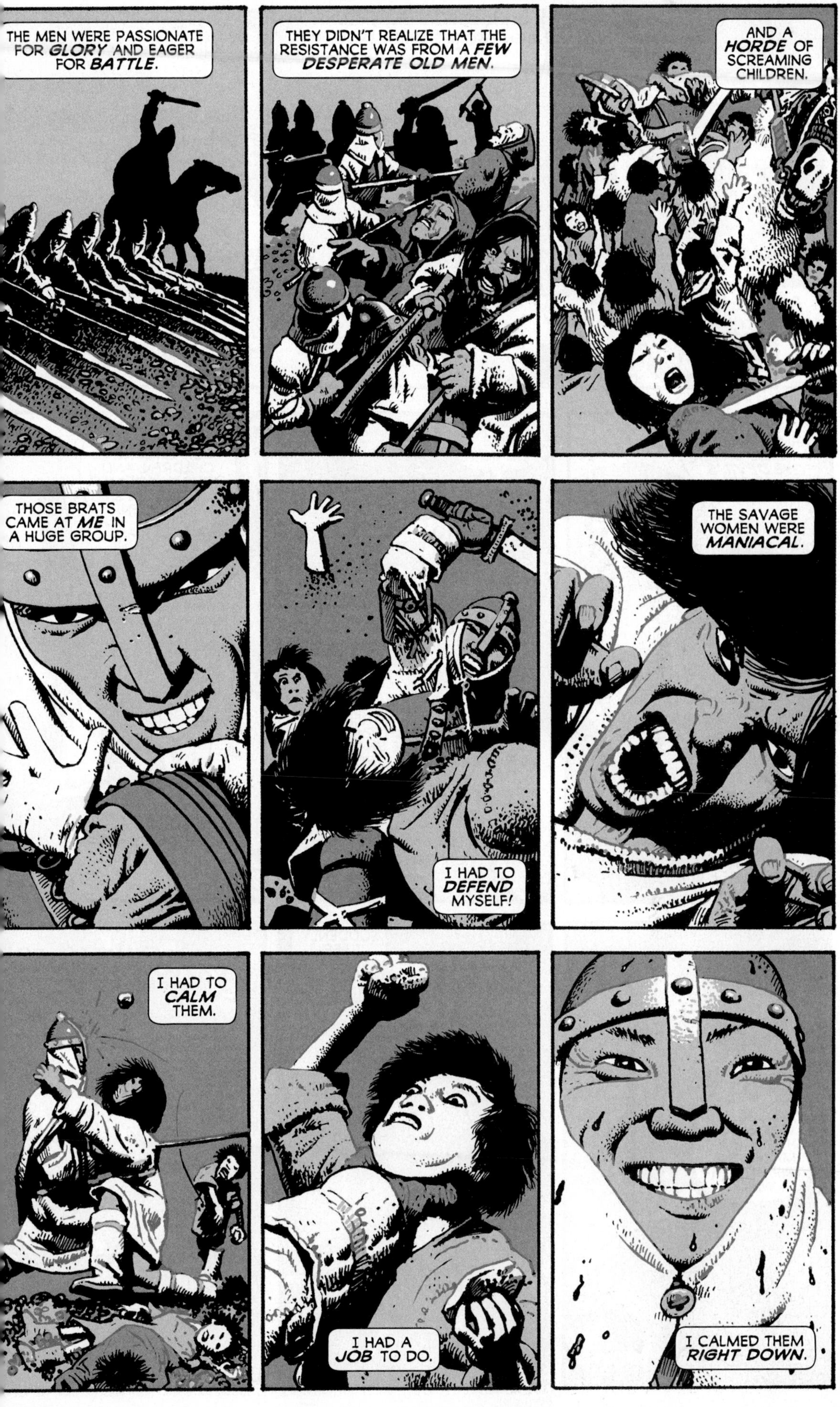
THE MEN WERE PASSIONATE FOR GLORY AND EAGER FOR BATTLE.
THEY DIDN'T REALIZE THAT THE RESISTANCE WAS FROM A FEW DESPERATE OLD MEN.
AND A HORDE OF SCREAMING CHILDREN.
THOSE BRATS CAME AT ME IN A HUGE GROUP.
I HAD TO DEFEND MYSELF!
THE SAVAGE WOMEN WERE MANIACAL.
I HAD TO CALM THEM.
I HAD A JOB TO DO.
I CALMED THEM RIGHT DOWN.

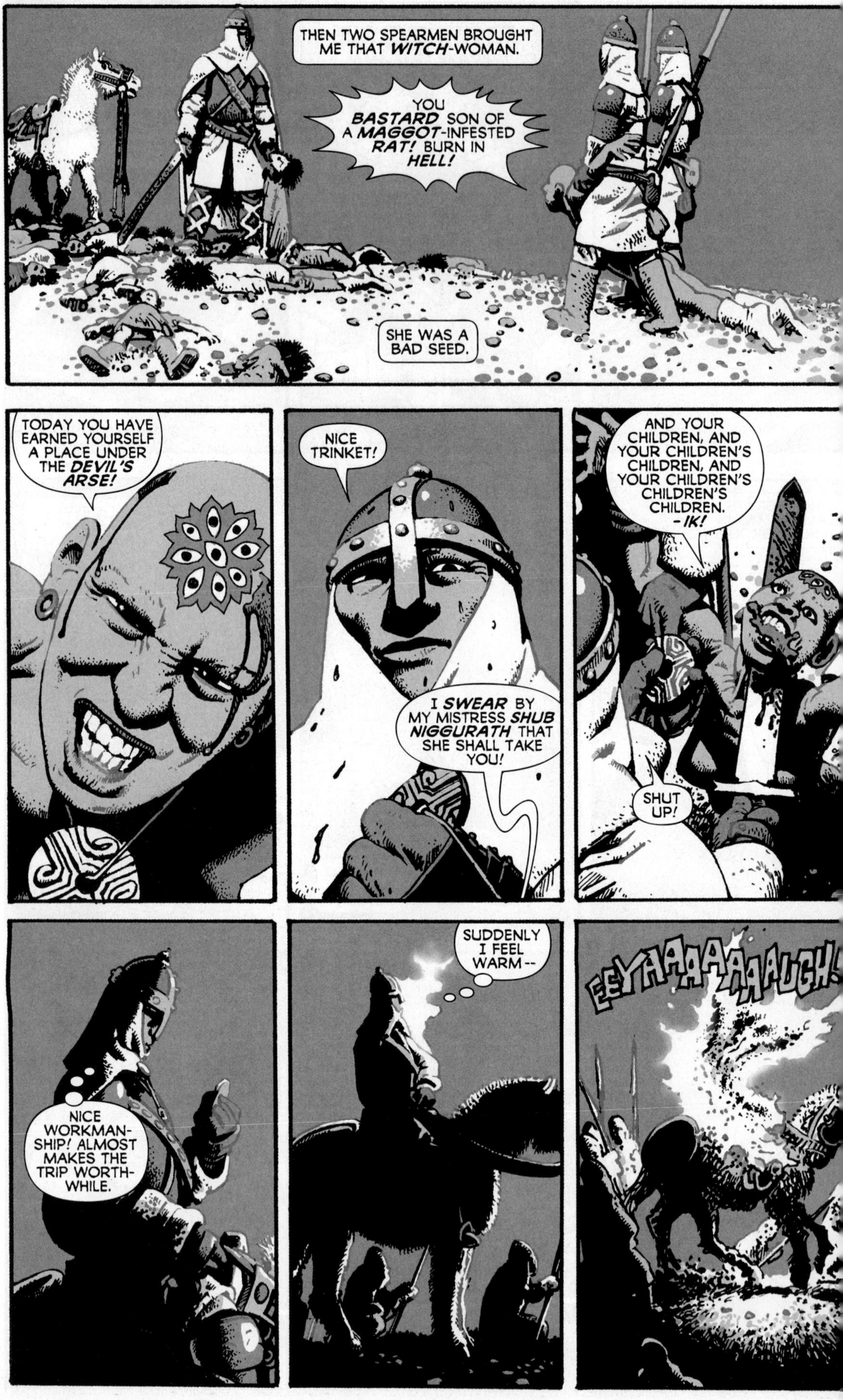
THEN TWO SPEARMEN BROUGHT ME THAT WITCH-WOMAN.
YOU BASTARD SON OF A MAGGOT-INFESTED RAT! BURN IN HELL!
SHE WAS A BAD SEED.
TODAY YOU HAVE EARNED YOURSELF A PLACE UNDER THE DEVIL'S ARSE!
NICE TRINKET!
I SWEAR BY MY MISTRESS SHUB NIGGURATH THAT SHE SHALL TAKE YOU!
AND YOUR CHILDREN, AND YOUR CHILDREN'S CHILDREN, AND YOUR CHILDREN'S CHILDREN'S CHILDREN. -IK!
SHUT UP!
NICE WORKMANSHIP! ALMOST MAKES THE TRIP WORTHWHILE.
SUDDENLY I FEEL WARM--
EEYAAAAAAAAUGH!

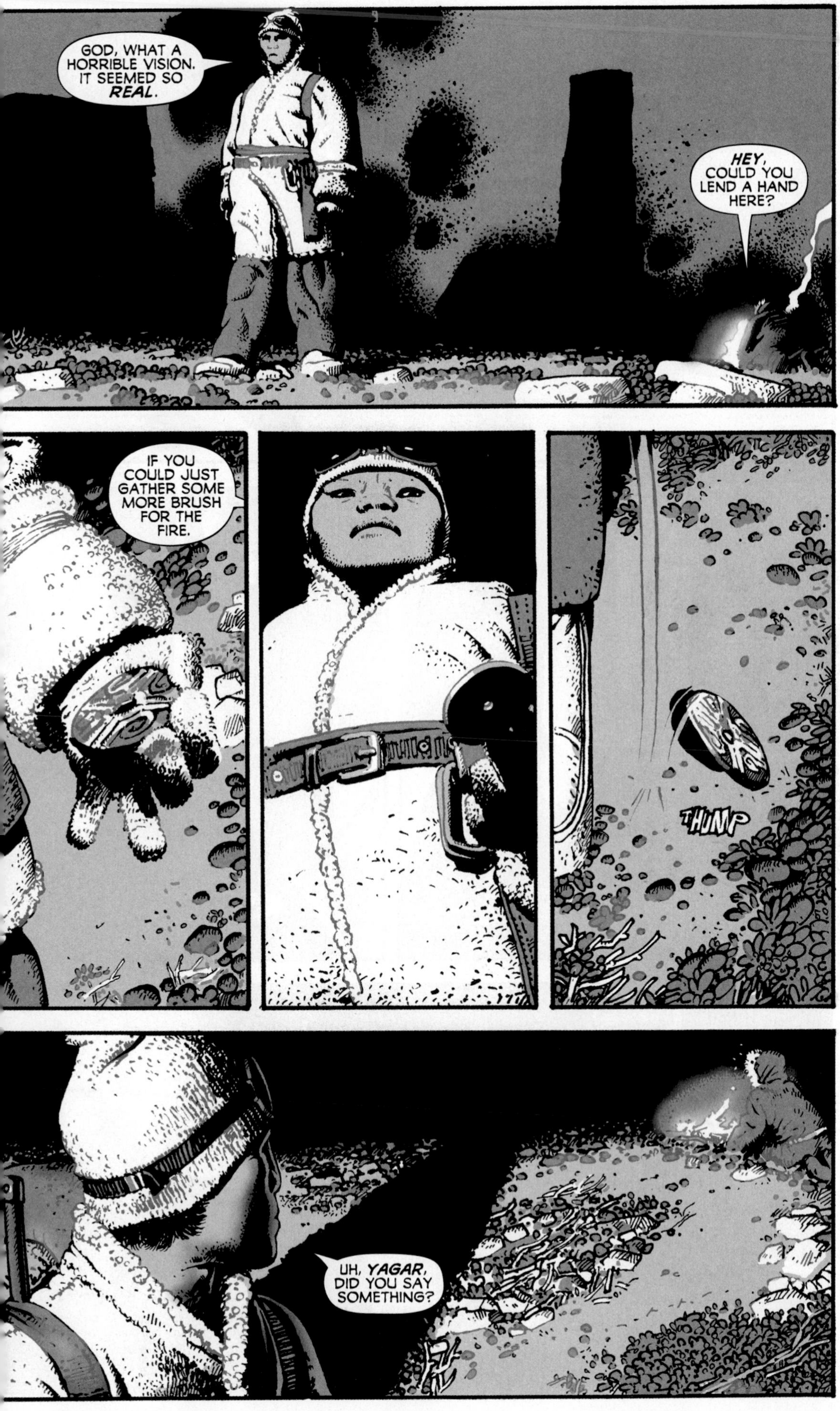

GOD, WHAT A HORRIBLE VISION. IT SEEMED SO *REAL*.
*HEY*, COULD YOU LEND A HAND HERE?
IF YOU COULD JUST GATHER SOME MORE BRUSH FOR THE FIRE.
THUMP
UH, *YAGAR*, DID YOU SAY SOMETHING?

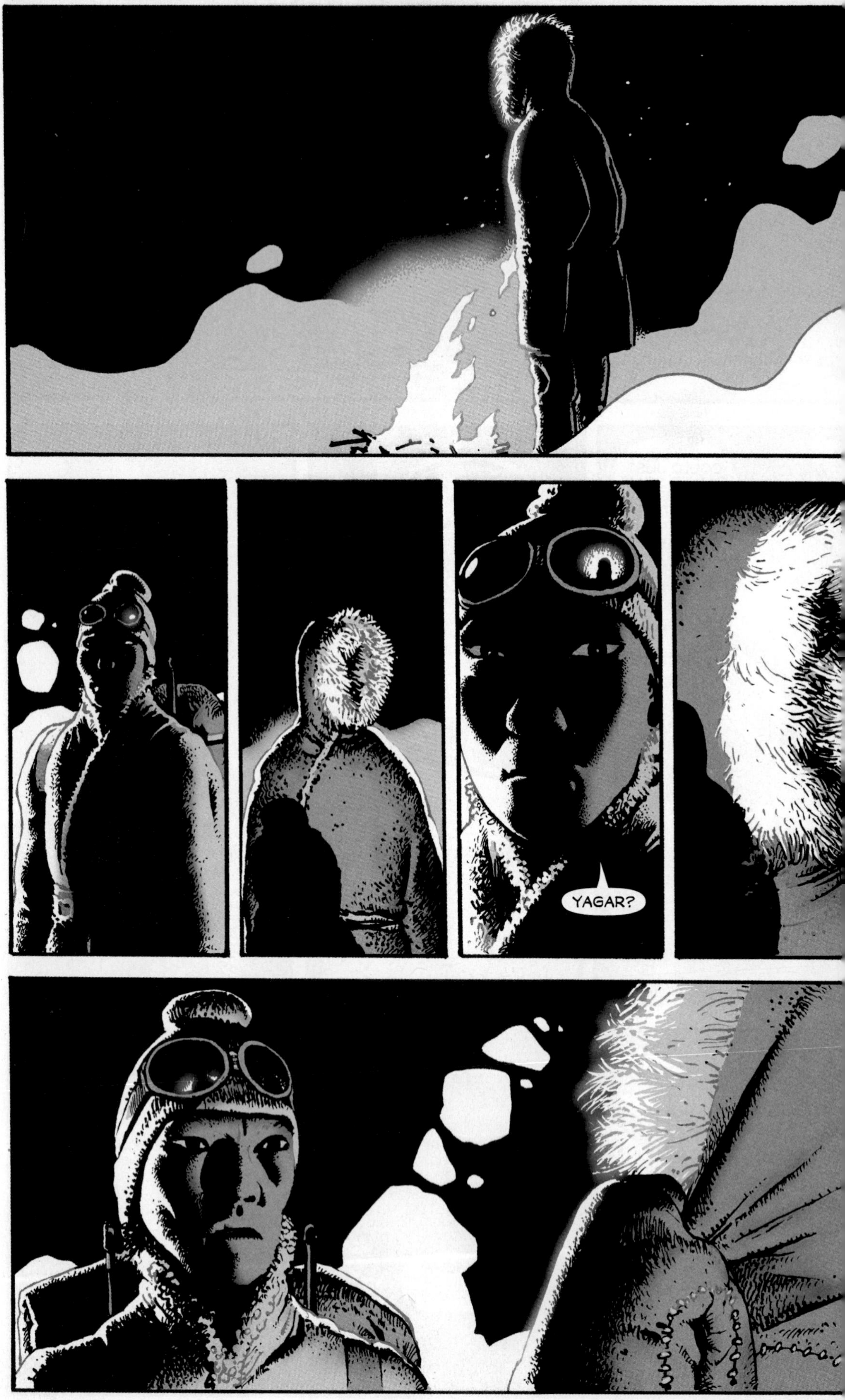
YAGAR?

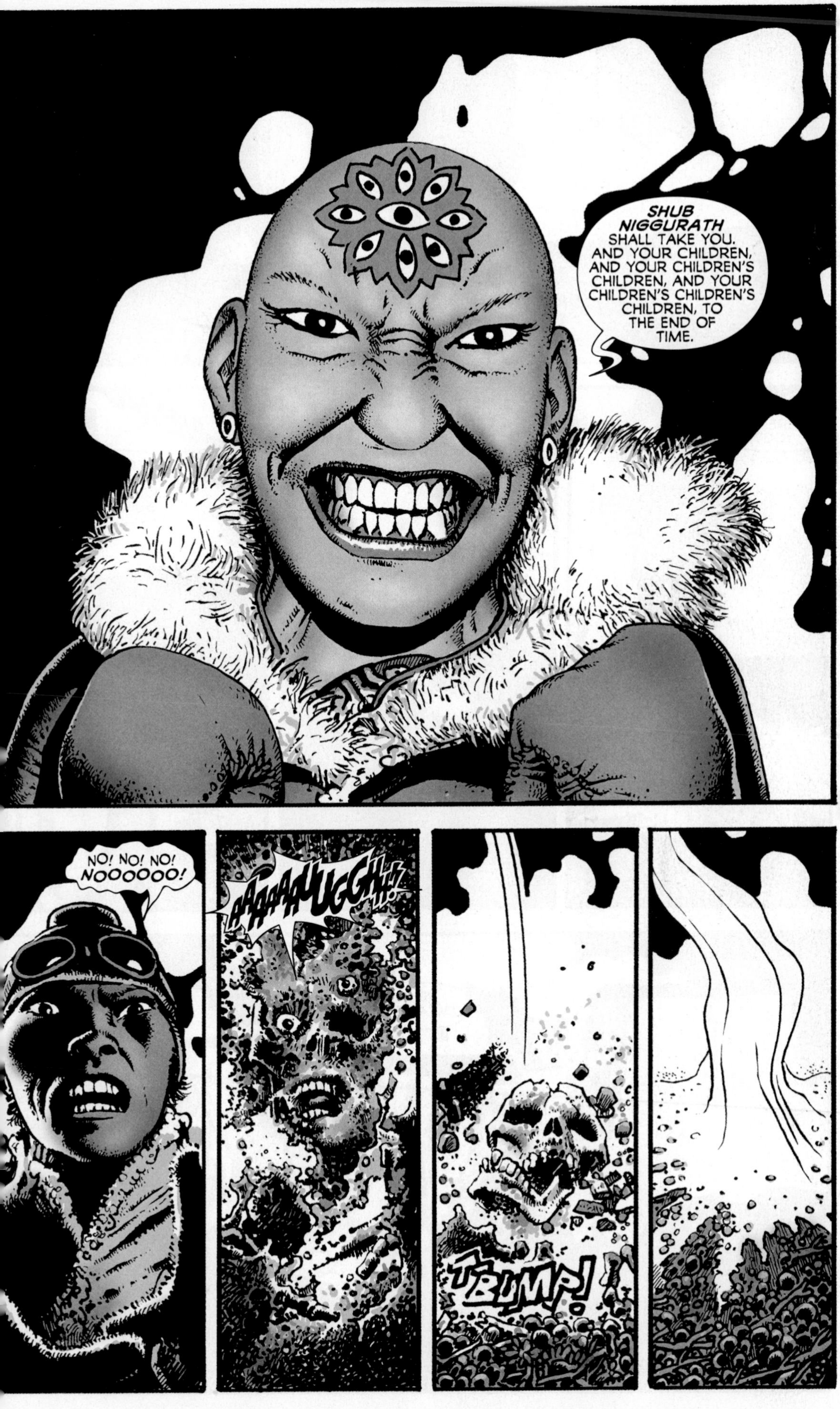
SHUB NIGGURATH SHALL TAKE YOU. AND YOUR CHILDREN, AND YOUR CHILDREN'S CHILDREN, AND YOUR CHILDREN'S CHILDREN'S CHILDREN, TO THE END OF TIME.
NO! NO! NO! NOOOOOO!
AAAAAAUGGHH!
TBUMP!

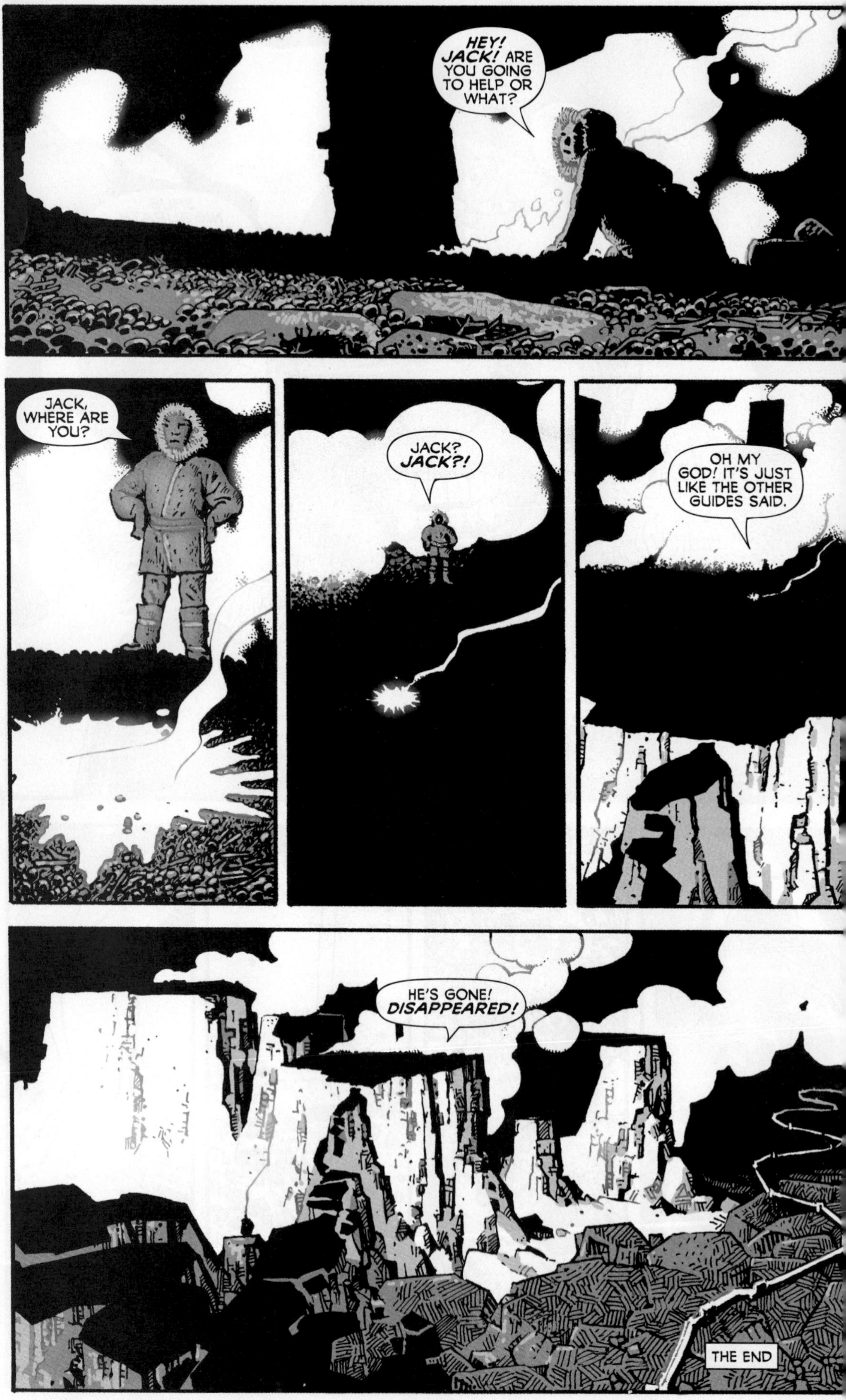
HEY! JACK! ARE YOU GOING TO HELP OR WHAT?
JACK, WHERE ARE YOU?
JACK? JACK?!
OH MY GOD! IT'S JUST LIKE THE OTHER GUIDES SAID.
HE'S GONE! DISAPPEARED!
THE END

#  A Memory (from "Fungi from Yuggoth")

There were great steppes, and rocky table-lands
Stretching half-limitless in starlit night,
With alien campfires shedding feeble light
On beasts with tinkling bells, in shaggy bands.
Far to the south the plain sloped low and wide
To a dark zigzag line of wall that lay
Like a huge python of some primal day
Which endless time had chilled and petrified.

I shivered oddly in the cold, thin air,
And wondered where I was and how I came,
When a cloaked form against a campfire's glare
Rose and approached, and called me by my name.
Staring at that dead face beneath the hood,
I ceased to hope - because I understood.

— H. P. Lovecraft

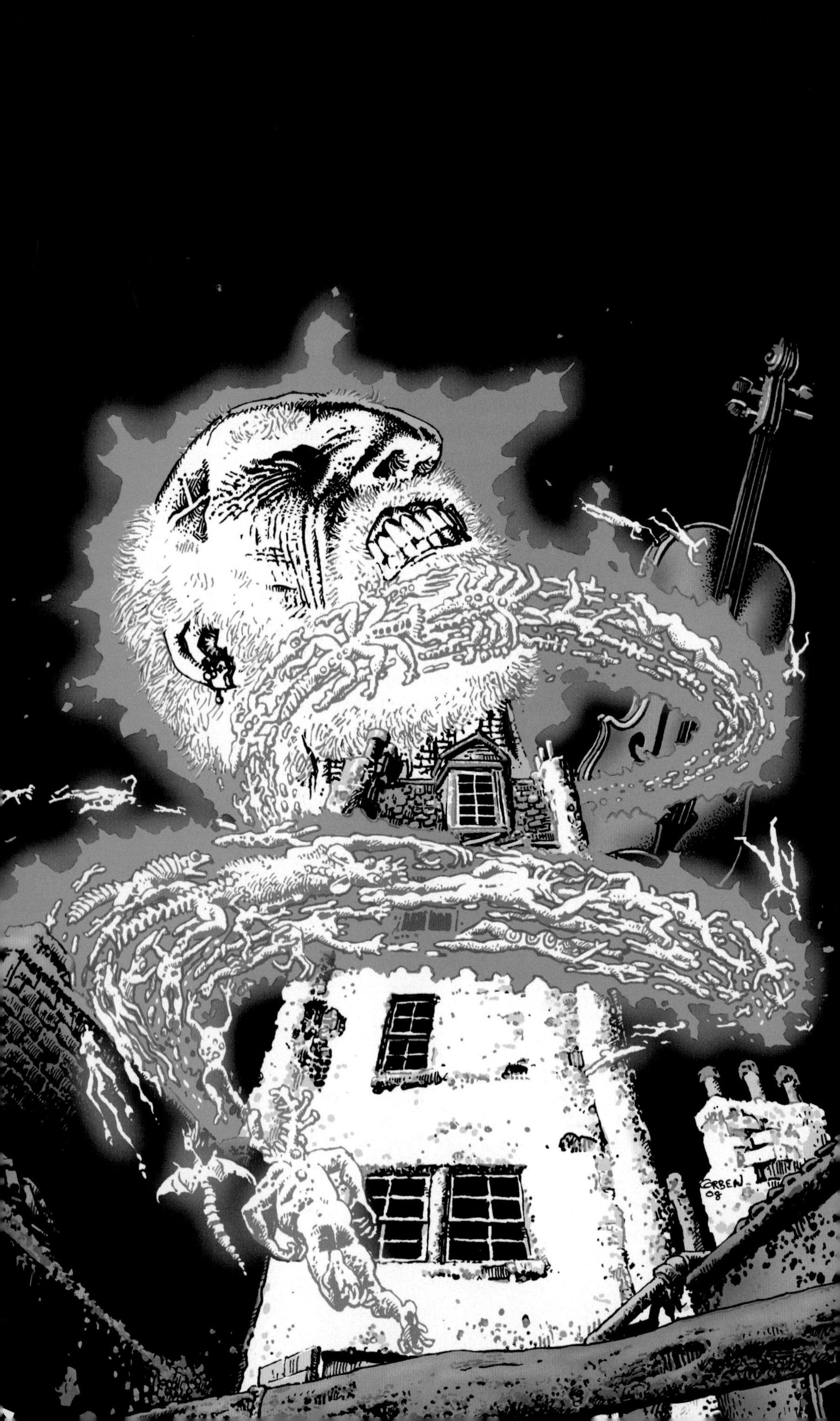
CORBEN
08

I CAN NO LONGER FIND THAT HATED *EVIL* HOUSE. MY MEMORY IS BROKEN, MY MENTAL AND PHYSICAL HEALTH DISTURBED SINCE MY STAY THERE. IT WAS *THERE* I HEARD:

# THE MUSIC OF ERICH ZANN
## BY H.P. LOVECRAFT

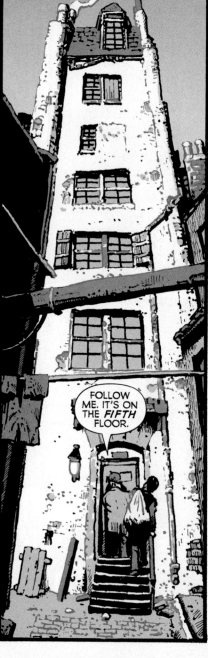

AS AN IMPOVERISHED STUDENT OF METAPHYSICS AT THE UNIVERSITY, I HAD TO FIND LODGINGS WITHIN MY *MEAGER* MEANS. THE RUE D'AUSEIL WAS IN WALKING DISTANCE.

STUDENT, EH? *YEH*, I HAVE A ROOM THAT *MIGHT* SUIT YOU.

FOLLOW ME. IT'S ON THE *FIFTH* FLOOR.

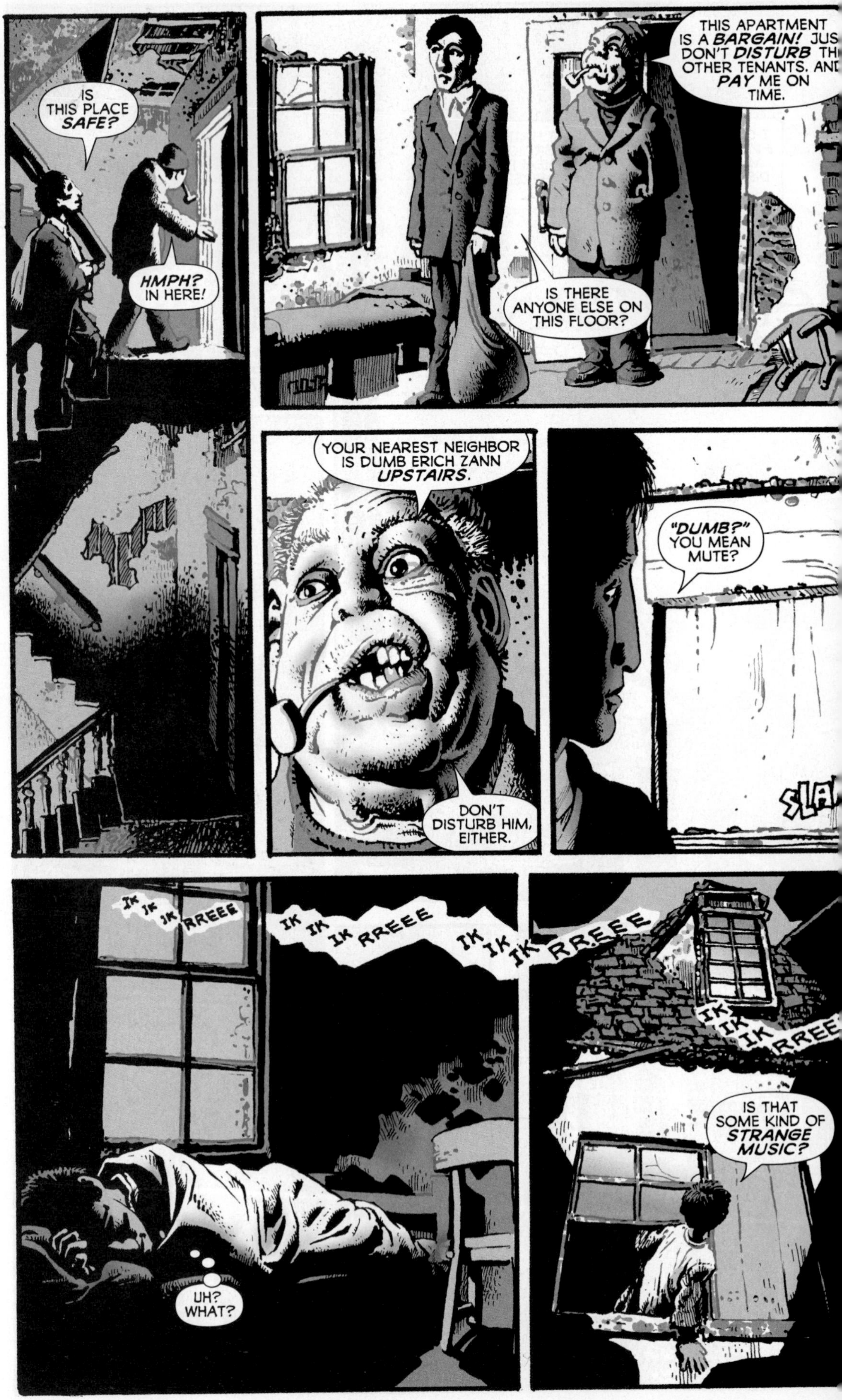
IS THIS PLACE SAFE?
HMPH? IN HERE!
THIS APARTMENT IS A BARGAIN! JUS DON'T DISTURB TH OTHER TENANTS. AND PAY ME ON TIME.
IS THERE ANYONE ELSE ON THIS FLOOR?
YOUR NEAREST NEIGHBOR IS DUMB ERICH ZANN UPSTAIRS.
DON'T DISTURB HIM, EITHER.
"DUMB?" YOU MEAN MUTE?
SLA
IK IK IK RREEE
IK IK IK RREEE
IK IK IK RREEE
UH? WHAT?
IK IK IK RREE
IS THAT SOME KIND OF STRANGE MUSIC?

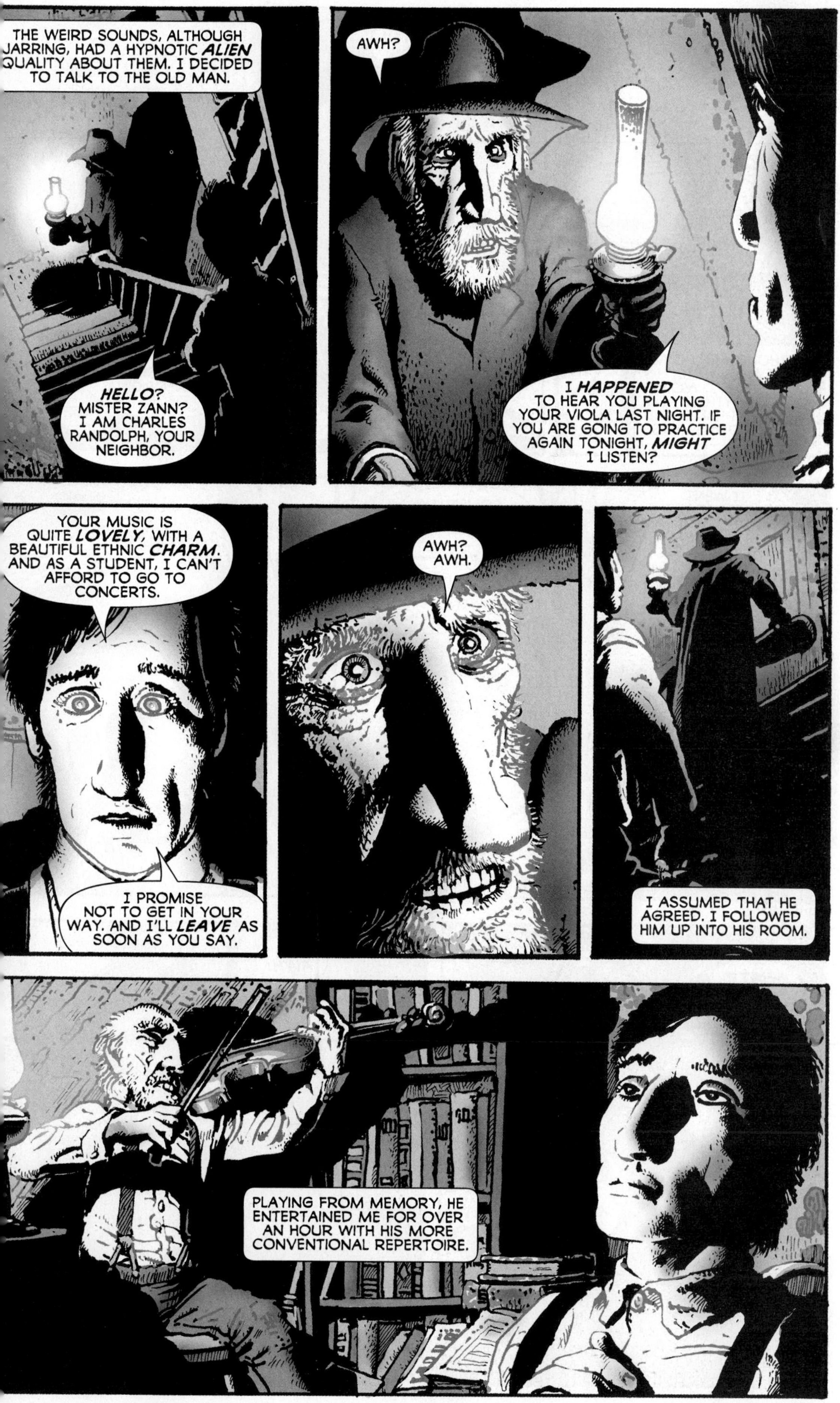
THE WEIRD SOUNDS, ALTHOUGH JARRING, HAD A HYPNOTIC ALIEN QUALITY ABOUT THEM. I DECIDED TO TALK TO THE OLD MAN.
HELLO? MISTER ZANN? I AM CHARLES RANDOLPH, YOUR NEIGHBOR.
AWH?
I HAPPENED TO HEAR YOU PLAYING YOUR VIOLA LAST NIGHT. IF YOU ARE GOING TO PRACTICE AGAIN TONIGHT, MIGHT I LISTEN?
YOUR MUSIC IS QUITE LOVELY, WITH A BEAUTIFUL ETHNIC CHARM. AND AS A STUDENT, I CAN'T AFFORD TO GO TO CONCERTS.
I PROMISE NOT TO GET IN YOUR WAY. AND I'LL LEAVE AS SOON AS YOU SAY.
AWH? AWH.
I ASSUMED THAT HE AGREED. I FOLLOWED HIM UP INTO HIS ROOM.
PLAYING FROM MEMORY, HE ENTERTAINED ME FOR OVER AN HOUR WITH HIS MORE CONVENTIONAL REPERTOIRE.

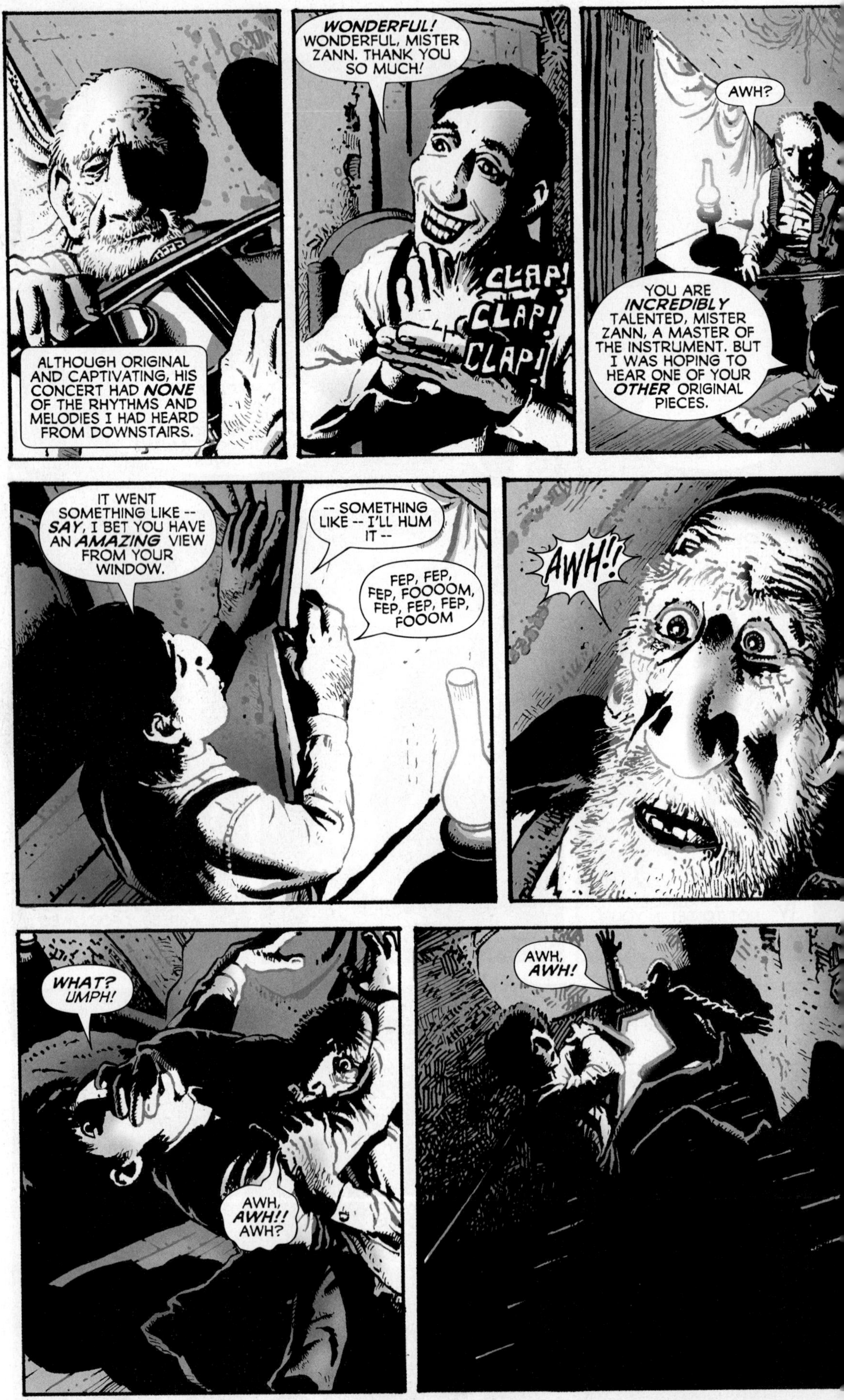
ALTHOUGH ORIGINAL AND CAPTIVATING, HIS CONCERT HAD NONE OF THE RHYTHMS AND MELODIES I HAD HEARD FROM DOWNSTAIRS.
WONDERFUL! WONDERFUL, MISTER ZANN. THANK YOU SO MUCH!
CLAP! CLAP! CLAP!
AWH?
YOU ARE INCREDIBLY TALENTED, MISTER ZANN, A MASTER OF THE INSTRUMENT. BUT I WAS HOPING TO HEAR ONE OF YOUR OTHER ORIGINAL PIECES.
IT WENT SOMETHING LIKE -- SAY, I BET YOU HAVE AN AMAZING VIEW FROM YOUR WINDOW.
-- SOMETHING LIKE -- I'LL HUM IT --
FEP, FEP, FEP, FOOOOM, FEP, FEP, FEP, FOOOM
AWH!!
WHAT? UMPH!
AWH, AWH!! AWH?
AWH, AWH!

HE PAYS HIS RENT, AND *I* DON'T HEAR ANYTHING.

I CAN MOVE YOU DOWN-STAIRS... AT *TWICE* THE RENT.

UGH. NEVERMIND.

IK IK IK RREEE IK IK IK RREEE IK IK IK RREEE

THE SOUNDS THAT I HAD ONCE FOUND STRANGELY ATTRACTIVE, WERE NOW LIKE *SANDPAPER* ON MY BRAINS.

IK IK IK RREEE IK IK IK RAEEE IK IK IK RREE

IT'S DRIVING ME *CRAZY!*

IT'S GOT TO *STOP!*

IK IK IK RREEE IK IK IK RREEE IK IK

BAM!

HEY IN THERE!

BAM!

AAAAAUUGH!

THE ROTTEN DOOR WAS EASY TO FORCE OPEN.

MISTER ZANN, WHAT IS IT?

OOOUUUUGGGHH!

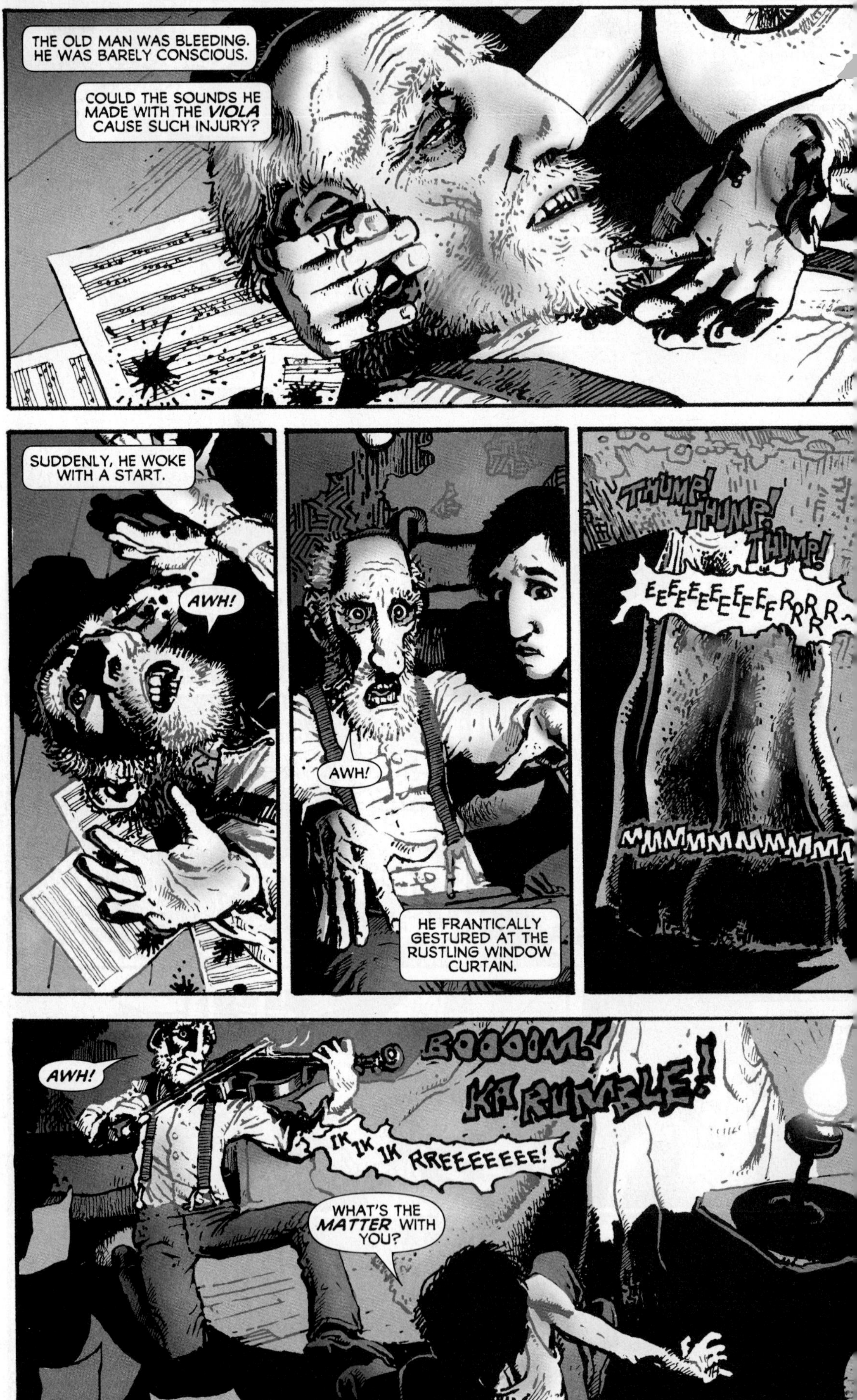

THE OLD MAN WAS BLEEDING. HE WAS BARELY CONSCIOUS.
COULD THE SOUNDS HE MADE WITH THE *VIOLA* CAUSE SUCH INJURY?
SUDDENLY, HE WOKE WITH A START.
AWH!
AWH!
HE FRANTICALLY GESTURED AT THE RUSTLING WINDOW CURTAIN.
THUMP! THUMP! THUMP!
EEEEEEEEEEERRRR-
MMMMMMMMMMMM
AWH!
BOOOOM!
KA RUMBLE!
IK IK IK RREEEEEEEE!
WHAT'S THE *MATTER* WITH YOU?

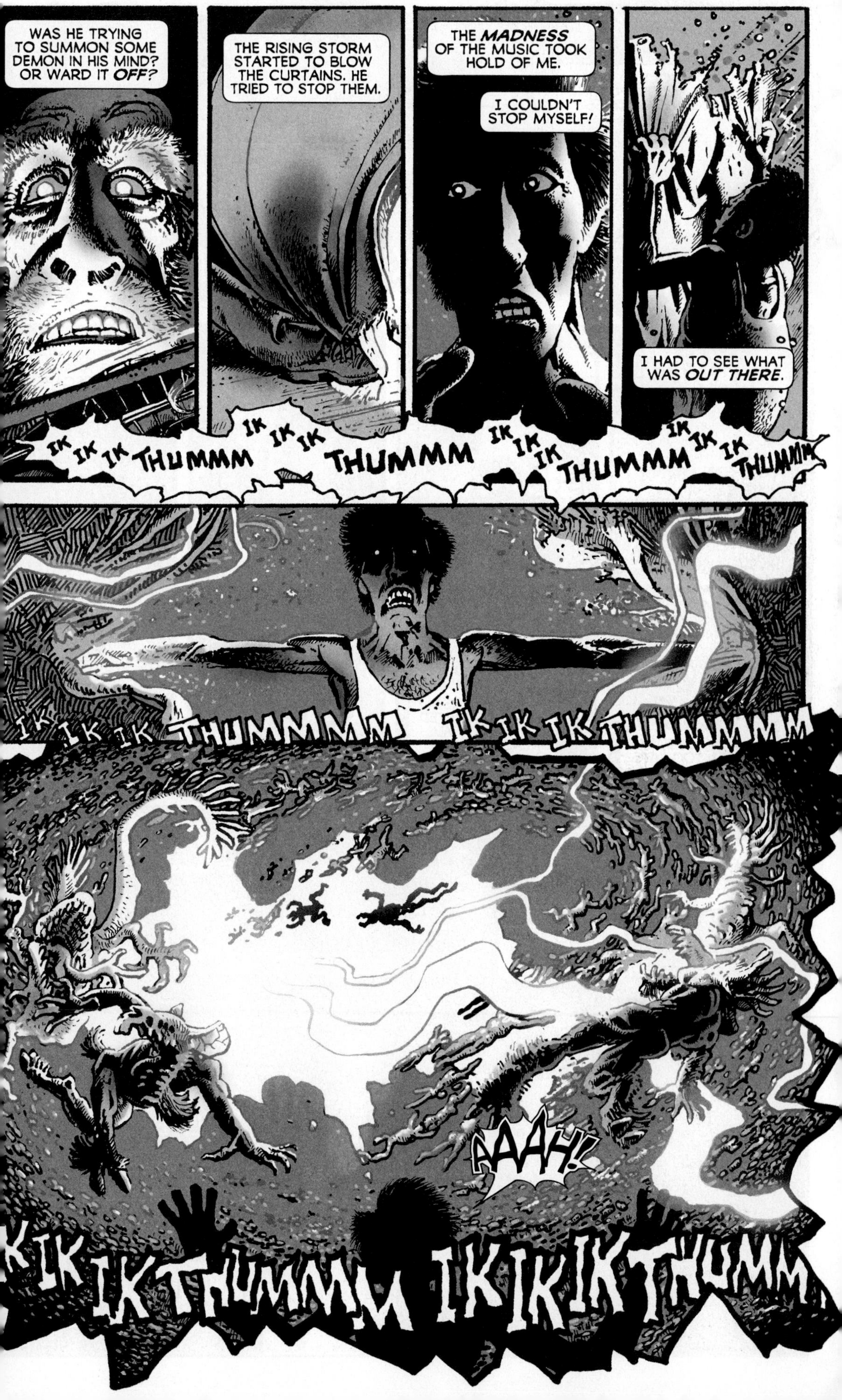

WAS HE TRYING TO SUMMON SOME DEMON IN HIS MIND? OR WARD IT *OFF?*
THE RISING STORM STARTED TO BLOW THE CURTAINS. HE TRIED TO STOP THEM.
THE *MADNESS* OF THE MUSIC TOOK HOLD OF ME.
I COULDN'T STOP MYSELF!
I HAD TO SEE WHAT WAS *OUT THERE*.
IK IK IK THUMMM IK IK THUMMM IK IK IK THUMMM IK IK IK THUMMM
IK IK IK THUMMMM IK IK IK THUMMMM
AAAH!
IK IK IK THUMMMM IK IK IK THUMM

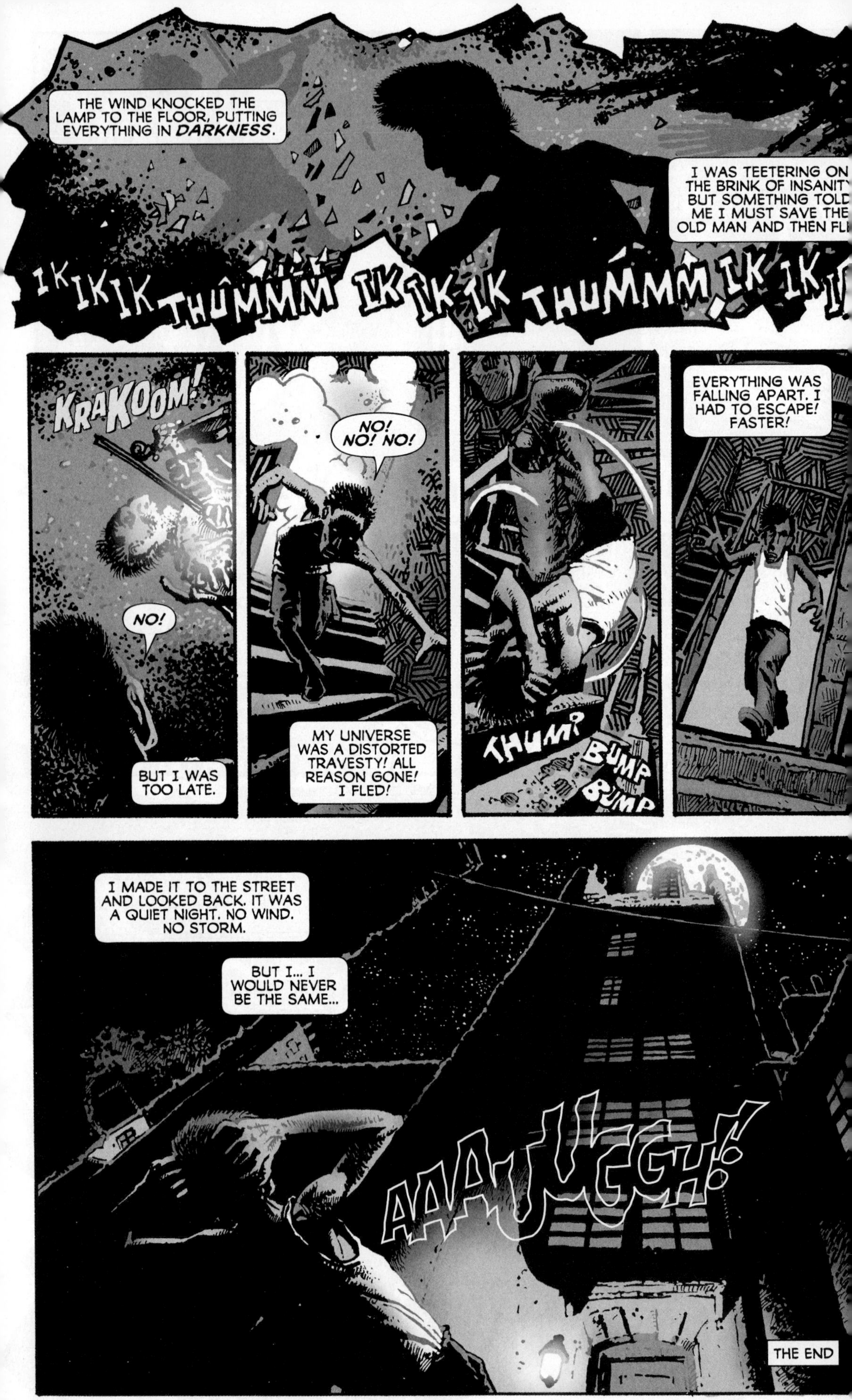
THE WIND KNOCKED THE LAMP TO THE FLOOR, PUTTING EVERYTHING IN *DARKNESS*.
I WAS TEETERING ON THE BRINK OF INSANIT BUT SOMETHING TOLD ME I MUST SAVE THE OLD MAN AND THEN FL
IK IK IK THUMMM IK IK IK THUMMM IK IK
KRAKOOM!
NO!
BUT I WAS TOO LATE.
NO! NO! NO!
MY UNIVERSE WAS A DISTORTED TRAVESTY! ALL REASON GONE! I FLED!
THUMP
BUMP
BUMP
EVERYTHING WAS FALLING APART. I HAD TO ESCAPE! FASTER!
I MADE IT TO THE STREET AND LOOKED BACK. IT WAS A QUIET NIGHT. NO WIND. NO STORM.
BUT I... I WOULD NEVER BE THE SAME...
AAAUGGH!
THE END

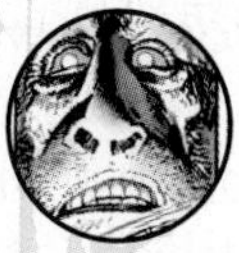

# The Music of Erich Zann

*I have examined maps of the city with the greatest care, yet have never again found the Rue d'Auseil. These maps have not been modem maps alone, for I know that names change. I have, on the contrary, delved deeply into all the antiquities of the place, and have personally explored every region, of whatever name, which could possibly answer to the street I knew as the Rue d'Auseil. But despite all I have done, it remains an humiliating fact that I cannot find the house, the street, or even the locality, where, during the last months of my impoverished life as a student of metaphysics at the university, I heard the music of Erich Zann.*

*That my memory is broken, I do not wonder; for my health, physical and mental, was gravely disturbed throughout the period of my residence in the Rue d'Auseil, and I recall that I took none of my few acquaintances there. But that I cannot find the place again is both singular and perplexing; for it was within a half-hour's walk of the university and was distinguished by peculiarities which could hardly be forgotten by any one who had been there. I have never met a person who has seen the Rue d'Auseil.*

*The Rue d'Auseil lay across a dark river bordered by precipitous brick blear-windowed warehouses and spanned by a ponderous bridge of dark stone. It was always shadowy along that river, as if the smoke of neighboring factories shut out the sun perpetually. The river was also odorous with evil stenches which I have never smelled elsewhere, and which may some day help me to find it, since I should recognize them at once. Beyond the bridge were narrow cobbled streets with rails; and then came the ascent, at first gradual, but incredibly steep as the Rue d'Auseil was reached.*

*I have never seen another street as narrow and steep as the Rue d'Auseil. It was almost a cliff, closed to all vehicles, consisting in several places of fights of steps, and ending at the top in a lofty ivied wall. Its paving was irregular, sometimes stone slabs, sometimes cobblestones, and sometimes bare earth with struggling greenish-grey vegetation. The houses were tall, peaked-roofed, incredibly old, and crazily leaning backward, forward, and sidewise. Occasionally an opposite pair, both leaning forward, almost met across the street like an arch; and certainly they kept most of the light from the ground below. There were a few overhead bridges from house to house across the street.*

The inhabitants of that street impressed me peculiarly; at first I thought it was because they were all silent and reticent; but later decided it was because they were all very old. I do not know how I came to live on such a street, but I was not myself when I moved there. I had been living in many poor places, always evicted for want of money; until at last I came upon that tottering house in the Rue d'Auseil kept by the paralytic Blandot. It was the third house from the top of the street, and by far the tallest of them all.

My room was on the fifth story; the only inhabited room there, since the house was almost empty. On the night I arrived I heard strange music from the peaked garret overhead, and the next day asked old Blandot about it. He told me it was an old German viol-player, a strange dumb man who signed his name as Erich Zann, and who played evenings in a cheap theater orchestra; adding that Zann's desire to play in the night after his return from the theater was the reason he had chosen this lofty and isolated garret room, whose single gable window was the only point on the street from which one could look over the terminating wall at the declivity and panorama beyond.

Thereafter I heard Zann every night, and although he kept me awake, I was haunted by the weirdness of his music. Knowing little of the art myself, I was yet certain that none of his harmonies had any relation to music I had heard before; and concluded that he was a composer of highly original genius. The longer I listened, the more I was fascinated, until after a week I resolved to make the old man's acquaintance.

One night as he was returning from his work, I intercepted Zann in the hallway and told him that I would like to know him and be with him when he played. He was a small, lean, bent person, with shabby clothes, blue eyes, grotesque, satyrlike face, and nearly bald head; and at my first words seemed both angered and frightened. My obvious friendliness, however, finally melted him; and he grudgingly motioned to me to follow him up the dark, creaking and rickety attic stairs. His room, one of only two in the steeply pitched garret, was on the west side, toward the high wall that formed the upper end of the street. Its size was very great, and seemed the greater because of its extraordinary barrenness and neglect. Of furniture there was only a narrow iron bedstead, a dingy wash-stand, a small table, a large bookcase, an iron music-rack, and three old-fashioned chairs. Sheets of music were piled in disorder about the floor. The walls were of bare boards, and had probably never known plaster; whilst the abundance of dust and cobwebs made the place seem more deserted than inhabited. Evidently Erich Zann's world of beauty lay in some far cosmos of the imagination.

Motioning me to sit down, the dumb man closed the door, turned the large wooden bolt, and lighted a candle to augment the one he had brought with him. He now removed his viol from its moth-eaten covering, and taking it, seated himself in the least uncomfortable of the chairs. He did not employ the music-rack, but, offering no choice and playing from memory, enchanted me for over an hour with strains I had never heard before; strains which must have been of his own devising. To describe their exact nature is impossible for one unversed in music. They were a kind of fugue, with recurrent passages of the most captivating quality, but to me were notable for the absence of any of the weird notes I had overheard from my room below on other occasions.

Those haunting notes I had remembered, and had often hummed and whistled inaccurately to myself, so when the player at length laid down his bow I asked him if he would render some of them. As I began my request the wrinkled satyrlike face lost the bored placidity it had possessed during the playing, and seemed to show the same curious mixture of anger and fright which I had noticed when first I accosted the old man. For a moment I was inclined to use persuasion, regarding rather lightly the whims of senility; and even tried to awaken my host's weirder mood by whistling a few of the strains to which I had listened the night before. But I did not pursue this course for more than a moment; for when the dumb musician recognized the whistled air his face grew suddenly distorted with an expression wholly beyond analysis, and his long, cold, bony right hand reached out to stop my mouth and silence the crude imitation. As he did this he further demonstrated his eccentricity by casting a startled glance toward the lone curtained window, as if fearful of some intruder—a glance doubly absurd, since the garret stood high and inaccessible above all the adjacent roofs, this window being the only point on the steep street, as the concierge had told me, from which one could see over the wall at the summit.

The old man's glance brought Blandot's remark to my mind, and with a certain capriciousness I felt a wish to look out over the wide and dizzying panorama of moonlit roofs and city lights beyond the hilltop, which of all the dwellers in the Rue d'Auseil only this crabbed musician could see. I moved toward the window and would have drawn aside the nondescript curtains, when with a frightened rage even greater than before, the dumb lodger was upon me again; this time motioning with his head toward the door as he nervously strove to drag me thither with both hands. Now thoroughly disgusted with my host, I ordered him to release me, and told him I would go at once. His clutch relaxed, and as he saw my disgust and offense, his own anger seemed to subside. He tightened his relaxing grip, but this time in a friendly manner, forcing me into a chair; then with an appearance of wistfulness crossing to the littered table, where he wrote many words with a pencil, in the labored French of a foreigner.

The note which he finally handed me was an appeal for tolerance and forgiveness. Zann said that he was old, lonely, and afflicted with strange fears and nervous disorders connected with his music and with other things. He had enjoyed my listening to his music, and wished I would come again and not mind his eccentricities. But he could not play to another his weird harmonies, and could not bear hearing them from another; nor could he bear having anything in his room touched by another. He had not known until our hallway conversation that I could overhear his playing in my room, and now asked me if I would arrange with Blandot to take a lower room where I could not hear him in the night. He would, he wrote, defray the difference in rent.

As I sat deciphering the execrable French, I felt more lenient toward the old man. He was a victim of physical and nervous suffering, as was I; and my metaphysical studies had taught me kindness. In the silence there came a slight sound from the window—the shutter must have rattled in the night wind, and for some reason I started almost as violently as did Erich Zann. So when I had finished reading, I shook my host by the hand, and departed as a friend.

The next day Blandot gave me a more expensive room on the third floor, between the apartments of an aged money-lender and the room of a respectable upholsterer. There was no one on the fourth floor.

It was not long before I found that Zann's eagerness for my company was not as great as it had seemed while he was persuading me to move down from the fifth story. He did not ask me to call on him, and when I did call he appeared uneasy and played listlessly. This was always at night—in the day he slept and would admit no one. My liking for him did not grow, though the attic room and the weird music seemed to hold an odd fascination for me. I had a curious desire to look out of that window, over the wall and down the unseen slope at the glittering roofs and spires which must lie outspread there. Once I went up to the garret during theater hours, when Zann was away, but the door was locked.

What I did succeed in doing was to overhear the nocturnal playing of the dumb old man. At first I would tip-toe up to my old fifth floor, then I grew bold enough to climb the last creaking staircase to the peaked garret. There in the narrow hall, outside the bolted door with the covered keyhole, I often heard sounds which filled me with an indefinable dread—the dread of vague wonder and brooding mystery. It was not that the sounds were hideous, for they were not; but that they held vibrations suggesting nothing on this globe of earth, and that at certain intervals they assumed a symphonic quality which I could hardly conceive as produced by one player. Certainly, Erich Zann was a genius of wild power. As the weeks passed, the playing grew wilder, whilst the old musician acquired an increasing haggardness and furtiveness pitiful to behold. He now refused to admit me at any time, and shunned me whenever we met on the stairs.

Then one night as I listened at the door, I heard the shrieking viol swell into a chaotic babel of sound; a pandemonium which would have led me to doubt my own shaking sanity had there not come from behind that barred portal a piteous proof that the horror was real—the awful, inarticulate cry which only a mute can utter, and which rises only in moments of the most terrible fear or anguish. I knocked repeatedly at the door, but received no response. Afterward I waited in the black hallway, shivering with cold and fear, till I heard the poor musician's feeble effort to rise from the floor by the aid of a chair. Believing him just conscious after a fainting fit, I renewed my rapping, at the same time calling out my name reassuringly. I heard Zann stumble to the window and close both shutter and sash, then stumble to the door, which he falteringly unfastened to admit me. This time his delight at having me present was real; for his distorted face gleamed with relief while he clutched at my coat as a child clutches at its mother's skirts.

Shaking pathetically, the old man forced me into a chair whilst he sank into another, beside which his viol and bow lay carelessly on the floor. He sat for some time inactive, nodding oddly, but having a paradoxical suggestion of intense and frightened listening. Subsequently he seemed to be satisfied, and crossing to a chair by the table wrote a brief note, handed it to me, and returned to the table, where he began to write rapidly and incessantly. The note implored me in the name of mercy, and for the sake of my own curiosity, to wait where I was while he prepared a full account in German of all the marvels and terrors which beset him. I waited, and the dumb man's pencil flew.

It was perhaps an hour later, while I still waited and while the old musician's feverishly written sheets still continued to pile up, that I saw Zann start as from the hint of a horrible shock. Unmistakably he was looking at the curtained window and listening shudderingly. Then I half fancied I heard a sound myself; though it was not a horrible sound, but rather an exquisitely low and infinitely distant musical note, suggesting a player in one of the neighboring houses, or in some abode beyond the lofty wall over which I had never been able to look. Upon Zann the effect was terrible, for, dropping his pencil, suddenly he rose, seized his viol, and commenced to rend the night with the wildest playing I had ever heard from his bow save when listening at the barred door.

It would be useless to describe the playing of Erich Zann on that dreadful night. It was more horrible than anything I had ever overheard, because I could now see the expression of his face, and could realize that this time the motive was stark fear. He was trying to make a noise; to ward something off or drown something out—what, I could not imagine, awesome though I felt it must be. The playing grew fantastic, dehnous, and hysterical, yet kept to the last the qualities of supreme genius which I knew this strange old man possessed. I recognized the air—it was a wild Hungarian dance popular in the theaters, and I reflected for a moment that this was the first time I had ever heard Zann play the work of another composer.

Louder and louder, wilder and wilder, mounted the shrieking and whining of that desperate viol. The player was dripping with an uncanny perspiration and twisted like a monkey, always looking frantically at the curtained window. In his frenzied strains I could almost see shadowy satyrs and bacchanals dancing and whirling insanely through seething abysses of clouds and smoke and lightning. And then I thought I heard a shriller, steadier note that was not from the viol; a calm, deliberate, purposeful, mocking note from far away in the West.

At this juncture the shutter began to rattle in a howling night wind which had sprung up outside as if in answer to the mad playing within. Zann's screaming viol now outdid itself emitting sounds I had never thought a viol could emit. The shutter rattled more loudly, unfastened, and commenced slamming against the window. Then the glass broke shiveringly under the persistent impacts, and the chill wind rushed in, making the candles sputter and rustling the sheets of paper on the table where Zann had begun to write out his horrible secret. I looked at Zann, and saw that he was past conscious observation. His blue eyes were bulging, glassy and sightless, and the frantic playing had become a blind, mechanical, unrecognizable orgy that no pen could even suggest.

A sudden gust, stronger than the others, caught up the manuscript and bore it toward the window. I followed the flying sheets in desperation, but they were gone before I reached the demolished panes. Then I remembered my old wish to gaze from this window, the only window in the Rue d'Auseil from which one might see the slope beyond the wall, and the city outspread beneath. It was very dark, but the city's lights always burned, and I expected to see them there amidst the rain and wind. Yet when I looked from that highest of all gable windows, looked while the candles sputtered and the insane viol howled with the night-wind, I saw no city spread below, and no friendly lights gleamed from remembered streets, but only the blackness of space illimitable; unimagined space alive with motion and music, and having no semblance of anything on earth. And as I stood there looking in terror, the wind blew out both the candles in that ancient peaked garret, leaving me in savage and impenetrable darkness with chaos and pandemonium before me, and the demon madness of that night-baying viol behind me.

I staggered back in the dark, without the means of striking a light, crashing against the table, overturning a chair, and finally groping my way to the place where the blackness screamed with shocking music. To save myself and Erich Zann I could at least try, whatever the powers opposed to me. Once I thought some chill thing brushed me, and I screamed, but my scream could not be heard above that hideous viol. Suddenly out of the blackness the madly sawing bow struck me, and I knew I was close to the player. I felt ahead, touched the back of Zann's chair, and then found and shook his shoulder in an effort to bring him to his senses.

He did not respond, and still the viol shrieked on without slackening. I moved my hand to his head, whose mechanical nodding I was able to stop, and shouted in his ear that we must both flee from the unknown things of the night. But he neither answered me nor abated the frenzy of his unutterable music, while all through the garret strange currents of wind seemed to dance in the darkness and babel. When my hand touched his ear I shuddered, though I knew not why—knew not why till I felt the still face; the ice-cold, stiffened, unbreathing face whose glassy eyes bulged uselessly into the void. And then, by some miracle, finding the door and the large wooden bolt, I plunged wildly away from that glassy-eyed thing in the dark, and from the ghoulish howling of that accursed viol whose fury increased even as I plunged.

Leaping, floating, flying down those endless stairs through the dark house; racing mindlessly out into the narrow, steep, and ancient street of steps and tottering houses; clattering down steps and over cobbles to the lower streets and the putrid canyon-walled river; panting across the great dark bridge to the broader, healthier streets and boulevards we know; all these are terrible impressions that linger with me. And I recall that there was no wind, and that the moon was out, and that all the lights of the city twinkled.

Despite my most careful searches and investigations, I have never since been able to find the Rue d'Auseil. But I am not wholly sorry; either for this or for the loss in undreamable abysses of the closely-written sheets which alone could have explained the music of Erich Zann.

*– H. P. Lovecraft*

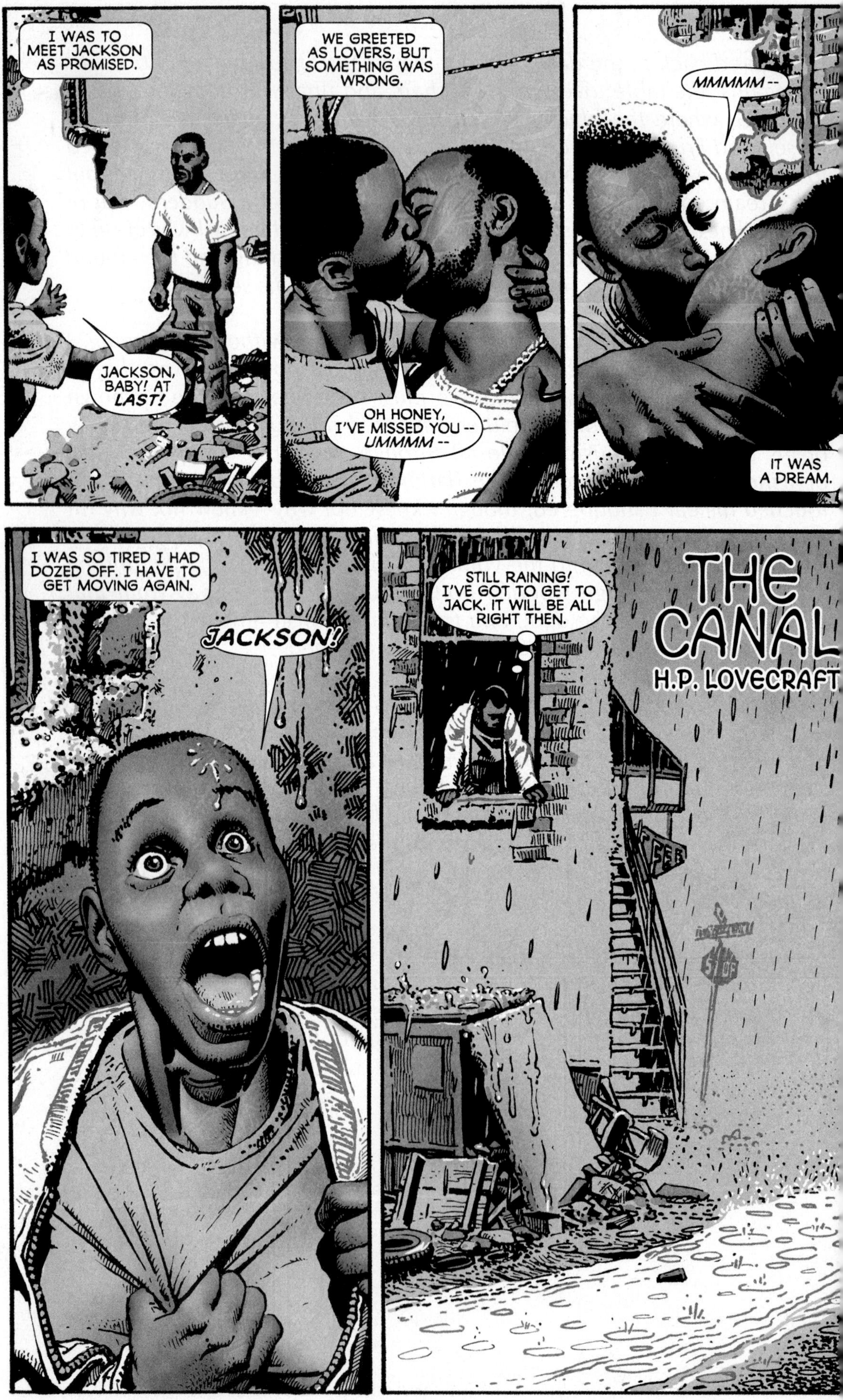
I WAS TO MEET JACKSON AS PROMISED.
JACKSON, BABY! AT LAST!
WE GREETED AS LOVERS, BUT SOMETHING WAS WRONG.
OH HONEY, I'VE MISSED YOU -- UMMMM --
MMMMM --
IT WAS A DREAM.
I WAS SO TIRED I HAD DOZED OFF. I HAVE TO GET MOVING AGAIN.
JACKSON!
STILL RAINING! I'VE GOT TO GET TO JACK. IT WILL BE ALL RIGHT THEN.
THE CANAL
H.P. LOVECRAFT
STOP

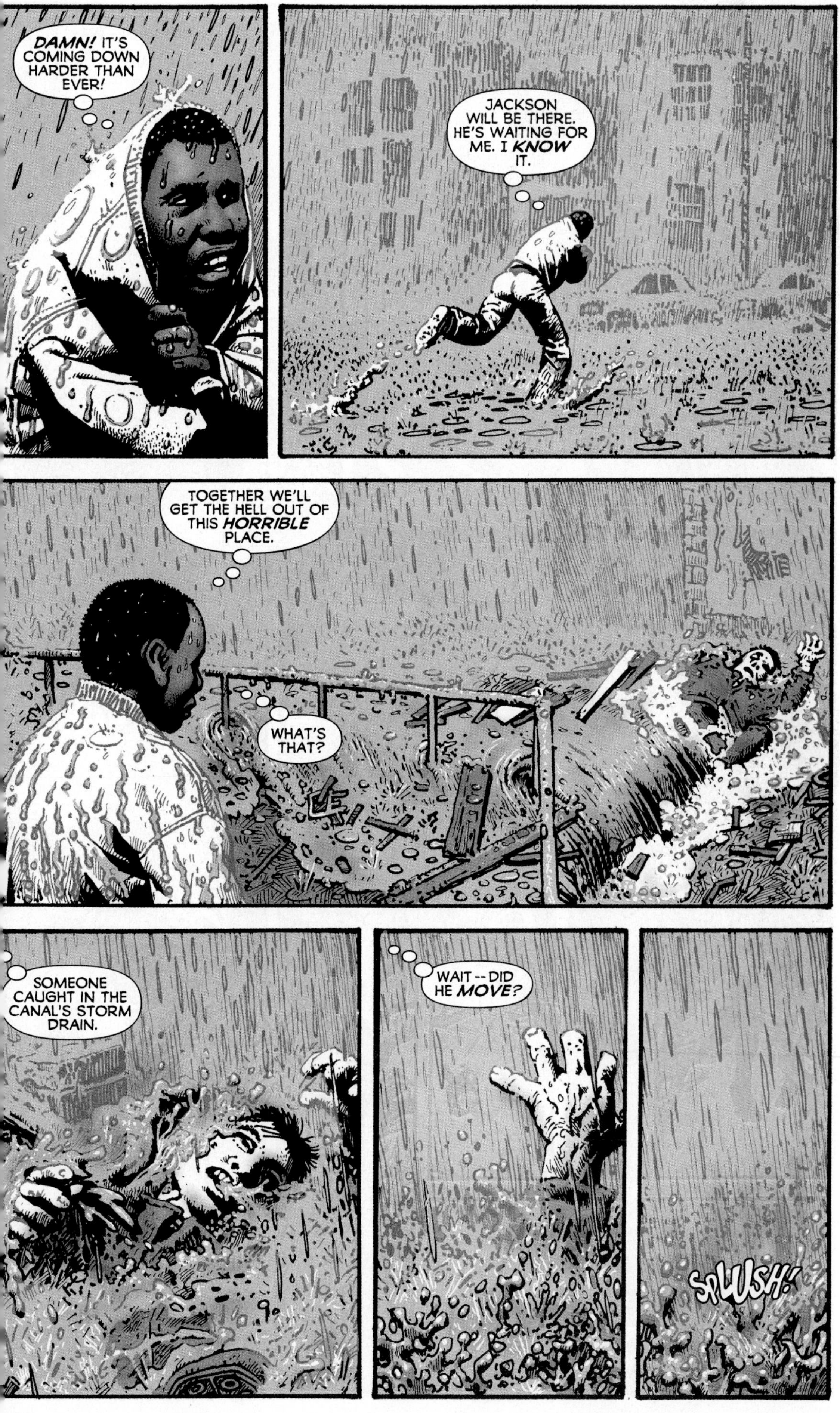
DAMN! IT'S COMING DOWN HARDER THAN EVER!
JACKSON WILL BE THERE. HE'S WAITING FOR ME. I KNOW IT.
TOGETHER WE'LL GET THE HELL OUT OF THIS HORRIBLE PLACE.
WHAT'S THAT?
SOMEONE CAUGHT IN THE CANAL'S STORM DRAIN.
WAIT -- DID HE MOVE?
SPLUSH!

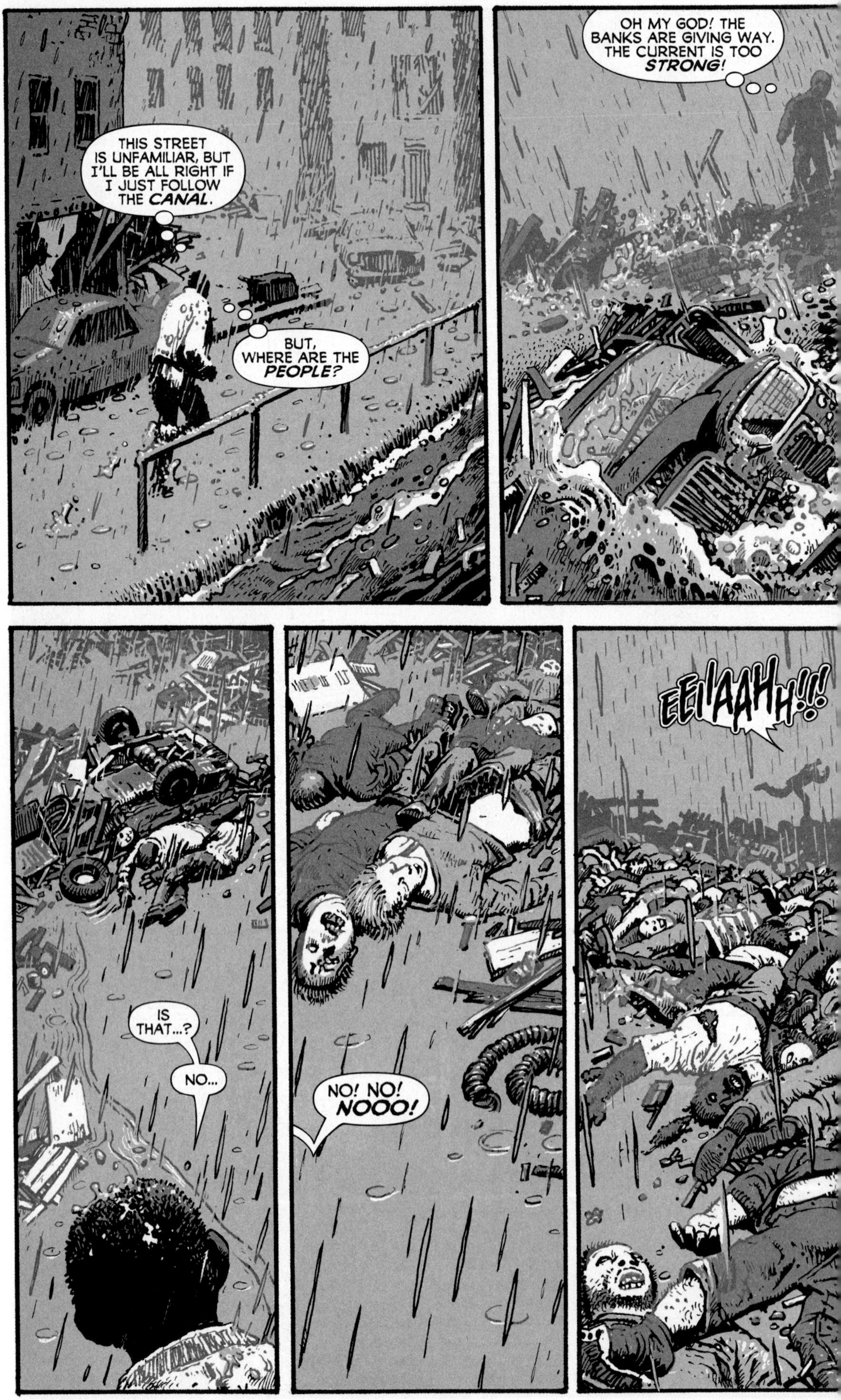
THIS STREET IS UNFAMILIAR, BUT I'LL BE ALL RIGHT IF I JUST FOLLOW THE *CANAL*.
BUT, WHERE ARE THE *PEOPLE?*
OH MY GOD! THE BANKS ARE GIVING WAY. THE CURRENT IS TOO *STRONG!*
IS THAT...?
NO...
NO! NO! *NOOO!*
EEIAAHH!!!

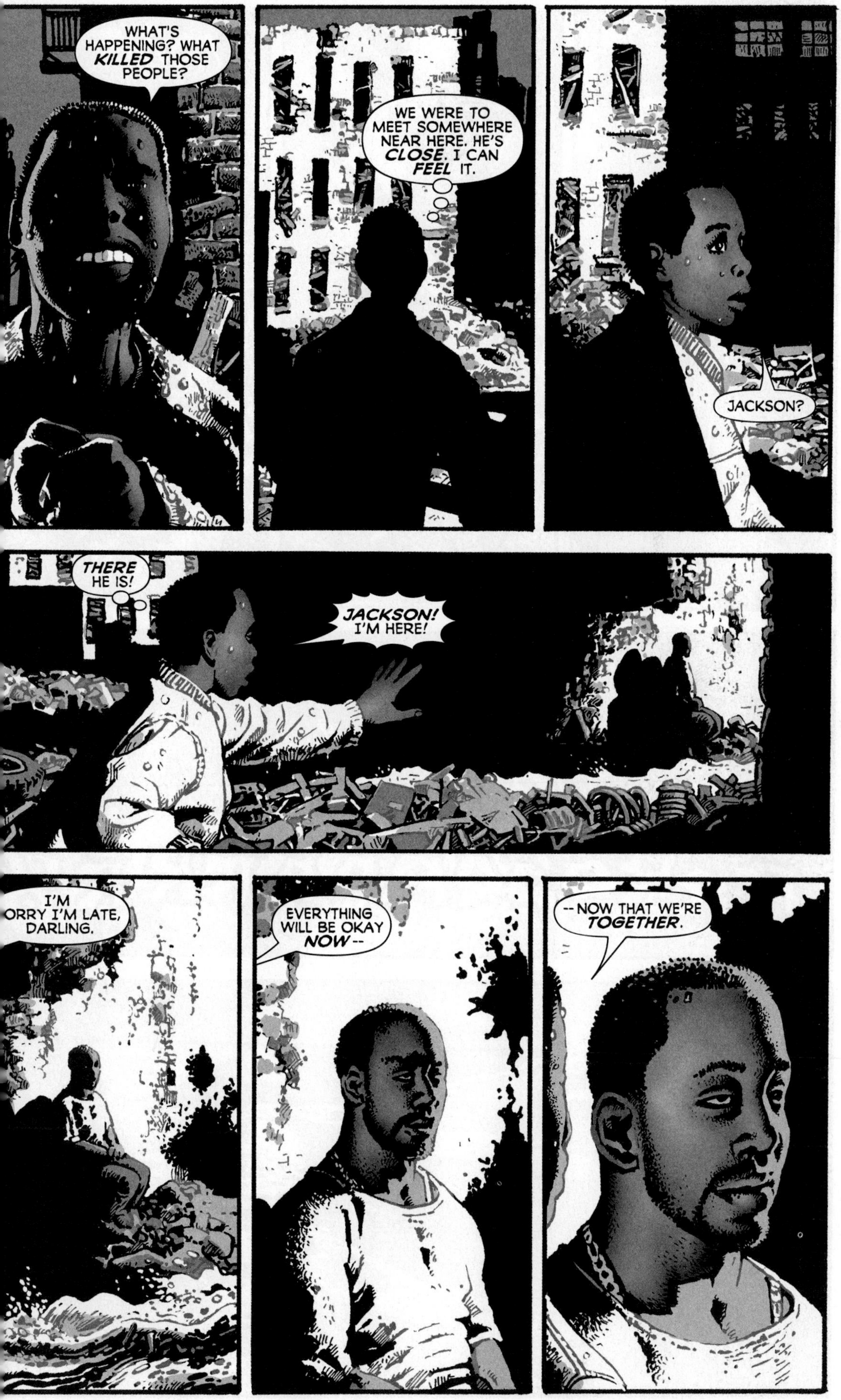
WHAT'S HAPPENING? WHAT KILLED THOSE PEOPLE?
WE WERE TO MEET SOMEWHERE NEAR HERE. HE'S CLOSE. I CAN FEEL IT.
JACKSON?
THERE HE IS!
JACKSON! I'M HERE!
I'M ORRY I'M LATE, DARLING.
EVERYTHING WILL BE OKAY NOW--
--NOW THAT WE'RE TOGETHER.

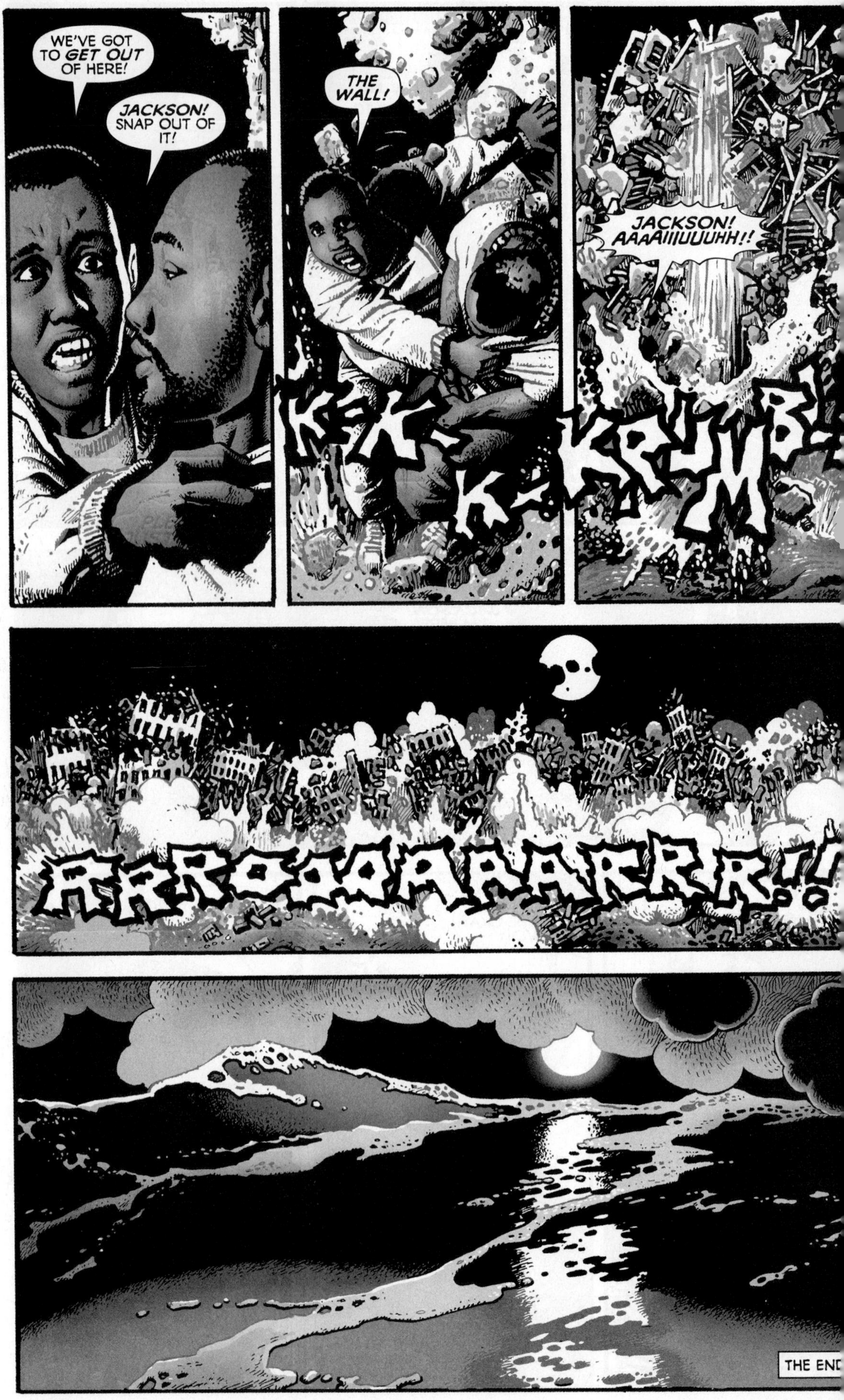
WE'VE GOT TO *GET OUT* OF HERE!
*JACKSON!* SNAP OUT OF IT!
*THE WALL!*
JACKSON! AAAAIIIIUUUHH!!
KRK-KRAKRUMBLM
RRROOOARARRR!!
THE END

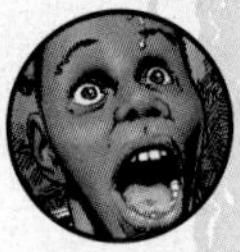

# The Canal (from "Fungi from Yuggoth")

Somewhere in dream there is an evil place
Where tall, deserted buildings crowd along
A deep, black, narrow channel, reeking strong
Of frightful things whence oily currents race.
Lanes with old walls half meeting overhead
Wind off to streets one may or may not know,
And feeble moonlight sheds a spectral glow
Over long rows of windows, dark and dead.
There are no footfalls, and the one soft sound
Is of the oily water as it glides
Under stone bridges, and along the sides
Of its deep flume, to some vague ocean bound.
None lives to tell when that stream washed away
Its dream-lost region from the world of clay.

*– H. P. Lovecraft*

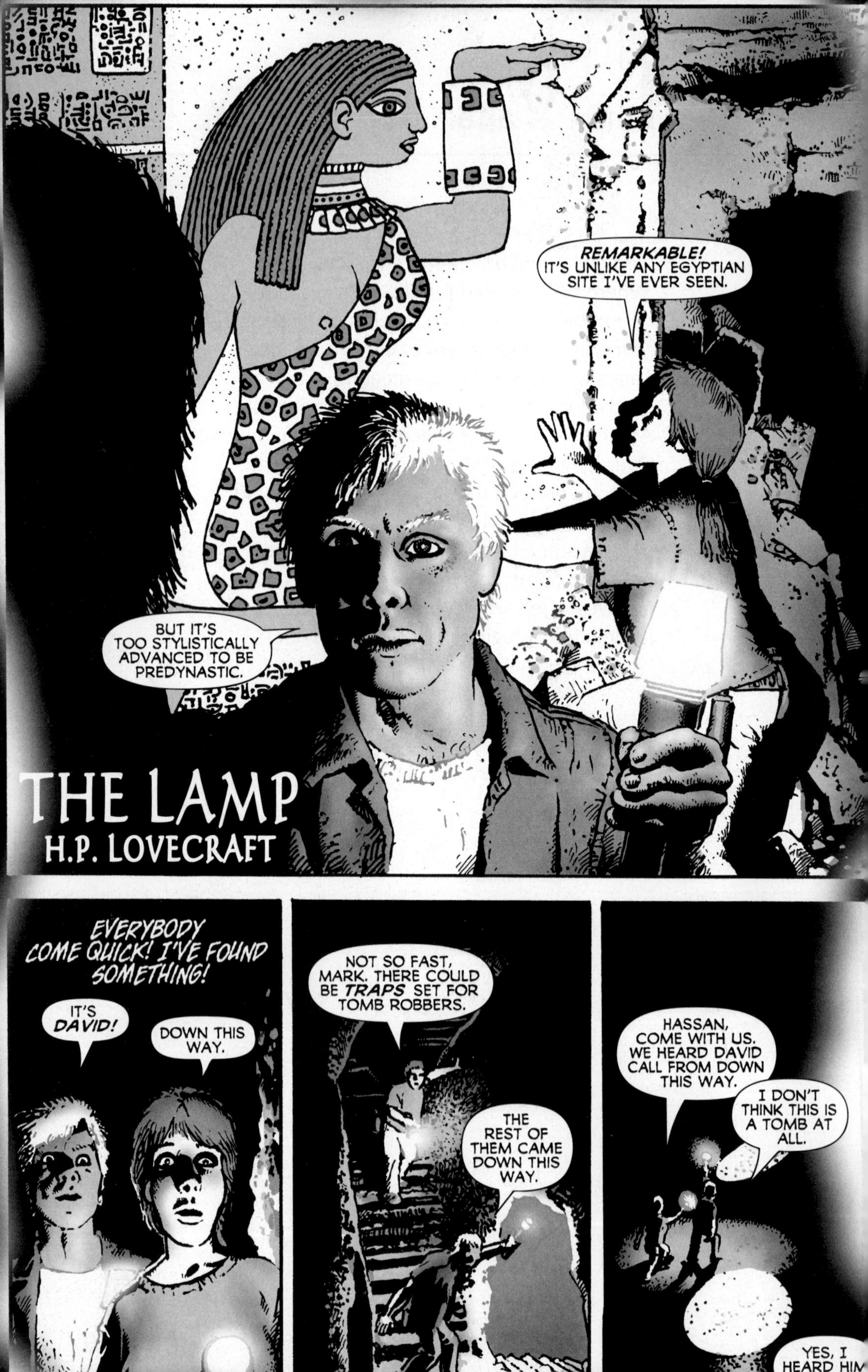
REMARKABLE! IT'S UNLIKE ANY EGYPTIAN SITE I'VE EVER SEEN.
BUT IT'S TOO STYLISTICALLY ADVANCED TO BE PREDYNASTIC.
THE LAMP
H.P. LOVECRAFT
EVERYBODY COME QUICK! I'VE FOUND SOMETHING!
IT'S DAVID!
DOWN THIS WAY.
NOT SO FAST, MARK. THERE COULD BE TRAPS SET FOR TOMB ROBBERS.
THE REST OF THEM CAME DOWN THIS WAY.
HASSAN, COME WITH US. WE HEARD DAVID CALL FROM DOWN THIS WAY.
I DON'T THINK THIS IS A TOMB AT ALL.
YES, I HEARD HIM ALSO.

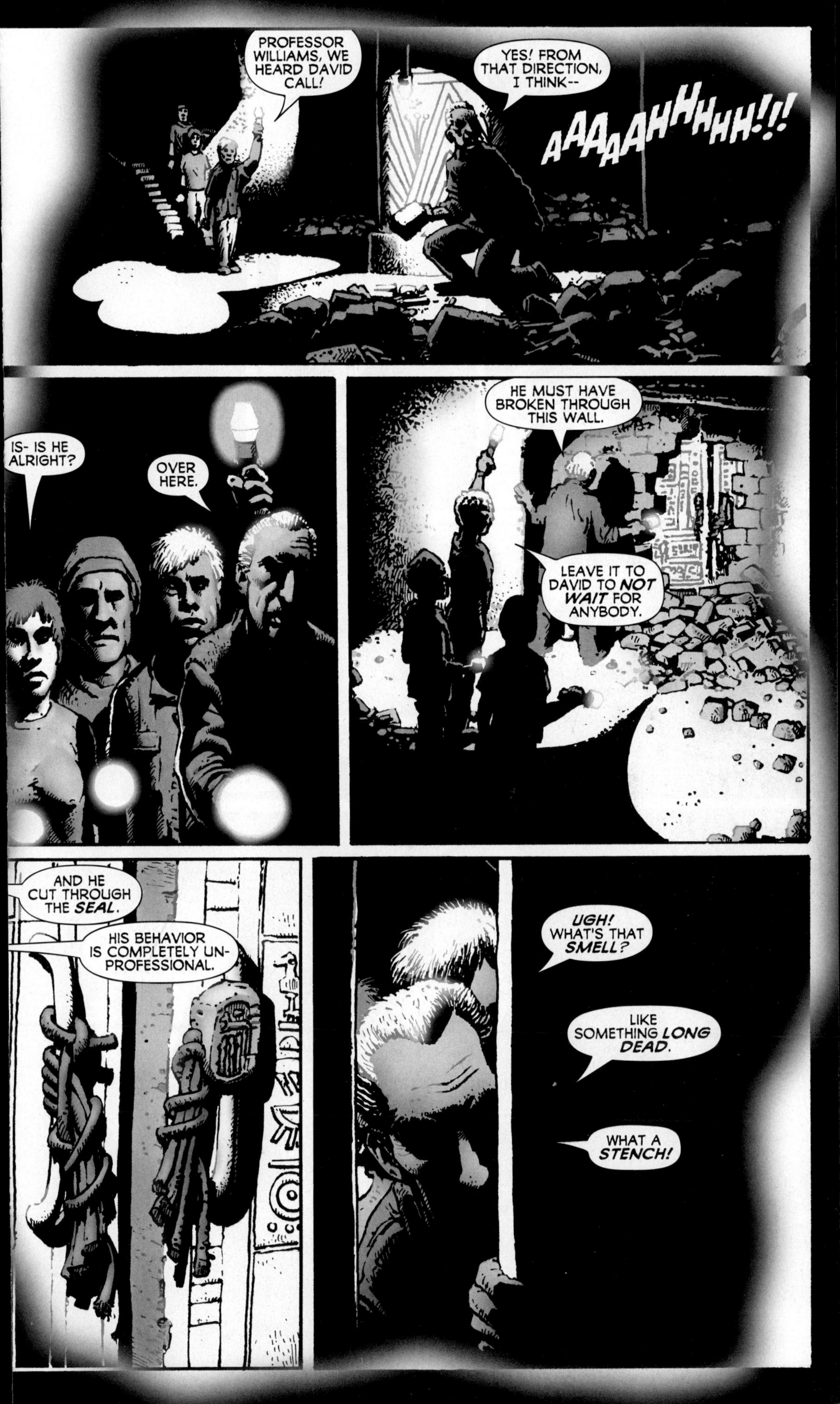
PROFESSOR WILLIAMS, WE HEARD DAVID CALL!
YES! FROM THAT DIRECTION, I THINK--
AAAAAHHHHHH!!!
IS- IS HE ALRIGHT?
OVER HERE.
HE MUST HAVE BROKEN THROUGH THIS WALL.
LEAVE IT TO DAVID TO NOT WAIT FOR ANYBODY.
AND HE CUT THROUGH THE SEAL.
HIS BEHAVIOR IS COMPLETELY UN-PROFESSIONAL.
UGH! WHAT'S THAT SMELL?
LIKE SOMETHING LONG DEAD.
WHAT A STENCH!

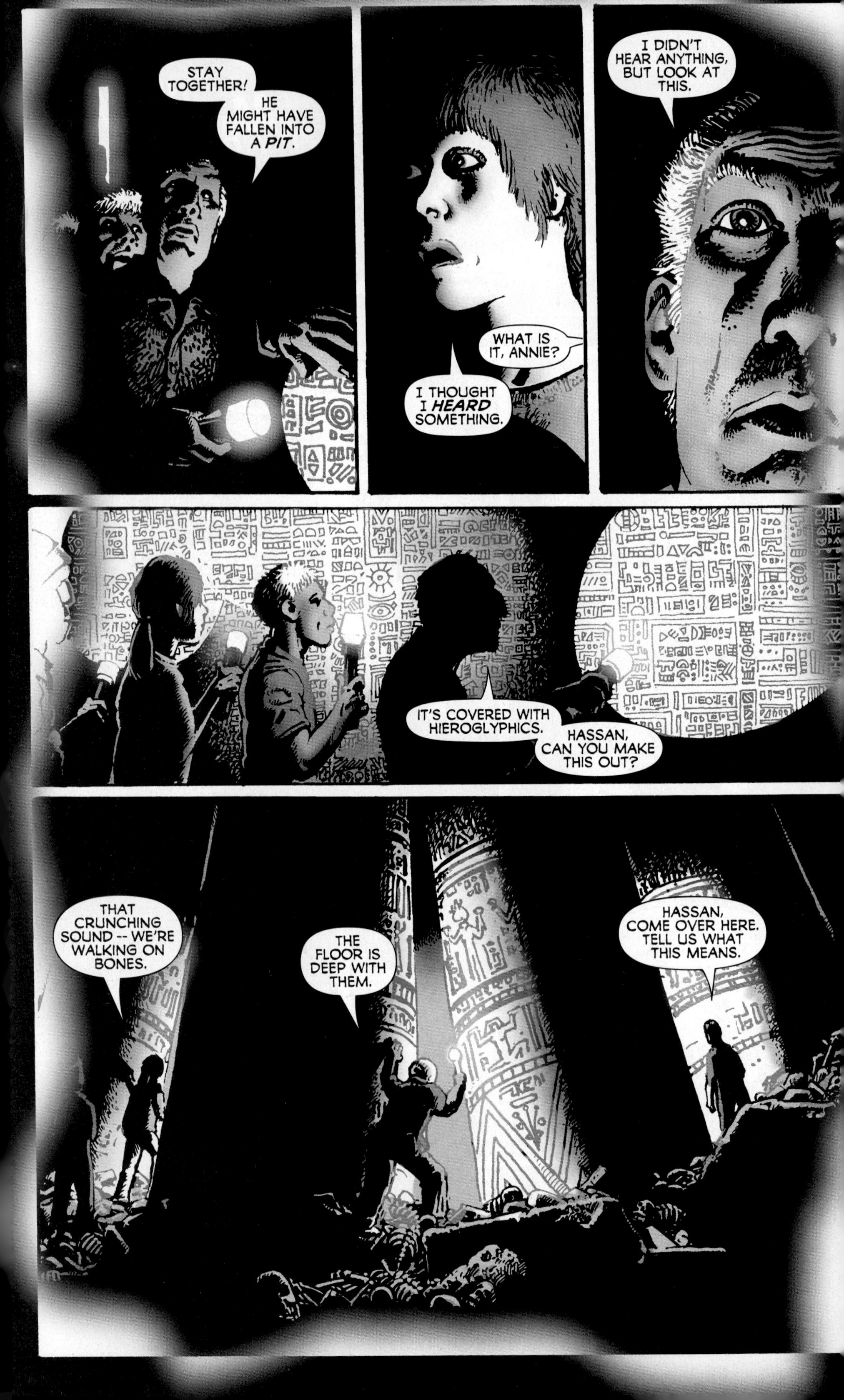
STAY TOGETHER!
HE MIGHT HAVE FALLEN INTO A *PIT*.
WHAT IS IT, ANNIE?
I THOUGHT I ***HEARD*** SOMETHING.
I DIDN'T HEAR ANYTHING, BUT LOOK AT THIS.
IT'S COVERED WITH HIEROGLYPHICS.
HASSAN, CAN YOU MAKE THIS OUT?
THAT CRUNCHING SOUND -- WE'RE WALKING ON BONES.
THE FLOOR IS DEEP WITH THEM.
HASSAN, COME OVER HERE. TELL US WHAT THIS MEANS.

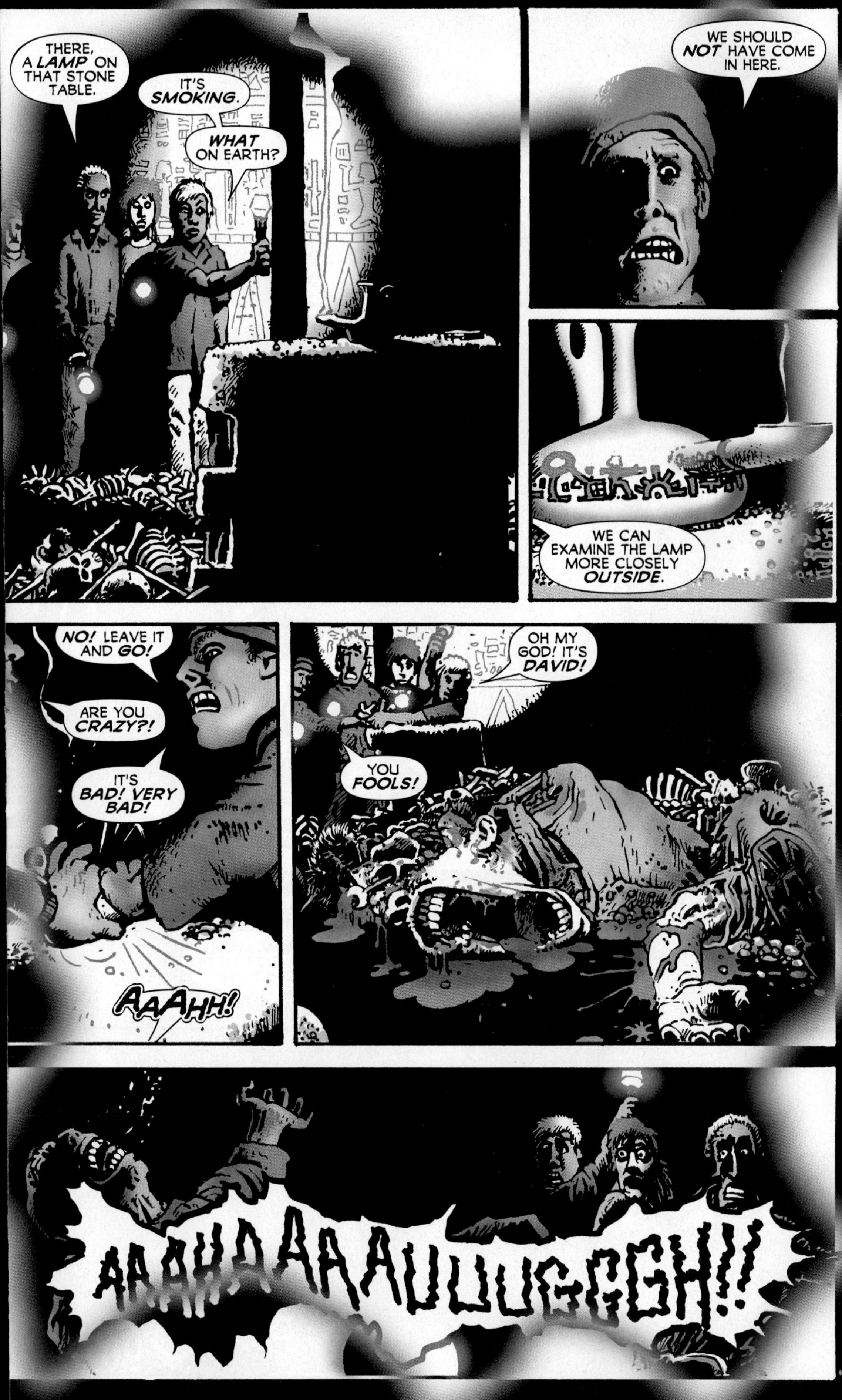

THERE, A LAMP ON THAT STONE TABLE.
IT'S SMOKING.
WHAT ON EARTH?
WE SHOULD NOT HAVE COME IN HERE.
WE CAN EXAMINE THE LAMP MORE CLOSELY OUTSIDE.
NO! LEAVE IT AND GO!
ARE YOU CRAZY?!
IT'S BAD! VERY BAD!
AAAHH!
OH MY GOD! IT'S DAVID!
YOU FOOLS!
AAAHAAAAUUUGGGH!!

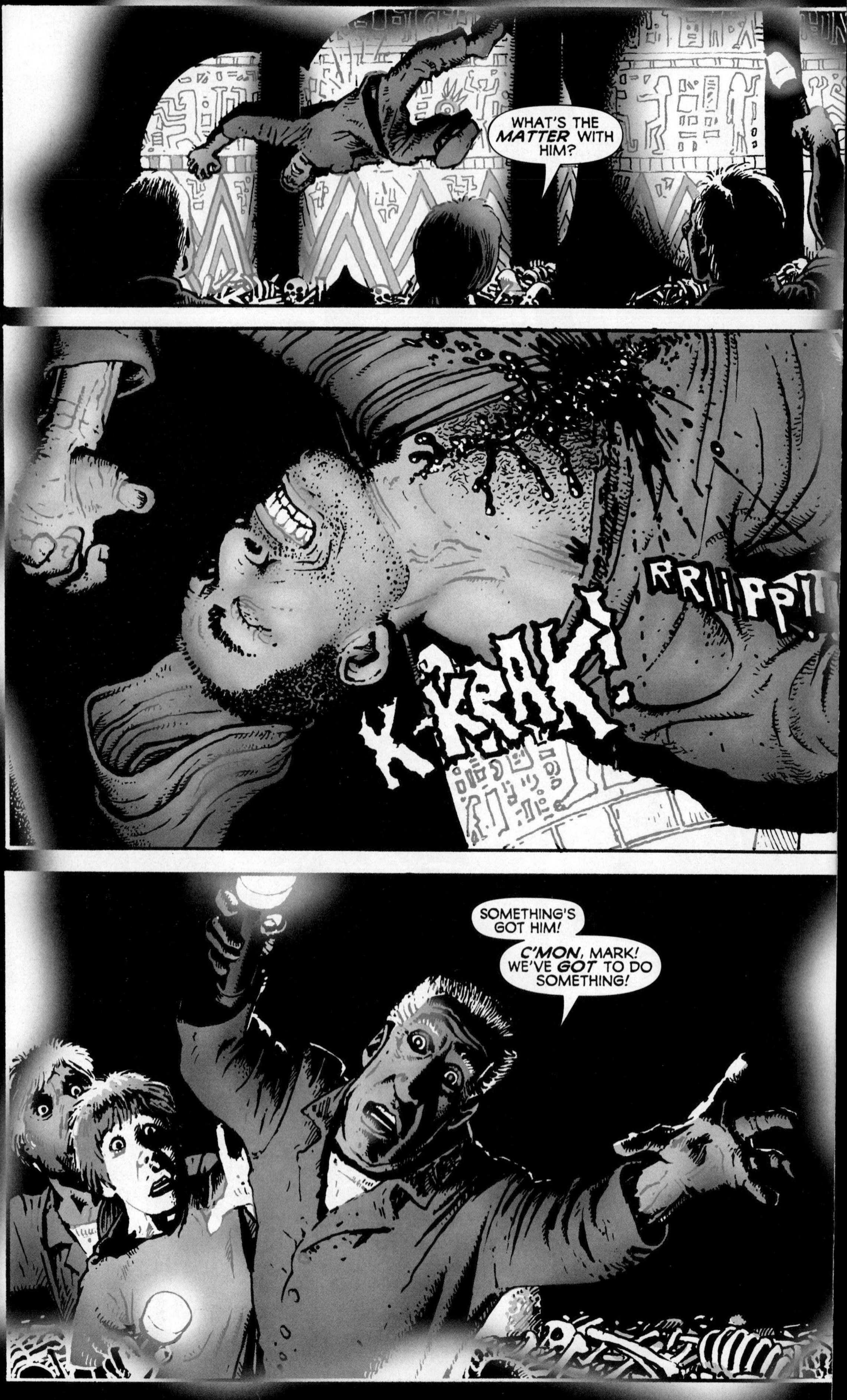
WHAT'S THE *MATTER* WITH HIM?
RRIIPPP!
K-KRAK!
SOMETHING'S GOT HIM!
*C'MON*, MARK! WE'VE *GOT* TO DO SOMETHING!

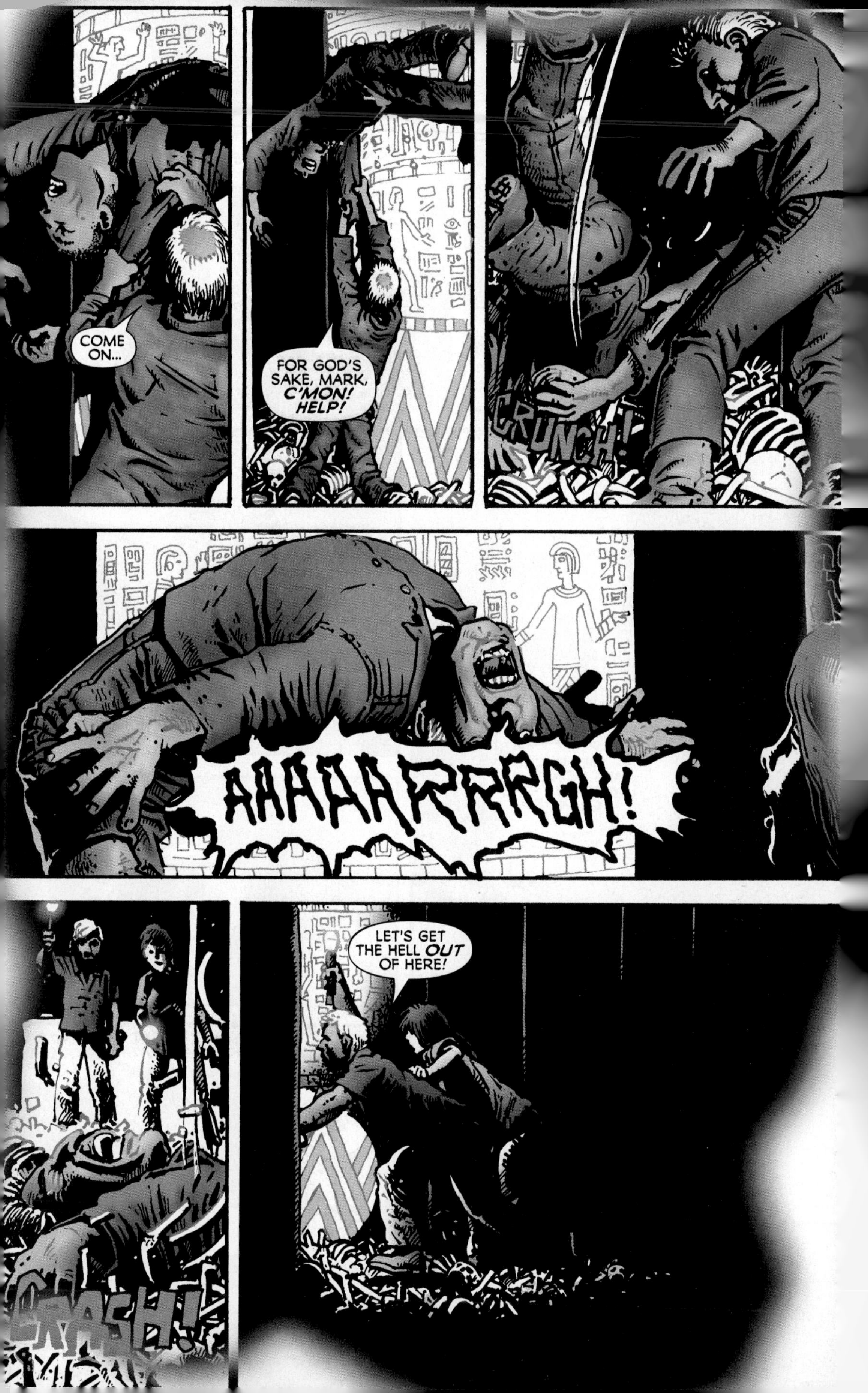
COME ON...
FOR GOD'S SAKE, MARK, C'MON! HELP!
CRUNCH!
AAAAARRRGH!
CRASH!
LET'S GET THE HELL OUT OF HERE!

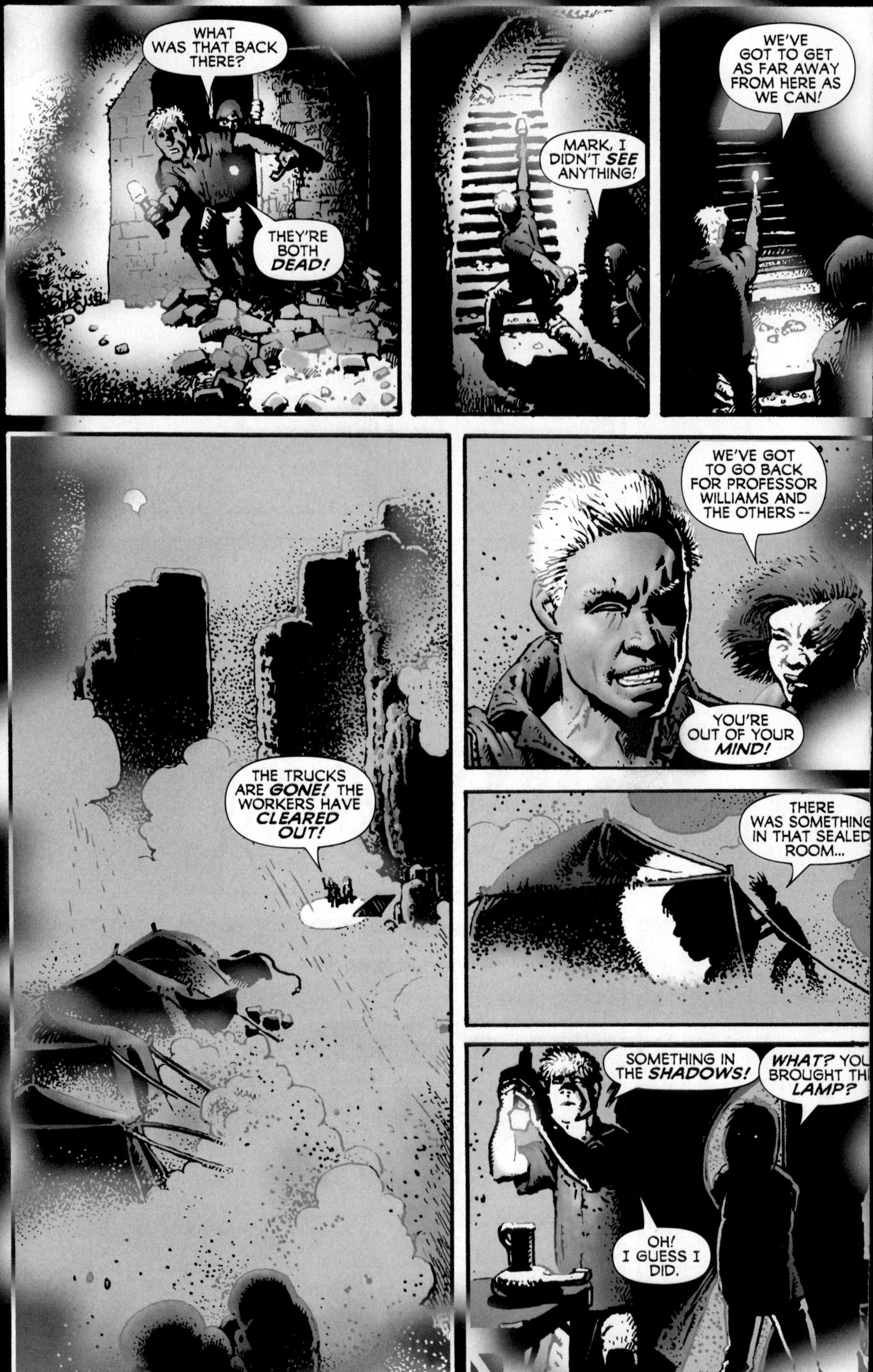

WHAT WAS THAT BACK THERE?
THEY'RE BOTH *DEAD!*
MARK, I DIDN'T *SEE* ANYTHING!
WE'VE GOT TO GET AS FAR AWAY FROM HERE AS WE CAN!
THE TRUCKS ARE *GONE!* THE WORKERS HAVE *CLEARED OUT!*
WE'VE GOT TO GO BACK FOR PROFESSOR WILLIAMS AND THE OTHERS --
YOU'RE OUT OF YOUR *MIND!*
THERE WAS SOMETHING IN THAT SEALED ROOM...
SOMETHING IN THE *SHADOWS!*
*WHAT?* YOU BROUGHT THE *LAMP?*
OH! I GUESS I DID.

THE HIEROGLYPHICS WARNED OF IT, BUT WE COULDN'T READ THEM!

BUT THE TOMB WAS CLOSED FOR OVER *FOUR THOUSAND YEARS!* HOW COULD ANYTHING BE *ALIVE* IN THERE?

I'M GOING TO TEST THE OIL AND *LIGHT* IT.

*NO!* WE'VE GOT TO RADIO FOR *HELP!*

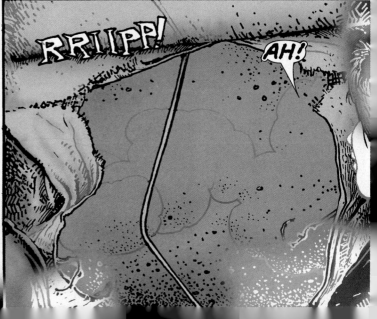

RRIIPP!

AH!

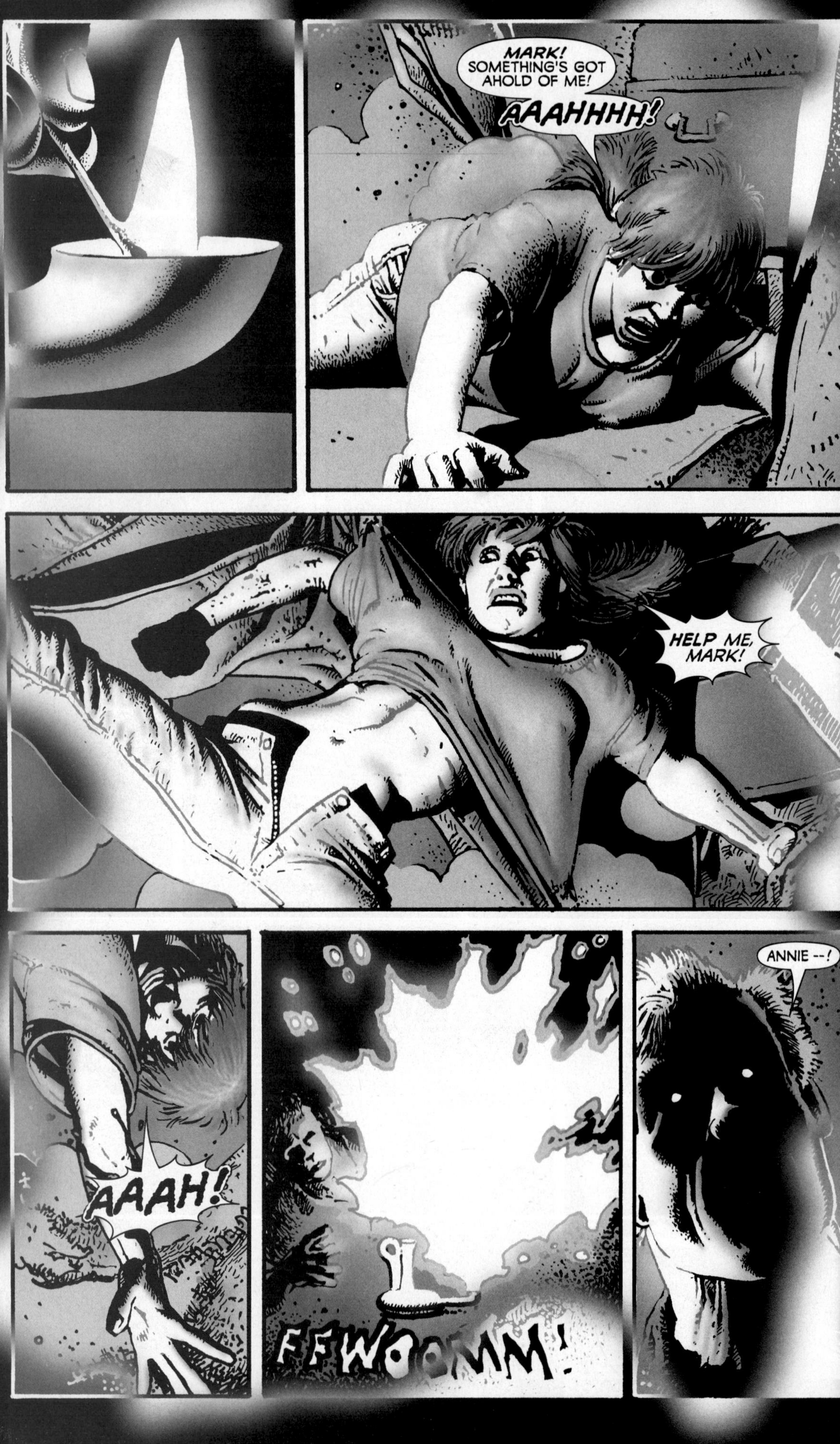
MARK! SOMETHING'S GOT AHOLD OF ME!
AAAHHHH!
HELP ME, MARK!
AAAH!
FFWOOMM!
ANNIE --!

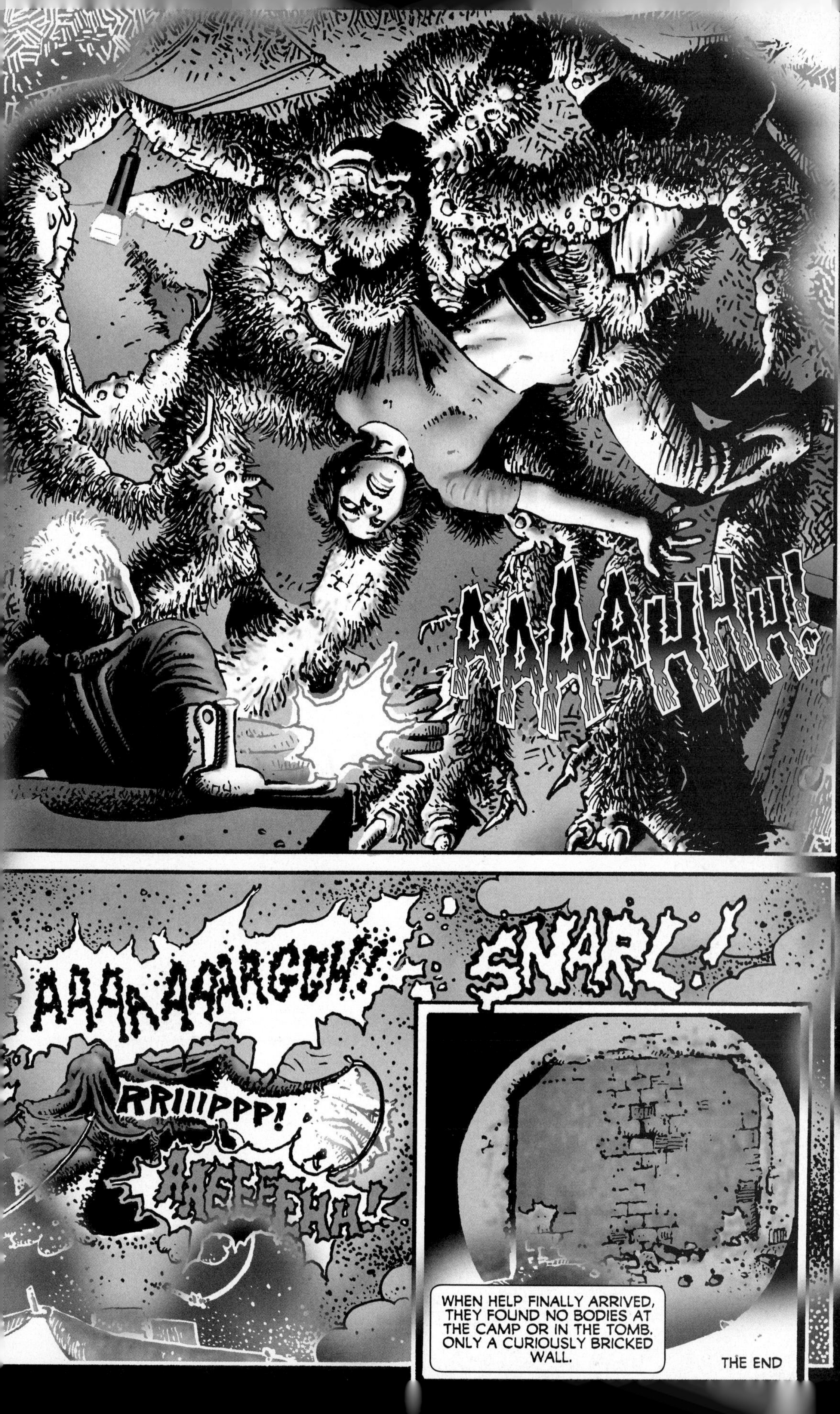
AAAAHHH!
AAAAAAARGGH!
SNARL!
RRIIIPPPP!
AHEEEHH!
WHEN HELP FINALLY ARRIVED, THEY FOUND NO BODIES AT THE CAMP OR IN THE TOMB. ONLY A CURIOUSLY BRICKED WALL.
THE END

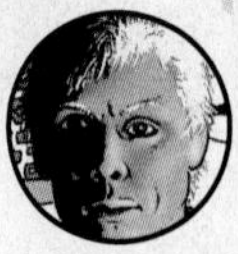

# The Lamp (from "Fungi from Yuggoth")

We found the lamp inside those hollow cliffs
Whose chiseled sign no priest in Thebes could read,
And from whose caverns frightened hieroglyphs
Warned every living creature of earth's breed.
No more was there - just that one brazen bowl
With traces of a curious oil within;
Fretted with some obscurely patterned scroll,
And symbols hinting vaguely of strange sin.
Little the fears of forty centuries meant
To us as we bore off our slender spoil,
And when we scanned it in our darkened tent
We struck a match to test the ancient oil.
It blazed - great God!... But the vast shapes we saw
In that mad flash have seared our lives with awe.

*– H. P. Lovecraft*

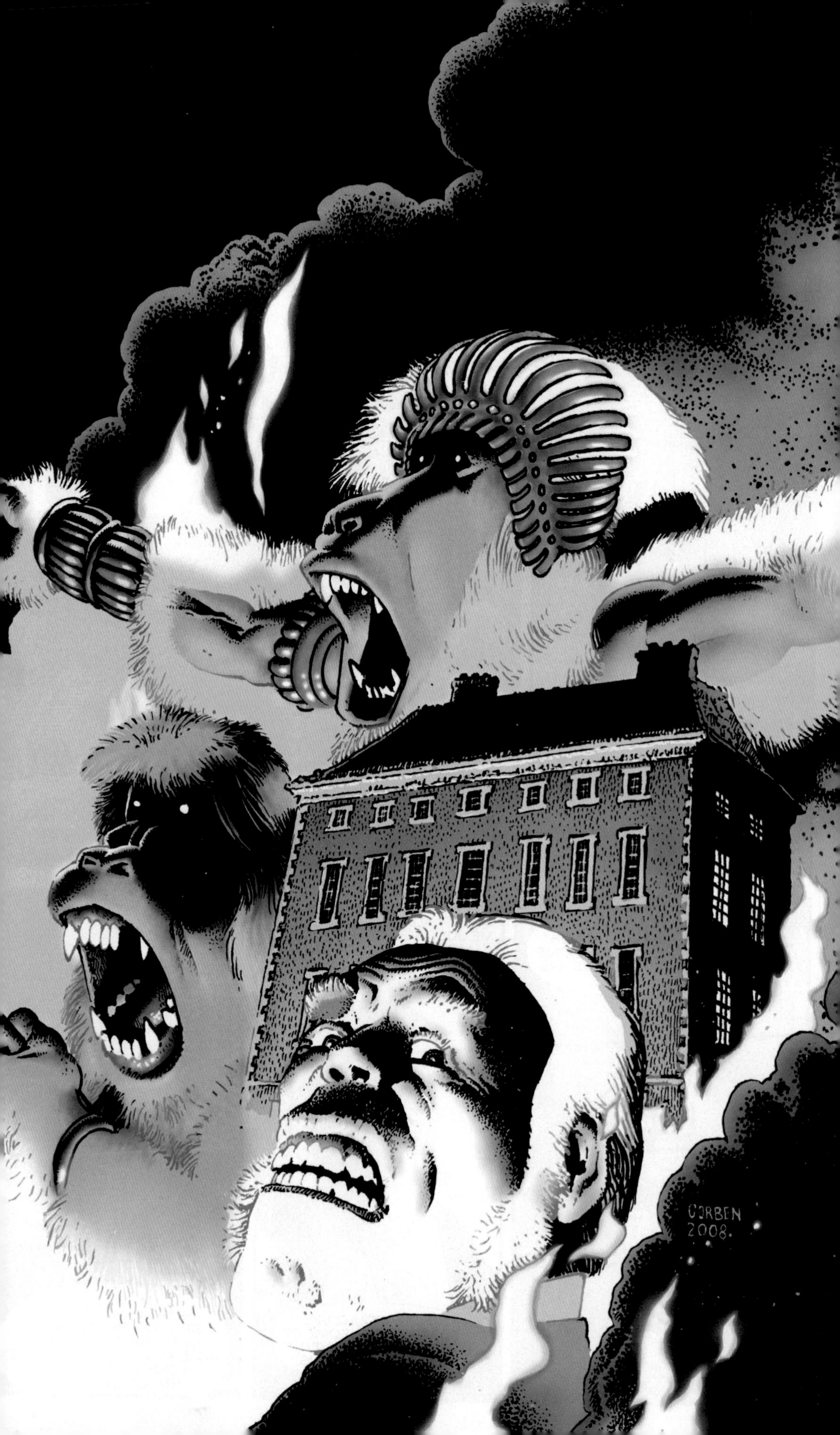
CORBEN
2008.

# Arthur Jermyn

H.P. Lovecraft

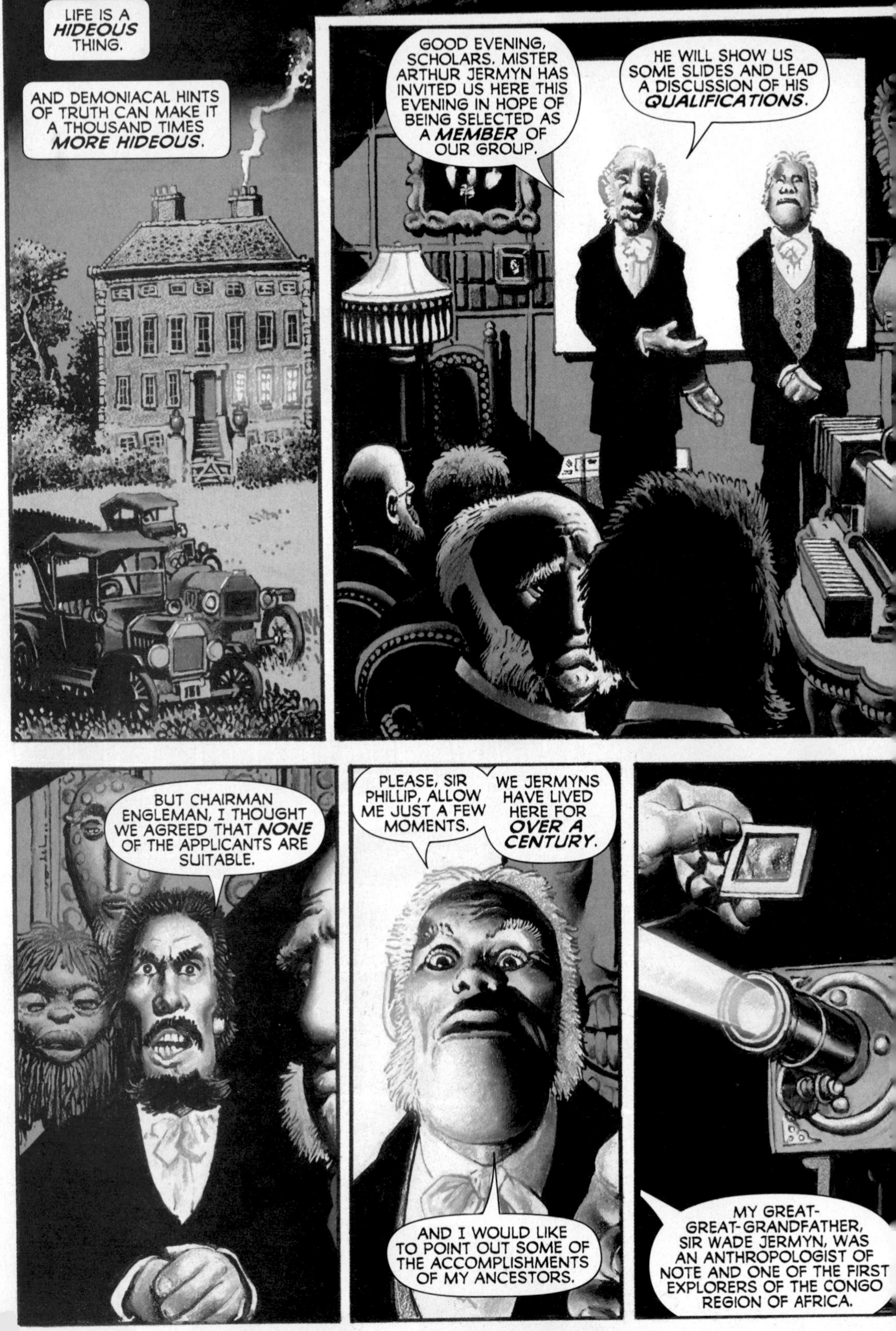

LIFE IS A *HIDEOUS* THING.
AND DEMONIACAL HINTS OF TRUTH CAN MAKE IT A THOUSAND TIMES *MORE HIDEOUS*.
GOOD EVENING, SCHOLARS. MISTER ARTHUR JERMYN HAS INVITED US HERE THIS EVENING IN HOPE OF BEING SELECTED AS A *MEMBER* OF OUR GROUP.
HE WILL SHOW US SOME SLIDES AND LEAD A DISCUSSION OF HIS *QUALIFICATIONS*.
BUT CHAIRMAN ENGLEMAN, I THOUGHT WE AGREED THAT *NONE* OF THE APPLICANTS ARE SUITABLE.
PLEASE, SIR PHILLIP, ALLOW ME JUST A FEW MOMENTS.
WE JERMYNS HAVE LIVED HERE FOR *OVER A CENTURY*.
AND I WOULD LIKE TO POINT OUT SOME OF THE ACCOMPLISHMENTS OF MY ANCESTORS.
MY GREAT-GREAT-GRANDFATHER, SIR WADE JERMYN, WAS AN ANTHROPOLOGIST OF NOTE AND ONE OF THE FIRST EXPLORERS OF THE CONGO REGION OF AFRICA.

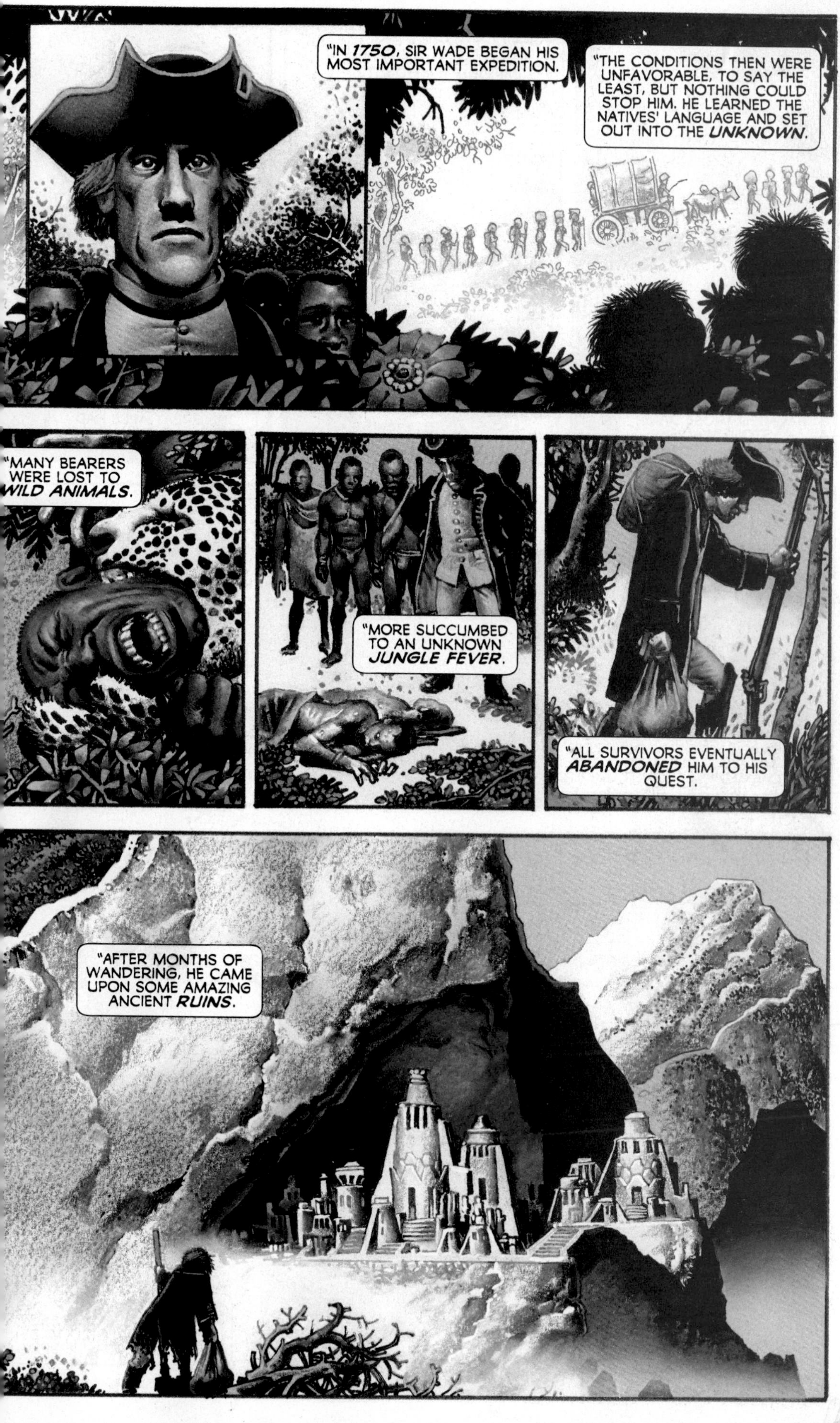
"IN 1750, SIR WADE BEGAN HIS MOST IMPORTANT EXPEDITION.
"THE CONDITIONS THEN WERE UNFAVORABLE, TO SAY THE LEAST, BUT NOTHING COULD STOP HIM. HE LEARNED THE NATIVES' LANGUAGE AND SET OUT INTO THE UNKNOWN.
"MANY BEARERS WERE LOST TO WILD ANIMALS.
"MORE SUCCUMBED TO AN UNKNOWN JUNGLE FEVER.
"ALL SURVIVORS EVENTUALLY ABANDONED HIM TO HIS QUEST.
"AFTER MONTHS OF WANDERING, HE CAME UPON SOME AMAZING ANCIENT RUINS.

"NOTHING COULD HAVE PREPARED HIM FOR THE CONFRONTATION WITH THE LIVING *THINGS* THAT HAUNTED THOSE DAMP STONE WALLS.

"*CREATURES*. HALF OF THE JUNGLE AND HALF OF THE IMPIOUSLY AGED CITY.

"*THINGS* THAT MIGHT HAVE SPRUNG UP AFTER THE GREAT APES HAD OVERRUN THE DYING CITY.

"THE MUSCULAR BRUTES QUICKLY *OVERPOWERED* THE LONE ARISTOCRAT AND CARRIED HIM TO THEIR LEADER...

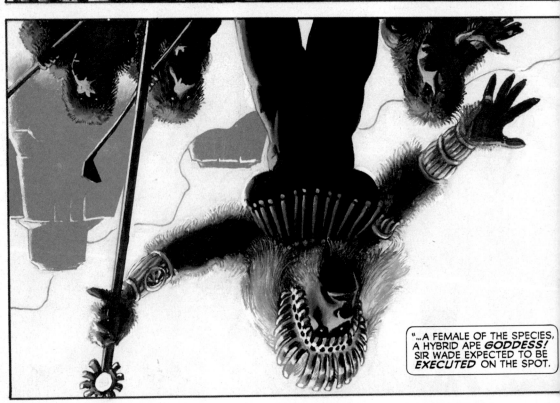

"...A FEMALE OF THE SPECIES, A HYBRID APE *GODDESS!* SIR WADE EXPECTED TO BE *EXECUTED* ON THE SPOT.

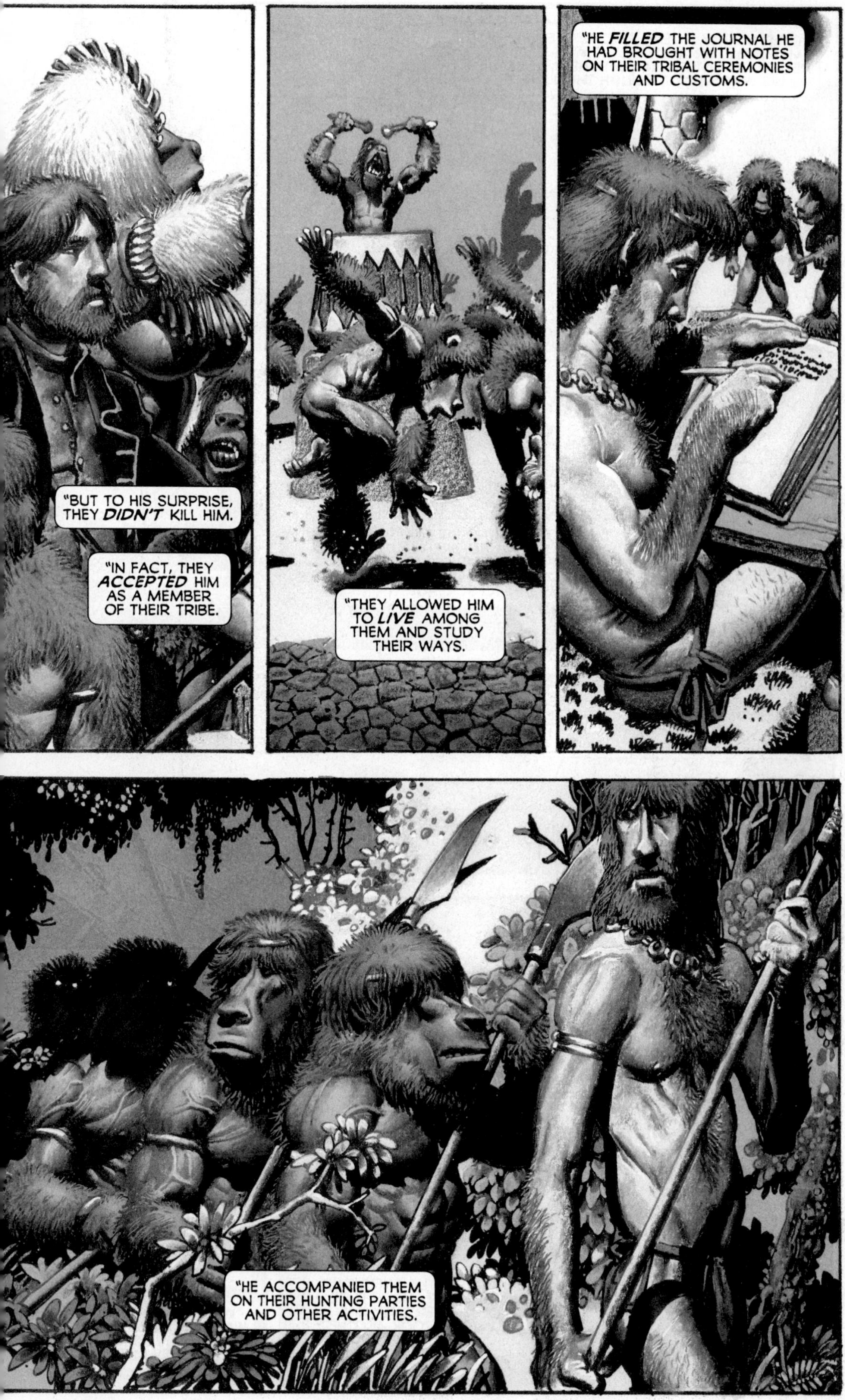
"BUT TO HIS SURPRISE, THEY *DIDN'T* KILL HIM.
"IN FACT, THEY *ACCEPTED* HIM AS A MEMBER OF THEIR TRIBE.
"THEY ALLOWED HIM TO *LIVE* AMONG THEM AND STUDY THEIR WAYS.
"HE *FILLED* THE JOURNAL HE HAD BROUGHT WITH NOTES ON THEIR TRIBAL CEREMONIES AND CUSTOMS.
"HE ACCOMPANIED THEM ON THEIR HUNTING PARTIES AND OTHER ACTIVITIES.

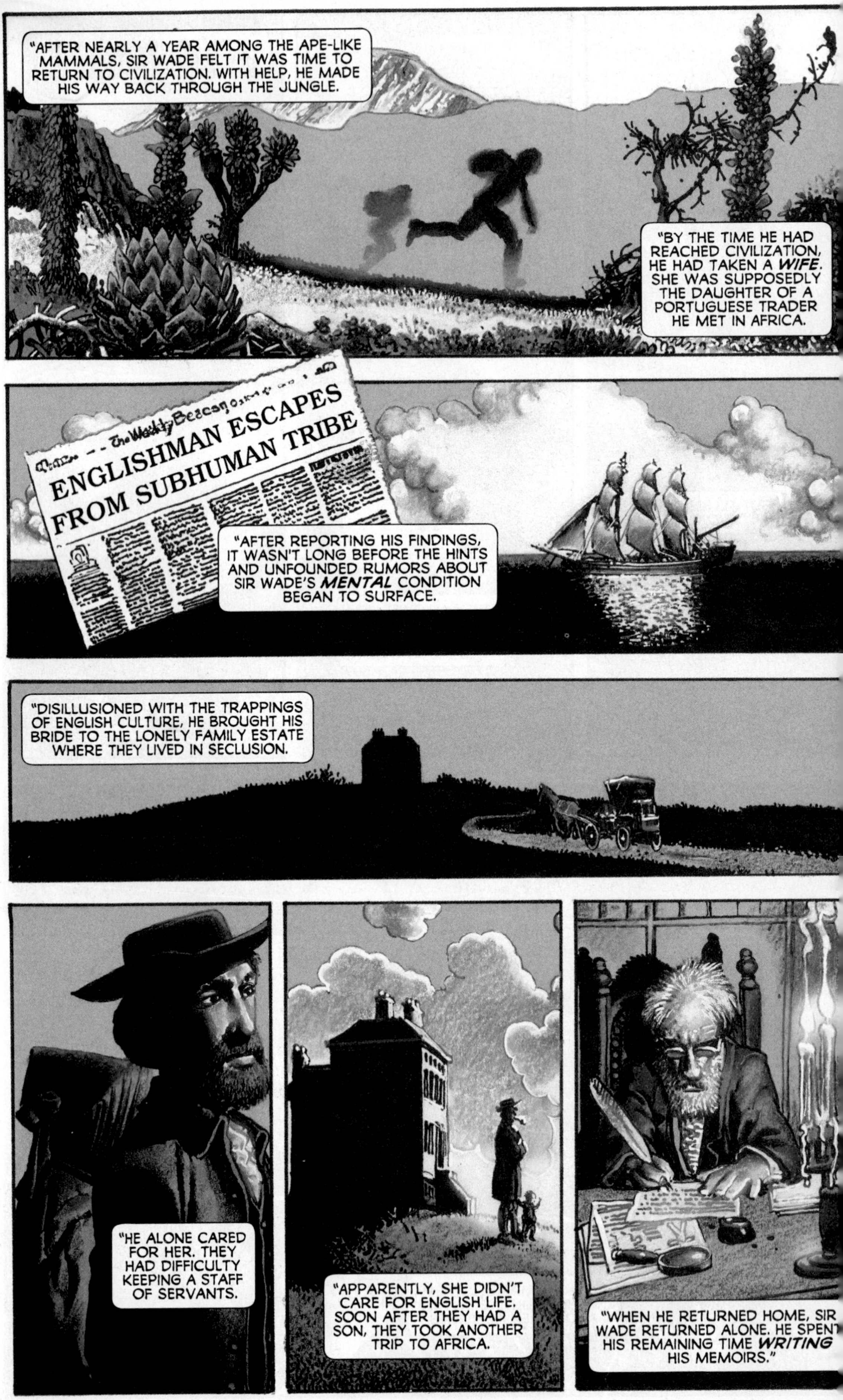
"AFTER NEARLY A YEAR AMONG THE APE-LIKE MAMMALS, SIR WADE FELT IT WAS TIME TO RETURN TO CIVILIZATION. WITH HELP, HE MADE HIS WAY BACK THROUGH THE JUNGLE.
"BY THE TIME HE HAD REACHED CIVILIZATION, HE HAD TAKEN A *WIFE*. SHE WAS SUPPOSEDLY THE DAUGHTER OF A PORTUGUESE TRADER HE MET IN AFRICA.
ENGLISHMAN ESCAPES FROM SUBHUMAN TRIBE
"AFTER REPORTING HIS FINDINGS, IT WASN'T LONG BEFORE THE HINTS AND UNFOUNDED RUMORS ABOUT SIR WADE'S *MENTAL* CONDITION BEGAN TO SURFACE.
"DISILLUSIONED WITH THE TRAPPINGS OF ENGLISH CULTURE, HE BROUGHT HIS BRIDE TO THE LONELY FAMILY ESTATE WHERE THEY LIVED IN SECLUSION.
"HE ALONE CARED FOR HER. THEY HAD DIFFICULTY KEEPING A STAFF OF SERVANTS.
"APPARENTLY, SHE DIDN'T CARE FOR ENGLISH LIFE. SOON AFTER THEY HAD A SON, THEY TOOK ANOTHER TRIP TO AFRICA.
"WHEN HE RETURNED HOME, SIR WADE RETURNED ALONE. HE SPENT HIS REMAINING TIME *WRITING* HIS MEMOIRS."

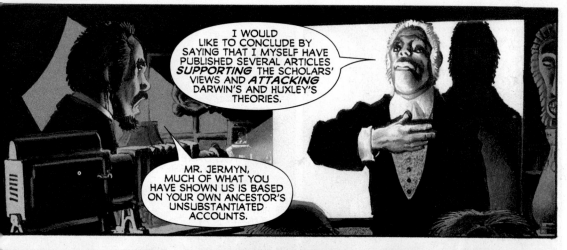

I WOULD LIKE TO CONCLUDE BY SAYING THAT I MYSELF HAVE PUBLISHED SEVERAL ARTICLES *SUPPORTING* THE SCHOLARS' VIEWS AND *ATTACKING* DARWIN'S AND HUXLEY'S THEORIES.

MR. JERMYN, MUCH OF WHAT YOU HAVE SHOWN US IS BASED ON YOUR OWN ANCESTOR'S UNSUBSTANTIATED ACCOUNTS.

YOU'VE CONVENIENTLY *SKIPPED* THE UNSAVORY PART OF THE PUBLIC RECORD.

OF HOW SIR WADE'S WIFE *ABANDONED* HIM IN AFRICA. AND HOW HE WAS COMMITTED TO AN *INSTITUTION* IN HIS LATER YEARS.

AND WHAT ABOUT SIR WADE'S SON, PHILLIP? A BRUTE WHO *RAPED* A WOMAN AND FLED.

"AND PHILLIP'S SON, ROBERT, WHO WENT ON A HOMICIDAL RAMPAGE, *KILLING* SEVERAL MEMBERS OF HIS FAMILY.

"ROBERT'S SON, NEVIL, WAS *MURDERED* BY HIS OWN FATHER."

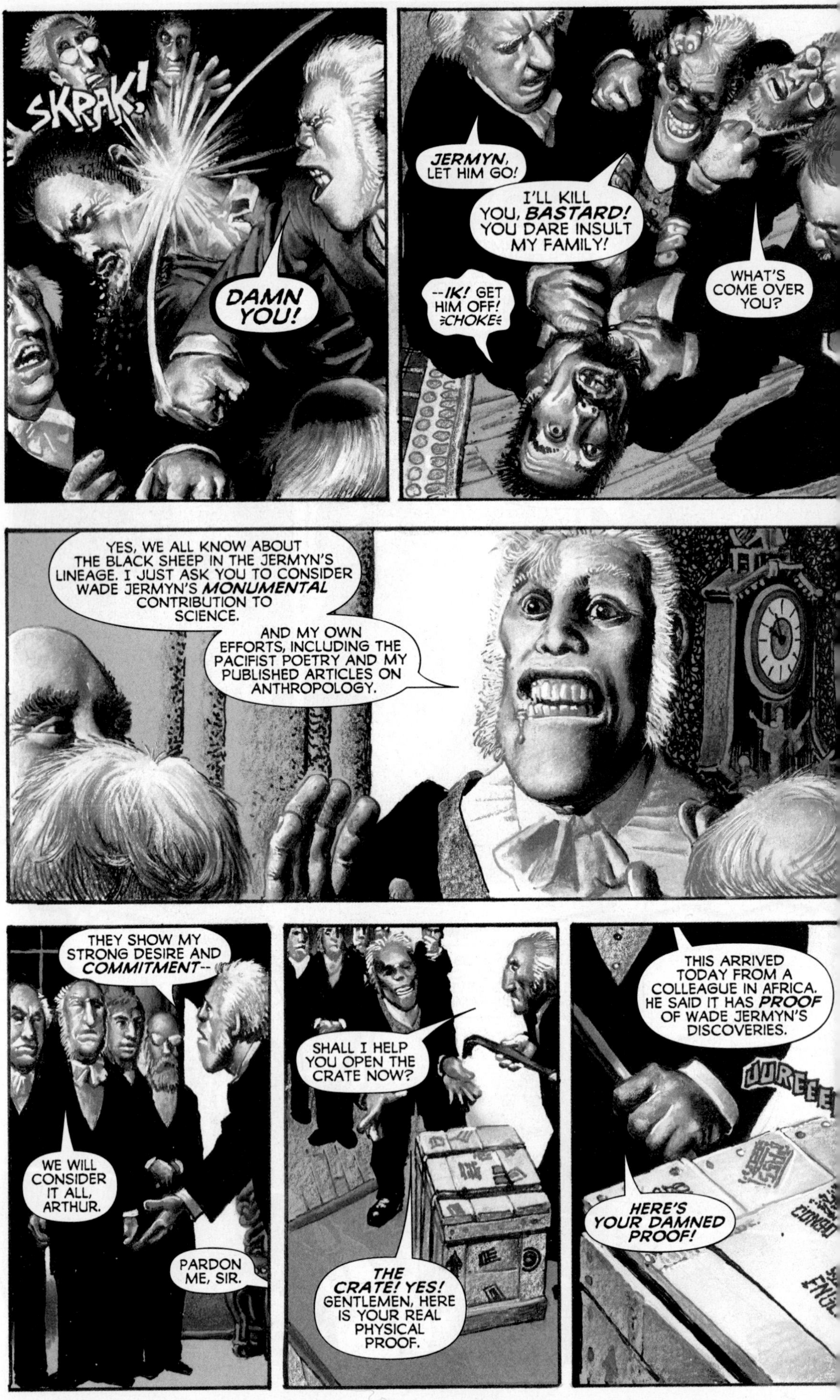
SKRAK!
DAMN YOU!
JERMYN, LET HIM GO!
I'LL KILL YOU, BASTARD! YOU DARE INSULT MY FAMILY!
--IK! GET HIM OFF! CHOKE
WHAT'S COME OVER YOU?
YES, WE ALL KNOW ABOUT THE BLACK SHEEP IN THE JERMYN'S LINEAGE. I JUST ASK YOU TO CONSIDER WADE JERMYN'S MONUMENTAL CONTRIBUTION TO SCIENCE.
AND MY OWN EFFORTS, INCLUDING THE PACIFIST POETRY AND MY PUBLISHED ARTICLES ON ANTHROPOLOGY.
THEY SHOW MY STRONG DESIRE AND COMMITMENT--
WE WILL CONSIDER IT ALL, ARTHUR.
PARDON ME, SIR.
SHALL I HELP YOU OPEN THE CRATE NOW?
THE CRATE! YES! GENTLEMEN, HERE IS YOUR REAL PHYSICAL PROOF.
THIS ARRIVED TODAY FROM A COLLEAGUE IN AFRICA. HE SAID IT HAS PROOF OF WADE JERMYN'S DISCOVERIES.
UREEEE
HERE'S YOUR DAMNED PROOF!

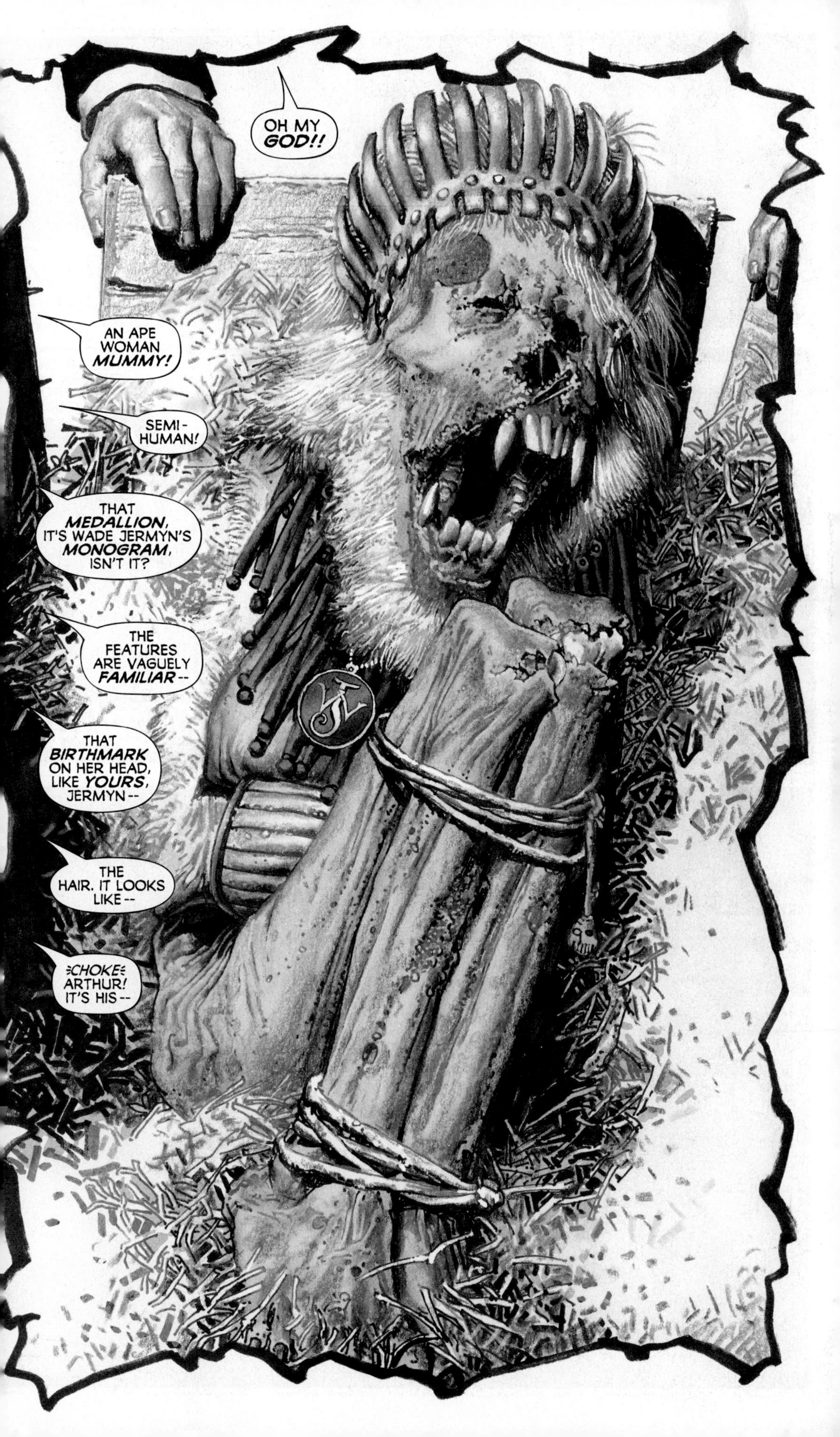
OH MY GOD!!
AN APE WOMAN MUMMY!
SEMI-HUMAN!
THAT MEDALLION, IT'S WADE JERMYN'S MONOGRAM, ISN'T IT?
THE FEATURES ARE VAGUELY FAMILIAR--
THAT BIRTHMARK ON HER HEAD, LIKE YOURS, JERMYN--
THE HAIR. IT LOOKS LIKE--
CHOKE ARTHUR! IT'S HIS--

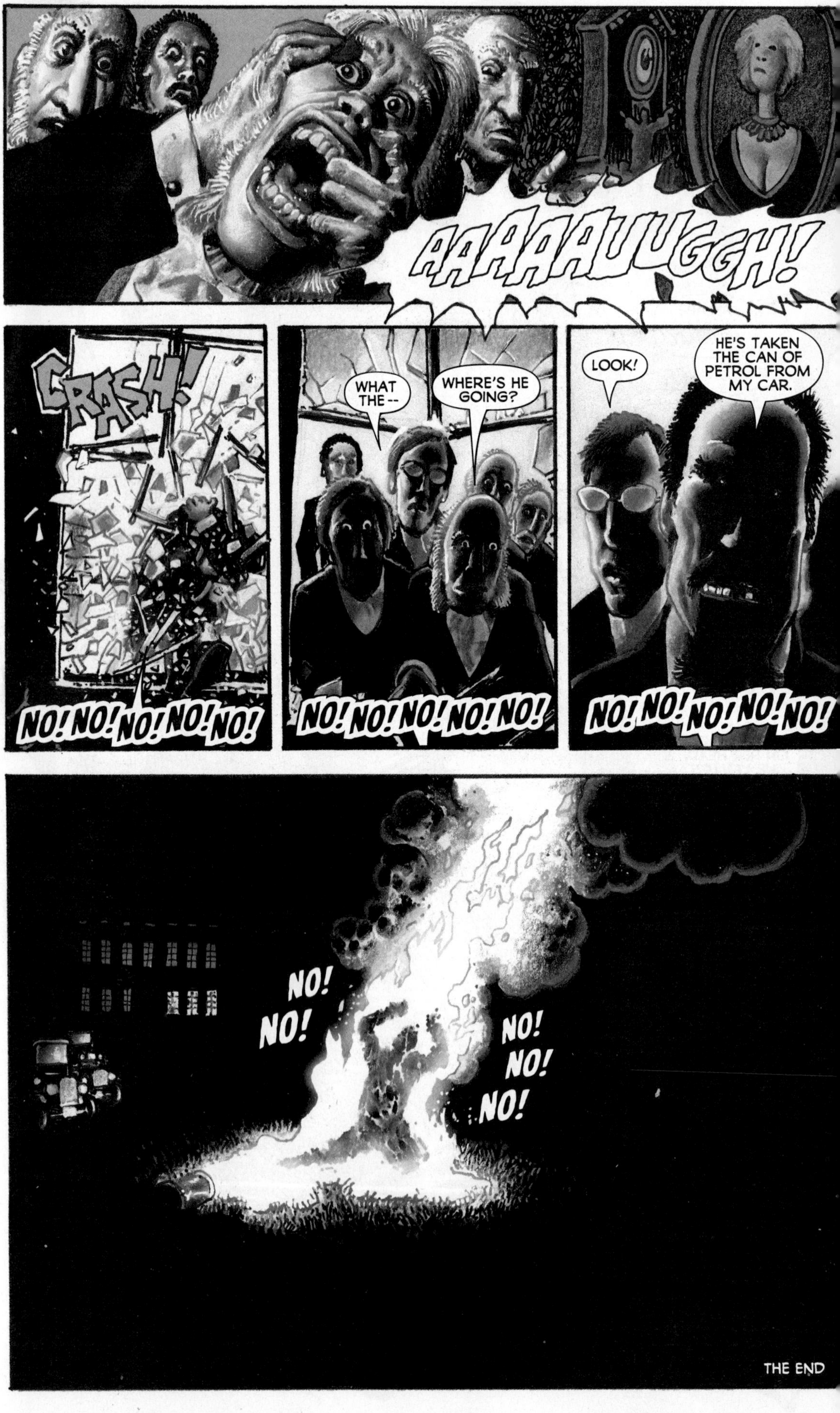
AAAAAUUGGH!
CRASH!
NO! NO! NO! NO! NO!
WHAT THE --
WHERE'S HE GOING?
NO! NO! NO! NO! NO!
LOOK!
HE'S TAKEN THE CAN OF PETROL FROM MY CAR.
NO! NO! NO! NO! NO!
NO!
NO!
NO!
NO!
NO!
THE END

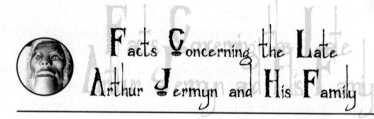

# Facts Concerning the Late Arthur Jermyn and His Family

## I

Life is a hideous thing, and from the background behind what we know of it peer daemoniacal hints of truth which make it sometimes a thousandfold more hideous. Science, already oppressive with its shocking revelations, will perhaps be the ultimate exterminator of our human species – if separate species we be – for its reserve of unguessed horrors could never be borne by mortal brains if loosed upon the world. If we knew what we are, we should do as Sir Arthur Jermyn did; and Arthur Jermyn soaked himself in oil and set fire to his clothing one night. No one placed the charred fragments in an urn or set a memorial to him who had been; for certain papers and a certain boxed object were found which made men wish to forget. Some who knew him do not admit that he ever existed.

Arthur Jermyn went out on the moor and burned himself after seeing the boxed object which had come from Africa. It was this object, and not his peculiar personal appearance, which made him end his life. Many would have disliked to live if possessed of the peculiar features of Arthur Jermyn, but he had been a poet and scholar and had not minded. Learning was in his blood, for his great-grandfather, Sir Robert Jermyn, Bt., had been an anthropologist of note, whilst his great-great-great-grandfather, Sir Wade Jermyn, was one of the earliest explorers of the Congo region, and had written eruditely of its tribes, animals, and supposed antiquities. Indeed, old Sir Wade had possessed an intellectual zeal amounting almost to a mania; his bizarre conjectures on a prehistoric white Congolese civilisation earning him much ridicule when his book, Observation on the Several Parts of Africa, was published. In 1765 this fearless explorer had been placed in a madhouse at Huntingdon.

Madness was in all the Jermyns, and people were glad there were not many of them. The line put forth no branches, and Arthur was the last of it. If he had not been, one can not say what he would have done when the object came. The Jermyns never seemed to look quite right – something was amiss, though Arthur was the worst, and the old family portraits in Jermyn House showed fine faces enough before Sir Wade's time. Certainly, the madness began with Sir Wade, whose wild stories of Africa were at once the delight and terror of his few friends. It showed in his collection of trophies and specimens, which were not such as a normal man would accumulate and preserve, and appeared strikingly in the Oriental seclusion in which he kept his wife. The latter, he had said, was the daughter of a Portuguese trader whom he had met in Africa; and did not like English ways. She, with an infant son born in Africa, had accompanied him back from the second and longest of his trips, and had gone with him on the third and last, never returning. No one had ever seen her closely, not even the servants; for her disposition had been violent and singular. During her brief stay at Jermyn House she occupied a remote wing, and was waited on by her husband alone. Sir Wade was, indeed, most peculiar in his solicitude for his family; for when he returned to Africa he would permit no one to care for his young son save a loathsome black woman from Guinea. Upon coming back, after the death of Lady Jermyn, he himself assumed complete care of the boy.

But it was the talk of Sir Wade, especially when in his cups, which chiefly led his friends to deem him mad. In a rational age like the eighteenth century it was unwise for a man of learning to talk about wild sights and strange scenes under a Congo moon; of the gigantic walls and pillars of a forgotten city, crumbling and vine-grown, and of damp, silent, stone steps leading interminably down into the darkness of abysmal treasure-vaults and inconceivable catacombs. Especially was it unwise to rave of the living things that might haunt such a place; of creatures half of the jungle and half of the impiously aged city – fabulous creatures which even a Pliny might describe with scepticism; things that might have sprung up after the great apes had overrun the dying city with the walls and the pillars, the vaults and the weird carvings. Yet after he came home for the last time Sir Wade would speak of such matters with a shudderingly uncanny zest, mostly after his third glass at the Knight's Head; boasting of what he had found in the jungle and of how he had dwelt among terrible ruins known only to him. And finally he had spoken of the living things in such a manner that he was taken to the madhouse. He had shown little regret when shut into the barred room at Huntingdon, for his mind moved curiously. Ever since his son had commenced to grow out of infancy, he had liked his home less and less, till at last he had seemed to dread it. The Knight's Head had been his headquarters, and when he was confined he expressed some vague gratitude as if for protection. Three years later he died.

Wade Jermyn's son Philip was a highly peculiar person. Despite a strong physical resemblance to his father, his appearance and conduct were in many particulars so coarse that he was universally shunned. Though he did not inherit the madness which was feared by some, he was densely stupid and given to brief periods of uncontrollable violence. In frame he was small, but intensely powerful, and was of incredible agility. Twelve years after succeeding to his title he married the daughter of his gamekeeper, a person said to be of gypsy extraction, but before his son was born joined the navy as a common sailor, completing the general disgust which his habits and misalliance had begun. After the close of the American war he was heard of as sailor on a merchantman in the African trade, having a kind of reputation for feats of strength and climbing, but finally disappearing one night as his ship lay off the Congo coast.

In the son of Sir Philip Jermyn the now accepted family peculiarity took a strange and fatal turn. Tall and fairly handsome, with a sort of weird Eastern grace despite certain slight oddities of proportion, Robert Jermyn began life as a scholar and investigator. It was he who first studied scientifically the vast collection of relics which his mad grandfather had brought from Africa, and who made the family name as celebrated in ethnology as in exploration. In 1815 Sir Robert married a daughter of the seventh Viscount Brightholme and was subsequently blessed with three children, the eldest and youngest of whom were never publicly seen on account of deformities in mind and body. Saddened by these family misfortunes, the scientist sought relief in work, and made two long expeditions in the interior of Africa. In 1849 his second son, Nevil, a singularly repellent person who seemed to combine the surliness of Philip Jermyn with the hauteur of the Brightholmes, ran away with a vulgar dancer, but was pardoned upon his return in the following year. He came back to Jermyn House a widower with an infant son, Alfred, who was one day to be the father of Arthur Jermyn.

Friends said that it was this series of griefs which unhinged the mind of Sir Robert Jermyn, yet it was probably merely a bit of African folklore which caused the disaster. The elderly scholar had been collecting legends of the Onga tribes near the field of his grandfather's and his own explorations, hoping in some way to account for Sir Wade's wild tales of a lost city peopled by strange hybrid creatures. A certain consistency in the strange papers of his ancestor suggested that the madman's imagination might have been stimulated by native myths. On October 19, 1852, the explorer Samuel Seaton called at Jermyn House with a manuscript of notes collected among the Ongas, believing that certain legends of a gray city of white apes ruled by a white god might prove valuable to the ethnologist. In his conversation he probably supplied many additional details; the nature of which will never be known, since a hideous series of tragedies suddenly burst into being. When Sir Robert Jermyn emerged from his library he left behind the strangled corpse of the explorer, and before he could be restrained, had put an end to all three of his children; the two who were never seen, and the son who had run away. Nevil Jermyn died in the successful defence of his own two-year-old son, who had apparently been included in the old man's madly murderous scheme. Sir Robert himself, after repeated attempts at suicide and a stubborn refusal to utter an articulate sound, died of apoplexy in the second year of his confinement.

Sir Alfred Jermyn was a baronet before his fourth birthday, but his tastes never matched his title. At twenty he had joined a band of music-hall performers, and at thirty-six had deserted his wife and child to travel with an itinerant American circus. His end was very revolting. Among the animals in the exhibition with which he travelled was a huge bull gorilla of lighter colour than the average; a surprisingly tractable beast of much popularity with the performers. With this gorilla Alfred Jermyn was singularly fascinated, and on many occasions the two would eye each other for long periods through the intervening bars. Eventually Jermyn asked and obtained permission to train the animal, astonishing audiences and fellow performers alike with his success. One morning in Chicago, as the gorilla and Alfred Jermyn were rehearsing an exceedingly clever boxing match, the former delivered a blow of more than the usual force, hurting both the body and the dignity of the amateur trainer. Of what followed, members of "The Greatest Show On Earth" do not like to speak. They did not expect to hear Sir Alfred Jermyn emit a shrill, inhuman scream, or to see him seize his clumsy antagonist with both hands, dash it to the floor of the cage, and bite fiendishly at its hairy throat. The gorilla was off its guard, but not for long, and before anything could be done by the regular trainer, the body which had belonged to a baronet was past recognition.

## II

Arthur Jermyn was the son of Sir Alfred Jermyn and a music-hall singer of unknown origin. When the husband and father deserted his family, the mother took the child to Jermyn House; where there was none left to object to her presence. She was not without notions of what a nobleman's dignity should be, and saw to it that her son received the best education which limited money could provide. The family resources were now sadly slender, and Jermyn House had fallen into woeful disrepair, but young Arthur loved the old edifice and all its contents. He was not like any other Jermyn who had ever lived, for he was a poet and a dreamer. Some of the neighbouring families who had heard tales of old Sir Wade Jermyn's unseen Portuguese wife declared that her Latin blood must be showing itself; but most persons merely sneered at his sensitiveness to beauty, attributing it to his music-hall mother, who was socially unrecognised. The poetic delicacy of Arthur Jermyn was the more remarkable because of his uncouth personal appearance. Most of the Jermyns had possessed a subtly odd and repellent cast, but Arthur's case was very striking. It is hard to say just what he resembled, but his expression, his facial angle, and the length of his arms gave a thrill of repulsion to those who met him for the first time.

It was the mind and character of Arthur Jermyn which atoned for his aspect. Gifted and learned, he took highest honours at Oxford and seemed likely to redeem the intellectual fame of his family. Though of poetic rather than scientific temperament, he planned to continue the work of his forefathers in African ethnology and antiquities, utilising the truly wonderful though strange collection of Sir Wade. With his fanciful mind he thought often of the prehistoric civilisation in which the mad explorer had so implicitly believed, and would weave tale after tale about the silent jungle city mentioned in the latter's wilder notes and paragraphs. For the nebulous utterances concerning a nameless, unsuspected race of jungle hybrids he had a peculiar feeling of mingled terror and attraction, speculating on the possible basis of such a fancy, and seeking to obtain light among the more recent data gleaned by his great-grandfather and Samuel Seaton amongst the Ongas.

In 1911, after the death of his mother, Sir Arthur Jermyn determined to pursue his investigations to the utmost extent. Selling a portion of his estate to obtain the requisite money, he outfitted an expedition and sailed for the Congo. Arranging with the Belgian authorities for a party of guides, he spent a year in the Onga and Kahn country, finding data beyond the highest of his expectations. Among the Kaliris was an aged chief called Mwanu, who possessed not only a highly retentive memory, but a singular degree of intelligence and interest in old legends. This ancient confirmed every tale which Jermyn had heard, adding his own account of the stone city and the white apes as it had been told to him.

According to Mwanu, the gray city and the hybrid creatures were no more, having been annihilated by the warlike N'bangus many years ago. This tribe, after destroying most of the edifices and killing the live beings, had carried off the stuffed goddess which had been the object of their quest; the white ape-goddess which the strange beings worshipped, and which was held by Congo tradition to be the form of one who had reigned as a princess among these beings. Just what the white apelike creatures could have been, Mwanu had no idea, but he thought they were the builders of the ruined city. Jermyn could form no conjecture, but by close questioning obtained a very picturesque legend of the stuffed goddess.

The ape-princess, it was said, became the consort of a great white god who had come out of the West. For a long time they had reigned over the city together, but when they had a son, all three went away. Later the god and princess had returned, and upon the death of the princess her divine husband had mummified the body and enshrined it in a vast house of stone, where it was worshipped. Then he departed alone. The legend here seemed to present three variants. According to one story, nothing further happened save that the stuffed goddess became a symbol of supremacy for whatever tribe might possess it. It was for this reason that the N'bangus carried it off. A second story told of a god's return and death at the feet of his enshrined wife. A third told of the return of the son, grown to manhood – or apehood or godhood, as the case might be – yet unconscious of his identity. Surely the imaginative blacks had made the most of whatever events might lie behind the extravagant legendry.

Of the reality of the jungle city described by old Sir Wade, Arthur Jermyn had no further doubt; and was hardly astonished when early in 1912 he came upon what was left of it. Its size must have been exaggerated, yet the stones lying about proved that it was no mere Negro village. Unfortunately no carvings could be found, and the small size of the expedition prevented operations toward clearing the one visible passageway that seemed to lead down into the system of vaults which Sir Wade had mentioned. The white apes and the stuffed goddess were discussed with all the native chiefs of the region, but it remained for a European to improve on the data offered by old Mwanu. M. Verhaeren, Belgian agent at a trading-post on the Congo, believed that he could not only locate but obtain the stuffed goddess, of which he had vaguely heard; since the once mighty N'bangus were now the submissive servants of King Albert's government, and with but little persuasion could be induced to part with the gruesome deity they had carried off. When Jermyn sailed for England, there-fore, it was with the exultant probability that he would within a few months receive a priceless ethnological relic confirming the wildest of his great-great-great-grandfather's narratives – that is, the wildest which he had ever heard. Countrymen near Jermyn House had perhaps heard wilder tales handed down from ancestors who had listened to Sir Wade around the tables of the Knight's Head.

Arthur Jermyn waited very patiently for the expected box from M. Verhaeren, meanwhile studying with increased diligence the manuscripts left by his mad ancestor. He began to feel closely akin to Sir Wade, and to seek relics of the latter's personal life in England as well as of his African exploits. Oral accounts of the mysterious and secluded wife had been numerous, but no tangible relic of her stay at Jermyn House remained. Jermyn wondered what circumstance had prompted or permitted such an effacement, and decided that the husband's insanity was the prime cause. His great-great-great-grandmother, he recalled, was said to have been the daughter of a Portuguese trader in Africa. No doubt her practical heritage and superficial knowledge of the Dark Continent had caused her to flout Sir Wade's tales of the interior, a thing which such a man would not be likely to forgive. She had died in Africa, perhaps dragged thither by a husband determined to prove what he had told. But as Jermyn indulged in these reflections he could not but smile at their futility, a century and a half after the death of both his strange progenitors.

In June, 1913, a letter arrived from M. Verhaeren, telling of the finding of the stuffed goddess. It was, the Belgian averred, a most extraordinary object; an object quite beyond the power of a layman to classify. Whether it was human or simian only a scientist could determine, and the process of determination would be greatly hampered by its imperfect condition. Time and the Congo climate are not kind to mummies; especially when their preparation is as ama-teurish as seemed to be the case here. Around the creature's neck had been found a golden chain bearing an empty locket on which were armorial designs; no doubt some hapless traveller's keepsake, taken by the N'bangus and hung upon the goddess as a charm. In commenting on the contour of the mummy's face, M. Verhaeren suggested a whimsical comparison; or rather, expressed a humorous wonder just how it would strike his corespondent, but was too much interested scientifically to waste many words in levity. The stuffed goddess, he wrote, would arrive duly packed about a month after receipt of the letter.

The boxed object was delivered at Jermyn House on the afternoon of August 3, 1913, being conveyed immediately to the large chamber which housed the collection of African specimens as arranged by Sir Robert and Arthur. What ensued can best be gathered from the tales of servants and from things and papers later examined. Of the various tales, that of aged Soames, the family butler, is most ample and coherent. According to this trustworthy man, Sir

Arthur Jermyn dismissed everyone from the room before opening the box, though the instant sound of hammer and chisel showed that he did not delay the operation. Nothing was heard for some time; just how long Soames cannot exactly estimate, but it was certainly less than a quarter of an hour later that the horrible scream, undoubtedly in Jermyn's voice, was heard. Immediately afterward Jermyn emerged from the room, rushing frantically toward the front of the house as if pursued by some hideous enemy. The expression on his face, a face ghastly enough in repose, was beyond description. When near the front door he seemed to think of something, and turned back in his flight, finally disappearing down the stairs to the cellar. The servants were utterly dumbfounded, and watched at the head of the stairs, but their master did not return. A smell of oil was all that came up from the regions below. After dark a rattling was heard at the door leading from the cellar into the courtyard; and a stable-boy saw Arthur Jermyn, glistening from head to foot with oil and redolent of that fluid, steal furtively out and vanish on the black moor surrounding the house. Then, in an exaltation of supreme horror, everyone saw the end. A spark appeared on the moor, a flame arose, and a pillar of human fire reached to the heavens. The house of Jermyn no longer existed.

The reason why Arthur Jermyn's charred fragments were not collected and buried lies in what was found afterward, principally the thing in the box. The stuffed goddess was a nauseous sight, withered and eaten away, but it was clearly a mummified white ape of some unknown species, less hairy than any recorded variety, and infinitely nearer mankind – quite shockingly so. Detailed description would be rather unpleasant, but two salient particulars must be told, for they fit in revoltingly with certain notes of Sir Wade Jermyn's African expeditions and with the Congolese legends of the white god and the ape-princess. The two particulars in question are these: the arms on the golden locket about the creature's neck were the Jermyn arms, and the jocose suggestion of M. Verhaeren about certain resemblance as connected with the shrivelled face applied with vivid, ghastly, and unnatural horror to none other than the sensitive Arthur Jermyn, great-great-great-grandson of Sir Wade Jermyn and an unknown wife. Members of the Royal Anthropological Institute burned the thing and threw the locket into a well, and some of them do not admit that Arthur Jermyn ever existed.

– H. P. Lovecraft

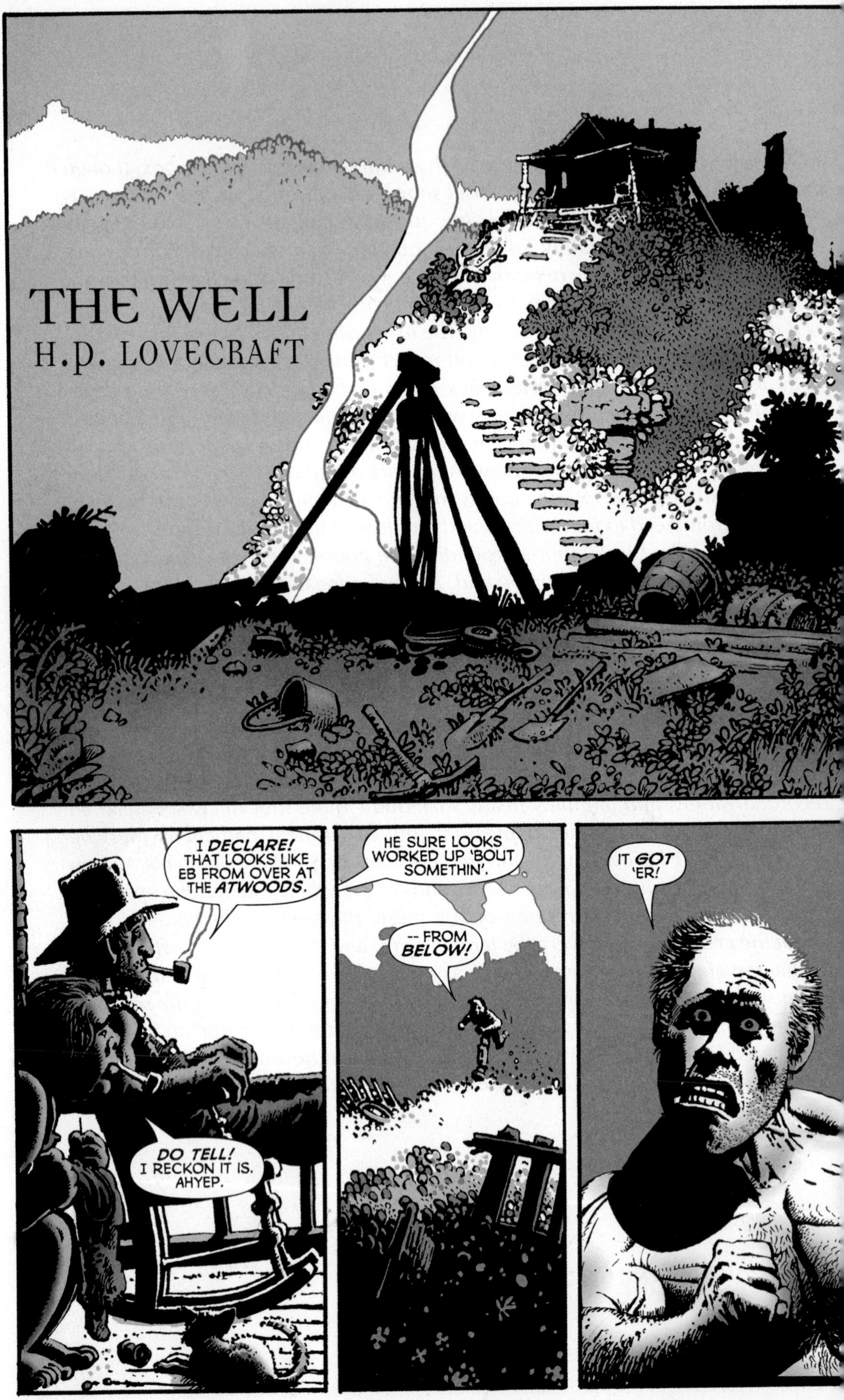
THE WELL
H.P. LOVECRAFT
I DECLARE! THAT LOOKS LIKE EB FROM OVER AT THE ATWOODS.
DO TELL! I RECKON IT IS. AHYEP.
HE SURE LOOKS WORKED UP 'BOUT SOMETHIN'.
-- FROM BELOW!
IT GOT 'ER!

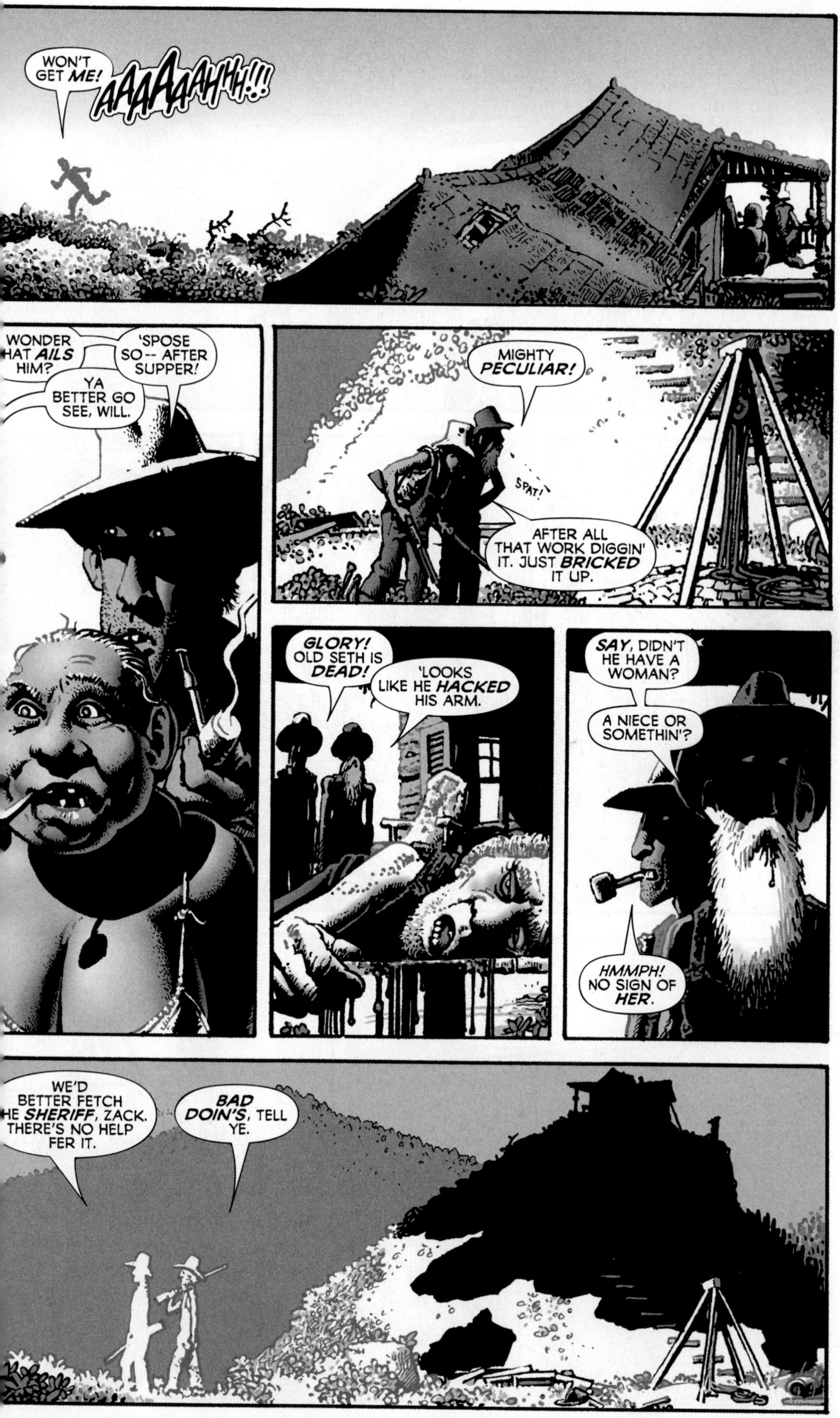
WON'T GET ME!
AAAAAAHHH!!!
WONDER HAT AILS HIM?
'SPOSE SO -- AFTER SUPPER!
YA BETTER GO SEE, WILL.
MIGHTY PECULIAR!
SPAT!
AFTER ALL THAT WORK DIGGIN' IT. JUST BRICKED IT UP.
GLORY! OLD SETH IS DEAD!
'LOOKS LIKE HE HACKED HIS ARM.
SAY, DIDN'T HE HAVE A WOMAN?
A NIECE OR SOMETHIN'?
HMMPH! NO SIGN OF HER.
WE'D BETTER FETCH HE SHERIFF, ZACK. THERE'S NO HELP FER IT.
BAD DOIN'S, TELL YE.

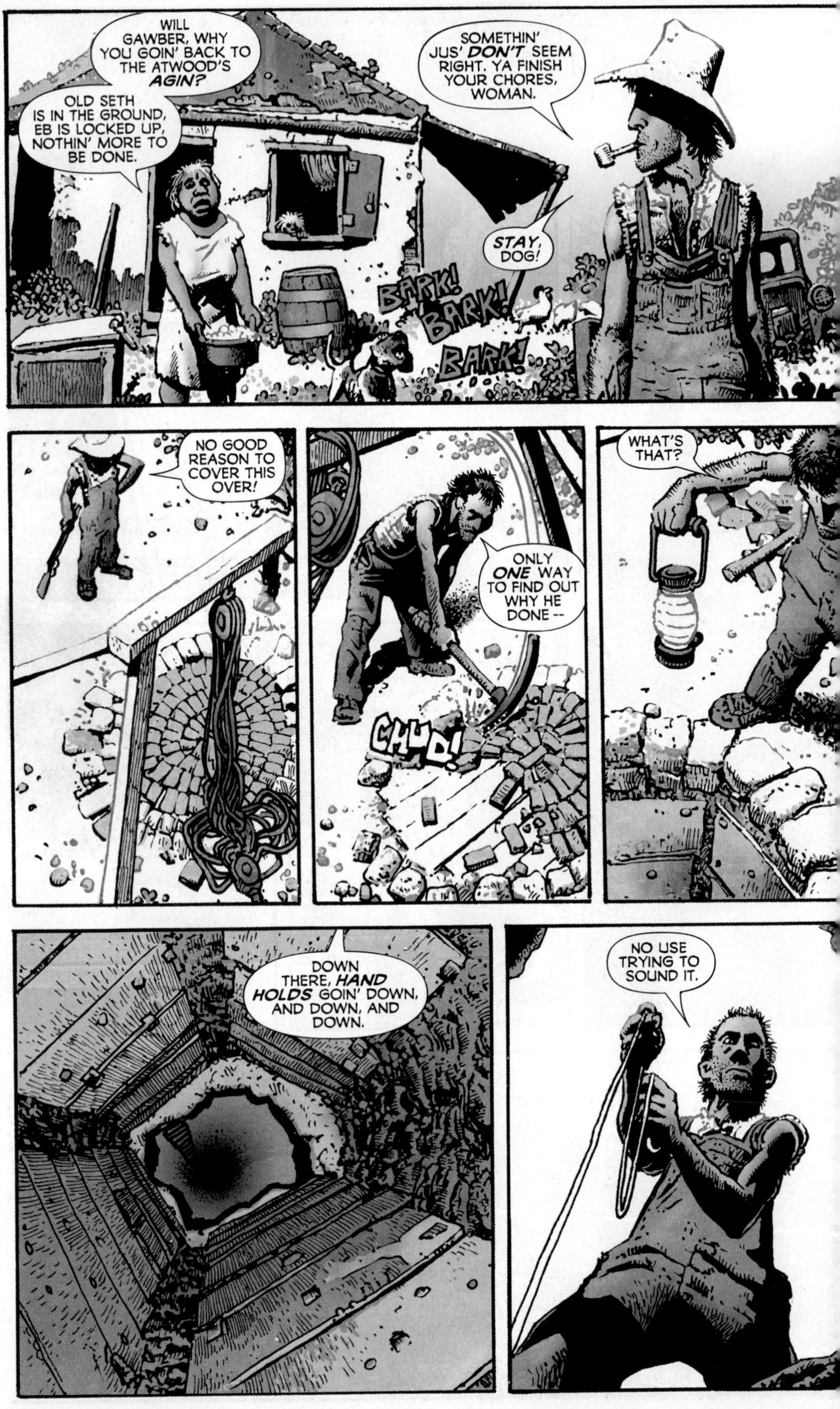
WILL GAWBER, WHY YOU GOIN' BACK TO THE ATWOOD'S AGIN?
OLD SETH IS IN THE GROUND, EB IS LOCKED UP, NOTHIN' MORE TO BE DONE.
SOMETHIN' JUS' DON'T SEEM RIGHT. YA FINISH YOUR CHORES, WOMAN.
STAY, DOG!
BARK! BARK! BARK!
NO GOOD REASON TO COVER THIS OVER!
ONLY ONE WAY TO FIND OUT WHY HE DONE --
CHUD!
WHAT'S THAT?
DOWN THERE, HAND HOLDS GOIN' DOWN, AND DOWN, AND DOWN.
NO USE TRYING TO SOUND IT.

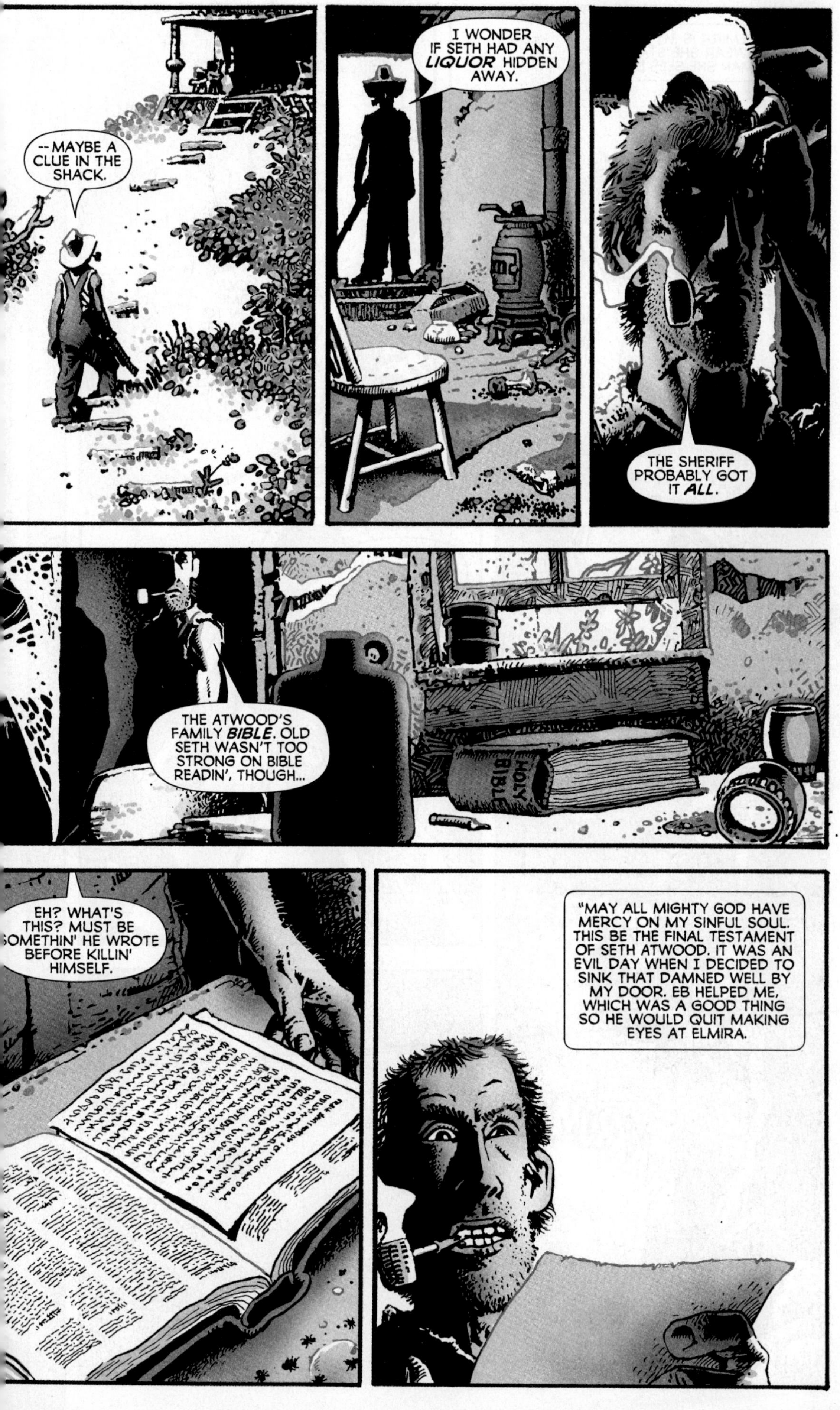
--MAYBE A CLUE IN THE SHACK.
I WONDER IF SETH HAD ANY LIQUOR HIDDEN AWAY.
THE SHERIFF PROBABLY GOT IT ALL.
THE ATWOOD'S FAMILY BIBLE. OLD SETH WASN'T TOO STRONG ON BIBLE READIN', THOUGH...
HOLY BIBLE
EH? WHAT'S THIS? MUST BE SOMETHIN' HE WROTE BEFORE KILLIN' HIMSELF.
"MAY ALL MIGHTY GOD HAVE MERCY ON MY SINFUL SOUL. THIS BE THE FINAL TESTAMENT OF SETH ATWOOD. IT WAS AN EVIL DAY WHEN I DECIDED TO SINK THAT DAMNED WELL BY MY DOOR. EB HELPED ME, WHICH WAS A GOOD THING SO HE WOULD QUIT MAKING EYES AT ELMIRA.

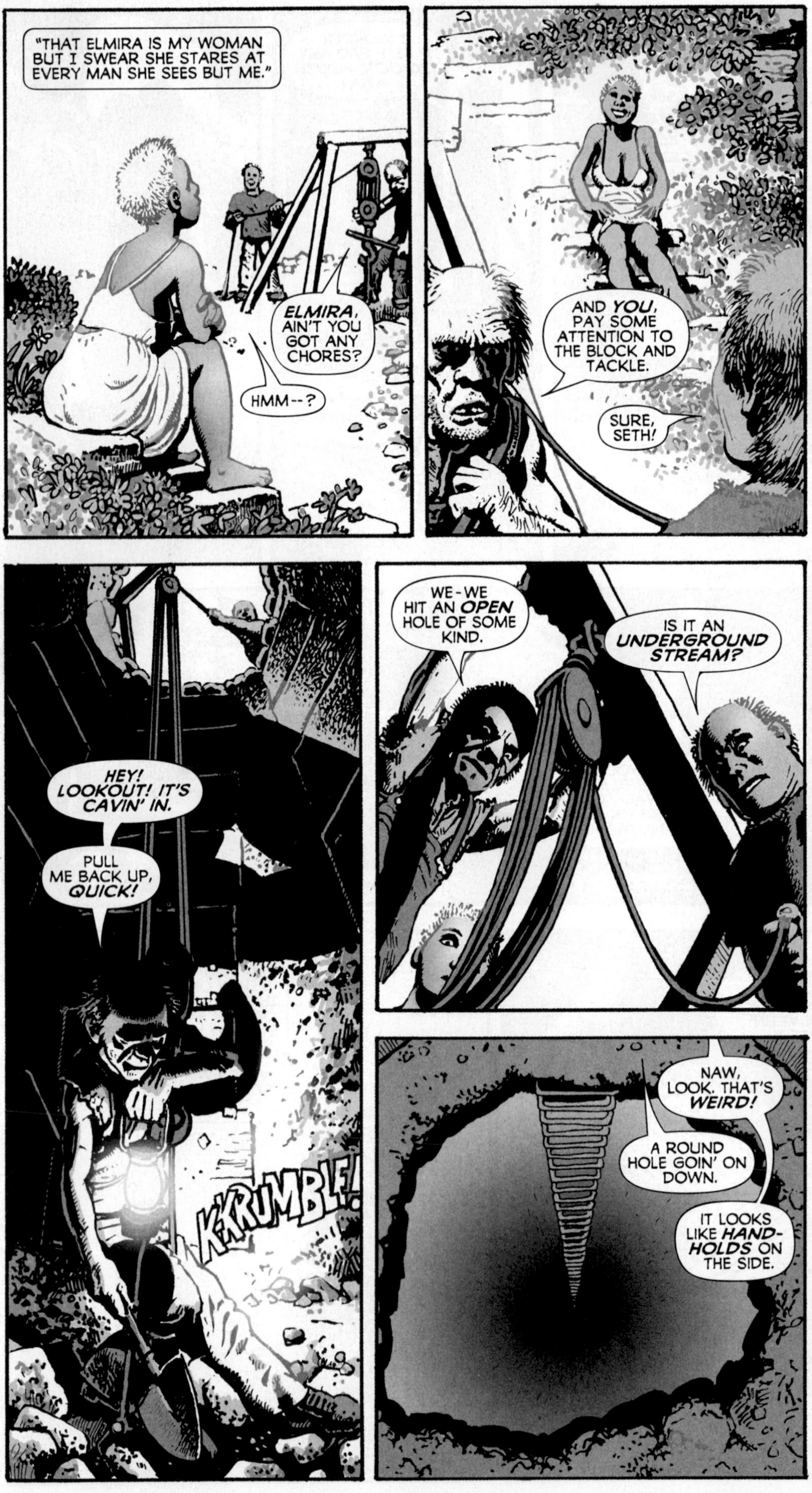
"THAT ELMIRA IS MY WOMAN BUT I SWEAR SHE STARES AT EVERY MAN SHE SEES BUT ME."
ELMIRA, AIN'T YOU GOT ANY CHORES?
HMM--?
AND YOU, PAY SOME ATTENTION TO THE BLOCK AND TACKLE.
SURE, SETH!
HEY! LOOKOUT! IT'S CAVIN' IN.
PULL ME BACK UP, QUICK!
K-KRUMBLE!
WE-WE HIT AN OPEN HOLE OF SOME KIND.
IS IT AN UNDERGROUND STREAM?
NAW, LOOK. THAT'S WEIRD!
A ROUND HOLE GOIN' ON DOWN.
IT LOOKS LIKE HAND-HOLDS ON THE SIDE.

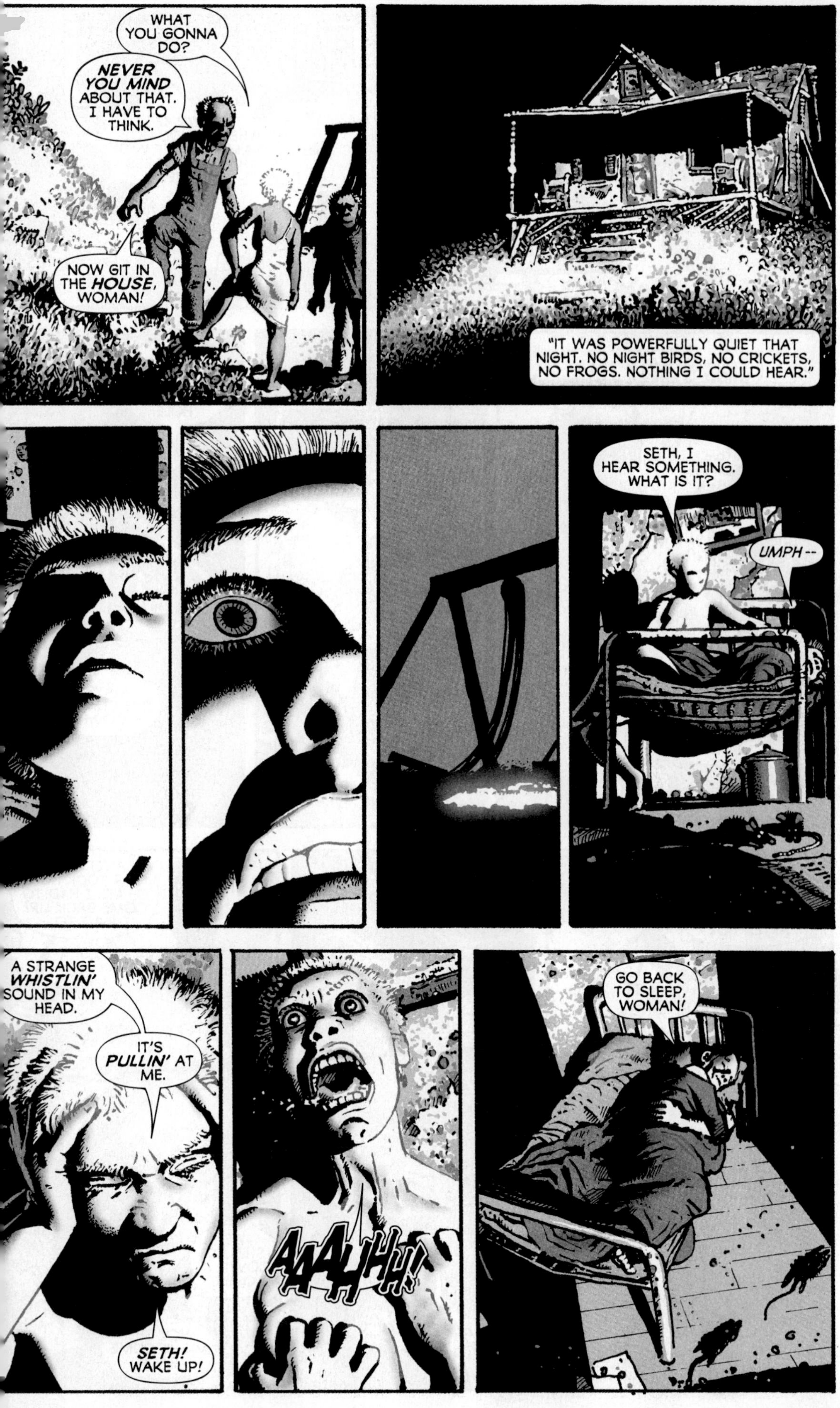
WHAT YOU GONNA DO?
NEVER YOU MIND ABOUT THAT. I HAVE TO THINK.
NOW GIT IN THE HOUSE, WOMAN!
"IT WAS POWERFULLY QUIET THAT NIGHT. NO NIGHT BIRDS, NO CRICKETS, NO FROGS. NOTHING I COULD HEAR."
SETH, I HEAR SOMETHING. WHAT IS IT?
UMPH--
A STRANGE WHISTLIN' SOUND IN MY HEAD.
IT'S PULLIN' AT ME.
SETH! WAKE UP!
AAAHHH!
GO BACK TO SLEEP, WOMAN!

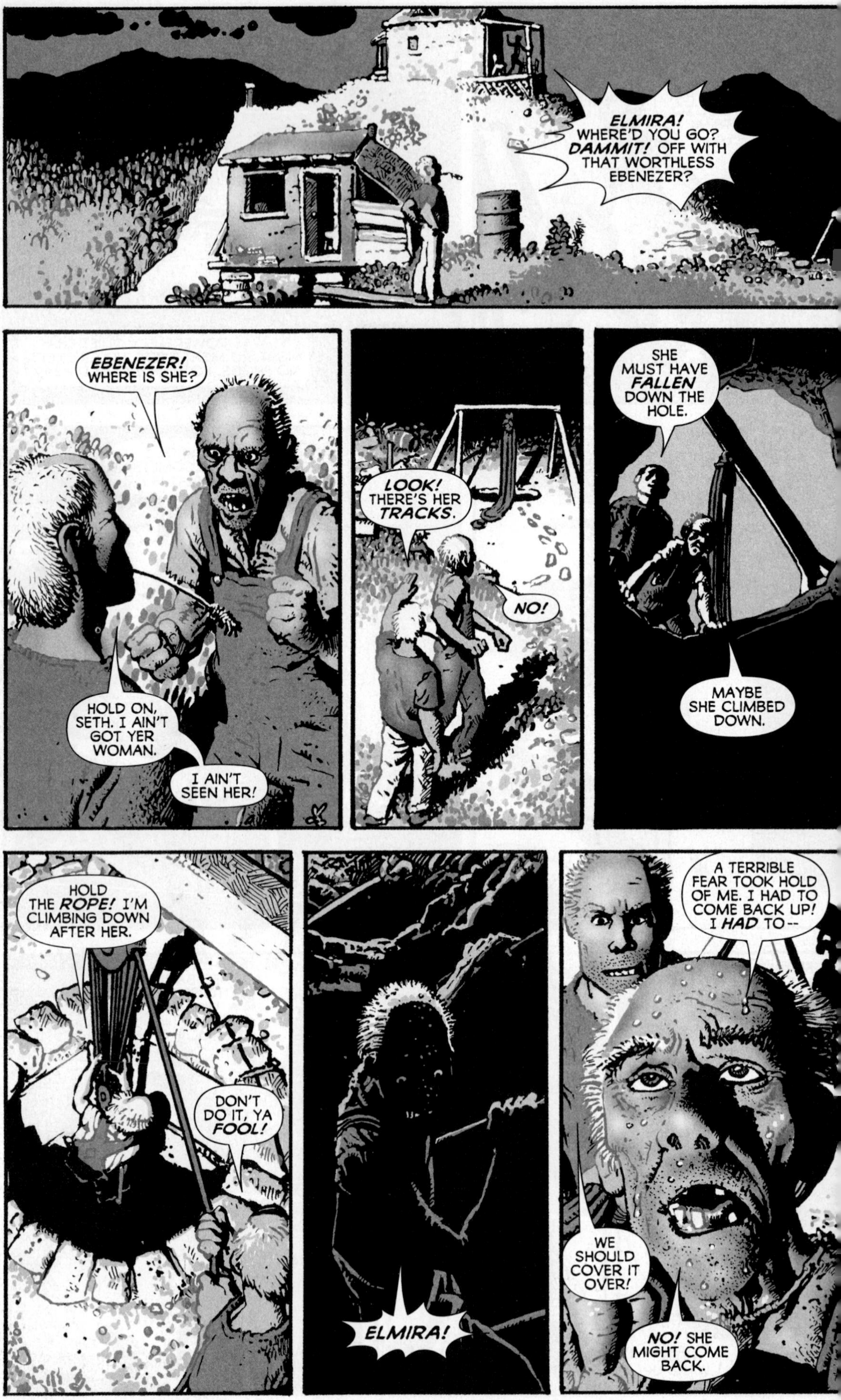
ELMIRA! WHERE'D YOU GO? DAMMIT! OFF WITH THAT WORTHLESS EBENEZER?
EBENEZER! WHERE IS SHE?
HOLD ON, SETH. I AIN'T GOT YER WOMAN.
I AIN'T SEEN HER!
LOOK! THERE'S HER TRACKS.
NO!
SHE MUST HAVE FALLEN DOWN THE HOLE.
MAYBE SHE CLIMBED DOWN.
HOLD THE ROPE! I'M CLIMBING DOWN AFTER HER.
DON'T DO IT, YA FOOL!
ELMIRA!
A TERRIBLE FEAR TOOK HOLD OF ME. I HAD TO COME BACK UP! I HAD TO --
WE SHOULD COVER IT OVER!
NO! SHE MIGHT COME BACK.

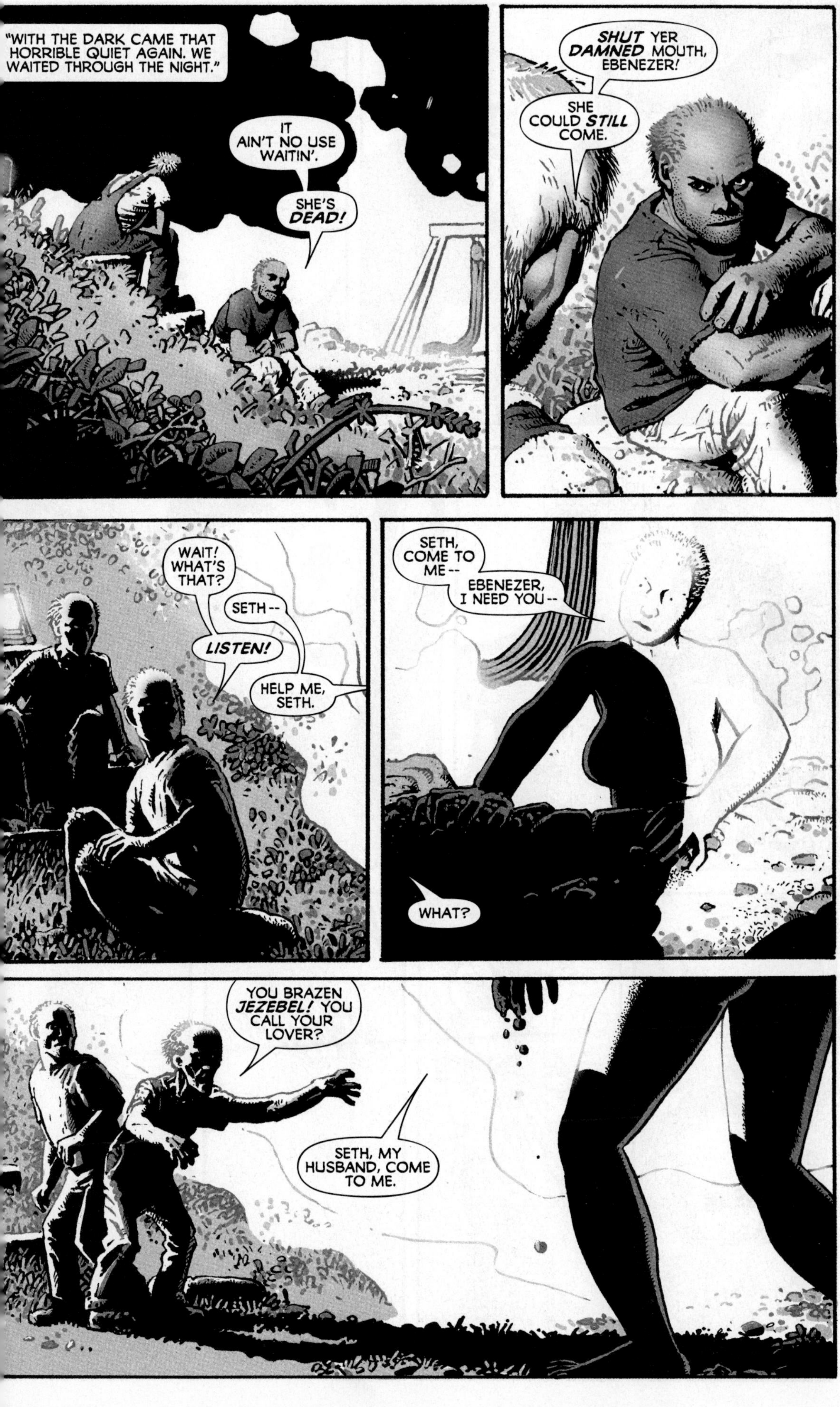
"WITH THE DARK CAME THAT HORRIBLE QUIET AGAIN. WE WAITED THROUGH THE NIGHT."
IT AIN'T NO USE WAITIN'.
SHE'S DEAD!
SHUT YER DAMNED MOUTH, EBENEZER!
SHE COULD STILL COME.
WAIT! WHAT'S THAT?
SETH--
LISTEN!
HELP ME, SETH.
SETH, COME TO ME--
EBENEZER, I NEED YOU--
WHAT?
YOU BRAZEN JEZEBEL! YOU CALL YOUR LOVER?
SETH, MY HUSBAND, COME TO ME.

SHE'S JUST *OUT* OF HER *MIND*. THAT'S ALL. EB, GIVE HER YOUR SHIRT. WE GOT TO GET HER INTO THE HOUSE.

ELMIRA, DARLIN', WHAT IS IT?

SETH --

DON'T HOLD BACK, ELMIRA. YOU NEED SOME *REST*.

SHE'S PULLIN' *BACK!*

OOF!

THUM

SETH, *HELP* ME!

EB, *PLEASE!*

*AAAGGHHH!!*

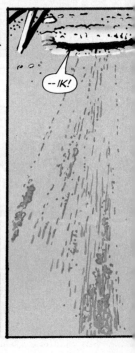

--IK!

YAAAAAAHHH!

"EB RAN OFF. IT CAME TO ME WHAT I HAD TO DO. THE WELL HAD TO BE BRICKED OVER. THERE'S SOMETHING DOWN THERE THAT'S BEYOND MY KIN. PRAY TO GOD THAT LAST FALL KILLED ELMIRA. GOD GRANT THAT THE WELL WILL NEVER AGAIN BE OPENED."

"-- NEVER AGAIN BE OPENED."

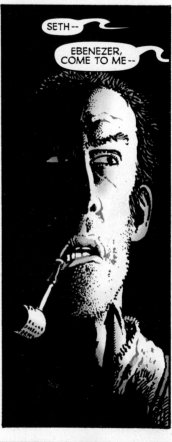

SETH --

EBENEZER, COME TO ME --

WILL, IS THAT YOU?

HELP ME, WILL. COME TO ME.

THE END

# 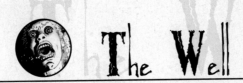 The Well

Farmer Seth Atwood was past eighty when
He tried to sink that deep well by his door,
With only Eb to help him bore and bore.
We laughed, and hoped he'd soon be sane again.
And yet, instead, young Eb went crazy, too,
So that they shipped him to the county farm.
Seth bricked the well-mouth up as tight as glue--
Then hacked an artery in his gnarled left arm.

After the funeral we felt bound to get
Out to that well and rip the bricks away,
But all we saw were iron hand-holds set
Down a black hole deeper than we could say.
And yet we put the bricks back -- for we found
The hole too deep for any line to sound.

— H. P. Lovecraft

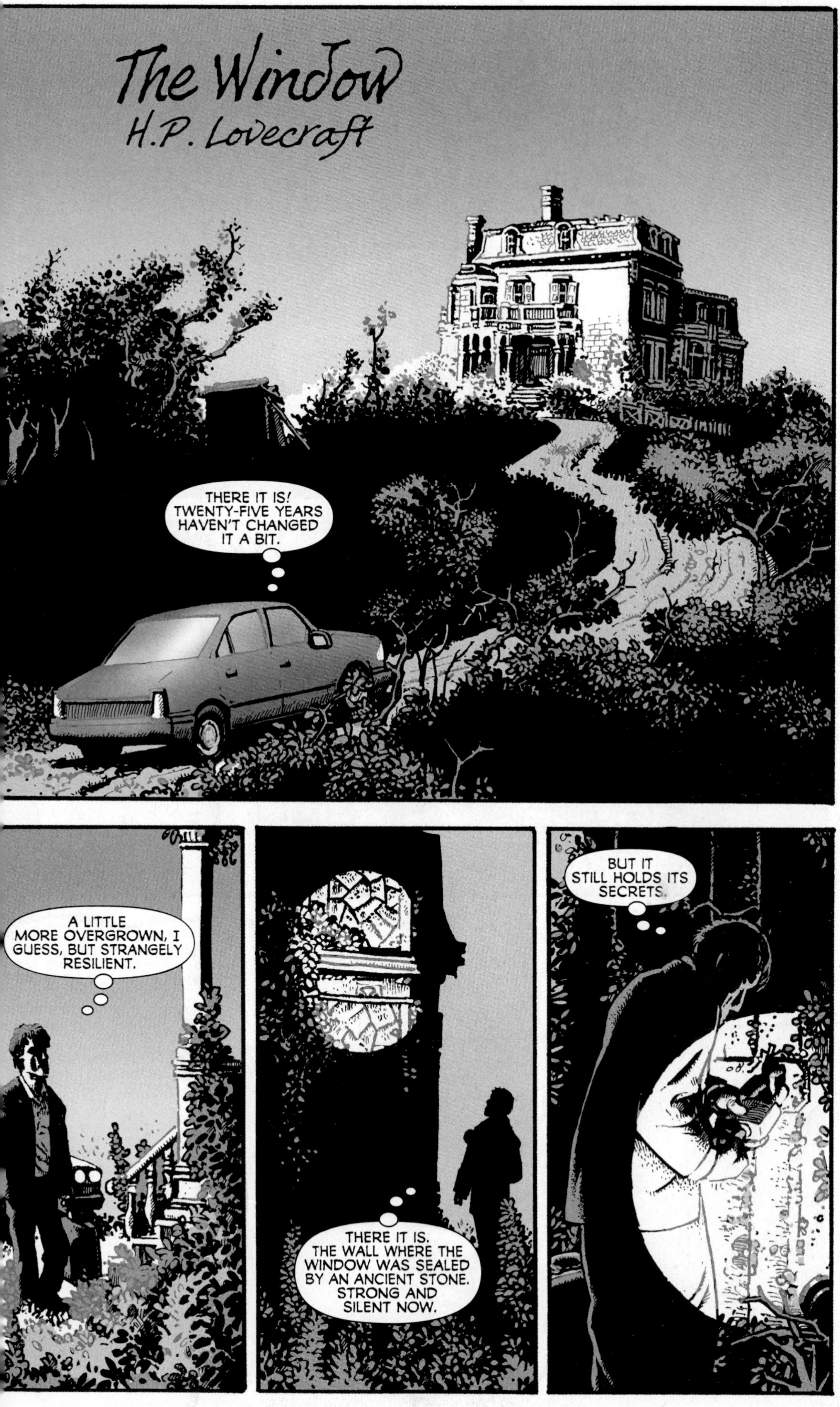
The Window
H.P. Lovecraft
THERE IT IS! TWENTY-FIVE YEARS HAVEN'T CHANGED IT A BIT.
A LITTLE MORE OVERGROWN, I GUESS, BUT STRANGELY RESILIENT.
THERE IT IS. THE WALL WHERE THE WINDOW WAS SEALED BY AN ANCIENT STONE. STRONG AND SILENT NOW.
BUT IT STILL HOLDS ITS SECRETS.

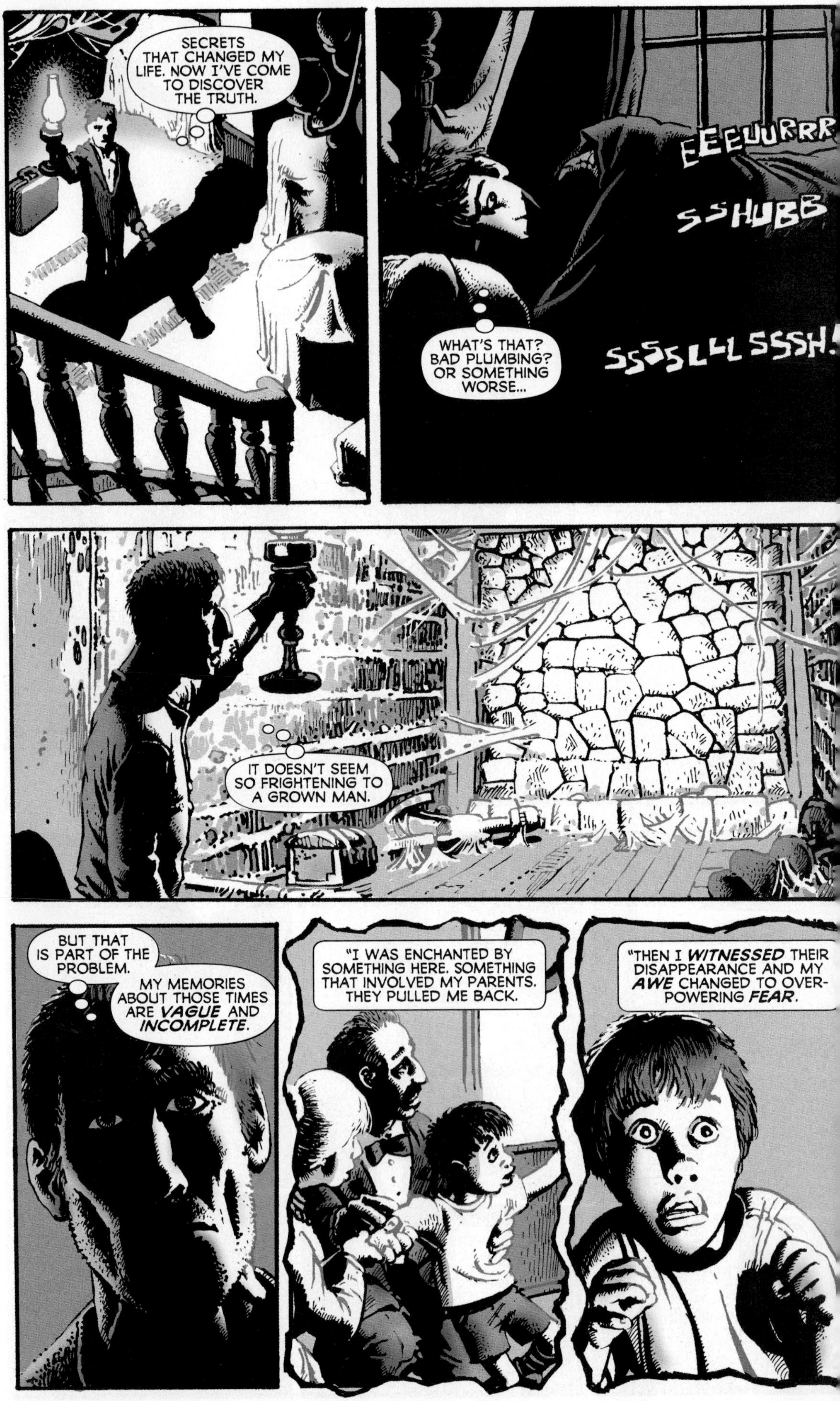
SECRETS THAT CHANGED MY LIFE. NOW I'VE COME TO DISCOVER THE TRUTH.
EEEUURRR
SSHUBB
WHAT'S THAT? BAD PLUMBING? OR SOMETHING WORSE...
SSSSLLLSSSH!
IT DOESN'T SEEM SO FRIGHTENING TO A GROWN MAN.
BUT THAT IS PART OF THE PROBLEM.
MY MEMORIES ABOUT THOSE TIMES ARE *VAGUE* AND *INCOMPLETE*.
"I WAS ENCHANTED BY SOMETHING HERE. SOMETHING THAT INVOLVED MY PARENTS. THEY PULLED ME BACK.
"THEN I *WITNESSED* THEIR DISAPPEARANCE AND MY *AWE* CHANGED TO OVER-POWERING *FEAR*.

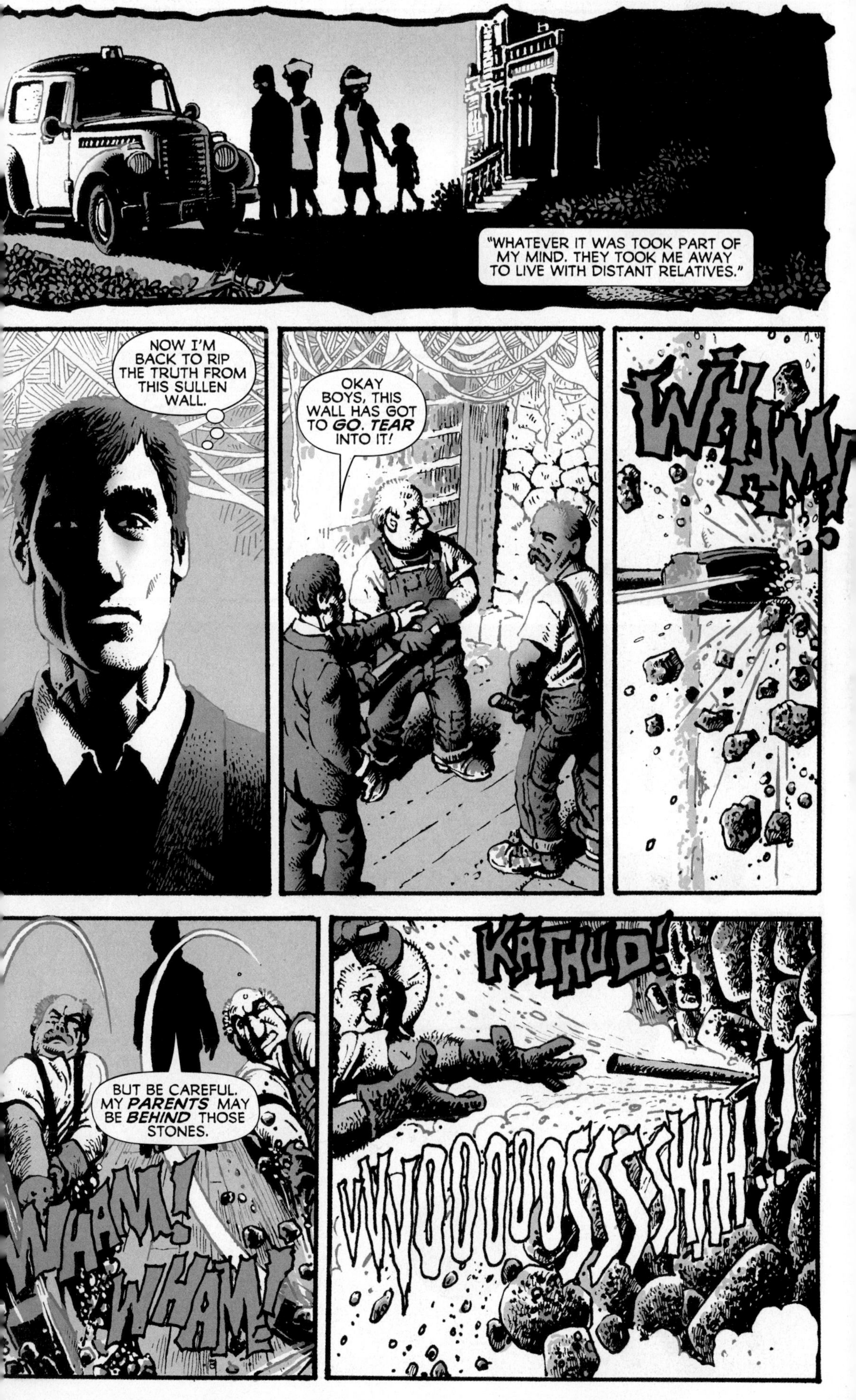

"WHATEVER IT WAS TOOK PART OF MY MIND. THEY TOOK ME AWAY TO LIVE WITH DISTANT RELATIVES."
NOW I'M BACK TO RIP THE TRUTH FROM THIS SULLEN WALL.
OKAY BOYS, THIS WALL HAS GOT TO GO. TEAR INTO IT!
WHAM!
BUT BE CAREFUL. MY PARENTS MAY BE BEHIND THOSE STONES.
WHAM!
WHAM!
KATHUD!
VVVOOOOOSSSSHH!!

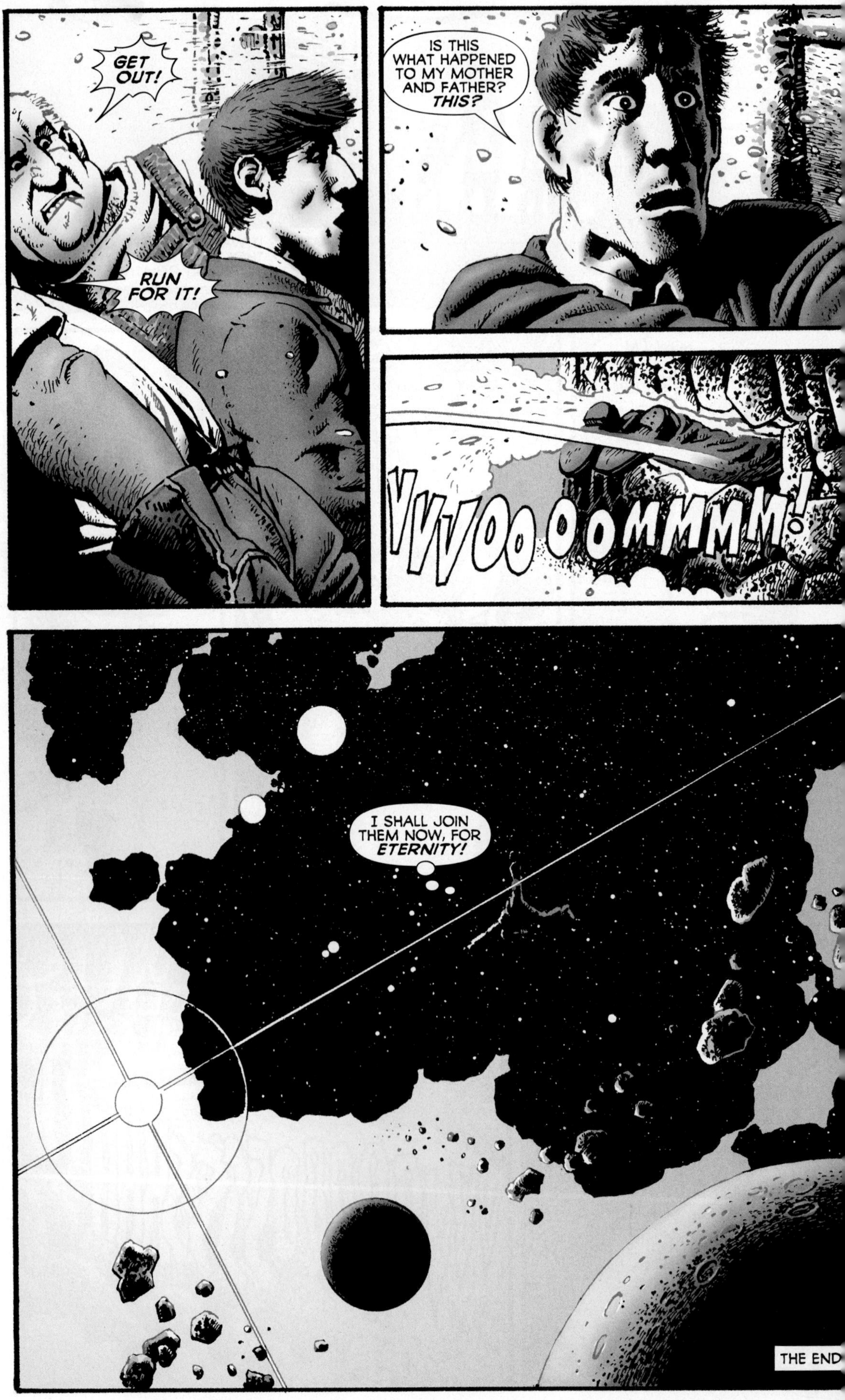
GET OUT!
RUN FOR IT!
IS THIS WHAT HAPPENED TO MY MOTHER AND FATHER? *THIS?*
VVVOOOOOMMMMM!
I SHALL JOIN THEM NOW, FOR *ETERNITY!*
THE END

#  The Window

The house was old, with tangled wings outthrown,
Of which no one could ever half keep track,
And in a small room somewhat near the back
Was an odd window sealed with ancient stone.
There, in a dream-plagued childhood, quite alone
I used to go, where night reigned vague and black;
Parting the cobwebs with a curious lack
Of fear, and with a wonder each time grown.
One later day I brought the masons there
To find what view my dim forbears had shunned,
But as they pierced the stone, a rush of air
Burst from the alien voids that yawned beyond.
They fled -- but I peered through and found unrolled
All the wild worlds of which my dreams had told.

– H. P. Lovecraft

## EDGAR ALLAN POE'S HAUNT OF HORROR #1

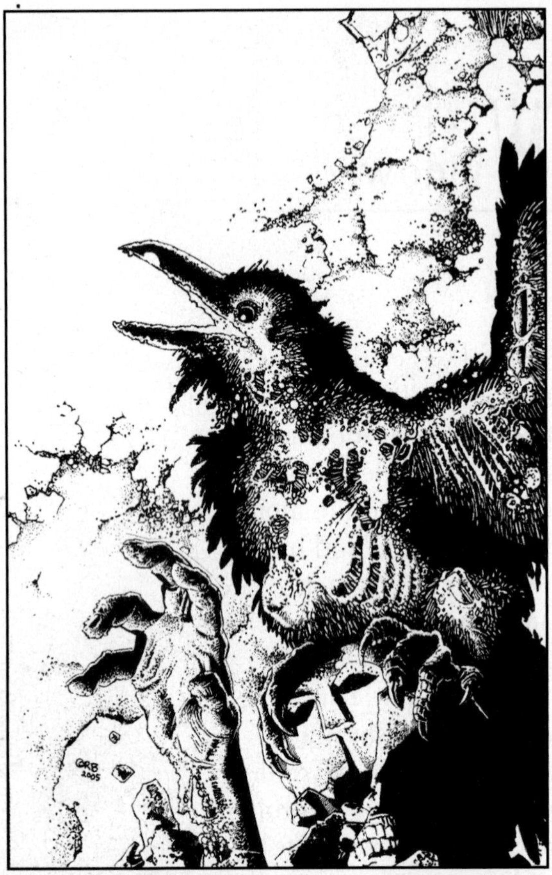

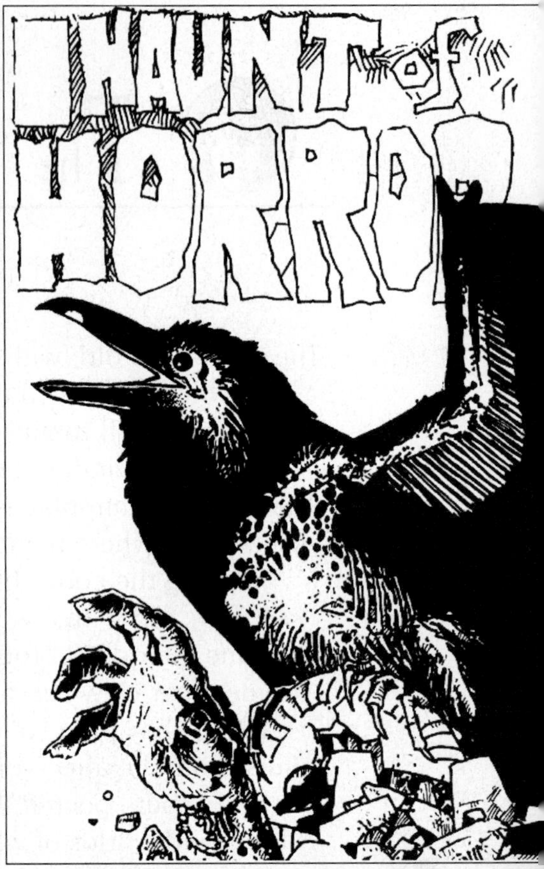
HAUNT of
HORROR

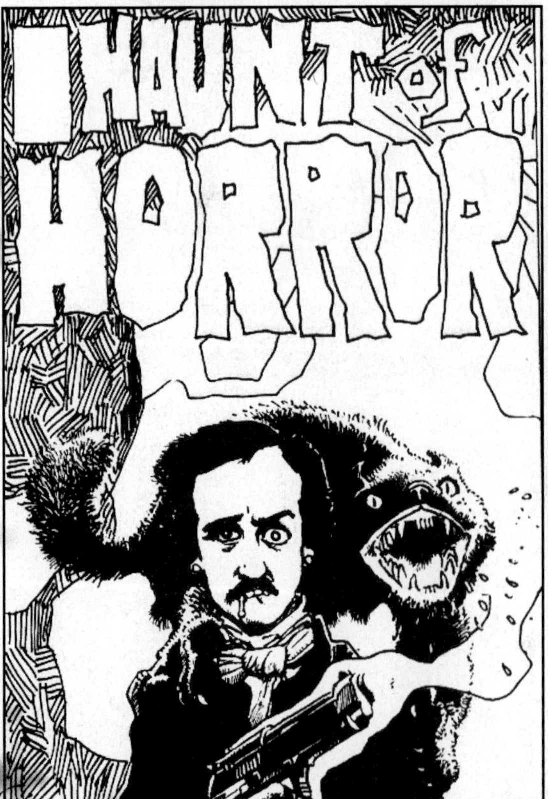
HAUNT of
HORROR

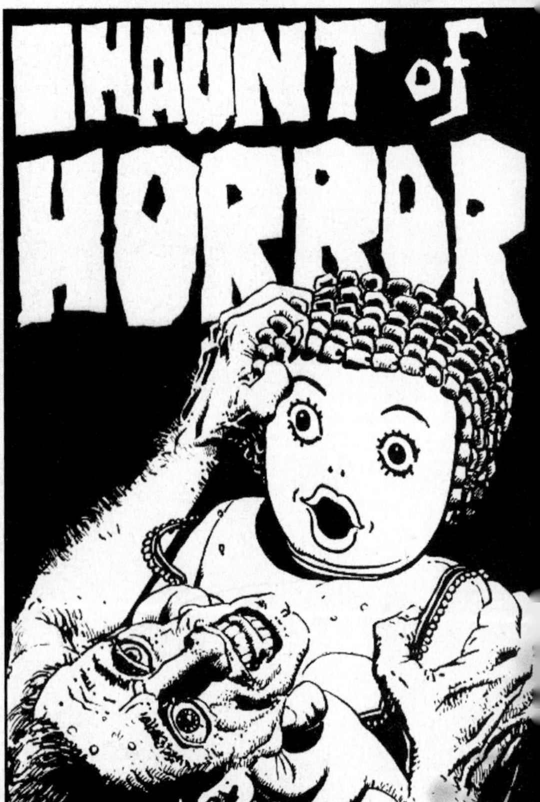
HAUNT of
HORROR

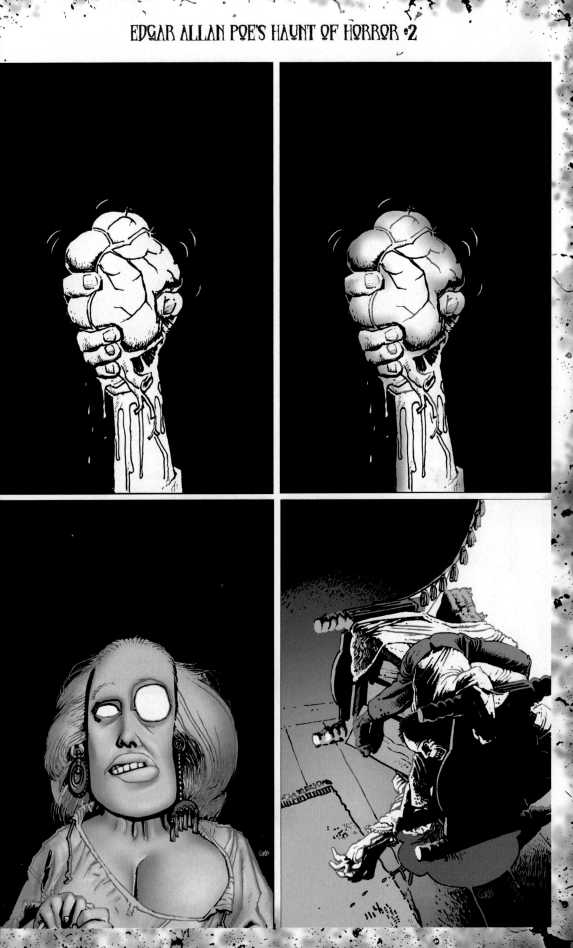

# EDGAR ALLAN POE'S HAUNT OF HORROR #3

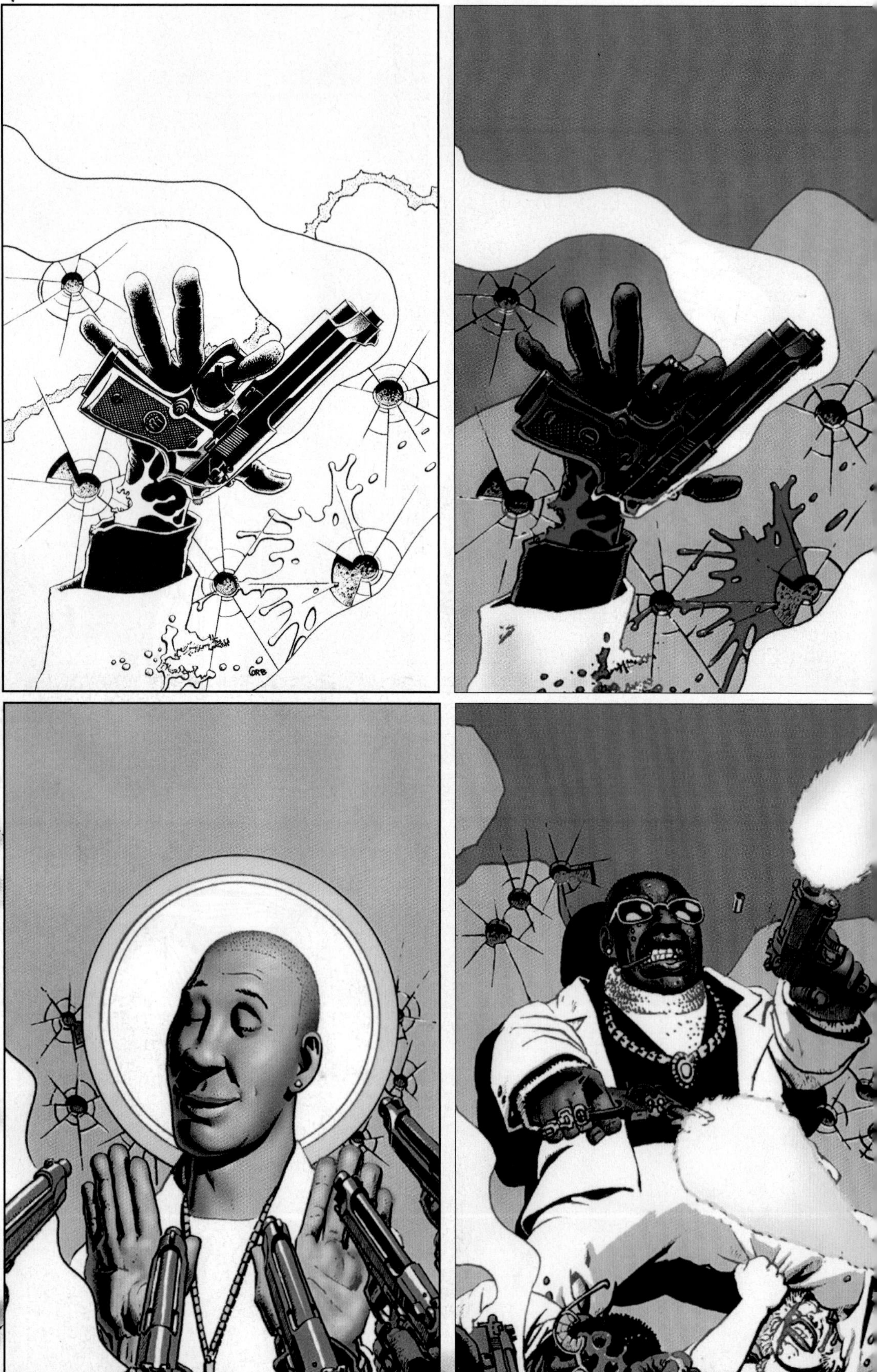

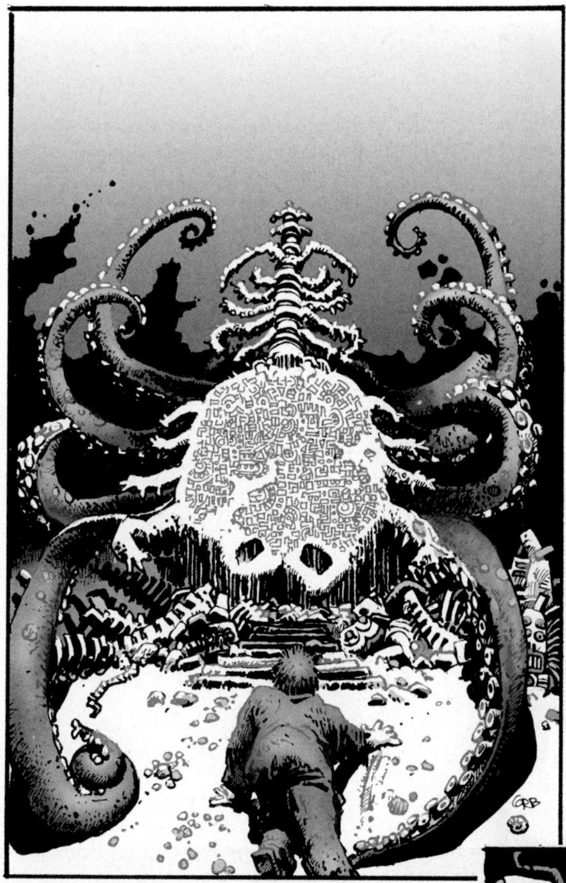
CORB

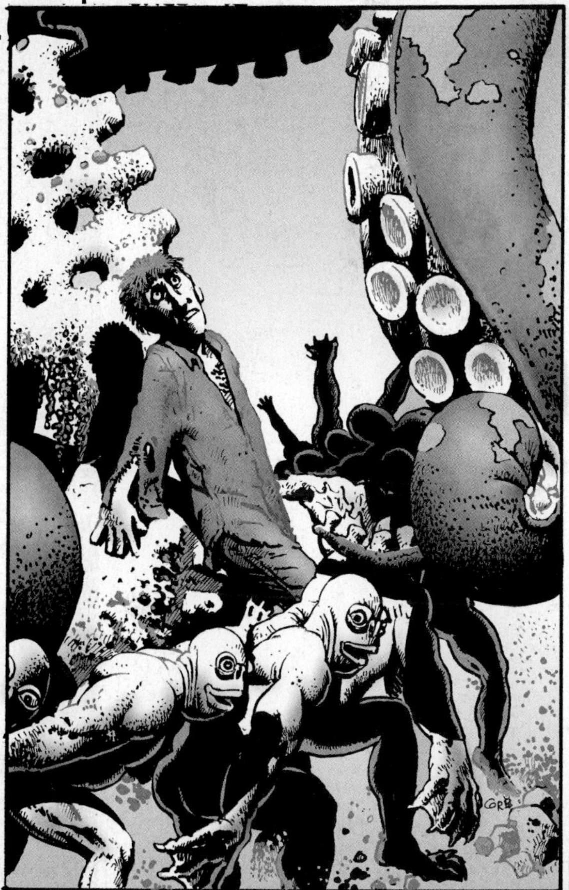
CORB

SAMPLE PAGES FROM OTHER POTENTIAL POE ADAPTATIONS, FROM THE INITIAL PROJECT PROPOSAL

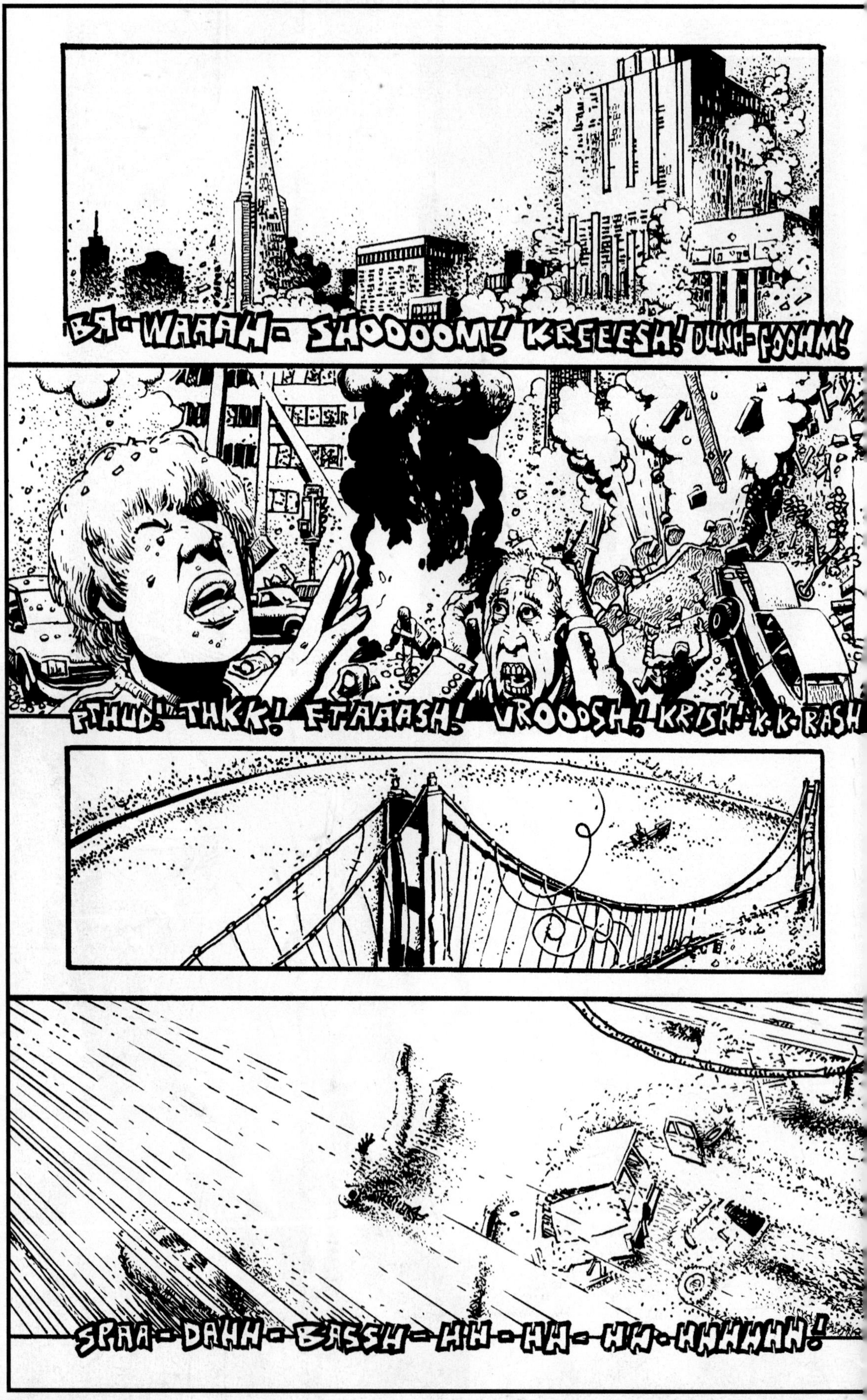
BR-WAAAH- SHOOOOM! KREEESH! DUNH-FOOHM!
PTHUD! THKK! FTAAASH! VROOOSH! KRISH-K-K-RASH
SPAA-DAHH-BASSH-HH-HH-HH-HHHHHH!

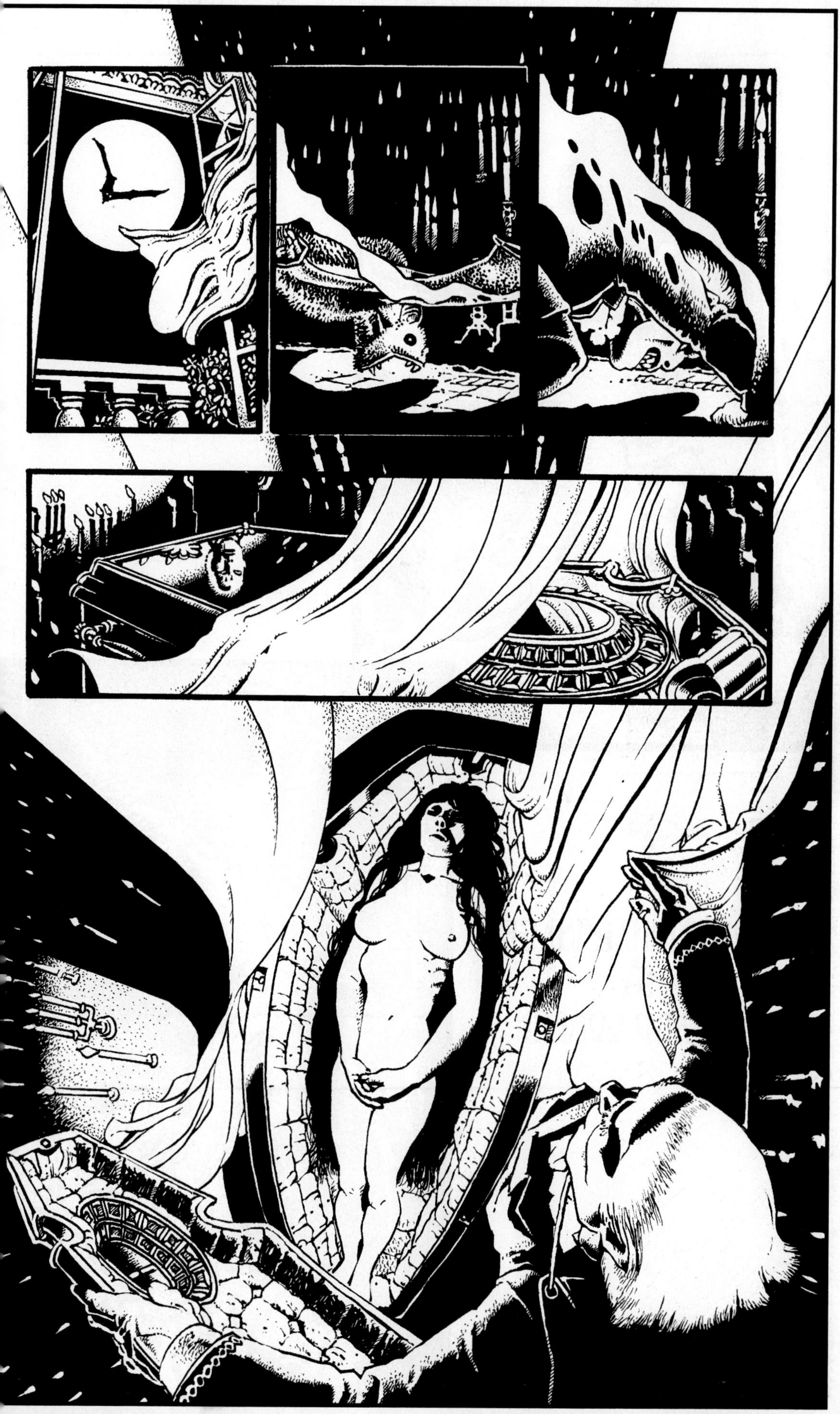

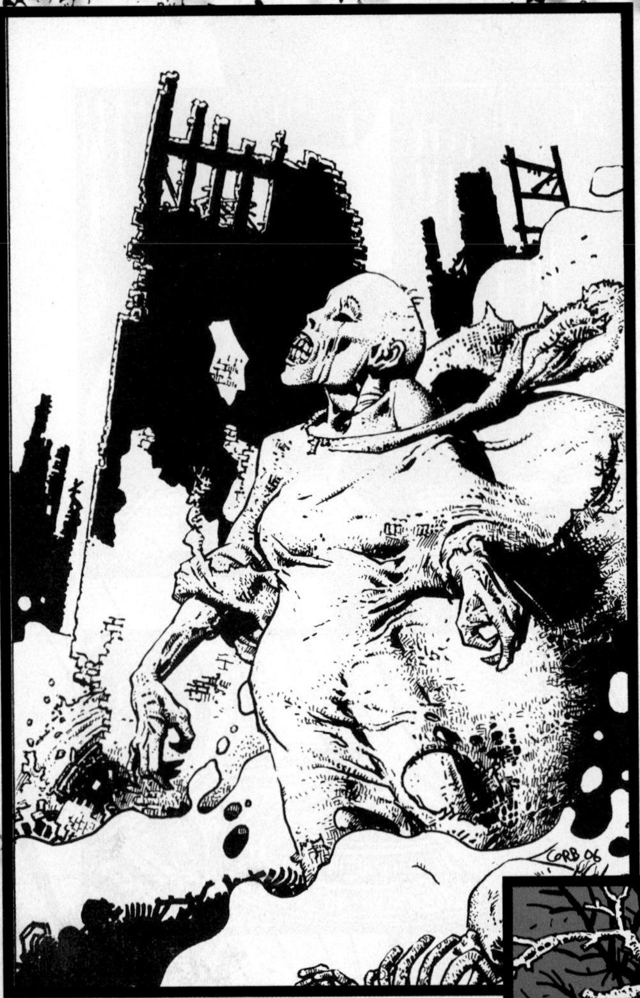

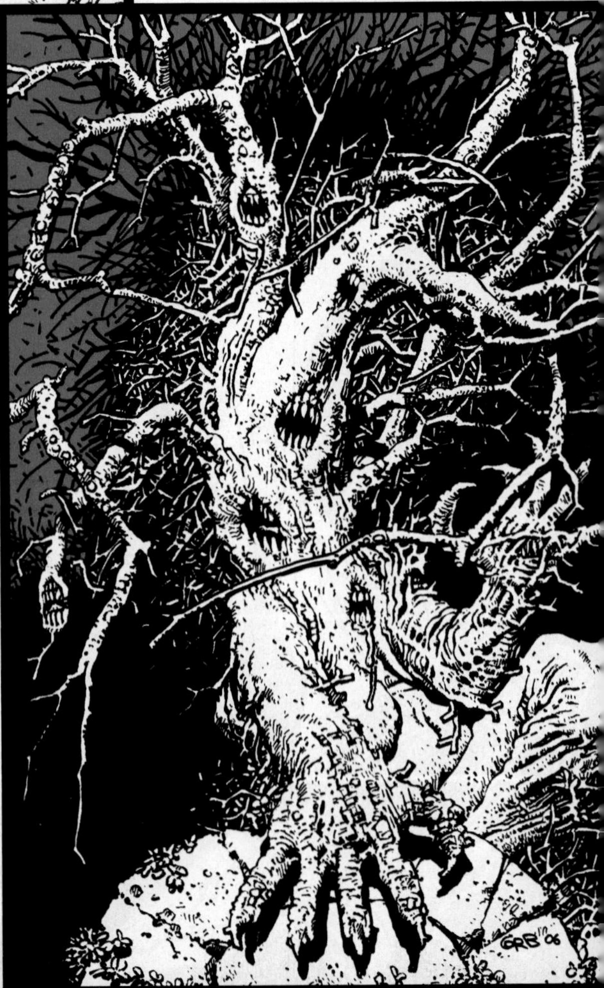

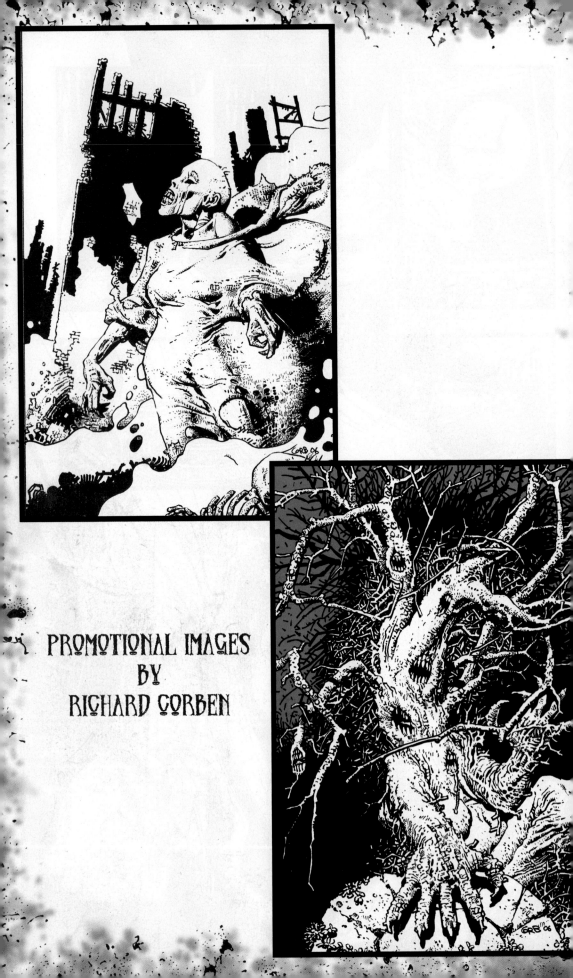

PROMOTIONAL IMAGES
BY
RICHARD CORBEN

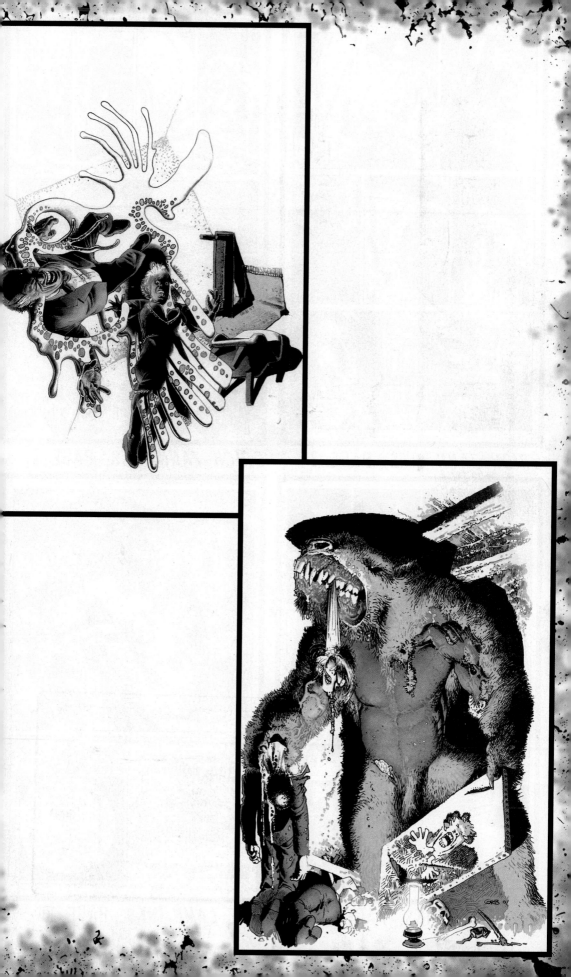

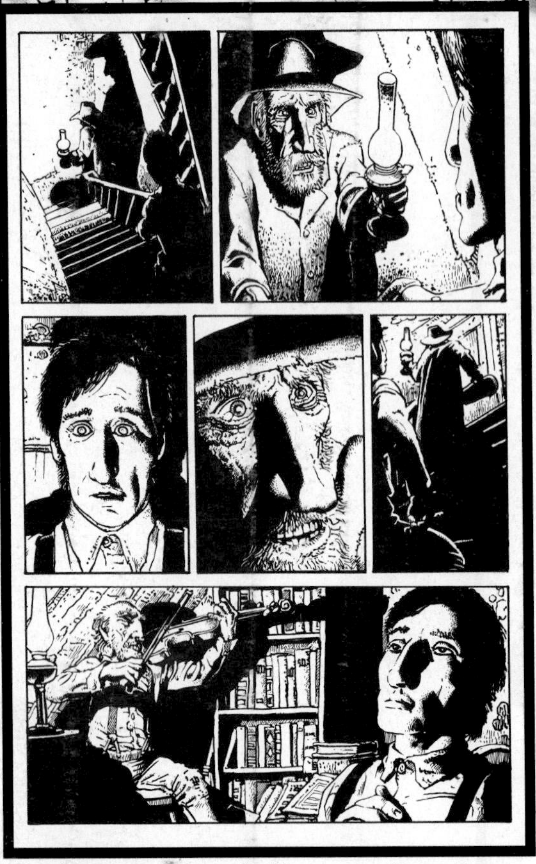

*ERICH ZANN* INKS, PAGE 3

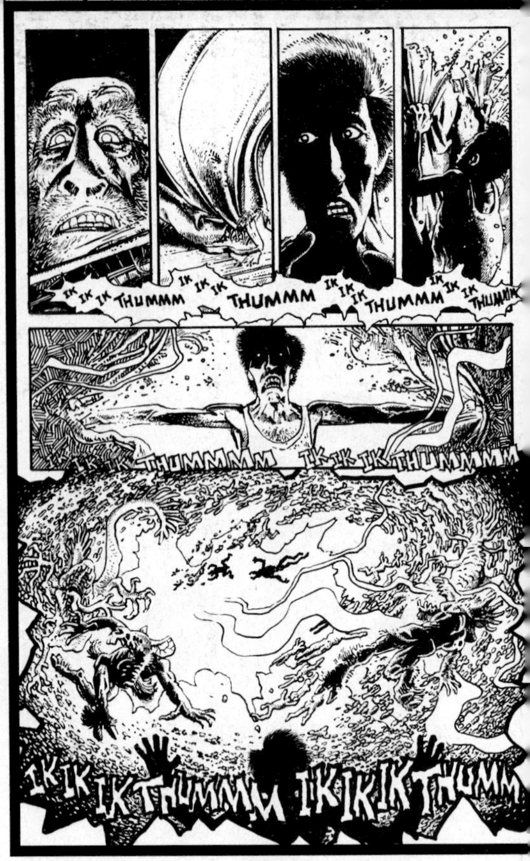

IK IK IK THUMMM
IK IK THUMMM
IK IK THUMMM
IK IK THUMMM
THUMMMM IK IK IK THUMMMM
IK IK IK THUMMM IK IK IK THUMM


*ERICH ZANN* INKS, PAGE 7

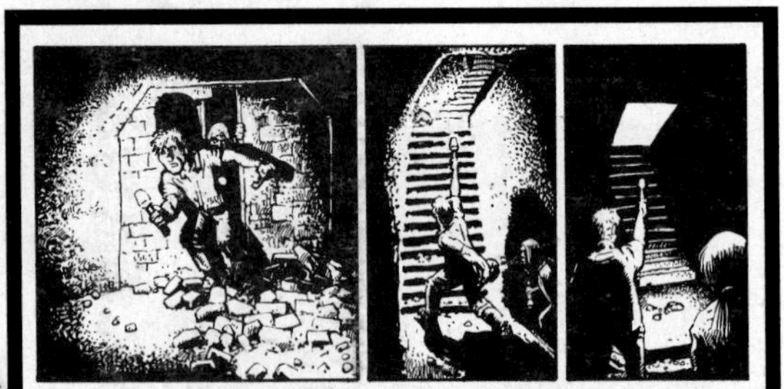

*THE LAMP* INKS, PAGE 7

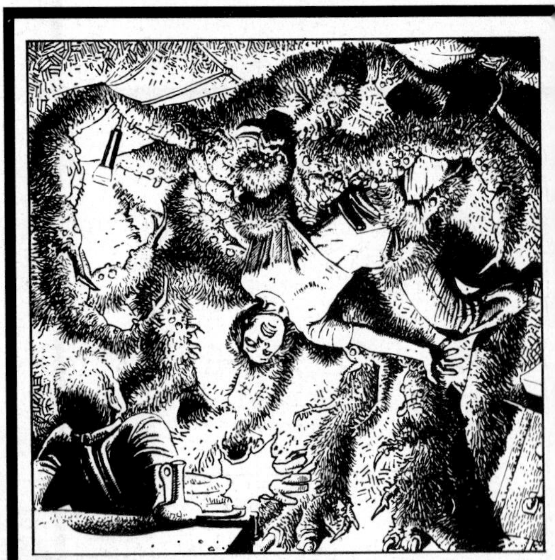

AAAAAAARGGH!
SNARL!
RRIIIPPP!
AHEEEEHH!

*THE LAMP* INKS, PAGE 10